D1542970

Essays on
THE ECONOMY OF
THE OLD NORTHWEST

Essays on
THE ECONOMY OF
THE OLD NORTHWEST

Edited by
David C. Klingaman
and
Richard K. Vedder

Ohio University Press, Athens

Library of Congress Cataloging-in-Publication Data

Essays on the economy of the old Northwest.

Bibliography: p.
1. Northwest, Old–History.   2. Northwest, Old–
Economic conditions.   I. Klingaman, David C.   II. Vedder,
Richard K.
F479.5.E87   1987   977   87–24701
ISBN 0–8214–0875–5

Contents

Introduction

TWO CENTURIES AGO, in 1787, two remarkable documents were formulated that served as the major institutional framework for the development of the United States and its midwestern heartland. Most scholarly attention has focused on the U.S. Constitution, but the Northwest Ordinance of 1787 was of perhaps equal importance in terms of the role it played in the creation of the greatest American phenomenon of the nineteenth century, the Westward Movement. Not only did the Ordinance help provide for the orderly settlement of the five East Central states, but it served as a model for development that was emulated throughout the West, as Jonathan Hughes demonstrates in the opening essay. In the century following 1787, the area to the west of the original northern states—the new states of Ohio, Indiana, Illinois, Michigan and Wisconsin—moved from being the unpopulated frontier of a young country that itself was a frontier, to being the geographic and economic center of an emerging colossus that by 1887 was already becoming the world's leading economic power as measured by gross national product or many of the other indicators that economists have devised to evaluate economic magnitudes.

This volume tells us some important parts of the story of the economic development of the Old Northwest, especially in the first century or so after the passage of the Northwest Ordinance. It is not a comprehensive survey, and readers can find many aspects of the extraordinary economic history of the region that are not extensively explored in this volume, such as the development of the railroad, the Chicago commodity markets, and the Detroit automobile industry. At the same time, the volume expands our insight into a number of important facets of the region's development, including the settlement of the land, the emergence of agriculture, industry, river transportation, banking, education, and the distribution of wealth.

As William Parker suggests towards the end of his paper surveying the industrialization of the region, the Old Northwest (and indeed, the entire Midwest) has been much neglected and even unconsciously maligned as a subject of serious study. For every important study on the Old Northwest before the Civil War, there are probably five or ten studies on the South. Similarly, for every account of the midwestern region for the half century between the Civil War and World War I, there are perhaps two accounts of the American West, despite the fact the Midwest had far more economic importance in this period.

This regional neglect is seen in our popular culture. Books and movies have romanticized the antebellum South, but no one has ever written or produced a "Gone with the Wind" or "High Noon" about antebellum Illinois or Ohio. For every song on television about the Ohio or Wabash rivers, there seem to be more about the Sewanee, the Shenandoah, and the Missouri. Even the practitioners of culture born in the region largely abandoned it. Hemingway, who lived his youth in Illinois and summers in Michigan, fled to Europe to write his greatest works. T.S. Eliot, born a stone's throw from the region in St. Louis, even went so far as to renounce his citizenship. Even many of the popular novels with a setting in the Midwest—*Sister Carrie, The Jungle, Babbitt*—present a grim or even satiric portrayal of the region.

Why has the region been treated with neglect and contempt, by scholars and popular writers and artists alike? Certainly not because of a lack of importance. By many measures the region was the most important in the nation by 1900, and certainly the economically most vibrant and growing throughout most of the nineteenth century. From the 1850s to the 1970s, the population center of the country was in the region.

Perhaps it is precisely this centrality, this importance, that explains the region's neglect. As Professor Parker says, from 1880 to 1930, "the Midwest was America." The region's character has been so indelibly mainstream, so commonplace, that it has not been perceived to be worth talking about. People are more interested in the exotic, in the cultural and economic outliers. The South with its "peculiar institution" and distinctly un-American class system, the West with its frontier romanticism, and perhaps even New England with its unique historical heritage were different, were outside the mainstream of American (meaning Midwestern) life.

This volume, like an earlier one published in 1975 (*Essays in Nineteenth Century Economic History: The Old Northwest*) is a modest attempt to partially correct for the scholarly neglect of the region's economic history. It begins where the modern regional history begins: with the Northwest Ordinance and the subsequent development of the land. Essays by Jonathan R. T. Hughes, Douglass C. North, Stanley Lebergott, and Terry Anderson deal with the emerging institutional framework and the land settlement.

Professor Hughes in the opening essay describes the Northwest Ordinance of 1787 and the critical role it played in delineating property rights in the unsettled lands to the west. He shows how alternative property tenure arrangements might have evolved, and how the provisions in the Ordinance and other pieces of legislation in the eighteenth century provided the basis for the modern American acquisitive spirit. Particularly interesting is his discussion of the development of the township and the six-by-six unit that prevailed not only in the Old Northwest but in later developed states. He also speaks of the selling off of the land, a theme developed further by Professors North, Lebergott, and Anderson.

In many respects, Professor North covers much of the same ground as Professor Hughes, but with a somewhat different perspective. He frames his discussion in the transactions cost framework for which he is well known. Also in his paper, Professor North discusses the political tradeoffs that went into the Ordinance's provisions and policy implementation, showing how concern over slavery entered into the framework establishing land policy. He introduces the concept of "adaptive efficiency," suggesting the Northwest Ordinance "gets high marks" for its role in permitting institutions to change in light of changing circumstances (especially altered relative prices).

Professors Lebergott and Anderson turn their focus primarily to the disposition of public lands. Using many pieces of historical evidence, Lebergott shows that land speculation was perhaps a far less remunerative and nefarious activity than is often presented. Indeed, entrepreneurs in western (meaning midwestern) lands in the early nineteenth century were both speculators in land and moneylenders, and were at least as successful at the latter as the former activity, despite high reported returns on land sales.

In his paper, Terry Anderson utilizes the analytically useful concept of economic rent and discusses how rent-seeking entrepreneurs operated at the margin in the context of American land policy. He analyzes behavior of speculators and squatters in a rent-seeking context, showing how squatting imposed resource costs on the economy. Squatting, in turn, was encouraged by minimum sale prices for land. Like Lebergott, Anderson is skeptical of the alleged evils of speculation.

The dominant use to which the public lands were put was agriculture, and Professors Atack and Bateman use the Bateman-Foust sample of agriculture to compare and contrast agriculture in the Old Northwest with its development in the East. In particular, they painstakingly compare farmers of Yankee origins in the Old Northwest with those remaining in the East. There are some clear differences in agriculture in the two regions, and the migrants from the East did things differently in the Midwest than their friends and relatives who stayed behind, although the authors also note that old habits died hard. In some ways, the similarities between the two groups of farmers are more striking than the differences.

Professors von Ende and Weiss provide us with a detailed analysis of labor force growth by state in the nineteenth century. Extending a procedure pioneered by Professor Lebergott, the authors show how the region's rise in labor force participation in both an absolute and relative sense contributed to its economic growth, as did the relatively sharp shift in human resources out of agriculture. Their state specific data show fairly significant variations in labor force behavior between states, suggesting it is sometimes misleading to refer to the Northwest Territory as a homogenous economic unit.

The fruits of work are consumption and wealth accumulation. In his paper, Professor Soltow describes an extraordinary sample of well over one hundred thousand Ohioans for 1835 classified by real estate wealth. He shows that although wealth in Ohio was unequally distributed, it was no more so than for real estate wealth in contemporary America. Indeed, by international standards of the era, Ohio wealth was relatively equally distributed, perhaps explaining de Tocqueville's emphasis on the equality of condition among Americans. Wealth inequality varied markedly between small geographic units (townships), but relatively little between the four quadrants of the state. Moreover, differences in wealth distribution between Ohio and Illinois do not seem large. The data are consistent with the view that the region was growing rapidly, a growth shared by rich and poor alike.

As Professor North noted, declining transactions costs are important in economic growth, and Professors Stevens, Smiley and Walton explore various aspects of the decline in such costs in the nineteenth century. Professor Stevens expands a point made by Professor Soltow, namely that the acquisition of wealth was positively associated with literacy and cultural development. As Professor Stevens notes, the growth in population and wealth in Ohio was accompanied by the rise of subscription and common schools. Learning was not confined to the institutional settings of schools, however, as the rise in the popular press and ownership of books attests.

Economic development had to be financed, and the greatest period of economic growth was between the Civil War and World War I. Professor Smiley describes in detail the extraordinary growth in banking during this era. Interest rate differentials declined, but even shortly before World War I some differences persisted. Smiley critically analyzes alternative explanations, concluding that "the regional interest rate differentials arose as a result of the rapid industrial development and rapid geographic growth into relatively capital poor and resource areas of the United States." The region's financial institutions moved to respond to market signals in order to meet the needs for financial capital, becoming a capital exporting region by the end of the period.

No matter was more important than falling transportation costs in the development of regional specialization. Although the railroad was important in the Old Northwest, the region was bordered by water on all sides: the Great Lakes on the north, the Ohio River on the east and south, and the Mississippi River on the west. Water transportation, steamboats in particular, played an important role in antebellum development. Dean Gary Walton outlines that growth, stressing the importance of river transportation in the ever-growing flows of commodities to and from the region. He shows that the steamboat actually helped the preservation of a competing transport mode, the flatboat. Before 1850 river transportation productivity rose at an impressive 5-6 percent annual rate, helping the region evolve from a frontier economy to a major integrated region within the national and even world economy.

The regional specialization arising from falling transactions costs manifested itself in many ways, but the single most important structural change in the economy of the East North Central states in the nineteenth and very early twentieth centuries was the massive industrialization of the region. At a time when the nation was undergoing an industrial revolution, the region moved from being relatively nonindustrial to rivaling the East as the nation's manufacturing heartland, a topic explored by William Parker and David Klingaman. Professor Parker uses broad strokes to paint the picture of nineteenth-century industrialization. He discusses the critical roles of labor and migration in the development of industrialization, including the importance of the shift in human resources to towns from the countryside. The mechanics of resource shifts ultimately, however, reflected the *zeitgeist* of the Midwest, a Puritan-like ethic that embraced both the norms of capitalism and the liberal society, in the process assimilating massive numbers of immigrants instilled with a "semi-feudal class consciousness." The new employer-employee relationships associated with larger-scale enterprise, and the changing market structures resulting from scale economies, created dilemmas and tensions for the growing region, the resolution of which awaited the twentieth century.

David Klingaman complements Professor Parker's essay with descriptive detail of Midwestern manufacturing in 1890. Nearly one-fourth of the nation's industrial output emanated from the Old Northwest by 1890, an impressive proportion for a region barely one hundred years old. Manufacturing largely took place in the rapidly growing cities, and Professor Klingaman looks at the characteristics of industrialization in five of the largest: Chicago, Cincinnati, Cleveland, Milwaukee, and Detroit. Comparison of manufacturing with older industrial cities (i.e., New York, Philadelphia, Boston, Baltimore) reveals similarities, and some differences, including larger average firm size in the Midwestern cities. Professor Klingaman concludes by noting the sheer magnitude of the Midwestern growth, quoting the 1900 census, "No where else in the world has there been so rapid a transformation of the occupations of the population."

Richard Vedder and Lowell Gallaway conclude the volume by tying the nineteenth-century growth to the maturity and stagnation of the twentieth century. They look at three measures of economic vitality—income per capita, net migration, and unemployment—and argue that the region grew rapidly in a relative sense up to 1880, "matured" and maintained rapid but not unusual growth to about 1930 or 1940, and began a slow but accelerating relative decline after 1940. Although they portray a decline in regional vitality, they conclude the volume on a speculatively optimistic note, suggesting reasons why the region's recent relative stagnation should not continue indefinitely.

This volume owes its existence to the encouragement and financial support of several individuals and institutions. At Ohio University, Dean F. Donald Eckelmann of the College of Arts and Sciences provided both generous financial resources and enthusiastic encouragement. Helping us with the administrative details of the project was our colleague Professor Ismail Ghazalah. Finally, a special thanks is due to the Earhart Foundation, whose financial support allowed us to materially expand both the quantity and the quality of this volume.

1.

THE GREAT LAND ORDINANCES
Colonial America's Thumbprint on History

Jonathan Hughes
Northwestern University

GEORGE DALTON ONCE SAID that the European imperialists of the nineteenth century "left their thumbprints all over Africa." Americans also had an historical thumbprint: the way they settled empty land. It is a pity that popular knowledge of the great land ordinances of 1784, 1785, 1787, and 1790 should have become so slight. American history textbooks typically say very little about them. Compared to the federal constitution, the average college student today knows almost nothing about the land ordinances of the 1780s. Yet, as legal guidelines directing the nation's physical and political growth the ordinances were as fundamental as was the federal constitution itself.

With the land ordinances in place, the Americans did an amazing thing: they surveyed and settled an empty continent in about a century, dividing it into small pieces of private property, peaceably, with few exceptions. This was done by a planned process of political mitosis: the organism created by the ordinances in the "Old Northwest" spread westward, recreating itself in measured townships and the sequence of territories and states again and again. This settlement system was cut into the wilderness primarily by privately motivated frontiersmen making small family farms acquired by purchase or homesteading from an undifferentiated wilderness systematically reduced to townships and sections clearly delineated by celestial surveys. The process was only stopped by nature and government action. Nature left great areas too poor in rainfall to support farming without irrigation, and the federal government finally withdrew the remaining public domain from occupation by homesteading in the interests of conservation and public amenity.

In the long run, the new country's freedom-spawning land tenure produced a social system that was generalized to the landless citizen, property qualifications were abandoned and the civil rights of the colonial New England "freeman" became the rights of all. What the frontiersman achieved by possession, ordinary citizens would come to achieve by birth or naturalization. The land ordinances became the great American colonizing machine: they left the intellectual mark of the Americans on the nation's geography as indelibly as did the Roman roads on physical England, still cutting straight across the undulating English countryside. The Northwest

1

Ordinances were the colonial Americans' institutional thumbprint on the American continent all the way from the Ohio River to the Pacific.

CONTEMPORARY EVENTS AND JEFFERSON'S ROLE

THE COUNTRY'S LAND AREA in the 1780s was an outcome of the War of Independence, and much of the policy governing that land was conceived while the future was still at risk to the fortunes, sometimes entirely by chance, of battles between contending forces of colonists, British, Indians, Spanish, and others. Settlement of the interior land was thus halting and uneven until after the War of 1812. By then the British had settled with us on division and control of the eastern half of the continent, the French had sold us Louisiana, and the Spanish role in Florida was at an end. But in addition to the political disorder that formed the background to the land ordinances and their operations, the establishment of the apparatus of survey and sale set out in the 1785 ordinance was uneven both in planning and execution.

It is therefore all the more impressive that a single conception, a single geopolitical mind, should have guided and shaped so much of our history connected with land acquisition and settlement. Mr. Jefferson's enthusiasm for Louisiana is well known. Not so well remembered is his decisive role in acquiring the old Northwest even before he outlined how to map, organize, and settle it.

The 1787 ordinance was in part a revision, expansion, and readoption of Jefferson's Ordinance of 1784,[1] which originally laid out conditions for self-government in all of the western lands. Jefferson included a provision to ban slavery after 1800 in his original plan, but it lost in Congress by only a single vote. Jefferson wrote of his defeat in 1784 on slavery in the western lands:

> There were ten states present. Six voted unanimously for it, and one was divided; and seven votes being requisite to decide the proposition affirmatively, it was lost. The voice of a single individual of the state which was divided, or one of those which were of the negative, would have prevented this abominable crime from spreading itself over the new country. Thus we see the fate of millions unborn hanging on the tongue of one man— and Heaven was silent in that awful moment.[2]

And thus did Thomas Jefferson narrowly miss being the man in American history who did more than any other single person to determine the peaceful demise of chattel slavery! In 1787 slavery was excluded only from the territories north of the Ohio, and the new states entering south of that line under the 1790 ordinance thus armed the coming Civil War.

Generally speaking, Thomas Jefferson, our national prodigy, can be given major credit for the entire project of settling the continental United States. This was so even during the Revolution when Jefferson, as governor of Virginia, on 25 December, 1780 ordered General George Rogers Clark to assemble an expedition: "... under your command at a very early season of the approaching year [to go] into the hostile country beyond the Ohio, the principle object of which is to be the reduction of the British post at Detroit and incidental to it the acquiring possession of Lake Erie."[3] Clark did not capture Detroit, but did capture Vincennes, and in consequence of General Clark's expedition, the treaty of peace in 1783 had to recognize, as *fait accompli*, the American national claim to the old Northwest. It was also as Governor of Virginia that Jefferson shepherded in 1781 the legislation to hand over Virginia's vast claim to western territory to the new national government. Jefferson drafted the actual deed of cession in 1784.[4] The famous scheme followed faithfully to the present day, of celestial surveys of the American land and subdivision into 36-square-mile townships—the Northwest Ordinance of 1785, was also Jefferson's work, if not solely his inspiration.

The Northwest Ordinance of 1787 was thus one part of a complex set of events, one island in a stream, that was destined to create a completely novel political organism, a giant amoeba-like social system that would grow (mainly without central direction or motivation) and subdivide itself steadily until the empty land was full. From start to finish, the new system, as well as the 1787 ordinance at the political heart of it, was among Jefferson's lesser-known achievements.

ESTABLISHMENT OF PROPERTY RIGHTS
UNDER THE 1787 ORDINANCE

PRESSURE WAS PUT ON Congress in 1787 when the Reverend Manasseh Cutler asked Congress to provide a settled plan of self-government for the proposed settlers of the huge blocs of land Congress had granted to the Ohio and Scioto Companies—the Act of 1785 not withstanding. The Committee of 1787 was the result.[5] Jefferson was in France in 1787 when the committee drafted the new Ordinance for the Northwest Territories. Committee members Nathan Dane and Rufus King, both of Massachusetts, seized the opportunity to reinstate the antislavery provision, and it became law.[6] The 1787 ordinance also settled the rule for the descent of land ownership by a simplification of the Massachusetts practice. There, the system of gavelkind of County Kent in England had been changed to be not merely equal division among sons, but equal division among all children, with a double portion going to the eldest son, the so-called Mosaic practice. The latter was now dropped. The 1787 ordinance reads:

> The estates both of resident and non-resident proprietors in the
> said Territory, dying intestate, shall descend to and be distrib-
> uted among their children and the descendants of a deceased
> child in equal parts among them; and where there shall be no
> children or descendants, then in equal parts to the next of kin, in
> equal degree; and among collaterals, the children of a deceased
> brother or sister of the intestate shall have in equal among them
> their deceased parent's share; and there shall in no case be a dis-
> tinction between kindred of the whole and half-blood; saving in
> all cases to the widow of the intestate her third part of the real es-
> tate for life, and one third part of the personal estate...[7]

Dane said the idea was taken directly from the laws of Massachusetts,
with the double portion dropped.[8] This was the famous rule, in equal parts
in equal degrees of consanguinity, that would determine the basic way private ownership of a continent would pass peacefully from generation to
generation. Jefferson himself had favored the adoption of gavelkind,[9] but
that divided the land equally among the sons only.

From the time of Henry VIII, owners of property rights in free socage
tenure (the American tenure) had been allowed to pass real property by
will. After the *Statute of Frauds* of 1667, the English had established rules for
making wills, rules that were followed even in the backwoods of colonial
America.[10] Consequently, the 1787 ordinance provided for intergenerational
land transfers by will: "...estates in the said Territory may be devised or
bequeathed by wills in writing signed and sealed by him or her in whom
the estate may be (being of full age) and attested by three witnesses."[11]

This was the practice established by the *Statute of Frauds*, except in that
legislation special provisions were made for soldiers and mariners fatally
wounded in military actions.[12] It is interesting, considering the violence attending the occupation of the Northwest Territories, including decades of
Indian wars to come, that loopholes were not made in the law to accommodate the consequences of military violence. You needed to have your will
made out and properly witnessed before you went off to your military ad-
ventures.

One reason for legislating the *Statute of Frauds* in England had been to
end the ancient common-law practice of conveying ownership in real property by "delivery" (the only method recognized by the common law). The
1787 ordinance provides for transfer of personal property by delivery, but
real property ultimately will have to be conveyed by deed.

> ...real estates may be conveyed by lease and release, or bargain
> and sale, signed, sealed, and delivered by the person, being of
> full age, in whom the estate may be, and attested by two wit-
> nesses, provided such wills be duly proved, and such convey-

ances be acknowledged, or the execution thereof duly proved, and be recorded within one year after a proper magistrate, courts, and registers, shall be appointed for the purpose; and personal property may be transferred by delivery...[13]

Although "signed, sealed, and delivered" now conveys no real meaning, it is reasonable to believe that until a deed of conveyance could be duly registered, an actual act of delivery (turning over property at the site before witnesses) would achieve a working, or practical, right to occupy the land for the lessee or the buyer. Such had been the case in the backwoods of New England, where it could be *years* before a deed of conveyance could be registered after land had been sold and occupied by new owners.[14]

Since parts of the territories had been in Virginia, where primogeniture had been the rule, and there were French occupants who followed their own customs, the ordinance left loopholes for them. "...saving...the French and Canadian inhabitants, and other settlers of Kaskaskias, St. Vincents, and the neighboring villages, who have heretofore professed themselves citizens of Virginia, their laws and customs now in force among them relative to the descent and conveyance of property."[15] Jefferson himself had written these provisions in 1783 in the Virginia Act of Cession,[16] and they reappear in the 1787 ordinance.

Until this ordinance the legal right to ownership of real property in the United States had descended one way or another from royal power, through land grants and royal charters. Now there had been a revolution and the power of England's kings was considered finished. *Dartmouth College v. Woodward* (1819) would amend this conception later on.[17] Nevertheless, the committeemen of 1787 believed they were finished with the British crown, in law at least. Therefore their grant from the "old Congress" (the Constitutional Convention was meeting in the summer of 1787) was thought a truly revolutionary act, or at least it was the use of power created by revolution. There had been a change of sovereignty, and Nathan Dane believed that the 1787 ordinance spoke directly to that change. Writing years later (26 March 1830) to Daniel Webster, Dane's opinion was: "...I believe these were the first titles to property, completely republican, in Federal America: being in no part whatever feudal or monarchical...."[18] Jefferson's own interpretation was that the royal power, that of the "donor," had passed to the United States by the state land grants to Congress, and that once sold off to private owners, the residual donor's rights (escheatment for nonpayment of taxes, failure of heirs, etc.) would go to the new states that were to come into existence as the land was sold, settlers arrived, and the succession to statehood was accomplished. The federal government would step out of its donor's rights *when the land was sold*, and "never after in any case" reenter the land.[19] Jefferson feared that a great endowment of land or rights left in the central government's hands would necessarily breed tyranny. In the end both Dane and Jefferson would be confounded by history. The King's powers stood against the revolution in *Dartmouth College v. Woodward,* and the federal government was never totally separated from its lands and related rights to those lands. It now reenters by eminent domain and by direct appropriation for failure by owners to pay their federal income taxes.

Article III exhorts the forthcoming settlers to a life on a high plane of public and private morality and fair dealing with the Indians.

> Religion, morality, and knowledge, being necessary to good government and the happiness of mankind, schools and the means of education shall forever be encouraged. The utmost good faith shall always be observed toward the Indians; their lands and property shall never be taken from them without their consent; and, in their property, rights, and liberty, they never shall be invaded or disturbed, unless in just and lawful wars authorized by Congress; but laws founded in justice and humanity shall...be made, for preventing wrongs being done to them and for preserving peace and friendship with them.[20]

Dane said of this article, as well as the famous prohibition of slavery in Article VI, that they were meant for New England people. The committee had not intended to throw down a gauntlet before the southerners. Hence, the 1790 ordinance, extending that of 1787 to the south, apart from the prohibition against slavery, was a perfectly natural development to Dane. He did not foresee, in 1830, that extending the nation westward with two totally different agricultural labor systems was necessarily breeding an irrepressible conflict.

> ...in the years 1784, '85, '86 and '87, the Eastern members of the Old Congress really thought they were preparing the North-Western Territory for New England settlers, and to them the third and sixth Articles of the compact more especially had reference; therefore, when North Carolina ceded her western territory, and requested this ordinance to be extended to it, except for the *slave* article, that exception had my full assent, because slavery had taken root in it, and it was then probable it would be settled principally by slave-owners.[21]

In coming years other states followed the rule of the 1787 ordinance and an ancient and marvelously arcane history ended. Primogeniture in the U.S. ended, was abolished by Virginia in 1776, and in the last case, by Rhode Island in 1798. The double portion lingered until Pennsylvania finally abolished it in 1810. Massachusetts had already abolished the practice in 1801.[22]

What was the content of the ownership of real property whose descent was regularized by the 1787 ordinance? The substantive content of ownership was (is) contained in the tenure granted. That of the English new-world mainland colonies seems simple enough: from the original Virginia charter in 1606 to the final charter, that of Georgia in 1732, only land ownership in "free and common socage" was allowed. There were some variations in Maryland, Delaware, Pennsylvania, and (originally) in Georgia, but they were transitory. The tenure remains essentially today what it was then. We now call it fee simple—the simple feud. The basic rights are:

1. Descent is directly to the heir without escheatment.

2. The tenure is "perpetual," usually shown by the words "heirs and assigns forever."

3. There is complete freedom of alienation and devise (right of will).

4. There is the right of "waste" (the right to change the nature of the property, cut the trees, dig mines, etc.)

5. There is the freedom from "incidents uncertain," all the dues and obligations of the ownership are known when it is conveyed. Neither the conveyor nor the donor can add on incidents (conditions for transfer of title) after the title is settled.

The American land tenure was the historical product of a long evolution in England that I have treated elsewhere.[23] There are many other characteristics of it not listed above. The variations on it, allowance for certain "feudal" rights and practices in Maryland, Delaware, Pennsylvania, and New York (to accommodate the Dutch tenures) vanished in time, in New York, only by constitutional revision in 1846. The custom of the British, when land was acquired already settled under the laws of other nations was to leave unchanged all practices that did not positively conflict with British laws. The Americans, in their turn, followed the same routine, so in Louisiana and the Southwest there are certain practices associated with real property rights that are not entirely the same as those in other states; e.g., "pueblo right" in California. Chancellor James Kent, in his *Commentaries on American Law* in 1826, tried to make sense of it all by the assertion that in the United States "the title to lands is essentially allodial, and every tenant [owner] has an absolute and perfect title, yet, in technical language, his estate is called an estate in fee simple, and the tenure free and common socage."[24] The reference to allodial ownership is an assertion that there is no donor, that ultimately an American property owner holds in the same ownership as did the King of England—a grant from God. This is not so in the U.S., as anyone knows who does not meet the modern incidents of his tenure—does not pay his property taxes—his "ownership" simply vanishes, and his property escheats to the donor, the state.

As a practical matter, after 150 years or so of living with the common law of England and free and common socage, the colonial Americans understood their land tenure inside and out—so much so that the federal constitution, in the fifth amendment (and elsewhere) could guarantee secure property rights without ever specifying what the rights were it guaranteed. The tenure, along with the common law, went straight through the Revolution into federal America via the conduits of the state courts and constitutions.[25] So the 1787 ordinance was not burdened with the need to establish any definitions of property rights in the lands about to be conveyed by the federal government to individuals, except to straighten out their descent in cases of intestacy.

MEASURING THE CONTINENT

THE 1787 ORDINANCE, AS we have seen, was largely an update of the legislation of 1784, and it embraced the 1785 ordinance. That law laid out the scheme for celestial surveys, before the land went up for sale, with the lands divided into square townships of 36 square miles each, 6 miles by 6 miles. The 1785 survey system is part of the metaphorical American thumbprint and is deserving of some kind of an explanation since it is still the way Americans measure their lands.

Although Jefferson's ideas were embodied in the 1785 ordinance, they represented an amalgam of colonial experience and ideals. The original idea of selling land in townships with specific (land) parcels set aside to support a school, and in New England a church (the glebeland), were examples. The New England way of westward expansion had been by planned settlements of groups committed to forming complete new social organisms, towns, at the very beginning of each extension into the wilderness.[26] Indeed, that is how Marietta, Ohio, was settled, and Brigham Young, of Whittingham, Vermont,[27] continued the practice in Zion, far into the nineteenth century. The Puritan commitment to an orderly existence, including the establishment and support of a church, motivated the settlement technique. The fact that the New England communities were church-centered is still apparent to the tourist's eye.

Expansion into Vermont on the New Hampshire government's authority in the mid-eighteenth century demonstrates the technique in its perfected form. Beginning in 1749 with Bennington Township, New Hampshire's governor, Benning Wentworth, began laying out square townships along the southern edge of present-day Vermont. The ideas involved—advance survey, advance sales (promises to settle)—were old colonial ideas going all the way back to the Virginia colony. Massachusetts had expanded that way, mostly. Consider the instructions for the surveyors laying out Marlboro town in 1751 in southern Vermont. The adjacent town, Halifax, had been chartered the year before. There was no celestial-survey base line. The base line was by "metes and bounds." "Beginning at a marked tree standing half a mile west of Green River, in the boundary line between the government of Massachusetts Bay and New Hampshire, and from thence due west one said boundary line six miles. . . ." This is the Halifax charter. It instructs the surveyors around by lengths of six miles at 90-degree angles to come back to the same tree. That was one town.[28] A year later Marlboro town picked up the line. Marlboro's charter reads: "Beginning at the North West Corner of a Township called Halifax lately granted. . .thence running by the Needle North Ten degrees East Six miles from Thence East Ten Degrees South Six miles from thence South Ten Degrees West Six miles & from thence West Ten degrees North by Halifax aforesaid Six Miles to the corner first mentioned. . ." [29] They were using a compass. More towns were laid out thusly, without regard to the topography. Mountains, streams, gorges, all were ignored. It is a true inspiration for a celestial survey with transit and rod. Political organizations, counties, and, later, states, took topography into account, but not townships. They were to be surveyors' lines only. In New England these little thirty-six square mile units, arbitrarily laid out, actually embraced, as they still do today, tiny direct democracies ruling over miniature domains.

Where the six-by-six mile unit came from is a mystery.[30] Each town contained thirty-six square miles, equal to 23,040 acres. Later on these would seem rational enough; each township divided into thirty-six sections, each one a square mile section containing 640 acres, or four farms of 160 acres each: the "squatter's 160" of colonial New England, and later on the size of a homestead farm under the Homestead Act of 1862. When you fly over Iowa, that is what you see. However, in the mid-eighteenth century, the Vermont townships were not so divided. They were divided instead into sixty-four lots of 360 acres each; not a natural multiple of 160 acres. So what was there later on, was not there at the beginning.

One can see the attraction of squares in the wilderness easily enough. Once you decided to ignore topography, a square is the easiest regular shape. It is believed that both William Penn and Lord Shaftsbury (a Carolina proprietor), early-day enthusiasts for square settlements, were inspired thusly by the work of Sir William Petty. He was a famous "Political Arithmetician" of the mid-seventeenth century and was surveyor general of England in 1655. Cromwell ordered the division of Northern Ireland's ten counties to pay off back wages to his soldiers, and Petty responded by dividing the counties into squares.[31] But why the thirty-six square miles per township in New England? Scholarship (Amelia Clewley Ford) cannot take us further, and neither can theory. Why six by six? Why not ten by ten? In 1717 Sir Robert Montgomery proposed a colony organized as a Margravate in what became Georgia. The colony, Azilia, was laid out in 640-acre squares—square miles but not thirty-six square mile townships: no such colony was ever actually established. After 1727 there was legislation in Massachusetts ordering new towns to be laid out in rectangles. Governor Oglethorpe had some square towns laid out in Georgia, but they were never developed. Then in 1749 came Benning Wentworth and Bennington—six miles by six miles square. Then came more towns in Vermont of the same size. Jefferson accepted the idea of the township as the basic survey unit, ignoring actual topography. But being an eighteenth-century rationalist, he naturally wanted a unit that made some kind of sense mathematically. He wanted, in fact, ten miles by ten miles. The New England men wanted their thirty-six square mile unit. A compromise left the proposed townships at seven miles by seven miles, but the New England men had their way and the township in 1785, and forevermore, was declared to be six miles by six miles square, even if it made no obvious sense.[32]

Given the importance the New England saints had placed on religion it is not surprising that the New England townships typically provided for the support of it. The land for support of the established church was called the *glebe*—and that word was not to be known beyond New England because of the 1785 ordinance. The New England towns also provided for schooling in their land grants. The 1751 royal charter for Marlboro Vermont reads in these matters: "...one Shear [share] for the First Settled Minister one Shear for the benefit of the School forever, one Shear for to remain as a Glebe for the benefit of the Church of England as by Law Established...for the Benefit of the Church there 'till an Episcopal Clergyman is Settled in the town...then to remain for the Sole Benefit of the Ministry there..."

In that case one sixty-fourth of the town was a gift for the first minister of faith willing to settle there. A second share was for the established church whenever an Anglican clergyman was willing to go live in the Vermont backwoods, and one share would support the school. During the American revolution, the established church was, of necessity, on the losing side. It was to be left out when new lands were up for settlement. What lay behind this change was doubtless as much a distaste for establishing another state church as it was due to Jefferson's famous "atheism." In any case, anticipating the first amendment (first proposed in 1789) to the upcoming federal constitution, the support for religion was now omitted altogether and 150 years of colonial tradition were assigned to history's famous trashcan. One tradition did survive: a 640-acre section in each town (section 16) was set aside to support schooling and four sections were reserved to support government.

Under the 1785 ordinance, the first base line was to run due west from the point where the border of Pennsylvania crossed the Ohio River. The first seven north-south range lines were measured at intervals westward from the Ohio River, and the land was scheduled to be offered for sale once the first seven ranges were surveyed.[33] That plan for survey and sales, and the 1787 ordinance's provision for intergenerational transfers of real property, together with the conditions for establishing self-government were the "constitution" of the Old Northwest. The ordinances were destined to provide the geographic, political, and property rights systems on the land for the nation's westward expansion. The actual historical process to come was far less orderly than the committees of the "old congress" could have imagined in 1787. But the system held together in the decades of change and stress that absorbed the newly independent nation.

SELLING IT OFF

THE ORDINANCES PROVIDED A kind of rational expansion machine in the background—a *deus ex machina*—while the foreground was filled with drama and often enough, chaos. From the Treaty of Paris in 1783 to the end of the Blackhawk War in 1832, the Old Northwest was buffeted by a long sequence of upheavals. Yet the settlement process continued. The 1783 treaty left a northern boundary stretching eastward and southward from Lake of the Woods across Lake Superior, then down Lake Huron to Detroit, then around through Lake Erie to Niagara, and from there through Lake Ontario to the St. Lawrence. But British military and trading posts below that meandering line were kept manned for years on various pretexts, and Hudson's Bay Company traders roamed far and wide below the lakes. Given the problems involved for the new nation in acquiring the hunting lands of the resident and unwilling Indian tribes, supported by British policies that targeted a hoped-for *de facto* buffer Indian state between the old colonies and lower Canada, there were many bloody and violent episodes to come in the Northwest territories after the American Revolution had cancelled out the Quebec Act of 1774. Nevertheless, by the cessions of the original states the new government in 1786 had nominal control of the Northwest, apart from the Virginia and Connecticut reserves, the Indians, the British.

The Southwest had an even more traumatic future coming. Its fate was to include not only the several Yazoo land scandals emanating from the Georgia legislature, but murky and sometimes bloody intrigues involving the Spaniards based in Florida and New Orleans, together with their would-be Indian allies. In addition, a host of frontier adventurers of mercurial loyalties played for and against all sides. The settlement, when it came, the Louisiana Purchase, was mainly the outcome of European power politics together with some adroit military bluffing by (then) President Thomas Jefferson. He bought an empire for $15 million from the French in 1803. They had just swindled it from the helpless Spaniards.[34]

By 1785 there already were several thousand squatters in the Ohio territory. They were described by Colonel Josiah Harmar as "banditti" who entered and claimed their "undoubted right to pass into every vacant country, and there to form their own constitution."[35] Conflicts with the Indians came thick and fast, and perforce often enough drew in the regular American forces in the neighborhood. Several expeditions against the Indians in 1786–87, including one led by George Rogers Clark, had failed to pacify the tribes and a widespread Indian war seemed inevitable.

Nevertheless, against all odds the first seven mountain ranges, westward from the Ohio River, had been surveyed according to the 1785 ordinance in the years 1785–87. The Ohio Company had acquired a massive land grant from Congress just to the southwest of the seven ranges. New England settlers had set out for those lands in the winter of 1787–88 and on 7 April 1788 they came ashore and founded Marietta.[36] A few months later, in January 1789, Arthur St. Clair, the new governor of the territory, tried to dictate a treaty with the Indians at nearby Fort Harmar.

War was the immediate result. St. Clair himself was in command of a disaster in the fall of 1791 in which the Americans sustained nearly a thousand casualties in a single engagement. After that, for many months most of the white settlements in Ohio were abandoned. For two more years the Ohio frontier was aflame. Then, in late August of 1794, General Anthony Wayne had his way with the Indians at the battle of Fallen Timbers. The British did not come out of their fortress at Detroit to help their allies, and in early 1795, in the Treaty of Greenville, dictated by Wayne, the Indians abandoned most of Ohio. By then the British, at war with revolutionary France, had bigger fish to fry and gave the American representative, John Jay, a promise that the British military posts in the Old Northwest would be given up by 1 June 1796. Wayne's treaty of Greenville, together with Jay's Treaty, gave the Northwest peace until nearly 1812.

Widespread frontier fighting resumed again in 1811 with the Indians now led by Chief Tecumseh and his crippled brother, "the Prophet." By then the Indians were being pushed back to the Mississippi and beyond by a series of treaties in which their lands had been taken. They were now losing Indiana, Illinois and Wisconsin piece by piece. The Battle of Tippecanoe, 7 November 1811, opened this final phase of Indian wars and the Battle of the Thames, 5 October 1813, in which Tecumseh was killed, ended it. The Indian power was broken forever east of the Mississippi, and despite their successes against American arms in the Northwest in 1812–14, the British would soon withdraw their influence south of the lakes for good.

After 1815 the legendary emptying-out of the eastern backwoods was on, the time had come when "the whole country is breaking up and moving west." Settlers flooded into the new lands. Ohio filled up first, then came the invasions of Michigan and Illinois, then the Indiana prairies above the river valleys that had been ignored. The tide swept into Wisconsin and Minnesota. The Blackhawk War of 1832 was a pitiable and desperate piece of hopelessness on the part of the Indians remaining east of the Mississippi. It did serve to focus attention on the swamplands at the portages at the base of Lake Michigan, from which Chicago soon mushroomed. By 1830 the states of the Old Northwest contained a population of 1,470,000 which had grown to 2,934,000 by 1840, a total greater than New England's 2,235,000. In terms of settlement, farms, towns and industry, the Northwest was fulfilling its promise in a hurry.[37]

Most of the sales under the new federal government had been made by the General Land Office. But before 1800 the secretary of the treasury (under a land act of 1796) had been the official responsible for making the sales. The internal history of the General Land Office has been told incomparably by Malcolm Rohrbough. The details of that internal history are sometimes thrilling, and nearly always just this side of easy belief. One pictures with difficulty the survey crews in the field during the War of 1812 following the line of fighting with rod and chain, retreating when the army retreated, fleeing into the few safe white strong points chased by irate Indians, then venturing forth again and again.[38] In the Washington offices a hopelessly understaffed bureaucracy struggled, decade after decade, under an increasing avalanche of paper—quill pens in hand. The treasury secretary, Albert Gallatin, with his singular long vision was an early hero of the office in the history of land sales. Surveyor General Jared Mansfield, the mathematician, also achieved immortality by settling the survey techniques on scientific principles—creating the system of base lines and principal meridians that would last for all time.[39] There was the pragmatic commissioner, Edward Tiffin, who loaded up the precious land office records in August 1814, and as the British entered Washington, D.C., with arson in their hearts, had his staff busy drafting plats, posting accounts, and correcting arithmetic in temporary quarters safely across the Potomac in Virginia. One member of the land office staff thought the flames of Washington, seen at night, "an interesting event." Tiffin, despite such heroics, was destined to be thrown out of office by President Jackson years later when the spoils system took over federal appointments.[40]

At other levels, of course, the record was notoriously less heroic: it was heavily flavored with fraud and corruption, not only by the appointed district land office officials, but by the landbuying public as well. But fraud and corruption had been common enough even before there was a land office, when the U.S. Treasury handled the sales under the direction of Congress. The Scioto Company was a piece of fraudulence from stem to stern, yet its needs directly motivated passage of the great Ordinance of 1787. The distribution of the public land seemed to offer temptation beyond the capacity of common humanity to resist, decade after decade. The corruption and fraud, however, "made a market," and the lands went quickly enough into private hands, which was, after all, the object of it all. That the federal government hoped for a profit was a secondary consideration.

What was important in the long run was that the land be distributed into private hands in the standard American land tenure, and that the titles be perfectiy secure, and that the American political democracy be expanded in its pure form from east to west as the continental nation was formed, piece by piece, township by township. The people and wagons moved ever westward and a stable institutional framework of settlement went with them until the nation extended from ocean to ocean, the remote heritage of the original Virginia Company charter of 1606.

After the fiascos of the Ohio and Scioto companies, the powers of the old Congress ended. In 1790 the new federal Congress gave the responsibility to the Treasury to sell off the public domain. Then began the long series of efforts to find the best vending techniques: the means of payment, extent of credit allowed, and optimal sizes of parcels for sale. The sizes became smaller and the amount of credit larger as time went on—democratization. Up to 1837 Congress had passed 375 laws governing the land distribution,[41] including acts of preemption, acts of donation, warrants for military service, settlements of titles derived from foreign grants. The land office, within the Treasury but after 1800 with its own commissioner, in 1800 set up the first district offices. Attached to them were the district surveyors, the registrars (who collected the money and had the greatest opportunities for fraud). The technique of survey before sales together with public auctions persisted, sometimes with difficulty. It could take just 30 seconds to "cry off" a parcel of land at an auction, but usually five years to get all the paperwork completed and a title, signed by the president, into the purchaser's hands. Rohrbough suggests that the inevitable delay guaranteed that there would be no property qualifications on voting in the new lands. Inefficiency bred popular democracy.[42]

The surveys made it possible for every parcel of land for sale to have a distinct trigonometric identity. Rohrbough wrote of the rectangular surveys: "One of the principal objects of the rectangular survey was a usable system of land description, and here the surveys proved successful. But much of the surveying was bad, and all of it was tardy."[43] It was done though, and the Washington bureaucracy was forever behind in the resulting paperwork. At one point President Jackson faced ten thousand separate land patents awaiting his quill-pen signature. It was all done by hand, from the survey team in the forest to the president in the White House.[44]

In 1854 the Graduation Act was applied to liquidate the remaining public holdings east of the Mississippi. Only the West remained public. The government, according to Vernon Carstensen, actually lost money overall on the land sales.[45] Rigged auctions and larcenous district officials accounted for much of the loss. Millions of people had poured into the public lands and yet the primary seller lost money. There was a huge rent to be realized from the lands, and the federal government did not realize its possible maximum share.

Then in 1862 the Homestead Act was passed and the frontiersman's dream of free land was nearly realized, except this meant there was a return to the practices of colonial times and the land so occupied had to be improved by the occupier. Once again raw labor could acquire land. Those lands so acquired were mainly quarter sections, 160 acres, and were also laid out in square miles. Ten percent of the public domain of 1850 was destined to be given away to the railroads as construction subsidies. Finally, some 174,000,000 acres of desert and mountains were left in the contiguous forty-eight states, and they remained as part of the "national land reserve", used mainly for mining, timbering, and grazing under federal license. It is all surveyed in thirty-six square mile sections according to the act of 1785 and New England custom. Owyhee County, Idaho, huge and empty, is laid out in little thirty-six square mile townships, just like southern Vermont. And it all lies in the states that were initially territories, organized according to the ordinances of 1787 and 1790.

Uncelebrated in history books, unknown to the average citizen, the land ordinances of the "old Congress" achieved an almost ubiquitous domination beyond the Appalachians. The objects of those acts were achieved in a century of unparalleled economic development. Arizona came into the union in 1912 after passing through the traces of a territorial government according to the eighteenth-century land acts. It is true that the machinery of the land distribution was oiled by fraudulence. But no amount of wisdom and virtue could have distributed without sin a legacy taken "from others of the sons of Adam"[46] by military force, or the threat of it, from the beginning. From the Ohio River to the Pacific Ocean, the American thumbprint covered it all.

Notes

1. The Ordinance of 1784 is reprinted in *Old South Leaflets* no. 127 (Boston, Mass., Directors of the Old South Work, 1896–1903). Hereafter, *OSL* 127.
2. *OSL* 127, 43. Jefferson wrote the lines quoted in 1786.
3. *OSL* 127, 27. In this place the entire letter from Jefferson to Clark is reprinted.
4. *OSL* 127, 33–34.
5. Ray Allen Billington, *Westward Expansion: A History of the American Frontier* (New York, Macmillan, 1949), 212–16.
6. Dane's account is given in Albert Bushnell Hart, ed., *American History Told By Contemporaries* (New York, Macmillan, 1901), 3: 155–58.
7. Jay Barrett, *The Evolution of the Ordinance of 1787* (New York, Putnam's Sons, 1891), 82.
8. Hart, *American History,* 155–57.
9. Marshall Harris, *Origin of the Land Tenure System in the United States* (Westport, Conn.: Greenwood Press, 1970), 389. However, Jefferson said he preferred the rule of descent in Virginia lands to be: "...the lands of any person dying intestate will be divisible equally among his children, or other representatives of equal degree (*Notes on the State of Virginia* [London: John Stockdale, 1788], 227). Dane may have written it in the 1787 Ordinance, but obviously Jefferson advocated it.
10. For more discussion by the present author on these matters, see J. R. T. Hughes, *Social Control in the Colonial Economy* (Charlottesville, University Press of Virginia, 1976), 43–44, 81–82.
11. Barrett, *Evolution of the Ordinance of 1787,* 182.
12. Hughes, *Social Control,* 82.
13. Barrett, *Evolution of the Ordinance of 1787,* 82.
14. In my paper, "A World Elsewhere: The Importance of Starting English," (forthcoming in *Essays in Honour of Sir John Habakkuk,* Oxford University Press), I give an example from the deed book of Halifax township in southern Vermont. Jeremiah Read, who calls himself "husbandman," conveys 26 March, 1773 to William Scot, "yeoman," in fee simple, for cash in exchange for "delivery" of the land (transfer of property rights before witnesses). The use of the old-style identification yeoman continues for some years after the Revolution, when all persons are equally "citizens." The archaic word *husbandman* does not recur in the Halifax records. In the case of the conveyance from Read to Scot, it is March 1778, five years after the delivery, before the deed is entered in the town deed book (Halifax Vermont Town Deedbook, vol. 1.A.)
15. Barrett, *Evolution of the Ordinance of 1787,* 82.
16. Francis Newton Thorpe, ed., *The Federal and State Constitutions, Colonial Charters, and Other Organic Laws*...(Washington, D.C., Government Printing Office, 1909), 956.

17. That is, Dartmouth's charter had been granted by King George III, and the charter was upheld by the U.S. Supreme Court against an attempted seizure by the state of New Hampshire, thus sustaining by implication all the prior grants of the English crown, i.e., all the vested property rights derived therefrom. As Chief Justice Marshall phrased it: "It is too clear to require the support of argument that all contracts, respecting property, remained unchanged by the revolution." 4 Wheaton, 518 (1819), 651.

18. Hart, *American History,* 155.

19. Harris, *Origin of the Land Tenure System,* 389.

20. Barrett, *Evolution of the Ordinance of 1787,* 87.

21. Hart, *American History,* 157.

22. Hughes, *Social Control,* 86.

23. Details and citations for the general information in the next four paragraphs may be found in Hughes, *Social Control,* "The Background of Tenures," 23-31, and "The American Tenure and Its Establishment," 37-50.

24. James Kent, *Commentaries on American Law,* 13th ed. (Boston: Little, Brown and Co., 1884) 3: *488-*489.

25. As a practical matter the constitutional continuity of the common law and hence the old practices regarding land-holding is covered by the tenth amendment to the federal constitution—the powers reserved to the "States respectively, or to the people."

26. Billington, *Westward Expansion,* 206-7.

27. Leonard Arrington, *Great Basin Kingdom: An Economic History of the Latter-day Saints* (Boston, Houghton Mifflin, 1958), 24-25.

28. Amelia Clewly Ford (Philadelphia), says of Wentworth's methods: "In the interval between King George's war and the last French and Indian War, Governor Benning Wentworth began to grant townships in the region beyond the Connecticut, with the hope of strengthening the claim of New Hampshire to the disputed country, as against New York. He mapped out on paper a large part of the present Vermont into townships six miles square." This after a long period of failed efforts to settle the new land elsewhere in squares of various dimensions. Settlement followed and a new system had begun "a brilliant innovation" (*Colonial Precedents of Our National Land System As It Existed in 1800* [Philadelphia: Porcupine Press, 1976 reprint, 1st ed., 1910]).

29. Both charters remain today in the custody of the townships. I am indebted to Laura Sumner and Harold Makepeace, the town clerks (as of the summer of 1986) of Halifax and Marlboro, respectively, for their assistance.

30. Ford, *Colonial Precedents,* 33-37 on square townships, and pp. 43-83 on 640-acre sections.

31. Ford, *Colonial Precedents,* 21-22, n. 53.

32. Ford, *Colonial Precedents,* 45-54, 65.

33. Malcolm J. Rohrbough, *The Land Office Business: The Settlement and Administration of American Public Lands, 1789-1837* (New York, Oxford University Press, 1971), 9-10.

34. Billington, *Westward Expansion*, 199, 228–44.

35. Billington, *Westward Expansion*, 210.

36. Billington, *Westward Expansion*, 217–18. The following two paragraphs are drawn from Billington's full account, pp. 174–245.

37. Rohrbough, *Land Office Business*, 89–136, covers the postwar (1815–19) surge into the midwest beyond Ohio.

38. Rohrbough, *Land Office Business*, 57–58.

39. Rohrbough, *Land Office Business*, 55.

40. Rohrbough, *Land Office Business*, 68–69.

41. Rohrbough, *Land Office Business*, 295. Jonathan Hughes, *American Economic History* (Glenview, Illinois: Scott, Foresman, 1983), 103–4 For a summary of parcel sizes and prices.

42. Rohrbough, *Land Office Business*, 301; Hughes, *American Economic History*, 105.

43. Rohrbough, *Land Office Business*, 297.

44. Rohrbough, *Land Office Business*, 271–94 ,for a description of the land office business in the 1830s, at the height of public land sales. The volume of the 1830s was never reached again; 20.1 million acres were sold in 1836. Two years later the figures were down to 3.4 million. The highest level ever reached again in a single year was 12.8 million acres in 1854.

45. Vernon Carstensen, ed., *The Public Lands: Studies in the History of the Public Domain* (Madison: University of Wisconsin Press, 1962), xviii.

46. John Winthrop's (attributed) description of the American Indians in 1629 just before the Puritans sailed for Massachusetts. Indian tenure, unless granted by the crown, was simply right of occupancy. Its extinction from 1607 to the closing of the frontier in 1890 is the history of the public lands. The Northwest Ordinances spelled inevitable disaster for the Indians, of course. It was so from the beginning. Winthrop wrote: "The whole earth is the Lord's garden and hee hath given it to the sons of Adam to bee tilled and improved by them, why then should we stand starving now for places of habitation. . . and in the meane tyme suffer whole countryes as profitable for the use of man, to lye waste without any improvement?" (*General Considerations for the Plantation in New England*, Thomas Hutchinson, *The Hutchinson Papers* [Albany, New York: The Prince Society, 1865], 1: 32–33). The logic was inexorable. Two-and-a-half centuries later, one need not question. T. R. Roosevelt wrote: "To recognize the Indian ownership of the limitless prairies and forests of this continent—that is, to consider the dozen squalid savages who hunted at long intervals over a territory of a thousand square miles as owning it outright—necessarily implies a similar recognition of the claims of every white hunter, squatter, horsethief, or wandering cattle-man" (*The Winning of the West*, [New York, Putnam, 1889], 1: 331).

2.

THE NORTHWEST ORDINANCE IN HISTORICAL PERSPECTIVE

Douglass C. North
Andrew R. Rutten
Washington University

A MAJOR TASK OF economic history is explaining the path of economic change through time. Doing so requires understanding the constraints that cause the economy to follow the particular path it does. Thus the role of the economic historian is not only to examine the economic consequences of each particular step along the path, but also to examine the determinants of the particular path the economy followed. In this essay we attempt to explain the factors involved in the passage of a landmark in American economic history, the Northwest Ordinance, and we explore its role in the evolution of the American economy. In section 1 we lay out the logical connections between institutions and economic performance. Section 2 outlines the Northwest Ordinance and its relationship to earlier land policy. Section 3 explores the major issues of the 1780s that led to the passage of the ordinance and shaped its specific provisions. Section 4 looks at the downstream consequences, that is, how the structure provided in the ordinance affected decisions about land policy in the early nineteenth century, and how that structure was itself modified. Section 5 summarizes the ordinance's implications for the institutional issues laid out in section 1.

I

Institutions define and narrow the choice set that exists at any moment, in contrast to the standard approach of economists, who typically take a tabula rasa approach, assuming that institutions impose no constraints on choice. Institutions are, as well, the connecting links in the sequential pattern of economic history. They not only define the alternatives at any moment, but as they evolve they connect previous choices with subsequent choices. Institutions are altered in light of new problems and issues, but they are altered at the margin, with the margin determined by the previous choices.

Thus the role that institutions play in an economy is to define the manmade constraints on choices that in turn affect economic performance. The cost of producing a good or service is usually taken as the cost of the land, labor, capital, and entrepreneurial talent that when combined through a production function produce output. Recently it has been recognized that this simple neoclassical approach needs to be radically altered, since the costs of transacting appear nowhere in this formula. It is as though all of the 'gains from trade' could be realized with no resources going into organizing and integrating production, devising markets, maintaining the political structure. The costs of production are actually the sum of production costs, here called transformation costs, and transactions costs, which are those costs incurred in carrying out exchange. Because the extent of specialization and division of labor depends on transaction costs, they have played a critical role in determining how well economies have realized their productive potential throughout history.

Transaction costs in turn depend on the institutional structure, which ultimately is shaped by the political decisions that define and enforce the rules of the game. This is why political and economic institutions play a critical role in the performance of an economy. They define the opportunities, which in turn determine the cost of transforming and transacting, and, hence, what is produced and how it is distributed. It is for these reasons that the decisions that produced the institutional structure of early America are important.

It is not just the rules themselves that are important, but also the degree to which the rules are enforced, the way they are enforced, and the preferences of the players. These three aspects interact to determine the choices actually made in the economy. The second and third are important because it is costly to measure performance of agents or the attributes of the goods and services being traded.[1] The more costly measurement is, the more likely it is that enforcement will be imperfect, particularly since third parties enforce rules and are themselves agents of principals. Accordingly, the contracts that embody economic decisions will be structured to attempt to take into account the effectiveness of enforcement by minimizing the dissipation of rent at the margins where compliance is difficult to determine. In addition, however, the attitudes of the parties to the rules in terms of their fairness or justice will (given the costliness of measuring performance) influence the costs of contracting. The price of ideological convictions is the premium individuals are willing to incur not to free ride. Although the strength of convictions varies with the issues and the individual, the premium is surely negatively sloped. That is, the higher the costs one incurs, the less ideological conviction matters.

The preference structure that affects the costs of contracting derives from the broad ideological constructs that everyone possesses as an essential part of the decision-making process. We know little about norms of behavior. Clearly, however, they are an important determinant of the choice set at a particular moment; even more important is their role in determining the path of institutional evolution. Without anything as elegant as a theory, we can say they are transmitted intergenerationally by family, schooling, and religion, and that they change slowly (although the rate of change is surely related to the cost of information). Changes in relative prices surely play a major role in changing individual perceptions of reality and hence norms of behavior. Differences in norms of behavior can dramatically modify the consequences of formal rules. For example, the adoption of the United States Constitution by some Latin American countries has led to very different results than in the United States. Since norms appear to change more slowly than formal rules, their interaction with rules can result in radically contrasting paths of institutional evolution.

It is one thing to understand the role of institutions, measurement costs, enforcement characteristics, and ideology in determining choices at any moment. It is much more difficult to understand the role institutions play in determining the path of economic development over time. We know very little about this subject, so the framework we suggest is not only tentative but far from complete. At any moment, there is an institutional framework that reflects decisions made in the past. This framework will change when participants are confronted with a new set of issues that makes them feel they can improve on the old forms of contracting based on the existing institutional structure (to put it in an economist's terms, there must be a change in some critical relative price). The participants will not change all the rules, but only those that, given the relative bargaining strength of the parties, appear to them to affect the new problem. In other words, institutional evolution occurs at the margin in response to new situations. The new institution will be a complex of inherited, old rules with modifications or new parts added to them to solve the new problems that are faced.

Thus, as institutions evolve, new rules will become embedded in the institutional structure and provide the basis for subsequent policymaking. This very simple view of institutional change is incomplete. To understand institutional evolution, we also need to know which rules will get thrown aside. The tentative answer is that it is those rules that, as a consequence of changing relative prices, become controversial given the bargaining power of the players. Although it is easy *ex post* to observe a pattern in the evolution of institutions, it is very difficult to forecast beforehand which will be adopted. History provides many examples of decisions that in retrospect appear inevitable but in fact were very close. We are far from being able to predict which institution will be chosen, even though we may be able to make sense out of history by looking at the paths that were chosen and observing which alternatives were foregone.

The two aspects of institutions, their ability to restrict choices and their responsiveness to changing situations, are illustrated by the history of the development and implementation of the Northwest Ordinance. The development of the ordinance was a process of changing existing land policy in response to changes in incentives brought on by the War of Independence.

In the nineteenth century, land policy continued to evolve in response to changes in incentives. However, the path of evolution was largely determined by the structure provided by the Northwest Ordinance. Before examining this process, we will examine the ordinance and how it resembled colonial land policies and how it differed from them.

II

The Northwest Ordinance was passed "by the United States in Congress assembled" on 13 July, 1787. Like the Constitution, which was devised and structured at the same time, it is simple and quite brief. There are three sections. The first established "the law of descent and conveyance of estates" for the territories. It provided that the estate of one who died without a will would be divided equally among all heirs, and explicitly established fee simple ownership of real property for the first time, so that property could be easily transferred by sale or lease. The second established "the territorial government." It provided the basic provisions of a territorial government and established the timetable by which the territories would eventually become self-governing. The final section established "the compact between the original States and the people and States." Its six articles effectively gave the territories a bill of rights, which provided for: (1) freedom of religion; (2) the use of writs of *habeas corpus*, jury trials, the common law, and bail (except in capital cases); and prohibitions against cruel and unusual punishment, the seizure of property without due process or compensation, or laws interfering with contracts; (3) encouragement of schools and the means of education because of the importance of religion, morality, and knowledge to good government and happiness; and encouragement of the utmost good faith towards the Indians; (4) the obligations of the territories to the United States, including remaining in the United States, sharing in the payment of federal debt, not interfering with federal land sales, not taxing nonresident owners higher than residents, and not interfering with shipments on the Mississippi or St. Lawrence; (5) the division of the territories into states, which were to have republican governments and to be admitted as full members of the United States after reaching specified populations; and finally, (6) a prohibition on slavery or involuntary servitude, with the proviso that fugitive slaves could be returned.

The land policy embodied in the ordinance included more than these provisions since the ordinance implicitly accepted many aspects of existing policy. The most important of these were established by the 1780 Resolution on Public Land and the 1785 land ordinances. The first established that the unsettled lands ceded by the states to the national government would be disposed of for the common benefit, and that the territories formed from them would become distinct republican states fully participating in the union.[2] The 1785 ordinance provided the mechanism for actually disposing of the public lands by specifying that presurveyed contiguous parcels would be sold at auction.

As several generations of historians have documented, there are antecedents for almost every provision of the Northwest Ordinance and its sister ordinances. Many were taken directly from colonial or state practices. These include not only such mechanical details as the method of sale, but also the clauses dealing with governance issues.[3] Those dealing with personal freedoms and rights came preponderantly from the Massachusetts and Virginia Constitutions. For example, the article on religious freedom comes from sections 2 and 12 of the Declaration of Rights in the Massachusetts Constitution of 1780. The articles on inheritance, fee simple ownership of land, and education were authored by Nathan Dane of Massachusetts and were based on his understanding of Massachusetts law.[4] The clauses guaranteeing access to the protections of the common law can be traced to colonial charters.[5] Those provisions that cannot be traced to actual practices, such as the antislave clause or the ultimate incorporation of the colonies as full-fledged states, can be traced to earlier policy proposals.[6] In turn, almost all of the American roots of these practices can themselves be traced to English practices.[7]

But simply finding these precedents does not constitute an explanation of the Northwest Ordinance. After all, land policies varied widely among the colonies and states, and many aspects of these policies were *not* embodied in the ordinance. Furthermore, there is little precedent in colonial practices for the emphasis on land sales as a source of revenue, and none for the promise of eventual statehood for the territories or the antislavery clause. Indeed, the antislavery clause even conflicted with the Constitution, which sanctioned slavery through the three-fifths rule. We believe that the explanation for this particular mixture of the old and familiar practices with the radically new lies in the changes in incentives facing policy makers from 1776 to 1787.

III

Independence dramatically changed the incentives guiding decisions about American land policy. These decisions were no longer made by English politicians running an empire, but by American politicians running a nation. Since their interests were very different, it is not surprising that Americans did not simply adopt British policies wholesale. Their choice of policies reflected not only the difference between American and English control, but also the American political structure. Under the Articles of Confederation, control over land policy lay with the states. Agreement among the states on land policy was complicated by the unequal distribution of its costs and benefits across the states. The attempt by each state to get a favorable land policy led to a protracted political war.[8] To understand the particular provisions of the Northwest Ordinance, it would be necessary to examine this fight in detail. Since this obviously cannot be done briefly, we will focus on how three issues that emerged with American independence shaped land policy from 1776 to 1787. These issues are: the need to finance the war, the commitment to representative government, and the antislavery sentiment of the northern states.

Land policy became a national issue because of the need to finance the war against the British. Since the Articles of Confederation left the power of taxation with the states, the unsettled lands were the major asset of the new nation. Americans could not raise revenue from land in the same way as the British because British policies relied on the manipulation of the imperial economy to generate revenue from the colonies. Because the British wanted large settlements, their land policy made use of such inducements to settlement as the promise of such English institutions as the common law[9] and representation in local government,[10] as well as marketing strategies such as settlement ahead of surveying and the granting of preemption rights to actual settlers.[11] These policies were unsuitable for Americans, who needed a policy that would generate revenue directly from the land.

The first method used to finance the war with the unsettled lands involved the use of land bounties, certificates for specified amounts of unsettled land, as a means of paying the army. This began with the states providing for their share of the troops out of their claims on unsettled land. Since the states differed in the extent of their claims on unsettled lands, this policy resulted in dramatic differences among the states. For example, Virginia, which had the largest endowment of unsettled land, offered ten times as much land to officers as the national government.[12] This led Maryland, which had no claims to either western land or land within its own border, to argue "that the back lands acquired from the Crown of Great Britain in the present war, should be a common stock for the benefit of the United States."[13] The threat by Maryland not to join the confederation unless its proposal was accepted led to the resolution of 10 October, 1780. Among other things, the resolution provided that "the unappropriated lands that may be ceded or relinquished to the United States [would be] disposed of for the common benefit of the United States."[14] Despite this agreement on principles of land policy, the final cession of Virginia lands was not accepted until 1784.

The signing of the peace treaty did not end the search for a method of paying for the war. If anything, it intensified the search. Not only did the debt incurred during the war have to be paid, but land bounties could no longer be used. In addition, the army was threatening rebellion if its claims were not satisfied. Indeed, one of the proposals that was considered was to settle former soldiers directly on the western lands. The national government decided on a dramatic new method of generating revenue—selling land to settlers (or to land companies).

This decision was a break not only with British policy, but also with the policies followed by the states during the early confederation period.[15] Paying for the war was such a pressing problem that previous policies were never given serious consideration by the national government. Perhaps nothing illustrates this shift better then the changing attitude of Jefferson. In 1776 he argued that "the idea of Congress selling out unlocated lands has sometimes dropped, but we have always met the hint with such determined opposition that I believe it will never be proposed.—I am against selling the lands at all"; by 1780 he was referring to them as a "precious resource" for financing the war.[16]

If the need to finance the war led to agreement that the western lands should be sold, the different landholdings of the states led to disagreement about how to actually sell the lands. Those states that managed to preserve claims to western lands, such as Virginia, New York, and Connecticut,[17] favored a land policy that increased the value of their western lands. They wanted to encourage western settlement, but with federal lands priced high enough to make their lands attractive. Those states that had unsold lands within their own borders, such as Pennsylvania and Massachusetts, favored a land policy that would diminish the value of this land as little as possible. They wanted to encourage western settlement, but at a far slower rate than states such as Virginia. Finally, those states that had no claims over unsettled lands favored policies that maximized national revenue from land sales.

It would seem that these widely divergent interests would prevent the states from reaching agreement about how to handle land sales. Although the scheme of the Ordinance of 1785, which was implicitly adopted by the Northwest Ordinance, seems to imply that an acceptable sales scheme existed, this was not the case. As we shall see in the next section, the fight over who was to benefit, both directly and indirectly, from land sales continued into the nineteenth century.

The politics of the revolution also played an important role in determining land policy. The fundamental political issue of the American revolution was the representation of colonists in central government. Until the early 1770s, Americans had accepted the British theory of 'virtual representation.' It relied on the interest of British politicians in the common good to justify the denial of direct representation of the colonies in Parliament. This theory was abandoned by 1776. It was replaced by theories that justified government by the use of some form of actual representation.[18] The universal acceptance of this idea meant that any politically feasible plan for the government of the territories (the American colonies) would have to include their eventual incorporation into the national government as states. This meant that the political structure of the British colonial system was as unattractive to Americans as its economic policies.

Since incorporating the new states into the Union would inevitably change the balance of power among the states, there was disagreement as to how the states should be incorporated. Each faction sought to ensure that the new states would not shift the balance of power in a manner that would overwhelm it. Among the factions were the northern and southern states, large and small states, and agricultural and industrial states. Among the issues that were raised were the number of states, the size at which territories would become eligible for statehood, and the manner in which the new states would be represented in the national government. From 1776 to 1787, a variety of different positions were adopted on these issues. For example, the number of states in the Northwest went from ten in Jefferson's original proposal to five in the Northwest Ordinance. Unlike the economic aspects of land policy, controversy over the political mechanisms provided by the Northwest Ordinance ceased with the passage of the ordinance.

One political issue that deserves separate treatment is the effect of the Northwest Ordinance on the balance between slave and free states. The antislave proviso in the ordinance appears to be in direct conflict with the Constitution, and has been the subject of immense controversy. In the Constitution slavery was sanctioned by counting slaves as three-fifths of a person for the purpose of determining representation in Congress; the ordinance explicitly prohibits slavery. The most likely explanation for these contradictory actions is that they resulted from a vote trade, in which northern states agreed to the three-fifths rule at the Constitutional Convention in return for southern states agreeing to the Northwest Ordinance's antislavery proviso at the Old Congress.[19] Despite the lack of direct evidence, such a trade is plausible. There was a substantial amount of communication between the convention and the congress, and the final votes on the three-fifths rule and the Northwest Ordinance occurred within two days of each other. Certainly the trade makes sense. The size of states, in terms of representation, was a major issue in both the Constitution and the Northwest Ordinance. The three-fifths rule increased the representation of southern states, making slavery more secure. On the other hand, southerners may not have feared the increasing political power of the free Northwest states because of their view that these states would share interests (such as navigation of the Mississippi) with southern states.

These examples show how American independence allowed new issues to determine American land policy. To be truly satisfactory, analysis would have to be extended to include more detail about how exactly these issues affected land policy, as well as examine other important issues. For example, we assumed that each state's position on land policy depended on how that state would be affected by those policies. However, this assumption ignores the possibility that the preferences of the actual representatives might reflect peculiarities of internal state politics. We have also ignored some of the most divisive issues of the period, such as free navigation on the Mississippi. Southern states favored it, since they believed it would not only encourage settlement of the Southwest, but also give a 'southern' tilt to states in the Northwest. It was opposed by northern states, since without free navigations freight would be shipped east, and by those states that wanted to discourage rapid settlement of the west.

IV

The Northwest Ordinance (together with its companion, the Act of 1785) did not settle policy on the disposal of the public lands. Indeed, the next fifty years were marked by almost constant controversy over who would benefit, and by how much, from the disposal of the public lands, with almost every aspect of land policy undergoing several major changes.[20] This does not mean that the Northwest Ordinance was unimportant. Each new policy reflected what was politically and economically feasible at any moment; but feasibility, particularly political feasibility, depended crucially on what had been done in the past. To see how the passage of the Northwest Ordinance shaped subsequent policy, we will look at the evolution of three different aspects of land policy: the political development of the territories, the distribution of benefits from the public lands, and the terms of sale.

The Northwest Ordinance's most direct impact was on policy regarding the political development of the territories. Subsequent law did little to alter the ordinance's provisions for the steps in the incorporation of the territories into national politics. The changes that occurred were all minor, mostly concerned with procedural details.[21] By and large, they corrected problems that had occurred with the government of the earlier territories. Their relative unimportance suggests that the most important and enduring contribution of the Northwest Ordinance to subsequent institutional development was its underlying view "that the Territories are to be regarded as inchoate states, as future members of the Union."[22] As we shall see below, it would only be a slight exaggeration to say that the most important change in the politics of public land policy after 1787 was the growing participation of westerners.

As the discussion of the politics of land policy in the previous section showed, there was no one land policy that was preferred by everyone.[23] Not only did different states have divergent preferences over land policy, but these preferences depended on their preferences on other policies, such as slavery or tariffs. A change in either the preferences of participants or the political structure would change policy. The incorporation of the frontier states was important because they preferred a different mix of policies than any of the existing factions. Furthermore, their interests on some issues changed over time, with divergences among them sometimes occurring, depending on the level of economic development.[24] The result was that the policy equilibrium was continually being shifted towards the policies favored by the frontier states. This process can be seen by looking at the evolution of policy concerning the distribution of benefits and the terms of sale.

All land policy implicitly distributes the benefits from public lands, so any change in land law can be considered as a change in distribution policy. However, there were a series of proposals that treated distribution directly. Each of these aimed at changing the status quo (set by the Act of 1784 and implicitly accepted in the Northwest Ordinance), which was (with some exceptions for the public land states) that the direct benefits from the public lands were to go to the federal government for national business. They fall naturally into two categories: increasing the grants to public land states and distributing land to nonpublic land states.

For the public land states, the *status quo* was fairly high. Not only did they get the land reserved for schools, but after the admission of Ohio in 1803, they received grants for the construction of roads to the state from the east. Beginning in 1817 they proposed a series of bills enlarging these grants to include more for public improvements. Although the original bills failed (actually, they were vetoed by President Madison), a coalition of western, northeastern, and mid-Atlantic congressmen emerged and was able to gradually increase internal improvement subsidies. It began with grants to improve the Cumberland Road (itself partially financed by land grants under the Ohio Enabling Act) and surveys for canals and roads, finally extending to support for new projects in 1830.[25] Although these included projects outside of the public land states, the bulk of the projects were in the public land states. These grants increased so much that Ohio, the first public land state, received only 10 percent of its land in grants, and Michigan and Wisconsin, the last of the Northwestern states settled, ultimately received grants totaling almost 30 percent of their land.[26]

Attempts to change policy to distribute benefits directly to nonpublic land states were also successful. This issue was first raised seriously in the 1820s by Maryland and Rhode Island, states that had few public lands of their own, either in-state or in the West.[27] They advocated giving the nonpublic land states grants for education, with each state's grant proportional to its share of the original land. These proposals failed because of opposition from the South and the West. Finally, in 1837 the combination of a budget surplus, a land boom, and congressional realignment led to the passage of a distribution bill, which gave 80 percent of the surplus to nonpublic land states.[28]

An examination of the evolution of sales policy from the *status quo* implicit in the Northwest Ordinance also shows an increasing Western tilt to policy. However, this tilt cannot be attributed solely to the growing political power of the western states. Even without direct political participation, the settlers could restrict the federal government's options. They could do this because of the weakness of the federal government in the distant territories, and because of the government's need to compete with other options available to settlers. These two factors often allowed the settlers to ignore federal land policies. For example, auctions were used to sell land in the hope that competitive bidding would drive the price of prime land above the minimum. However, claims clubs, which were locally more effective at enforcing their will than was the federal government, could prevent competitive bidding and ensure that their members got their choice of land.[29]

The federal government's need to compete for sales with other sources of land led to the first major change in sales policy. The Frontier Land Bill of 1800 proposed by William Henry Harrison, the (nonvoting) congressional delegate from the Indiana Territory, and containing measures favored on the frontier, was passed before there were any western states. Before its passage sales policy had been governed by the Act of 1784, as modified in 1796. It provided for sale of tracts larger than 640 acres for two dollars per acre, with payment in specie or government securities, due immediately. Sales under this regime were disappointing, largely because settlers could get land more easily either by buying it on better terms in existing states or in the nonfederal tracts in the public land states, or simply by squatting in the federal lands. To meet this competition, the new law not only allowed sale of smaller parcels, but offered four-year credit at 6 percent interest, with one quarter due in forty days, one quarter due in two years, and the balance in four years.[30]

As had been predicted by foes, the credit system had serious problems from the beginning. Purchasers used all of their money for a down payment, hoping either that Congress would give them relief, or that they could avoid eviction and repossession. The result was a steady growth in the amount of money owed on land. The problem became intolerable after the land boom of 1816–18. In 1818 there was a total of $7 million owed on land, but land revenues totaled only $2 1/2 million. The increase in outstanding debt was due to the fact that Congress granted relief, as purchasers had hoped, passing ten relief laws between 1800 and 1820.[31]

The Act of 1820 abolished credit but was not a complete defeat for the West. It reestablished cash sales, but on more generous terms than before, with the minimum plot reduced to forty acres and the price to $1.25 per acre. In addition it was followed by a series of credit relief acts that not only extended the period of payment for purchases, but also allowed purchasers to relinquish some land in return for title to remaining portions.[32]

These acts did not meet all of the demands of westerners, especially those in fairly well settled states. In these states the presence of large parcels of still unsold (and thus untaxable) public lands—30 percent of Indiana, 50 percent of Ohio, and 70 percent of Wisconsin[33]—led to a series of proposals for graduation, so that the price of unsold land would gradually be reduced. The Graduation Act was passed in 1841.[34]

Another modification of sales policy that remained controversial during this period was preemption, which gave squatters the first chance to buy the land they occupied. Preemption had been commonly granted by states after the war, when it was motivated by the desire to settle the frontier.[35] However, the federal government had not followed this lead, going as far as having troops burn out squatters in the 1790s. This policy was made official in 1807 with the passage of the Intrusion Act, which provided that squatters could remain as long as they paid rent until the land was purchased. Those who failed to register or pay rent were subject to a fine or imprisonment. As with credit sales, this led to widespread abuse, and between 1799 and 1830 Congress passed twenty acts granting preemption rights to squatters in specific regions. Finally in 1830 these acts were replaced by a general preemption act, which was renewed several times until in 1841 a permanent general preemption was passed.[36]

The history of these three aspects of land policy illustrates the importance of the Northwest Ordinance. Since land policy changed, often dramatically, after 1787, the ordinance did not simply set the terms on which the western lands were settled. Instead, land policy continued to evolve in response to changing economic and political pressures. However, as we have shown, these political and economic changes were to a large extent due to the Northwest Ordinance.

V

What were the implications of the Northwest Ordinance for efficiency and the distribution of income? We are not aware of any studies that explore the second question (although some tentative work has been done on overall land policy), but both earlier research and our own essay allows us to provide some answers on the first issue.

First we should enter a caveat. The economic historian (and the economist for that matter) should be interested in efficiency in two distinct (if related) ways. The first is the traditional measure, allocative efficiency. It is concerned with the standard question of whether the existing institutional arrangements result in more output than any other conceivable arrangement. The second type is adaptive efficiency. It is concerned with how well the institutional structure adapts to new and unforeseen circumstances. An adaptively efficient institution must both maximize the alternatives available, so that in a world of uncertainty the chances of achieving an allocatively efficient solution in turn are maximized, and provide a competitive mechanism for eliminating less efficient solutions. Any evaluation of the efficiency of the Northwest Ordinance must consider both types.

The criterion of allocative efficiency has been at least provisionally examined.[37] Traditionally, historians have given land policy a bad press, complaining about too much land being made available, the evils of speculation, or sometimes, paradoxically enough, monopolization of land.

Economists, on the other hand, have by and large given land policy higher marks. However, it is probably true that the early policy tended to lead to too many resources going into settlement. This policy was continued and even exacerbated by the Homestead Act. It is also probably true that the size requirements of later land policy led to an economically inefficient initial distribution. However, the historian's notions of speculation and monopoly do not hold up. Finally, it should be noted that these inefficiencies were due not to the Northwest Ordinance but to either the 1785 ordinance or its subsequent modifications.

When we turn to the question of adaptive efficiency, the Northwest Ordinance gets high marks. By making land easily transferrable and inheritable, it widened the options of individuals and helped to resolve the allocative inefficiencies described above. The fact that individuals had clear title to land and could, after meeting the initial requirements for getting title, transfer it, lowered the cost of transacting downstream. This meant that despite the inappropriateness of the initial size of landholdings under the Homestead Act, it was possible to restructure landholdings to achieve allocative efficiency. Moreover, the governance provisions of the Northwest Ordinance provided for an assured and reasonably certain path from territory to statehood and thus involvement in the political system of the United States. The provisions of the Bill of Rights provided for the sort of safeguards that, however imperfectly enforced at times, nevertheless provided to settlers confidence in their ability to take up land and to utilize it, and more assurance about the outcome of decisions. In terms of adaptive efficiency, the Northwest Ordinance is a remarkable piece of legislation.

Bibliography

Allen, David. *In English Ways: The Movement of Societies and Traditions of English Local Law and Custom to Massachusetts Bay in the Seventeenth Century.* New York: Norton, 1982.

Barrett, Jay. *Evolution of the Ordinance of 1787.* New York: G. P. Putnam's Sons, 1891.

Barzel, Yoram. "Measurement Costs and the Organization of Markets." *Journal of Law and Economics,* vol. 25, no. 1, (April 1982), 27–48.

Becker, Gary. "A Theory of the Allocation of Time." *Economic Journal,* vol. 75, no. 29, (September 1965), 493–517.

Bestor, Arthur. "Constitutionalism and the Settlement of the West: The Attainment of Consensus, 1754–1784." Bloom, John, *The American Territorial System.* Athens: Ohio University Press, 1973.

Brown, Elizabeth Gaspar. *British Statutes in American Law, 1776–1836.* Ann Arbor: University of Michigan Law School,1964.

Cheung, Steven N. S. "The Contractual Nature of the Firm." *Journal of Law and Economics,* vol. 26, no. 1, (April 1983), 1–22.

Dane, Nathan. "Letter of May 12, 1831." *Indiana Historical Society Publications,* vol. 1, no. 2, (1897).

Dennen, Taylor. "Some Efficiency Effects of Nineteenth Century Federal Land Policy: A Dynamic Analysis." *Agricultural History,* vol. 51, no. 4 (October 1977), 718–736.

Farrand, Max. *The Legislation of Congress of the Government of the Organized Territories of the United States, 1789–1895.*Newark: William Baker, 1896.

Feller, Daniel. *The Public Lands in Jacksonian Politics.* Madison: University of Wisconsin Press, 1984.

Fogel, Robert,and Jack Rutner. "The Efficiency Effects of Federal Land Policy, 1850–1900: A Report of Some Provisional Findings." Edited by William Aydelotte, Allan Bogue, and Robert Fogel. *The Dimensions of Quantitative Research in History.* Princeton: Princeton University Press, 1972.

Ford, Amelia. *Colonial Precedents of Our National Land System as It Existed in 1800.* Madison: University of Wisconsin Press, 1910.

Freund, Rudolf. "Military Bounty Land and the Origins of the Public Domain." *The Public Lands: Studies in the History of the Public Domain.* Edited by Vernon Carstensen. Madison: University of Wisconsin Press, 1963.

Gates, Paul. *History of Public Land Law Development.* New York: Arno, 1979.

Harris, Marshall. *Origin of the Land Tenure System in the United States.* Ames: Iowa State College Press, 1953.

Hibbard, Benjamin. *A History of the Public Land Policies.* Madison: University of Wisconsin Press, 1965.

Howard, A. E. Dick. *The Road from Runnymede: Magna Carta and Constitutionalism in America.* Charlottesville: University Press of Virginia, 1968.

Hughes, Jonathan. "The Great Land Ordinances: Colonial America's Thumbprint on History," Paper prepared for this volume (October 1986).

Kammen, Michael. *Deputyes and Libertyes: The Origins of Representative Government in Colonial America.* New York: Alfred Knopf, 1969.

Lynd, Staughton. *Class Conflict, Slavery and The United States Constitution.* Indianapolis: Bobbs-Merrill, 1967.

New American State Papers, Public Lands, Vol. 1, General Administration. Wilmington: Scholarly Resources, 1973.

North, Douglass. *Structure and Change in Economic History,* New York: Norton, 1981.

Pole, J. R. *The Seventeenth Century: The Sources of Legislative Power.* Charlottesville: University Press of Virginia, 1969.

Tatter, Henry. "State and Federal Land Policy During the Confederation Period." *Agricultural History.* vol. 9, no. 4, (October 1935), 176–186.

Treat, Payson Jackson. *The National Land System, 1785–1820.* New York: E. B. Treat and Co., 1910.

Wood, Gordon. *Representation in the American Revolution.* Charlottesville: University Press of Virginia, 1969.

Wood, Gordon. *The Creation of the American Republic, 1776–1787.* New York: Norton, 1969.

Notes

1. See Lancaster (1969) and Becker (1965) for the origination of this consumer theory argument. It has been extended into the transaction cost framework by Cheung (1983), North (1981), and Barzel (1982).
2. Bestor (1973), 20–22.
3. The origins of such features of the land distribution system as rectangular surveys of townships, the 640–acre section, land bounties, and preemption are traced in detail in Ford (1910) and Harris (1953).
4. For details of the politics surrounding the Northwest Ordinance, see Barrett (1891). Dane's claims for authorship are advanced in Dane (1897).
5. For the history of grants of English "rights and privileges," including the common law, see Brown (1964). The origins of representative government are traced in Kammen (1969) and Wood (1969).
6. For a discussion of the policy proposals concerning land, see Bestor (1973). Dane understandably claims that Jefferson's influence has been overstated.
7. Examples of the adoption and adaptation of English institutions to colonial circumstances are found in Howard (1968), Allen (1982), and Hughes (1986).
8. Indeed, as we show in the next section, the controversy over land policy did not end with the passage of the Northwest Ordinance, but continued into the nineteenth century.
9. See Brown (1964).
10. See Kammen (1969), Pole (1969), and Wood (1969).
11. See Ford (1910) 112–42, and Tatter (1935).
12. Freund (1963), 19.
13. Freund (1963), 18.
14. Bestor (1973), 21.
15. See Tatter (1935) for a summary of early state policy.
16. Ibid. p. 184.
17. Connecticut maintained control of a large parcel of land in what is now Ohio. Known as the "western reserve," (as in Case Western Reserve) it included Cleveland.
18. The evolution of American thinking on representation is traced in Wood (1969).
19. Our analysis follows that of Staughton Lynd in his "Compromise of 1787," reprinted in Lynd (1967), 185–213.
20. The details of the evolution of land policy can be found in Treat (1910), Hibbard (1965), or Gates (1979).
21. The changes in the laws regarding political development are cataloged in Farrand (1896).
22. Farrand (1896), 53.
23. Our discussion of the politics of land laws relies heavily on Feller (1984), which contains a thorough analysis of Congressional votes on land legislation during the period.

24. For example, in 1826 two Ohio "congressmen opposed additional frontier land surveys...arguing that a glutted market depressed property values and retarded the sale of Ohio's remaining public domain." Feller (1984), 79.

25. Feller (1984), 48–67, 83–85, 91–97, 136–42.

26. Gates (1979), 384.

27. Feller (1984), 40–48.

28. Feller, (1984), 40–48.

29. Hibbard (1965), 198–208.

30. Treat (1910), 1–101.

31. The relief acts and their terms are listed in Treat, (1910), 143.

32. Feller (1984), 26–38.

33. Calculated from General Land Office, Statement of Annual Land Sales, 1830–1840, Table D, Recapitulation, reprinted in New American State Papers, Public Lands, Vol. 1, General Administration, p. 111.

34. Feller (1984), 101–10, 125–36, 156–71.

35. Tatter (1935), 176–86.

36. Hibbard (1965), 144–70.

37. See Fogel and Rutner (1972) and Dennen (1977).

3.

"O PIONEERS"
Land Speculation and the
Growth of the Midwest

Stanley Lebergott
Wesleyan University

Of all the occupations by which gain is secured, none is better than agriculture, none more profitable, none more delightful, none more becoming to a freeman.

—Cicero,
De Officiis

I

THE PREVAILING VIEW OF land purchase before the Civil War embodies a charming paradox. It describes ante bellum farmers as too poor to buy land at federal government prices—but not "speculator's" land, at still higher prices. Congress, we are told, set "a price for land beyond the capacity of the average settler."[1] It did not "provide that easy access to the public domain that Jefferson had seen as the foundation of political and economic democracy...."(thus) "the average settler found land too dear for outright purchase."[2]

But if government prices were too dear, then millions of farmers who bought land before the Homestead Act had to buy their land from speculators. Authorities agree on how they operated. Their companies early "spied out the best tracts, bought them at public auction, and sold them at higher prices to authentic settlers."[3] (It has even been asserted that "nearly three-fourths" of the 40 million acres sold by the U.S. in the 1835–37 boom "went to speculators—men acquiring land tracts in the hope of selling them at a profit—and only about a fourth to actual settlers."[4]) Thus the prevailing "land system allowed speculators to monopolize many million acres of land"[5] while farmers "were forced to borrow at high rates."[6] The paradox follows remorselessly: farmers too poor to pay the prices set by Congress somehow paid even higher prices to speculators—plus high interest rates as well. Nor did a mere handful of people manage to do so. Nearly seven million people set up farms in the Central states by 1860.[7] Most of their land had come from the public domain. So dramatic a paradox invites inquiry.

Closer inquiry into the history of U.S. land settlement and intervention by giant speculators, however, leads to quite different conclusions.[8] Federal policy did not in fact set a price for land "beyond the capacity of the average settler." Few farmer settlers appear to have bought their land from the large speculators of legend, even during the great land boom of the 1850s. Moreover, such speculators added little to the cost of the public domain land that farmers did as a whole buy.

II

The starting place for so different a view of land policy and speculation is the Northwest Ordinance of July 1787. For the Northwest is the arena to which the usual highly colored descriptions are intended to apply. The structure of its settlement turned on three primary elements that appear decade after decade.

One such factor was the exclusion of slavery from that huge territory. Concern with the morality of slaveholding had risen during the eighteenth century, in the U.S. as well as in England. Yet twelve of the thirteen colonies retained slavery after independence. In 1789 the new nation did so as well. (So, of course, did almost every other nation in Europe, Asia and Africa.)

It is all the more striking how many "founding fathers" planned a different future for the Northwest. In 1784 Jefferson proposed that "after the year 1800 of the Christian era there should be neither slavery nor involuntary servitude" in any state carved from that territory. But Maryland, Virginia and South Carolina opposed his bill. And it failed. In April 1787 a new ordinance was drafted, omitting any provision against slaveholding. So did the revised draft of July 11. But two days later the old Confederation adopted a final version as nearly its last act. It included a provision, offered by Nathan Dane of Massachusetts, that forbade slavery in the territory.[9]

Meanwhile the Constitutional Convention was at work in Philadelphia. The exclusion of slavery from the Northwest was retained, embodied in statute law by the new Congress.[10] The convention nonetheless accepted slavery in the rest of the U.S. The Constitution it wrote even guaranteed that the external slave trade would not end before January 1, 1808—if then. Slave holding was thus excluded from only one portion of the entire continent: the Northwest Territory.

Dane's amendment was adopted, with full agreement of the four Southern states voting. The next day Madison told the Constitutional Convention (then also meeting) "It now seemed to be pretty well understood that the real difference of interest lay, not between the large and small but between the northern and southern states. The institution of slavery and its consequences formed the line of discrimination."[11] Jefferson's 1784 draft had permitted the new states to use slaves for thirteen years. When he bought the Louisiana Territory from Napoleon in 1803 he made no mention of excluding slavery. The territory South of the Ohio was left open to slave settlement.[12] Only the Northwest Territory was denied the benefit of what some were already describing as "a positive good."

III

That denial, however, altered the economic (and political) future of the United States, for migration into the Northwest Territory became selective. The region attracted, disproportionately, those migrants who objected to slavery. Some had moral objections. Others refused to compete with slave labor. (John Adams attributed "the real cause" of the abolition of slavery in Massachusetts to the "multiplication of labouring white people, who would not longer suffer the rich to employ these sable rivals so much to their injury....The common people would not suffer the labour, by which they alone could obtain a subsistence, to be done by slaves."[13]) Ben Wade, fervent abolitionist leader from Ohio, declared that the high minded free man of the North would never "stoop to labor side by side with your miserable serf."[14] Both moral and economic factors were thus at work.

Migration to the Northwest Territory, the only U.S. region from which slavery was excluded, became increasingly dominated by independent minded men. The migrants did not search for beaver and muskrat, gold or silver. They looked forward to setting up their own farms. But they shared the fractious and independent spirit of the frontier. For centuries the mountaineers (in Afghanistan, Switzerland, Montenegro or Albania) had been the most fractious, the most independent, residents of their nations. Similarly the mountaineers of West Virginia and Kentucky expressed the independent frontier perspective. (And Shays's rebellion appeared in western Massachusetts, not the coastal regions.)

Washington understandably saw uncontrolled migration raising the spectre of

> the overspreading of the Western country...by a parcel of Banditti who will bid defiance to all Authority while they are skimming and disposing of the Cream of the Country at the expence of many suffering Officers and Soldiers who have fought and bled to obtain it and are now waiting the decision of Congress to point them to the promised reward of their past dangers and toils, or a renewal of Hostilities with the Indians, brought about more than probably, by this very means.[15]

As early as 1730 the Scotch-Irish in Pennsylvania broke the law by migrating onto Indian lands. The provincial authorities warned them against stealing the Indian's land, and by way of instruction burned their cabins. From 1763 to 1768 the Quaker Assembly warned off the immigrants on "pain of death."[16] In 1768 Governor William Penn ordered soldiers to forcibly remove them. Yet soon there were "double the number of inhabitants in those two Settlements than ever before." The infuriated governor then proclaimed that those settling on Indian lands would be executed. But no judges could be found for such prisoners, or compliant juries and secure lockups.[17] (The Virginia burgesses, by contrast, passed acts as early as 1752 "encouraging persons to settle on the waters of the Mississippi."[18])

As settlement continued westward, the Continental Congress forbade settlement on western lands to which title had not passed from the Indians by treaty. In 1779 General Brodhead was instructed to destroy the huts of settlers who trespassed "on the Indian lands" at the Muskingum and Ohio. Squatters continued to cross the rivers and hills seeking still more attractive land. Congress then called in the Army. Following orders in the Spring of 1785, Ensign Armstrong "dispossessed two families and destroyed their building....The 3rd we dispossessed eight families."[19] The next day Armstrong arrested the leader of a "party of armed men." In June Congress ordered the construction of Fort Harmar (at the mouth of the Muskingum) to prevent settlers from returning.[20]

In 1789 migrants again were settling on Pennsylvania frontier land owned by the Indians. President Washington ordered their cabins destroyed, their families removed. Within a few months, however, they, too, returned.[21] Their nesting instinct proved stronger than the power of the central government, more intense than the moral principles of the voters. As one enraged squatter declared: "I do certify that all mankind agreeable to every constitution formed in America, have an undoubted right to pass into every vacant country and...Congress is not empowered to forbid them."[22] Three months later Congress could only report its own continuing failure: "disorderly persons have crossed the river Ohio and settled upon the unappropriated lands of the United States, before they were offered for sale." Such conduct was "highly disrespectful to the Federal authority."[23] Indeed it was.

IV

So unrelenting a drive toward land acquisition cannot be attributed to transient malice, specialized greed, or hatred of an alien race. It expresses an "earth hunger," whose precedents reach back to early settlements, perhaps even to the earliest farmers. When births rose in ancient days the common solutions were harsh—death and/or forcible redistribution. Death was not uncommon. One historian notes that Rome's half million free people included fewer than 5,000 free-born boys. "Far more children were born to free parents"—only "to perish from exposure or be brought up as slaves."[24] Probably few mothers happily abandoned their offspring. Yet parents did not adjust their sexual activities to the needs of children whom they might conceive. The outcome? Three infants of every four were killed or sold into slavery.[25]

But redistribution to new lands was an alternative for some. "The characteristic slogan of Greek history...the redistribution of land" was, we are told, heard as early as the 7th century BC.[26] After Rome's external and civil wars, redistribution also took place—from defeated peoples and classes. Ex-soldiers were sent off to found colonies "at the expense of the former owners and cultivators of the soil."[27] Doing so had a further advantage. Soldiers who might revolt against the new government were sent to fight abroad. (That precedent was, of course, followed in later revolutions—in France, in Cuba.)

V

The Continental Congress acquired soldiers for the American Revolution by scattering promises to pay across the country side. Then, in 1781, it promised half pay for life to those officers who had survived the war, since earlier promises had been all but worthless. Some citizens were indignant. The Massachusetts legislature thought it outrageous to promise those soldiers the equivalent of one dollar a day for five years. So much money, Sam Adams declared, would be "inconsistent with that equality that ought to subsist among citizens of free and republican states....(It would) raise and exalt some citizens in wealth and grandeur to the injury and oppression of others." It was not an "appropriate award for their services," but "more than adequate."[28] Massachusetts then sent a memorial to Congress which, Madison observed, was "pregnant with the most penurious ideas" attacking the Congress for making any such promise.[29] In the face of such fierce popular objection, Congress could not fulfill its promises. The soldiers therefore dumped the certificates that commuted their half pay, selling for whatever they could get. And that proved to be twelve and one-half cents on the dollar.[30]

The Congress faced an additional difficulty: a military threat on its frontiers. The invading French, or English, might again hire Indians as cheap mercenaries. The Indians might even fight on their own.

Following classical precedents, Congress converted these two problems into a single solution. What better protection than to provide frontier land to the ex-officers? Rome's soldiers had frequently settled on the borders of lands they had conquered.[31] Moreover, they earned their own incomes. When farming in Switzerland, or making bricks in Jerusalem, they formed a living barrier against the enemy.

Similar protection in the U.S., declared General Putnam, would prevent "our Western territory (from) falling under the dominion of any European power. . . .; the frontier of the old states will be effectually secured from savage alarms, and the new will have little to fear from their insults."[32] Bounty lands were to be restricted to military districts on the frontiers.[33]

Eventually Congress did just that, not by setting up an agency and procedures, but by allowing the Reverend Manasseh Cutler and his associates to organize the Ohio Company for ex-officers and by assigning them a huge tract of land which they could buy with their certificates after the ordinance of 1787 was passed. Migration then accelerated. Three thousand one hundred and ninety six "souls" and twenty four hogs passed Fort Harmar on their way to the Kentucky country between June and December 1787.[34]

By the spring of 1788, the first thirty settlers arrived at Marietta with the new governor to colonize Ohio. Within fourteen years migration increased the state's population to sixty thousand.[35] It was the harbinger of the great tide of settlement that created the new Northwest.

VI

That migration would have taken a far different course, with far different political consequences, if Congress had pursued a different policy for paying soldiers than the one it actually adopted. Statesmen such as Madison and thinkers such as Harrington and John Stuart Mill, saw economic independence as the precondition of political freedom.[36] Marx complicated and narrowed that insight by focusing chiefly on ownership of "the means of production." In agricultural societies, however, economic independence and the "means of production" clearly centered in the land.[37] Farmers who owned land could produce, barter, and borrow. They could thereby acquire tools and animals and farm more profitably. Thus cheap land in the U.S. provided "a competence" to most Americans. It enabled them to reach a level of economic well being far exceeding that of the rest of the world. And it did so in the simplest way—by reducing the share of their income that farmers had to give up in economic rent.

Samuel Blodget, knowledgeable member of Congress, estimated rental rates from which Table 1 has been prepared.[38] It indicates that in 1800 U.S. farmers could rent ten acres for about 1 percent of their income. This was enough land to raise food for a family.[39]

TABLE 1

Land Rentals and Labor, 1787–1805

	1784	1790	1795	1800	1805
Land Rent	3-1/2%	4%	4-1/2%	4-1/2%	4-1/2%
Cultivated Land (price per acre)	$2.25	$2.10	$4.60	$5.50	$6.25
Rental of 10 acres	$0.71	$0.82	$1.95	$2.48	$2.81
Labor (per year)	$125	$125	$238	$340	$188
Percent of Annual Income Need to Rent 10 Acres	1%	1%	1%	1%	1%

Higher rents, however, were charged by the great "feudal" landlords of the Hudson Valley. And in the 1840s their tenants rioted. The rents at issue came to ten to fourteen bushels of wheat for one hundred acres, plus "four fat hens, and one day's service with carriage and horses."[40] The money value of such payments in kind came to about 7 percent of a farm laborer's yearly income.[41] A decade later the greatest "monopolistic" land owner in the country was William Scully. "No frontier landlord in the entire country ...was the object of as much ill feeling and political agitation." His rents were unusually high, Gates charges: Scully actually collected "5.7 percent on the cost."[42]

How do American rents of 1 percent (in 1800) or 7 percent (Rensellaer) or 5.7 percent (Scully) contrast with the historic past? In medieval England peasants rented five acres from the church in return for one day's labor every week.[43] To rent ten acres of land, therefore, they had to commit the equivalent of one third of their usual income. In 1800, too, English farm laborers had to allocate a third of their income to rent ten acres.[44] Hence U.S. farm laborers in the nineteenth century could rent as much land with 1 percent of their annual income as British farm laborers could when using one-third to one-half their income (see table 2.)

TABLE 2

Percent of Annual Income Required by Farm Laborer

to Rent Ten Acres

	YEAR	PERCENT
United Kingdom	1222, 1272	33%
	1800	33%
United States	1800	1%
	1840 (Rensellaer estates)	7%
	1870s (Scully estate)	6%

U.S. land ownership was never as concentrated as England's had been when nine followers of William of Normandy were given most of that "green and pleasant land." (Nor even when, as in 1876, 400 noblemen owned 17 percent of the UK's total acreage.[45]) Nothing like such concentration appeared in the U.S. despite all the talk of monopolization.

VII

One major factor held U.S. rents to so small a portion of farmer's income: federal policy. It was not explicit land policy, but the federal military policy of providing free land to veterans. Soldiers' bounties hark back to the lands George Rogers Clark promised Virginia volunteers, to the lands the South Carolina Yazoo Company promised men who fought for Mississippi land, and to the land the Confederation promised soldiers of the Revolution. But no precedent, ancient or modern, forecast the impact of Congressional military policy after the Mexican War. Congress had already provided two million acres of bounty land for the soldiers who fought the Revolution, five million to those in the War of 1812. But it legislated thirteen million acres for soldiers who fought Mexico.[46]

The inexorable logic of politics then summoned up legions of lobbyists and claimants who demanded equally generous treatment for soldiers of other wars. Between 1851 and 1860 Congress added 44 million acres for service in the Revolutionary War, the War of 1812, Indian Wars, etc.[47] No one expected the half million widows and elderly men who received them to form a barrier against foreign invasion. Their warrants only evidenced the nation's gratitude for past efforts. (And, of course, lobbying by Congressmen, lawyers, and warrant brokers.)[48]

Congressional bounty, however, attracted recipients to real estate offices —not to farms, for eighty-four recipients out of a hundred did not choose to settle on Congress land.[49] They threw their warrants on the market, selling them for whatever they could get. The earliest buyers located their warrants in the South—Alabama, Louisiana, and Arkansas.[50] But events in Europe soon shifted warrant locations to the old Northwest. Sir Robert Peel had recently opened British ports to American wheat (thereby deserting the country gentlemen who had supported him for so long). And in 1848 revolutions in Europe interrupted European grain production. The export prospects thus opened up helped concentrate land warrant locations in Illinois, Wisconsin, and Iowa. The new "midwest" became the bread basket of the U.S.

VIII

That transformation occurred because the flood of land warrants cut the price of Federal land. Between December 1847 and January 1848 its price fell by one third.[51] So substantial a decline generated a welter of investment opportunities. The mechanism of advantage can be examined through the record for the greatest speculators. Easley and Willingham of Virginia entered over 400,000 acres in Iowa, Missouri, Wisconsin, Minnesota, Kansas and Nebraska, "a volume of entries probably exceeding that made by any similar group before the Civil War." Altogether they loaned five hundred thousand dollars to some two thousand squatters.[52] In the great Iowa boom of the 1850s, they bought 328,000 acres, of which they sold 85 percent to "individuals who wished to take advantage of the 12-month credit advance—the so-called 'time-entry' system."[53] (Settlers gave promissory notes for the price of the land, plus interest. They got title to the land when they paid off the note.) The firm used the remaining 15 percent of its funds to buy land for sale in the indefinite future, to buyers who had yet to appear. Swierenga estimates that 71 percent of the land acquired by Iowa realtors was sold on time entry.[54] In the same boom, "William J. Barney, Dubuque loan shark and speculator, entered 191,000 acres." And Miles and Elias White of Baltimore loaned two hundred thousand dollars "to hard pressed squatters."[55] (The Whites entered 101,000 acres in central and eastern Iowa during the 1850s boom.[56])

Thus the great land speculators—from Virginia, Maryland, Iowa—were both "loan shark *and* speculator" (in Gates's phrase). They placed their money in loans and land. They bought land often as a means of getting security for those loans.[57] It is unlikely that these large lenders would have committed so much to loans, year after year, if their rate of return did not roughly equal that from long term land purchase, and vice versa. When the yield on loans for a period of years and over different locations did not equal the return from investing land, they reoriented their new investments.

IX

What was their rate of return? Milestone studies by Gates, Swierenga and others have described returns to land investment in particular areas. But they do not answer a quite different question—what speculative margin did most midwestern farmers pay when buying land before the Civil War? Frontier interest rates provide our most likely indicator. Large eastern investors frequently moved their funds between territories and states. Hence interest rates would be more uniform than the few careful estimates of returns to land in a single area. Moreover such rates are widely quoted by contemporaries.

What returns did Easley and Willingham and other great frontier investors achieve? Swierenga tells us that Iowa real estate mortgages in the 1850s yielded 3 to 5 percent per month.[58] Hibbard, too, refers to 3 percent to 5 percent yields (in Kansas on the frontier in 1858).[59] A circular from one of the leading speculators in 1851 offered 160 acre warrants "Cash $135; on one year's time, $200."[60] Or 48 percent interest. A local historian bitterly remembered Iowa settlers "would. . .allow and promise. . .40 percent per annum" on land for their homes."[61] And a Minnesota speculator charged a 40 percent to 60 percent time entry rate (in 1856-1858).[62] Swierenga, however, estimates a 79 percent rate of return on large Iowa land investments, far above such interest rates. If returns between the two types of investment really tended to equalize, why is his figure so much higher? In large part because his data relate to "nine selected counties, 1845-84."[63] And one of those nine counties constitutes a large proportion of his total sample. Since the variance in returns between counties was enormous (from 27 percent to 131 percent) that sample weighting is critical.

Suppose one's goal is not to establish rates of return for the nine counties, but the rate for the entire state, with its ninety-one counties, in the same boom decade.[64] To represent that rate, the return for the median county is preferable to the weighted mean average for nine counties. Now land in the median county of Swierenga's sample actually yielded 50 percent.[65] This is close to the 48 percent time entry rate offered by Byington and at the center of the 3 percent to 5 percent range of frontier interest rates.[66]

X

To determine by how much speculators forced up the price of land bought by farmer settlers that profit rate of 50 percent must be applied to the share of total farm land bought up by the speculators. A meaningful estimate can be derived beginning with the sale of the 47 million acres taken up during 1847-60 under warrants of the Acts of 1847-55.[67] Of that land, only 16 percent was retained by the original recipient.[68] Hence 39 million acres were bought with warrants.

How many went to speculators? The great speculators bought warrants. So did thousands of smaller ones. We include as speculators all those who bought more than a single warrant. (Adopting so broad a definition prevents understating the role of the speculator.) Now Oberly has listed every one in his extended sample who bought more than one bounty warrant. The great speculators cited in the historical literature all appear: Barney, Byington, Cook, Daniels, Easley, Sargent, Sanford, Sullivant, Van Martens, White—plus many others. It turns out that as a group all multiple warrant buyers purchased only 8 percent of his entire warrant total.[69]

Hence only 4 of 47 million acres bought with bounty warrants went to speculators. Oberly's sample, however, omits warrants sold to settlers on time entry. We therefore turn to Swierenga's study of holdings by "ten major Iowa real estate vendors whose entries exceeded 25,000 acres." His data indicate that they made perhaps half their purchases via time entry for other buyers.[70] If so, speculators bought and held four million acres, buying another four million on time entry, usually sold within a year. This sequence can be summarized simply in table 3.

TABLE 3

Millions of Acres Located

with Bounty Warrants, 1847 to 1860
(Acts of 1847-55)

Total located		47
By settlers		39
Original warrant holders	8	
Buyers of 320 acres or less	31	
By speculators		8
Sold to settlers on time entry	4	
Held and sold	4	

Of 47 million acres located during the massive settlement of the Midwest, 8 million were bought from speculators. (And still less from the legendary "large speculators.") Was this percentage large? It may perhaps be dimensioned by the redistribution of land under the French Revolution. A detailed study of that redistribution in one part of France indicates that 1.3 percent of the French buyers of church land got 53 percent of total acreage.[71] Study of another area indicates 1.6 percent got 36 percent.[72] A third finds the concentration so extreme that it concludes: "no doubt is possible; the rich were the only ones to profit from the sales of confiscated lands and property under the Revolution."[73] There is an enormous, and fervent, literature on "great speculators" in the U.S. Yet no handful of large buyers in the U.S. acquired anything like the share of public domain that buyers did in the celebrated Revolution for "equality and fraternity."

XI

Instead of gobbling up most of the 47 million acres of public domain land sold for bounty warrants, the speculators took no more than 17 percent of that huge total. The "great speculators" (who bought a thousand or more acres) took an even smaller share. If they achieved the 50 percent profit rates we have suggested, why were they so restrained?

One primary reason is associated with federal policy. The U.S. had priced its land at $1.25 an acre beginning in 1820. In fixing that price, Congress specified a clause of particular interest to speculators. It provided that "no land shall be sold, either at public or private sales," for "a less price than one dollar and twenty-five cents per acre." That clause pledged "the faith of the Government absolutely to the purchaser that the Government will not prejudice his interest by disposing of any of their lands below the price fixed by law."[74]

What was the "interest" of purchasers? It was at least not to sustain a capital loss, yet, if the government began to sell land for less than the $1.25 it had been charging, those who had bought most recently would sustain an immediate loss. To whom could they ever hope to resell their land for even the price they had just paid if equivalent quality could be had at a lower price?

The Government did not actually break the letter of its promise: the official $1.25 price did not change after December 1847. But the first Mexican bounty warrants became available in January 1848 at about 75 cents. With those warrants the government had created a second currency, sharply reducing the value of the land already owned. The *de facto* price of land recently bought from the Federal government was thus cut—by 40 percent. When might the government cut the price again? The great speculators surely realized the possibility of further losses. It becomes evident, then, why they bought only four of those 47 million acres "on spec", to be sold to some eventual buyer.[75] And why, in the Iowa boom, they sold half their purchases in less than a year[76]—rather than holding for great long run gains.

By how much did speculators increase the price of land bought by farmer settlers? Half the 8 million acres sold by U.S. "speculators" were sold on time entry. Their mark up typically included a year's interest, or roughly 38 cents per acre (Table 4). What was the profit margin on the remaining four million acres? If it equalled that achieved by the great Iowa speculators during the boom of the 1850s, the settlers paid them $1.37 an acre (Table 4). At 40 percent interest rates and 50 percent profit rates, the price farmers paid for 47 million acres in bounty land in the boom of the 1850s was increased by less than 5 percent:

4.1 percent for interest charges

0.6 percent for additional speculators margin

In earlier decades the charges may even have been less. During 1838-39, William Ogden and others charged "usurious interest rates" of 30 percent.[77] In late 1839, other speculators lent money to Iowa squatters at 20-28 percent and, in 1840, at 20-50 percent.[78] Hence the rate of speculators' profit on earlier sales of public domain land could well have been under the 50 percent Iowa rates used here. In either case prices paid for their farms by earlier settlers would have been increased less than 5 percent by the lenders and speculators with whom they dealt.

TABLE 4

The Purchase of Farm Land

(Iowa, 1850)
per acre

	BUYING ON TIME	BUYING FROM SPECULATOR
Extra Cost to farmer	+ .38¢	+ $1.37
Value of Land Clearing	$14.00	$14.00

Sources:

Credit: An interest rate of 40% is derived from Swierenga's pp. 190 n.11, 164, 165, 171, 117 n.42, 120. 40% of the cost of a warrant (77¢ average in 1850 according to Disbrow's figures in Swierenga, p. 145) plus 17 cents in fees (Swierenga, pp. 136, 190-191) is 38¢. The sum of .77 + .38, $1.15, is slightly below the land office standard of $1.25.

Speculators profit: Cf. p. 20, n. 2.

Value of land clearing: Lebergott, "The Demand for Land," *Journal of Economic History* (June 1985) p. 188.

XII

Thousands of settlers migrated into the North Central states during the 1840s and 1850s. Many passed through Ohio, Indiana or Illinois on their way West. They chose *not* to buy any of the acreage available in those states. Why on earth did they pay 40 percent interest rates in Iowa when 15 percent rates were available in Ohio or Illinois?[79] Why, e.g., could Jason Easton collect more than 350 percent from a single loan on a land warrant?[80] Three considerations help explain settler behavior. First, farmers were not concerned with rates—of interest or profit—but with the actual amount they had to pay. Because Easton's farmer repaid in 19 days (rather than 6 months) the lender's return was spectacular. But the farmer's interest cost was still only 17 cents per acre. The millions of bounty acres that farmers bought from speculators on time entry typically cost them an extra 38 cents an acre for interest, (Table 4) or less than a farm laborer could earn in half a day.

Second, loans guaranteed farmers legal title to land on which they had already squatted. These preemption acres were often well located. On many of them, farmers had already made improvements. With time entry farmers could lock away the particular piece of the public domain they coveted at a relatively modest interest charge (38 cents an acre). They thus secured title to some of the best land in the nation and then could utilize days when regular farm work was impossible (bad weather, etc.) to clear the land. Doing so, of course, made their farm that much more valuable. In Iowa in the 1850s their labor could thus add $14 to the land value per acre.

Third, other farmers paid speculators $1.37 per acre extra for four of the 43 million bounty acres sold in the boom of the 1850s.[81] The obvious reason they did so was that speculators had gotten hold of better than average land. It was land with richer soil or closer to wood and water or to a planned town or railroad. As Senator Thomas Benton of Missouri endlessly reiterated: "It is out of the question for this Federal Government to have but one price for all qualities, to demand the same for... broken, hilly ground, half barren, part rock, part swamp... (as) rich level land, well watered and timbered...."[82] But it did—thereby opening up prospects for capital gains.

Many who bought land from the U.S., certainly prior to 1848, in effect got lottery tickets sure to win. Some could win largely indeed. And where the promise of winnings was greatest the bidding and the boom was the greatest. Some 75 percent of Iowa land fell into the top U.S. land quality class.[83] And much of this fine land was taken up on bounty warrants during the 1850s, when the Indians were pushed from the region. Even if speculators had bought random parcels, some of their land would have been superior. But typically they had investigated the land themselves or paid local land lookers to do so. They then charged for their successful choices.

One of the greatest Iowa speculators during the 1850s declared that raw lands were "worth from $2.50 to $3.00 per acre... as soon as they were entered."[84] His implication was clear: the U.S. sold off the public domain below its market value. The extent and persistence of the boom in the 1850s, as in that of the 1830s, suggests that as a plausible hypothesis. Why else did speculators themselves sometimes borrow money at 40 percent?[85]

XIII

Through much of the 19th century the nation pursued a land sales policy that outdid Henry George. George, it will be remembered, had discovered that the gradual settlement of land, the building up of cities, roads, railroads, all added to the capital value of land. Even though the individual land owner did no more than hold title. Mill had previously proposed nationalizing the future "unearned increase in the value of land." George went on to propose taxing away all unearned increase, past and future.[86]

Congress, however, found a brilliant short cut. It sold land to farmers at prices below its long run value. It thereby conjured up endless opportunities for capital gains. Farmers then settled the land, broke the soil, and raised their crops. In so doing they increased land values. Such increases accrued chiefly to the very farmers whose land breaking and crop raising had generated the gains, for they owned the land.

A Georgian "single tax" policy would have taxed away such increases in value.[87] But it could have had one further consequence. Since 1789, Congress had allocated most of the nation's revenue to war. (To the military establishment *per se*, or for pensions and interest linked to prior wars.) By denying itself the opportunity of financing still more wars, Congress awarded most of those capital gains to the very farmers whose efforts had created them.

Some farmers, of course, collected short term capital gains, selling in the escalating boom years. When "raw land was worth from $2.50 to $3.00 per acre at entry," the government nonetheless sold such land for 80 cents to $1 an acre, in land warrants. It is no surprise, then, that farmers stood in line for days to be the first to bid at the U.S. auctions. Or that "claims clubs" sprang up, whose farmer members sought to block anyone from bidding above the legal minimum. (Over one-hundred clubs were formed in the Territory of Iowa alone.) William Parker has brilliantly evoked their attitude: "The squatters, with families, shotguns, and a strong sense of moral right, combined with local settlers to form a brooding, even a menacing, presence" at public land auctions.[88] They fiercely opposed anyone who tried to bid "their" land up to its market value.

Ohio settlers in 1801 expressed outrage at the prospect of appearing at "a Publick Vendue," and being "outbid by an unfeeling land-jobber or speculator, who perhaps had been preying on the vitals of his country until he has fill'd his pockets."[89] That these same farmers had simply settled on land which they did not own was irrelevant to their emotions. A trumpet call of the *Milwaukee Sentinel* summoned such Wisconsin settlers in 1838: We call to the attention "of the settlers on the public lands...the meeting of Saturday next.... Let dissension arise among claimants—let them but commence bidding against each other at the sale, and the door will be fairly opened. The Capitalist and speculator will then step in to take from them their land and improvements."[90] (Parsed in financial terms: they feared that speculators would bid up auction prices until the U.S. Treasury got something closer to the true market value of the land.)

The long steady gain in land prices accrued chiefly to those who owned most of the land. The super-Georgian land policy that Congress adopted therefore chiefly benefited farmers. That conclusion conflicts with the endless histories of land speculation. However, if one considers that most voters from 1789 to the Civil War were farmers, it may become more acceptable.

XIV

The gap between the uniform price which the Federal Government accepted for pieces of the public domain and the price which farmers willingly paid for the land marked a profit opportunity. Who would seize it? One English traveler provided the classic answer:

> Speculation in real estate has for many years been the ruling idea and occupation of the Western mind. Clerks, labourers, farmers, storekeepers, merely followed their callings for a living, while they were speculating for their fortunes.[91]

Historians of land investment in the United States have typically described settlers as victims of two mean spirited groups of "speculators"—greedy lords of grand acreage and "petty speculators."[92] Both groups, they tell us, sometimes bought land "intending" to profit from its sale. Farmers may sometimes have profited but did not "intend" to sell land at a profit. Clairvoyants and psychoanalysts may analyze "intent" very well—judging whether buyers only intended to sell later at a profit. Most other scholars, however, can more usefully focus on outcomes, seeking to ascertain who bought unimproved land, why they did, and who actually realized capital gains.It may be time to recur to Lewis Carroll's *Through the Looking Glass.* There Carroll described baby oysters trooping down to welcome the carpenter and the walrus, only to be gobbled up by both.

> "I like the walrus best," said Alice."You see he was a little sorry for the poor oysters." He ate more than the carpenter though, said Tweedledee. . . . "Then I like the carpenter best." But he ate as many as he could get, said Tweedledum.

Notes

1. Harry Scheiber *et al.*, *American Economic History* (1976), 110.
2. Maldwyn Jones, *The Limits of Liberty* (1983), 118.
3. John Blum *et al.*, *The National Experience* (1981), 205.
4. T. Harry Williams *et al.*, *A History of the United States* (1959), 385. It is not clear how the estimate of three-fourths was arrived at. No source is given, no procedure described.
5. Paul Gates, *History of Public Land Law Development* (1968), 207. "Some writers imply that public land was sold only to speculators before the Civil War: "The Homestead Act of 1862 opened the public lands to individual ownership and development." Robert Heilbroner and Aaron Singer, *The Economic Transformation of America, 1600 to the Present* (1977), 138.
6. Jones, *Limits*, 344.
7. 1900 Census, *Agriculture*, Part 1, 688.
8. The citations below indicate how much use has been made of the fundamental scholarly research by Robert Swierenga on bounty land sales.
9. William Poole, "The Early Northwest" and George Loring, in *Papers of the American Historical Association*, vol. 3, no. 1 (1888), 46, 59.
10. U.S. Statutes, First Cong. Sess. 1, Ch. 9, 1789, Article VI, 53.
11. Gaillard Hunt and James Scott, Eds., *The Debates in the Federal Convention* (1920), 257.
12. This was done indirectly by accepting conditions specified by North Carolina when ceding its Western land claims to the U.S. in December 1789. That cession provided for the continuation of slavery in that land.
13. Massachusetts Historical Society, *Collections*, 5th series, 3:402. In 1774 Connecticut forbid importation of slaves, summarizing its reasons succinctly: "whereas the increase of slaves in this colony is injurious to the poor and inconvenient." *Public Records* of the Colony of Connecticut, vol. 14, 329.
14. 1854 speech quoted in Henry N. Smith, *Virgin Land* (1950 r 1957) p. 193. In the 1832 struggle over ending slavery in Virginia a legislator from the Western area declared they would not yield "to the slothful and degraded African." Cf. Smith, p. 152.
15. J.C. Fitzpatrick, Ed., *The Writings of George Washington*, September 7, 1783. The Commander at Fort Pitt had just reported "400 men from the Western Frontier of Virginia has passed the Ohio in order to establish a settlement on the Muskingum."
16. Charles A. Hanna, *Historical Collections of Harrison County in the State of Ohio* (1900), 16.
17. Solon Buck and Elizabeth Buck, *The Planting of Civilization in Western Pennsylvania* (1939), 142.
18. Virginia statutes quoted in Peter Onuf, "Toward Federalism," *William and Mary Quarterly* (July 1977), 363.

19. Hanna, *Historical Collections,* 47-50.

20. Archer Hurlbert, *Ohio in the Time of the Confederation* (1918), 112.

21. Annals of Congress, *The Debates and Proceedings* (1834), 1:412, May 1789.

22. "Call for election of delegates to form a state convention West of the Ohio River" (March 1785). Hurlbert, *Ohio,* 99.

23. Hurlbert, *Ohio,* 113-114.

24. P.A. Brunt, *Italian Manpower, 225 B.C.—A.D. 14* (1971), 110, 383, 387. Because boys were entitled to a free grain allowance from the state, their number is likely to have been fully reported.

25. In the U.S. in 1980 there were 23,000 boys aged 5-10 per half million population —not 5,000. Allowance for different age composition would reduce Rome's 78%, but hardly to less than two-thirds. However the proportion for females was surely greater, female infanticide being common in Rome. (Brunt, 150-154.)

26. M.M. Austin and P. Vidal-Naquet, *Economic and Social History of Ancient Greece* (1977), 70.

27. Brunt, *Italian Manpower,* 246.

28. John S. Barry, *The History of Massachusetts, The Commonwealth Period* (1857), 223. The Congress bought Jeffersons' entire library to constitute the beginning of the Library of Congress. That $24,000 expenditure, Representative Cyrus King declared, would surely "bankrupt the Treasury, beggar the people, and disgrace the nation." Cf. Dumas Malone, *The Sage of Monticello* (1981), 178.

29. Henry Gilpin, Ed., *The Papers of James Madison* (1841), 1:562.

30. Given "inability to pay" on the part of Congress, and "inability to wait" on the part of the officers, the latter's certificates "were thrown on the market for cash, and soon fell to 12 1/2 cents on the dollar." 19th Cong., 2nd Sess., H.R. 6, *Revolutionary Officers* (1826), 12.

31. An ordinary soldier was promised 100 acres by the Colonial Congress in 1776. This figure may be compared with 10 acres provided to Roman foot soldiers who settled new colonies of Tenney Frank, *An Economic Survey of Ancient Rome* (1933), 1:117, 422.

32. Hurlbert, 56 ff. Related proposals by Pickering, Peletiah Webster, and others appear in Hurlbert.

33. Military reserves, as Hibbard wrote, were "to provide a screen of veterans between the older settlements and the Indians." Benjamin Hibbard, *A History of the Public Land Policies* (1924, r1965), 120.

34. Clarence Carter, Ed., *The Territorial Papers of the United States* (1934), 2:197.

35. Frazer Wilson, *Arthur S. Clair* (1944), 215.

36. Madison, of course, had emphasized the wide ownership of land as a condition of republican government. Cf. Drew McCoy, "Republicanism and American Foreign Policy," *William and Mary Quarterly* (1974), 31:640. John Stuart Mill, *On Liberty.* The importance of Harrington's views in shaping those of the Founding Fathers is reviewed in J.G.A. Pocock, *Politics, Language and Time* (1972), Ch. 3.

37. The central importance of land ownership in farming was even missed by American radicals. A.M. Simons, editor of the *International Socialist Review,* in his *The*

American Farmer (1902) p. 118 noted "the transfer of ownership away from the users of the tools. The hand-churn, the mule gin, the flail, the ox team and the simple granary all belonged to the producer—the farmer. But the creamery, steam ginnery....threshing machine...the railroad...have passed into the hands of another class." Noting the hand churn, he ignored the land.

38. Samuel Blodget, *Economica* (1805, r. 1964), 142. We use his rental data for "cultivated lands" since the English rentals applied to land under tillage. We assume a U.S. work year of 250 days.

39. Lebergott, *The Americans*, 1984, 15. In 1802 a Tennessee family could cultivate four acres (producing $250 worth of cotton) plus four more in corn or wheat for the family's food. Francois Michaux, *Travels to the West of the Alleghany Mountains* (1850), 241.

40. State of New York, Assembly Doc. 156 (March 28, 1846) "Leasehold Estates," 2.

41. The clerk representing the estate stated that for the past thirty years the rent of farms of the Western towns averaged $19 for 100 acres, and $14 in the Eastern towns. N.Y. *Assembly Document 156*, 49-50.

A day's labor in the Mid-Atlantic states in 1832 came to 71 cents plus board, or approximately $1. (Cf. Lebergott, *Manpower in Economic Growth*, 1964, 541.) Service with horses was usually double the laborers' daily rate. Wheat had a market price of $1.25 in 1835, $1.05 in 1840 in New York City. (47th Cong., Ist Sess., H.D. No. 2, *Annual Report, Secretary of the Treasury, 1881*, Table XXV .) Allowing for the 4 fat hens the total came to about $17 for 100 acres. Farm laborers' monthly earning in New York in 1830 came to $8. (*Manpower*, 539). Increased to $12 to allow for board, and multiplied by 12, the figure indicates an annual income of $244.

42. Paul Gates, *Landlords and Tenants on the Prairie Frontier* (1973), 266-268.

43. William Hale Hale, *The Domesday of St. Pauls of the Year MCCXXII* (1858), cviii, 5. A similar percentage for 1272 can be calculated from data in F.W. Maitland, "History of a Cambridgeshire Manor," *English Historical Review* (July 1984), 418, 420.

44. Annual earnings of farm labor averaged £30 in 1797 and £40 in 1805 according to Peter Lindert and Jeffrey Williamson, "English Workers Living Standards During the Industrial Revolution" (September 1980) p. 16. A charitable scheme that supplied small cottagers with allotments in 1800 rented land to them for £1 12s per acre, according to J.L. and Barbara Hammond, *The Village Labourer* (1911 r 1978), 104. Presumably a charitable scheme rented the land at or even below prevailing rates. Hence a 46% ratio for 10 acres is, if anything, likely to understate the percentage English farm laborers paid to rent land.

45. A.S. Turberville, *The House of Lords in the Age of Reform, 1784-1837* (1958), 409.

46. Thomas Donaldson, *The Public Domain* (1884), 237.

47. 36th Cong. 2nd Sess., S.D. 1, *Message of the President, 87*.

48. Among the most recent and skilled reviews is James Oberly's aptly titled "Acres and Old Men: Military Bounty Warrants, 1847-1860" (Dissertation, University of Rochester, 1982).

49. Data based on a systematic sample of one half percent of the entries in *Monthly Abstract of Bounty Locations*, U.S. National Archives.

50. *Ibid.*, for Cahaba, Huntsville, Ouachita, Natchitoches.

51. Natalie Disbrow's tabulations as reported in Swierenga, *Pioneers,* 145, indicate a 78-88 cent range in January 1848 compared to the usual $1.25 rate.

52. Paul Gates, *Landlords and Tenants on the Prairie Frontier* (1973) pp. 81, 145, 80.

53. Swierenga, *Pioneers,* 162.

54. *Pioneers,* 120. Stephen Schoene, *The Economics of U.S Public Land Policy Prior to 1860* (Unpublished dissertation, University of North Carolina, 1981), 242-243, contends that the procedure used to designate credit entries has contrary biases, but he does not indicate whether they offset or are important. Given Swierenga's 85% from Easley and Willingham, whose papers he reviewed in detail, we assume no substantial net bias in his 71% estimate.

55. Gates, *Landlords and Tenants,* 145-56, 154.

56. Swierenga, *Pioneers,* 27, 36. He describes White as "the largest Maryland speculator in Iowa lands." 135.

57. Gates, *Landlords and Tenants,* 147, described one who had to foreclose on some of these loans. The money lender, contrary to his intentions, thus found himself in possession of large quantities of partly improved western land.

58. Swierenga, 121, 136, 151, 152, 164, 165, 171.

59. Benjamin Hibbard, *A History of the Public Land Policies* (1924 r 1965), 128.

60. Reprinted in Swierenga, 136.

61. Joe Smith (1880) quoted in Gates, 80. Easley and Willingham realized 33% on 323 cash loans in 1856-59. Swierenga, 171.

62. Robert Jost, *An Entrepreneurial Study of a Frontier Financier* (University of Minnesota, 1957), 11, 20, 53, 113. In 1860 he was getting 40% to 50%, 122.

63. Computed from 201, 202.

64. Swierenga has carefully noted that excluding a handful of sales to the railroad reduces the Poweshiek average substantially. Cf. his "The Equity Effects of Public Land Speculation," *Journal of Economic History* (December 1974), 1015-1017. It falls from 132% to 50%.

65. Swierenga's median county in *Ibid.*, Table 8.3 has a 45% return. This table, however, values land warrants at $1.25. They are valued at market rates in Table 8.5, though for only six selected counties. Comparison between the two tables suggests that a 50% return (using market rates for warrants) would apply to the median county in his 9 county study.

66. Schoene, *Public Lands,* 193, revises Swierenga's 77% estimate, offers a "recalculated figure" of 531%. . . . The reason for the large increase is the large proportion of transactions that had short holding periods." He adds: "Other than the treatment of short period transactions there are no differences between Swierenga's calculation and the current revised calculation, that could have more than minor impact on the comparison." (p. 251)

His adjustment does not change Swierenga's estimate of the price charged the buyer. Nor the speculator's dollar profit. Since, then, his only significant change in Swierenga's calculation was the duration of the investment one can solve using his rate of return: $3.20 = $1.49 cost + 531%($1.49)(d:12). The implicit duration is then 4.1 months.

67. 36th Cong. Ist Sess., S.D. 1, *Message of the President*, 173, indicates 46.9 million acres were located through September 30, 1859.

68. Our sample of bounty abstract books is described in footnote 49 above.

69. We use listings and counts from his Tables 12, 17, 25, 30, 31, 32.

70. Swierenga, 120. Specifically: 28% of their sales were "clearly not credit entries." "Most" of the remaining 72% being time entry. His figures apply to those buying 25,000 and more acres. We assume that the smaller speculators, who bought 320 to 25,000 acres, did proportionately less selling on time. Hence we use a 50% ratio for the combined group of "speculators." Their acreage in time entries therefore equalled that in their own name.

71. G. Gerbaud, *et al. La Revolution dans le Puy-de-Dome* (1972) p. 133.

72. Rene Caisso, *La Vente des Biens Nationaux de Premiere Origine dans le District de Tours* (1967), 120, 121, 126, 314-381.

73. Jean Sentou, *La Fortune Immobilier des Toulousains et la Revolution Francaise* (1970), 174. 1 Cf. also 31,79, 163.

74. *Register of Debates in Congress* (May 20, 1830), 441.

75. The 4 million acres that speculators held under time entry were not directly liable to such an impact. For the buyers had already agreed to the sales price. They were borrowing money from the speculator using the land as collateral. At worst they would refuse to pay, leaving any improvements they had made to the land as an inadvertent gift to the speculator.

76. According to information kindly supplied by Swierenga about his sample.

77. Gates, *Landlords and Tenants*, 60.

78. Bogue, *From Prairie to Corn Belt*, 172.

79. For Ohio and Illinois cf. R.F. Severson, Mortgage Borrowing," *Journal of Economic History* (June 1966), 164. Allan Bogue (*From Prairie to Corn Belt*, 177) notes that even in Iowa in 1853, mortgage rates of 12% and 20% were recorded. Such rates exceeded those stipulated by the state's usury law.

80. Jost, *Financier*, 57-58. Easton made $20.45 on the loan. But since it was paid off in 19 days his annual rate yield was 350%.

81. Using the 50% interest/profit rate we estimate for all sales implies $1.37 profit (Table 4). Robert Swierenga, "The Equity Effects of Public Speculation in Iowa," *Journal of Economic History* (December 1979), 1015 gives data implying $1.71. Thus $3.20 per acre sales price = cost + [(77% of cost)(18/12)]. He estimates a 77% annual net rate of return and an average investment period of 18 months. Which leads to a cost figure of $1.49, and a profit residual of $1.71. Schoene's reestimation would shorten the implicit investment period—but yield much the same dollar figure.

82. Congress, *Register of Debates in Congress* (May 3, 1830), 407.

83. As judged by the U.S. Department of Agriculture. Cf. Swierenga, 21.

84. Quoted, Swierenga, *Pioneers*, 199, 166.

85. Swierenga, *Pioneers*, 165 n.10.

86. Henry George, *Progress and Poverty* (1881), 324-325.

87. Assuming it could somehow overcome the forces that long kept State legislatures from fully assessing land owned by farmers. Or rigorously taxing its assessed value.

88. In Lance Davis, *et al.*, *American Economic Growth* (1972), 105. Swierenga (p. 23) describes an 1848 claim club with 800 members. R.C. Buley, *The Old Northwest* (1851) 2:152 describes another, organized by about a thousand settlers.

89. Petition to Congress by the citizens of the Territory between the Muskingum and Sciota Rivers (February 1801) in Clarence E. Carter, *The Territorial Papers of the United States* (1934), 3:123.

90. Issue of January 6, 1838.

91. David W. Mitchell, *Ten Years in the United States* (1862), 325.

92. The distinction between speculators and settlers is made in the classic study by Paul Gates, *The Illinois Central Railroad and Its Colonization Work* (1939), 109. Gates finds that between 1849 and 1856 the railroad sold 12 million acres—at least 6 million to "speculators" and the rest to "settlers."

4.

THE FIRST PRIVATIZATION MOVEMENT

Terry L. Anderson
Montana State University

INTRODUCTION

IN CONTRAST TO TODAY when there is only lip service paid to the disposal of
public lands, the first one hundred years following the American Revolution witnessed a land policy aimed at disposing of the public domain into
private ownership. Of course, during these first years the domain of the
federal government was growing rapidly. States were ceding their western
lands to the newly formed federal government, and new territories such as
the Louisiana Purchase were helping fulfill our manifest destiny. The mood
during the Progressive Era when reservation of public lands was advocated
was very different than during the Federalist Era. The Progressives believed
there was ample evidence that good resource stewardship would not come
from private owners guided by the invisible hand of the market. They believed that market failure had been demonstrated by the "rape and run"
tactics of timber companies in the Great Lakes region and that such failure
could only be countered by governmental control. Centralized scientific
management conducted by "professionals" was to replace decentralized
private control.

The Federalists, on the other hand, led mainly by Jefferson and Hamilton, believed that a limited democratic government would function best if
power were fragmented, and that meant fragmentation of resource ownership. Jefferson in particular is famous for his insistence that the nation be
populated by yeoman farmers owning their lands. Hamilton's support of
disposal into private hands was more pragmatic; for him the public domain
represented a vast resource base that could provide badly needed revenue
for the infant government with large debts incurred during the revolution.
For these first privatizers, the main function of government was to set policies for disposing of the public domain.

In order to facilitate this disposal, there were two important questions
that had to be resolved by the early privatizers. First, what would be the
nature of land tenures? Would there be any vestiges of feudal tenures with
services to government or limitations on inheritance such as primogeniture? And second, how would private ownership be established so that title
could transfer from the government to individuals? Would squatting be allowed; would the federal government wholesale its land; or would govern-

ment land offices be retail establishments selling only small parcels?

This paper focuses on these questions with special emphasis on the Northwest Territory, the dominant frontier of the era. The passage of the Ordinance of 1787 was especially precedent setting. Daniel Webster doubted "whether one single law of any lawgiver, ancient or modern, has produced effects of more distance, marked, and lasting character than the Ordinance of 1787."[1] Later, Supreme Court Justice Story remarked, "American legislation has never achieved anything more admirable as an internal government than this comprehensive scheme."[2] This paper will discuss the establishment of freehold tenures and provide a framework for analyzing the various institutions used during this period for defining and enforcing property rights to land.

II. TENURE ARRANGEMENT

EVEN PRIOR TO THE arrival of Europeans, control or ownership of land determined the power and wealth of each native tribe. From the Atlantic to the Pacific, Indian tribes fought over hunting and fishing grounds and carved out boundaries in the wilderness. In New England the tribes parceled out the trapping grounds to clans and families who treated the resource as their own property, husbanding beavers like a modern rancher might his cattle. [3] On the Columbia River, tribes allocated rights to fishing locations where the salmon could be caught easily on their annual migration up stream to spawn.[4] Agreements among the many tribes that used the Columbia and its tributaries allowed enough fish to spawn so that a sustained migration from year to year was ensured.

When the Europeans arrived in the New World and began to exploit the bounty of the land, it was inevitable that they would come into conflict with the native Americans. The relatively sparse population had a comparative advantage in producing from the land, which meant that labor applied to natural resources could capture the rents. As long as resources remained abundant, conflicts could be avoided by moving on to unclaimed land, but exploitation of both the land and the animals eventually brought competition between the Indians and whites for the increased rents. There was also competition among the Europeans as their mother countries and companies sought returns for the risks undertaken. The British, French, and Spanish sent settlers to the New World at first with the idea that they would stay only a short time and return with gold and other precious metals. It soon became clear, however, especially to the British, that permanent settlement was necessary if the ventures were to succeed. Colonization of the New World was the answer for the British empire.

The institutional framework under which the permanent British settlements were established was steeped in the basic ideas of private ownership even by the seventeenth century.[5] Spain and France had been the dominant countries of Europe for centuries, but it was becoming obvious by 1700 that England would emerge as the industrial power to be emulated and copied. Out of the middle ages came the Magna Carta in 1215, with its fundamental change in the relationship between the powers of the state and the people. With the demise of serfdom, an individual's rights to the fruits of his labor were well established, and the enclosure movements of the seventeenth and eighteenth centuries culminated several centuries of evolution toward private property rights in land. More than any other factor, it was this institutional framework of personal and economic freedom that laid the foundation for the Industrial Revolution in England.

The tradition of private property in England was clearly reflected in the views of the founding fathers through their writing and leadership. Colonial constitutions explicitly protected the right to own property. The Pennsylvania Constitution of 1776, for example, was typical in its guarantee "that all men are born equally free and independent, and have certain natural, inherent and inalienable rights, amongst which are the enjoying and defending of life and liberty, acquiring, possessing and protecting property, and pursuing and obtaining happiness and safety." The Massachusetts and New Hampshire constitutions were almost identical; those of Georgia and South Carolina specifically listed "life, liberty and property" but left out happiness. Even the First Continental Congress guaranteed the inherent rights of acquiring and possessing property in the Declaration on the Violation of Rights.[6] This guarantee is not surprising in light of the position taken by Jefferson in the Declaration of Independence. Responding to the efforts of the British Government to prevent settlers from moving into western lands and to declare that those lands belonged to the king, Jefferson inserted these words into the Declaration of Independence: "He [the king] has endeavored to prevent the Population of these States; for that purpose obstructing the Laws for Naturalization of Foreigners; refusing to pass others to encourage their migrations hither, and raising the conditions of new Appropriation of Lands."The colonists were determined to prevent the ownership from becoming the sole right of nobility and saw the establishment of private property rights as the best way to prevent this.

To help protect private property rights from the vicissitudes of government, written laws and constitutions contained phrases specifically guaranteeing property rights unless the due process of law was followed. Of course, the Fifth Amendment of the Constitution is considered the cornerstone of the guarantee that no person shall "be deprived of life, liberty, or property, without due process of law," but these words were borrowed from earlier state constitutions and ordinances.

One of the more important documents establishing the sanctity of private property was the Ordinance of 1787. In the words of Thomas Donaldson, the Ordinance of 1787 was "the most progressive and republican act ever performed by a nation in relation to the estates of her people. It made the individual absolutely independent of the State, and the entire owner of his or her home."[7] The ordinance was designed primarily to establish the form of government for the Northwest Territory, but a by-product of the law was its impact of our land-tenure system.

Marshall Harris summarizes well the essential land-tenure elements of the Ordinance of 1787:

1. Estates of persons dying intestate would descent to the children, the descendants of a deceased child sharing their parent's share in equal parts. If no children, the next kin of equal degrees would share equally. Distinction between whole and half blood would not exist. The widow would receive a third part of the real estate for life and a third of the personal estate.

2. Estates could be bequeathed by wills in writing, signed and sealed and witnessed by three parties.

3. Real estate would be conveyed by lease and release, or by bargain and sale, signed and sealed and witnessed by three parties.

4. Wills and deeds would be duly proved and recorded within a year.

5. Personal property could be transferred by delivery.

6. Laws and customs in force among certain French and Canadian settlers would not be disrupted.

7. Residents and nonresidents would be taxed alike on their real estate, and no tax would be imposed on land belonging to the federal government.

8. No man would be deprived of property except that public exigencies made it necessary and then only upon full compensation for the same.[8]

On the last point it is worth quoting exactly the words in the ordinance:

No man shall be deprived of his liberty or property, but by the judgment of his peers, or the law of the land, and should the public exigencies make it necessary, for the common preservation, to take any person's property, or to demand his particular services, full compensation shall be made for the same. And, in the just preservation of rights and property, it is understood and declared, that no law ought ever to be made, or have force in the said territory, that shall, in any manner whatever, interfere with, or affect, private contracts or engagements, bona fide, and without fraud, previously formed.[9]

The Ordinance of 1787 did firmly establish the concept of fee simple ownership and provide the first guarantee of freedom of contract in the United States. Both of these, in turn, laid the foundation for the "release of energy" which came in the nineteenth century. With this ordinance the federal government followed the lead of states in completely abolishing the last vestiges of feudal incidence of tenure. The establishment of fee simple tenure meant estates were held in perpetuity with an unlimited power of alienation. This combined with the freedom of contract and the right to convey real estate by bargain and sale cleared the way for an efficient market in land and resources. The only remaining question was to whom initially should the land in the Northwest Territory go.

WHOLESALE OR RETAIL: SPECULATION OR SQUATTING

CESSIONS FROM THE STATES and acquisitions from Indians and the French endowed the federal government with vast tracts of public domain, but the holding was to be temporary. As Roy M. Robbins has noted, "Realizing that this relation should continue no longer than was absolutely necessary, it became the anxious desire of the Confederation government to transfer title into private hands."[10]

From our institutional inheritance, there was never really any question whether private land ownership would prevail over federal or state retention; there was, however, the question of who would get the lands and the rents therefrom. What ensued for the first several decades after the revolution and indeed after ratification of the Constitution was a struggle to decide this question. First, the smaller states were concerned that larger states such as Virginia had a disproportionate share of land. Since all fought for independence, the argument was that the unsettled land west of the Allegheny Mountains should be ceded to the federal government. That question finally was decided in favor of the small states, but there still remained the question of which individuals should get the lands. Land policy debates focused mainly on whether speculators or squatters should get the lands and on the revenue requirements of the federal government. M. Sakolski summarized the debate:

> The conflicting and overlapping claims to territory were gradually surrendered to the national government. The question arose: "What is to be done with it?" "Give it to the soldiers," demanded some. "Use it to pay off the national debt," said others. "Keep it for future use," still others counseled, and there were those who held that any who desired should have the right to settle on it.[11]

Before focusing on the answers to these questions and examining the impact of the Ordinance of 1787 on public disposal, it is useful to develop a framework within which the speculation-squatting debate can be analyzed. The first point to be kept in mind is that whenever rents are "up for grabs," individuals will undertake actions to capture those rents. Certainly this applies to the early American frontier lands.

If we define the frontier as a geographic point where the marginal rental value of land falls to zero because its productivity is not sufficient to cover transportation costs, it is easy to understand which factors caused the frontier to march westward. These factors were rising value of outputs produced from the resource base; declining transportation costs; and technological changes that reduced production costs. The Industrial Revolution in England played an important role in causing the value of agricultural outputs, especially cotton, to rise. The development of roads and canals also contributed to the expansion of the frontier as they brought distant land parcels closer to markets. And finally, learning-by-doing along with technological improvements in farm implements increased the rents associated with land on the frontier margin.

As the marginal land rents increased, it made sense for people to devote resources to capturing them. The question was what were the rules of the game within which competition for the rents would take place. If the lands were to be put up for sale, competition would have to be at the price margin, with the highest bidder getting claim to the land. On the other hand, if squatting was to allocate the land, competition would take place at the hardship margin associated with early frontier settlement.[12]

Consider figure 1, which depicts a hypothetical time path of annual rents associated with a parcel of frontier land. Suppose that the date is 1750 and that the value of output produced from a piece of land in the Ohio Valley is less than the costs of production including transportation costs. Under these conditions land rents would be negative; you would have to "pay" someone to settle and work the ground. However, over time as the value of output increases, transportation costs decrease, or costs of production fall, the rental value will rise and eventually become positive. For any given parcel of land on the frontier we could expect the annual rental value to be negative for some time span (origin to t^* in figure 1), to rise until it becomes zero (t^*), and to be positive thereafter (t^* and beyond).

Within the context of figure 1 we can ask two important questions regarding early American land disposal policy. First, if the goal is to obtain the maximum net present value from the land, what is the optimal time to bring the land into production? And second, if the land is disposed of before t^*, how much would speculators or squatters pay for the land?

The important implication for land policy and economic growth is that there is an optimal time for bringing land into production. The net present value of bringing a particular piece of land into production will be equal to

FIGURE 1

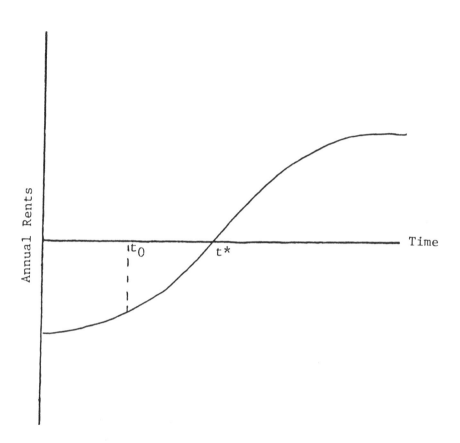

the discounted annual rents over the production period. It is clear that the net present value of annual rents will be maximized if land is put into production at the point t^*. If land is brought into production prior to t^*, the negative rents for the early period must be subtracted from the positive rents that follow t^*. On the other hand, if land is brought into production after t^*, some positive rents will not be captured. Of course it would be impossible given that the rental curve is not known with certainty to hit t^* exactly. Many different individuals will have different ideas about the shape of the rental curve and will act accordingly. The important question is whether land policies tended to encourage settlement at t^* and whether there is any tendency for correction if expectations about rents are incorrect.

To know whether the land policy tended to encourage optimal timing, we must consider the two major methods of competing for the land rents, speculation and squatting. To make the comparison simpler, assume that both the speculators and the squatters have the same expectations about the time path of annual rents shown in figure 1, that both have identical discount rates, and that capital markets are perfect so that discount rates between physical and human capital are the same. Under these conditions how much would speculators and squatters be willing to pay for a parcel of land and what form would their payments take?

How much each would be willing to pay would depend on the net present value at the time of "sale" which is given by the formula where R is

$$NPV = \sum_{i=1}^{n} \frac{R_i}{(1+r)^i}$$

the net rental value in any given time period i, and r is the discount rate. Suppose that a speculator were purchasing a piece of land at time t*. The amount she would be willing to pay would be the discounted value of the annual rents to the right of t* in figure 1. If the land were put up for sale prior to t*, the purchase price would decline since the speculator would have to incur the opportunity cost of money during the time when annual rental values are negative, i.e., any discounted negative cash flows associated with ownership before t* would have to be deducted from the positive rental values to the right of t*. The farther to the left of t* the land is offered for sale, the higher these opportunity costs and the lower the offer, until it is possible that the speculator would not make a positive bid. In the case of speculation, the transaction is in the form of an exchange of ownership claims on resources in general (money) from the speculator in return for ownership claims on specific land from government. If the land speculation market were perfectly efficient with competition and no transaction costs, the values exchanged would be equal at the margin.

Now consider the amount and form of payment from the squatter. Assuming identical expectations and discount rates, the value calculation and bid would be the same. At any point in time the present value of negative rents would have to be offset against the present value of positive rents. Prior to the point where the discounted value of the negative rents exceed the positive rents, no squatting will take place; as soon as the two are equal the value of a parcel of land turns positive and squatters would enter the land.

At any point in time the amount the speculator and squatter would pay will be equal, but there would be a big difference between the two forms of payment. The speculator *exchanges* claims on resources for land; the squatter *expends* time, effort, and capital to obtain the land. The discounted value of the positive rents will attract squatters who will compete for the land by squatting on it the longest. Each year spent squatting has an opportunity cost associated with it in the same way that capital invested by the speculator does. If capital markets are functioning perfectly, the opportunity costs will be exactly the same since the squatter could borrow against his human capital at the same rate that speculators could borrow against physical capital, making the cost of investing the same for each. The time, effort, and capital expended in the rent-seeking process of squatting are not received by anyone and therefore constitute a loss to society. In other words when speculation and squatting are compared, the former represents an efficient exchange where resources consumed in the process are minimized and the latter represents an inefficient expenditure process where the resources consumed are maximized.[13]

A second important distinction (though it is related to the first) between the two forms of land disposal is in the date of settlement. Consider the case of two identical parcels of land, one available for the speculator and the other for the squatter, each of which is offered at the point where the net discounted value of future rents is just positive, say t_0. At this point in time, both speculator and squatter would be willing to make a positive bid. The speculator would purchase the land for ownership claims on other assets and bring it into production at t^*. To bring it into production prior to or after t^* would reduce the return on his investment. The squatter, however, would make the same "bid" but would have to settle the land and bring it into production at the time of purchase. In other words the rent-seeking process of squatting necessitates premature settlement if ownership is to be obtained in competition with other squatters and in the limit dissipates the positive value rents associated with the land.

It is interesting to note that this analysis sheds light on the common accusation that speculators "held land out of the market for at least a time and so compelled settlement to pass around or across it."[14] If lands were available for both speculating and squatting, we would expect squatters to settle at t_0 and speculators to settle at t^*. It was not that speculators were trying to corner the market so as to drive land prices up (though of course they would have been happy to do so if they could). In a competitive market where returns are being maximized, the speculator has no choice but to settle at t^*. Edward Rastatter describes the competitive nature of land speculation:

> A speculator in any commodity reacts to expected changes in supply-demand conditions. To the extent his expectations are correct, he helps smooth out price fluctuations by buying in "glut" time and selling in "shortage" times. Seldom if ever can speculators "corner the market"; and even if they could do so,

they would not sit on their holdings indefinitely, since invested funds have opportunity costs. The speculator pays out his holdings at a rate which he hopes will maximize his profits or minimize his losses. Land speculation is no exception.[15]

To maximize profits, the speculator will pay out his holdings at t^*. By the same token, the competitive nature of squatting leaves the squatter no choice but to settle prior to t^* at t_0. It is not that land speculators held land off the market for "too long" thus compelling settlement to leap-frog over; it is that squatting caused premature settlement of the frontier costing the young nation valuable resources.[16]

Before applying this analysis to the Ordinance of 1787, let us relax the simplifying assumptions used above. It is certainly not the case that all individuals have identical expectations about the time path of rents and therefore that all will pay the same amount for land. In fact it is differences in expectations that drive the market. Those individuals who are most optimistic about the future land rents will be the ones who outbid others in the competitive process. If we imagine two expected time paths of annual rents as shown in figure 2, the person who holds expectations associated with path II will out compete the person who holds expectations associated with path I. If the two are competing speculators, II expects the land value to turn positive sooner and therefore will pay a higher amount for land at any given point in time. If the two are competing squatters, II will be willing to invest more in settlement and will settle at an earlier time. It is perhaps for this reason that people are often so optimistic about frontier settlement *ex ante*, but once they must face the period of negative rents, *ex post* pessimism sets in. We can expect the winners in the bidding for land to be more optimistic about the rents, but there is no reason *a priori* for speculators to have expectations systematically different from squatters.

Relaxation of the assumption of perfect capital markets and identical discount rates, on the other hand, is likely to introduce a systematic bias between those favoring speculation and those favoring squatting. In absence of transaction costs, arbitrage will equalize the discount rate with the marginal rates of substitution and transformation between present and future consumption for all individuals. Positive transaction costs in capital markets drive a wedge between rates at which people are willing to lend and borrow. Even by the time of the American Revolution, physical capital markets were quite well developed. Capital was flowing between Europe and America, and brokers were profiting from any differences in rates of return between the two areas. Land speculators were offering people across the Atlantic the opportunity to invest in American land even before the Ordinance of 1787. This is not to say that physical capital markets were perfect, but arbitrage was taking place to remove differentials in rates of return.

FIGURE 2

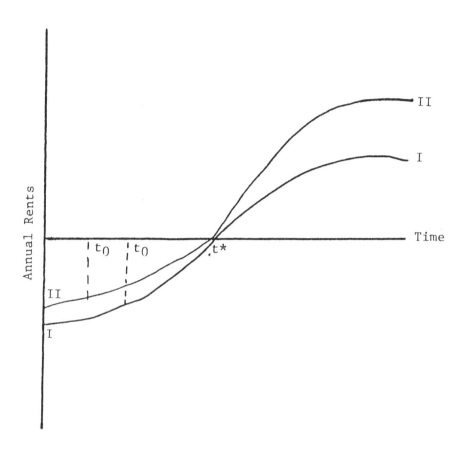

Human capital markets, however, were not nearly so well developed and, in fact, had probably deteriorated since the early colonial days when indentured servitude contracts were common.[17] Indenture contracts made it possible for individuals to borrow against their human capital in the same way that others were borrowing against physical capital. But concern over slavery, including its ban in the Northwest by the Ordinance of 1787, brought legal restrictions on indenture contracts making it more difficult to borrow against human capital. As a result of the high transaction costs associated with this borrowing, individuals with little physical capital could only obtain land through squatting, a form of borrowing against human capital. Squatting allowed these individuals to earn negative rents on land for a period of time in return for positive rents later. Had human capital markets been as efficient as physical markets, rates of return between the two would have been equalized. Squatters would have been able to borrow money against their human capital and compete in the speculation market exchanging claims against human assets for land. Unfortunately, high transaction costs forced them to compete through a rent-seeking process. This would suggest that those with less physical wealth would favor squatting as a means of disposing of the public domain, and those with more physical assets would favor speculation.

LAND DISPOSAL FOLLOWING THE REVOLUTION

THE MODEL PRESENTED ABOVE allows us to evaluate various land disposal policies centering around the Ordinance of 1787. It was necessity rather than a desire to maximize the net present value of land settlement that caused speculation to be the dominant form of land disposal after the revolution. For all practical purposes, the Continental Congress was bankrupt after the war save for the enormous tracts of land ceded it by the newly-formed states. Therefore the statesmen of the time were reluctant to give away the land resources until financial stability was attained. Though the federal government did have a vast national domain,

> it was a bankrupt national government. Its notes, "scrip," "certif-icates," "indents" and other forms of floating indebtedness were overdue and unpaid. The public land was proposed as a means of debt liquidation. Jefferson in 1782 estimated that 5,000,000 acres could readily be sold at a dollar per acre in government debt certificates and the whole national debt soon paid with the proceeds from additional sales.[18]

To be sure, Jefferson was overly optimistic for the potential of land sales during the early years of the Republic, but as table 1 suggests, disposal of the public domain in exchange for cash, certificates, public debt, and land warrants did contribute significantly to the elimination of the national debt by 1835.

Jefferson's optimism, however, was shared by a large number of land speculators eager to invest in the Old Northwest Territory. "Petitions for grants of vast tracts at nominal prices poured into Congress" after the passage of the Ordinance of 1787 provided a structure of government and a survey of land in the region.[19] Of all these, only two met with any success, the Ohio Company and the Symmes Purchase. The Reverend Manasseh Cutler represented the Ohio Company in the negotiations with the Continental Congress and eventually colluded with William Duer, secretary of the Board of the Treasury. Cutler originally proposed that the Ohio Company purchase one million acres, but when Congress demanded a mini-

TABLE 1

Receipts from the Public Domain, 1787–1840

	Receipts
Prior to 30 June, 1796	$ 1,201,726
1796–1799	99,340
1800–1805	1,550,195
1806–1810	3,018,149
1811–1815	5,010,251
1816–1820	11,226,071
1821–1825	6,133,580
1826–1830	7,754,470
1831–1835	29,417,081
1836–1840	46,157,758

Source: Thomas Donaldson, *The Public Domain* (New York: Johnson Reprint Corporation, 1970), 17.

mum price of one dollar an acre and payment within three months of purchase, he became discouraged. Duer suggested that Cutler might obtain better terms if he asked for a larger tract and offered to take the additional acres as part of the Scioto Project which he would secretly head. Eventually, Congress approved the purchase of approximately five million acres at a price of one dollar per acre "payable in specie, or in loan office certificates reduced to specie value, or certificates of liquidated debts of the United States."[20] After an initial payment of five hundred thousand dollars, remaining payments were to commence when the survey was completed and then would be spread over a three year period in six semiannual installments. "On October 27, 1787, Cutler paid over to the Board of the Treasury a half million dollars in debt certificates of the United States then worth anywhere from $60,000 to $130,000," and the Ohio Company was off on its efforts to settle the territory.[21] Unfortunately for Congress and the speculators, the investment was not overly successful. Before the second payment could be made, the company petitioned Congress to reduce the price to fifty cents per acre. Congress agreed, and "the Ohio Company, therefore, received about 1,000,000 acres of land for $500,000 in government debts, worth during the time of purchase from 12 1/2 to 50 cents on the dollar. For about 215,000 acres it presented soldiers' warrants."[22] That companies like the Ohio Company had a difficult time making their payments as originally agreed suggests that the early land speculators were overly optimistic. The fact that it was their money on the line, however, did force them to carefully consider the optimal time for investment and settlement. If they were wrong, they suffered the losses and others learned from their lesson.

Nonetheless, Payson Treat concluded that the Ohio Company venture was positive. "It extinguished a half million of the public debt at a time when the treasury was all but bankrupt; it was a concrete example of the wealth of the western lands; it seemed to pave the way for other remunerative sales, and better than all this, it placed on the frontier a most desirable body of settlers, many of them veterans of the Revolution."[23]

Now let us consider the disposal mechanisms used following the revolution in terms of the model. Efforts by the Continental Congress to sell the public domain discouraged rent seeking to the extent that speculators competed on the price margin. Nonetheless, the fact that Cutler and Duer were able to negotiate the terms of their purchase with Congress suggests that some rents were "up for grabs." The process of disposing of the public domain immediately following the revolution was far from competitive. Indeed, it was not at all uncommon for politicians and bureaucrats such as Duer to make their fortunes in land grabbing schemes that worked only because they had control of the political process that handed out the land rents.

In addition to the lack of competition among speculators bidding for land, another cause of rent seeking was the minimum price placed on the land by the Congress. Such minimum prices sometimes made it impossible for speculators to bid at the time of sale and successfully earn a normal rate of return. In other words the speculator would only bid the net present value of the expected land rents. If this was less than the minimum price, speculators would only bid on the land when the net present value of land rents was greater than or equal to the minimum. Since this could only occur after the net present value turned positive, t_0 in the model, a policy of minimum prices gave squatters the incentive to go out on the frontier in advance of speculators. Therefore minimum prices encouraged squatting and its accompanying resource expenditures.

The federal government did try to discourage those who were squatting without paying anything or who were not meeting their credit obligations, but the incentives for rent seeking were too great. Laws were enacted making it illegal to trespass on the public lands in some parts of the Northwest Territory. In some states those found guilty of squatting could be fined as much as one thousand dollars and imprisoned for up to one year.[24] Congress even authorized the use of troops to evict squatters. As early as 1783, General Harmar drove off squatters "who had planted themselves on 'all the most valuable land,' " and even burned their cabins.[25] With the net present value of land positive but below the minimum price set by Congress, there was enough incentive for the squatter to return as soon as the troops left so that "the government was never free from such illegal intrusions upon public lands."[26]

CONCLUSION

THE FIRST EFFORTS AT privatizing the public domain after the revolution set a precedent for speculation rather than squatting. Following the pattern established by the New England states, the Land Ordinance of 1785 required that lands be sold at auction and not be purchased any other way until an auction had been held. Given the interest in raising revenue, squatting was expressly prohibited by a resolution of the Continental Congress passed on 15 June, 1785, and the Secretary of War was even authorized to remove unlawful settlers from federal lands in the Northwest Territory.

The first effort at establishing land policy made it clear that the federal government intended to capture the rents from its land assets through exchanges with citizens. In so doing, the Continental Congress opened the door for a debate that would last until 1841, a debate over whether public land would be disposed of to speculators or squatters. Roy M. Robbins summarizes the first round of that debate: "Regardless of the comparatively democratic character of the Ordinance of 1785, the American settler found little within its provisions that was attractive. The policy appealed more to speculators and men of money than to hardy yeomen who were usually unable to compete with the former at the auction."

Most historians have looked at this era of speculation with disdain. They have argued that speculators made profits at the expense of settlers by monopolizing land markets and forcing settlers to go even further into the wilderness. Rastatter has argued that "the consensus among historians might be that speculation made an already poor public land policy even worse," but that his evidence "casts further doubt on this contention."[28] He found that speculators were not able to charge the high prices that confiscated all of the returns to land, that they brought the most valuable land into production first, and that they did not hold land off the market for long periods of time in an effort to drive up prices.

The model and evidence presented in this paper cast even further doubt on the evils of speculation.[29] A land disposal policy that required exchanges of private assets for the public domain was superior to one that encouraged squatters to expend effort rent seeking since the latter represents a social waste. Given the imperfections of capital markets, one might argue that squatting was the only way to allow those not endowed with physical wealth to compete with those who were. Unfortunately, such an effort to create equity cost the young nation by diverting resources with alternative uses to the frontier and imposed the "winners curse" on the squatters who had to spend years on the frontier earning negative rents that translated into hardship and misery. Only by considering early land markets as any other commodity market and by examining the efficiency of the disposal policies can we further the evolution of "a more dispassionate view of the speculator."[30]

Notes

1. Daniel Webster, *Works of Daniel Webster* (Boston: Little, 1860), 263.
2. Marshall Harris, *Origin of the Land Tenure System in the United States* (Ames: Iowa State College Press, 1953), 392.
3. Richard L. Stroup and John Baden, *Natural Resources: Myths and Management* (Cambridge, Mass.: Ballinger Press, 1983).
4. Robert Higgs, "Legally Induced Technical Regress in the Washington Salmon Fishery," *Research in Economic History*, vol. 7, 1982.
5. Jonathan R. T. Hughes, *The Governmental Habit: Economic Controls From Colonial Times to the Present* (New York: Basic Books, 1977).
6. Harris, 372–73.
7. Thomas Donaldson, *The Public Domain: Its History with Statistics* (New York: Johnson Reprint Corporation, 1970), 157.
8. Harris, 392.
9. For the full text, see Donaldson, 153–56.
10. Roy M. Robbins, *Our Landed Heritage* (New York: Peter Smith, 1952), 5–6.
11. A. M. Sakolski, *The Great American Land Bubble* (New York: Harper and Brothers Publishers, 1932), 99.
12. Terry L. Anderson and Peter J. Hill, "Privatizing the Commons: An Improvement?," *Southern Economic Journal*, October 1983; A. Taylor Dennen, "Some Efficiency Effects of Nineteenth-Century Federal Land Policy: Dynamic Analysis," *Agricultural History*, 1977.
13. Anderson and Hill.
14. Benjamin H. Hibbard, *A History of Public Land Policies* (New York: Macmillan, 1924), 219.
15. Edward H. Rastatter, "Nineteenth-Century Public Land Policy: The Case for the Speculator," *Essays in Nineteenth-Century Economic History*, David C. Klingaman and Richard K. Vedders, eds. (Athens: Ohio University Press, 1975), 118–19.
16. Robert William Fogel and Jack L. Rutner, "The Efficiency of Federal Land Policy 1850–1900: A Report of Some Provisional Findings, *The Dimensions of Quantitative Research in History*, William O. Aydelotte et al., eds. (Princeton: Princeton University Press, 1972).
17. David Galenson, "The Market Evaluation of Human Capital: The Case of Indentured Servitude," *Journal of Political Economy*, June 1981.
18. A. M. Sakolski, *The Great American Land Bubble* (New York: Harper and Brothers Publishers, 1932), 33.
19. Sakolski, 33.
20. Sakolski, 102.
21. Sakolski, 104.
22. Sakolski, 105; see also Shaw Livermore, *Early American Land Companies* (New York: Octagon Books, 1968), 134–46.

23. Payson J. Treat, *The National Land System of 1785–1820* (New York: E. B. Treat and Company, 1920), 57–58.

24. Paul W. Gates, *History of Public Land Law Development* (Washington, D.C.: Government Printing Office, 1968), 219.

25. Gates, 122.

26. Ibid.

27. Robbins, 9.

28. Rastatter, 135.

29. See Fogel and Rutner.

30. Rastatter, 118.

5

YANKEE FARMING AND SETTLEMENT IN THE OLD NORTHWEST: A COMPARATIVE ANALYSIS

Jeremy Atack
University of Illinois

Fred Bateman
Indiana University

THE CESSION OF CLAIMS to western lands by the original thirteen colonies paved the way for two legislative acts by the Continental Congress—the Land Ordinance of 1785 and the Northwest Ordinance of 1787—that were to have a profound effect upon both the pattern of American growth in general and development in the Old Northwest in particular. The first imposed order upon the land by providing a systematic basis for land sale and settlement; the second laid down the terms under which these newly settled lands would be governed and might enter the Union. Although authorship of these laws is still debated, both show the influence of New England thought and practice as well as the agrarian vision of Thomas Jefferson.[1] In this essay we focus upon the consequences of that New England legacy to the Old Northwest by looking at the settlement and agricultural practice of New England and Middle Atlantic farmers who had migrated to the Old Northwest. Their behavior and characteristics are then compared with those who stayed behind and with other groups in the same communities.[2]

In the Old Northwest, Yankee settlers found many familiar features from back home—a township form of local governance; contiguous, orderly settlement; public schooling; a similar climate; and no slavery. Indeed, in many ways the Old Northwest must have looked much better to many of the migrants who found more fertile soils and lower land prices. These advantages were doubtless tempered by the greater distance from markets and what must have been, at least initially for many, a much rougher and more precarious life. Nevertheless, settlers stayed west or pushed even farther westward and successive generations joined them in out-migration from the Northeast to settle the lands of the Old Northwest.[3] As the words of a New England ballad put it:

'Tis I can delve and plough, love,
And you can spin and sew;

And we'll settle in the banks
Of the pleasant Ohio.[4]

And so:

> By wagons, by rafts, hundreds of families from New England,
> along with their neighbors in the Middle States, followed the
> Mowhawk Valley or the old Braddock Road, or floated down the
> Ohio to plant a new state which should be but a younger New
> England on the shores of Lake Erie and on the banks of the
> Muskingom.[5]

In this westward trek, the Yankee is generally portrayed as well-informed
and with definite plans:

> First in order, as he is always first when speculation is con-
> cerned, comes the hardy, enterprising New Englander. Of all the
> emigrants to the West Brother Jonathan alone knows where he is
> going to—the cheapest mode of travel, and what he is going to
> do when he gets there; he alone has read the preemption laws,
> and knows what sum he must take with him, or notions in the
> way of trade, to secure a home in the wilderness. Already, before
> he gets there, he converses fluently about ranges, townships,
> and sections, has ascertained the number of acres in each subdi-
> vision, the amount reserved for schools, and is ready on his ar-
> rival to avail himself of his new position.[6]

Migration was not, however, for everyone. Most Yankees remained settled and resisted the urge to join the tide of westward migration to the new
lands of the Old Northwest. Even in Vermont where out-migration began
before settlement was completed, a recent study of some who did not move
westward concluded: "Those who stayed behind in older rural America
were not necessarily left there by the progressive advance of an urban and
industrial society. Many chose to stay and experienced a sense of stability
that eluded a good number of their contemporaries. But that order had its
price (life within the boundaries of community was rarely marred by social
conflict), those boundaries eventually became rigid and anachronistic and
excluded new people and outside ideas."[7]

The quantitative extent of the migration from New England and the Middle Atlantic states before 1850 is largely undocumented.[8] Beginning in that
year, however, the federal census office began collecting data on place of
birth. These data were eventually tabulated by the census office and published but only with the caveat that "time has not admitted of its examination. . . [and]. . . in many particulars it does not agree with other published
results."[9] Whatever their defects, actual or alleged, the data substantiated
claims by contemporaries of substantial out-migration from New England
and the Middle Atlantic states into the Old Northwest. Despite mortality

among the earlier and older migrants, almost nine hundred thousand former northeasterners had made the Old Northwest their home by 1850 (table 1).[10] Ten years later their numbers had swelled to well over a million, an increase of over 30 percent in the decade. However, this growth was less rapid than the growth of total population so that the Yankee-born were a declining proportion of total population in each state. Nevertheless, Yankees made up 33.9 percent of Michigan's population in 1860, over 25 percent of Wisconsin's, almost 17 percent of Illinois's, 14 percent of Ohio's, but only 8 percent of Indiana's. Only in Ohio did the absolute number of northeastern-born residents decline; elsewhere, and especially in Illinois and Wisconsin, their numbers increased sharply.[11]

TABLE 1

Yankee-Born Settlers in the Old Northwest, 1850–1860
(Figures in Parentheses are Percentages of State or Regional Population)

| State | | | Yankee-born Population | |
| | | | Net increase | % change |
	1850	1860	1850–1860	1850–1860
Illinois	148,549	286,700	138,151	93.0
	(17.4)	(16.7)		
Indiana	87,038	108,574	21,536	24.7
	(8.8)	(8.0)		
Michigan	179,703	254,225	74,522	41.5
	(45.2)	(33.9)		
Ohio	374,075	321,487	−52,588	−14.1
	(18.9)	(13.7)		
Wisconsin	106,761	199,334	92,573	86.7
	(35.0)	(25.7)		
OLD NORTHWEST	896,126	1,170,320	274,194	30.6
	(19.8)	(16.9)		

Source: Computed U.S. Census Office. Seventh Census, *The Census of 1850,* (Washington, D.C.: Robert Armstrong, 1853), p. xxxvi and U.S. Census Office. Eighth Census, *Population of the United States in 1860,* (Washington, D.C.: Government Printing Office, 1864), 616–19.

The census did not break down the other data by nativity and, consequently, analyses have generally been restricted to place-of-birth by place-of-residence cross-tabulations. The data underlying this study permit us to break out of this mold. They are a subset of the sample of quantitative information collected from the federal censuses of agriculture and population in 1860 for 21,118 rural households that was collected by Fred Bateman and James D. Foust.[12] These data were drawn from the population of all nonurban townships in twenty northern states (including Maryland and Missouri). From them we have selected those households operating farms and headed by northeasterners in the sampled northeastern states of Connecticut, New Hampshire, New Jersey, New York, Pennsylvania, and Vermont and those households with farms operated by Yankees in the Old North-west—Illinois, Indiana, Michigan, Ohio, and Wisconsin. The resultant usable sample sizes were 3,527 matched farms and households in the Northeast (over 99 percent of the sample farms in the area) and 1,199 matched farms and households (24 percent of the sample farms) in the Old Northwest (table 2).[13]

TABLE 2

Yankee Farmers in the Old Northwest, 1860

State	Proportion of Yankee-born:			Sample Size of Yankee Farmers
	Farmers	Residents	Household Heads	
(1)	(2)	(3)	(4)	(5)
Illinois	28%	17%	29%	232
Indiana	14%	8%	14%	395
Michigan	51%	34%	48%	294
Ohio	43%	14%	39%	179
Wisconsin	28%	26%	34%	99
OLD NORTHWEST	25%	17%	25%	1,199

Source: Columns 2, 4, and 5 computed from the Bateman-Foust sample.
Column 3 from Table 1.

In Michigan 51 percent of all the sample farms were operated by Yankees. In Ohio the proportion was 43 percent. In Illinois and Wisconsin, the proportion was lower, 28 percent. It was lowest in Indiana where only 14 percent of the farms were operated by Yankees. It will be noted that these proportions are higher than the proportion of Yankees among the general population in the Old Northwest.

Were Yankees thus more likely than other groups to establish farmsteads? Mathews, in his description of the out-migrants from New England and New York who settled the Old Northwest, especially in Illinois, described them as "wealthy farmers, enterprising merchants, millers, and manufacturers who built mills, churches, schoolhouses, cities, and made roads and bridges with astonishing public spirit."[14] In short, he attributed to the group a wide range of economic activities of which farming was but one. Our sample data bear this out, for migration analyses based upon the census place-of-birth by place-of-residence matrix (such as that in table 1) are flawed by the implicit assumption that all residents were independent decisionmakers who determined where they lived. In so doing they tend to understate the proportion of migrants because they count in the denominator the children born to migrant couples. Moreover, the matrix provides no information about migration within a state. The former flaw can be overcome by household reconstruction from the data in the manuscript census. This has been done in the Bateman-Foust sample. With these data we can then isolate the birthplace of the head of household who, we would argue, determined place of residency although place of birth of other household members simply represents happenstance. As a result, a somewhat different picture of interstate migration emerges as the proportion of migrants rises relative to nonmigrants. Thirty-nine percent of rural Ohio households in the Bateman-Foust sample were headed by native northeasterners. In Michigan the proportion was even higher, 48 percent; in Wisconsin somewhat lower, 34 percent. In Illinois 29 percent of the households were headed by people from the Northeast. Indiana still had the smallest proportion of Yankees among its household heads, only 14 percent, but the fraction is still substantially higher than that reported by the published census. Unfortunately, because the sampling technique was deliberately biased towards rural areas, we do not know whether these proportions hold true for the urban population as well. Based upon these proportions, therefore, northeasterners were farmers in the Old Northwest in about the same proportions as they were in rural population.

How did the personal characteristics of these Yankee farmers in the Old Northwest in 1860 compare with those of farmers who stayed behind in the Northeast? This comparison is particularly germane to the debate over the Safety Valve and whether or not the migrants were pushed out of the Northeast by land scarcity creating high prices in the face of relative poverty.

TABLE 3

Personal and Household Characteristics of Yankee-born Farmers
in the Northeast and Old Northwest, 1860

Characteristics	Northeast	Old Northwest
Age (Years)	46.5	46.3
Literacy (%)	97.3	95.9
Household size*	5.4	6.0
Number of Children*	2.0	2.8
Percentage of Tenants	6.4	5.9
Percentage of Part-Owners*	5.2	6.6
Period of Residency (years)*	41.4	17.1
Wealth:		
Real Estate ($)*	3,668	2,045
Personal Estate ($)*	1,192	780

*Significant difference between means at the 5 percent level.
Source: Computed from the Bateman-Foust sample.

The personal characteristics of the northeastern-born heads of farm households in each region are shown in table 3. In terms of average age, literacy rate, and the proportion who were tenants, the two populations are virtually identical. Mean age differs by less than three months, and though literacy rates and tenancy are somewhat higher in the Northeast than in the Old Northwest the differences are not statistically significant. The two populations do differ significantly from one another on the basis of the other characteristics in table 3. Western householders had more children and consequently larger overall size. Since households in both regions were at the same stage in their life cycle, the greater number of children can be interpreted as evidence of higher fertility in the Old Northwest. This is consistent with the findings of other studies that relate the higher fertility to land availability and the demand for child labor on the family farm.[15] The homogeneity of these two populations with respect to cultural background and life cycle stage reinforces these findings.

We have used the matched data to divide farmers into owner-occupiers, part-owners, and tenants based upon a comparison of the real estate value reported on the population schedules with the value of farm reported on the agricultural schedules. Tenants are identified as those farmers who satisfied the criteria proposed by Allan C. Bogue who argues that those persons named in the agricultural schedules as operating a farm and who listed their occupation as farmer but reported no real estate value on the population schedules were tenants.[16] Contrary to the usual practice, however, we have not simply divided farmers between tenants and yeomen. Instead, we identify a third group, namely those who listed their occupation as farmer or agriculturalist or who claimed to follow two or more occupations one of which was that of farmer and for whom a farm was located in the agricultural schedules but who probably owned only a fraction of the land that they farmed. They are identified by a value of real estate on the population schedules greater than zero but less than the value of the farm they operated. We refer to this group as "part-owners."[17] Such farmers are common today, and they also proved numerous in the mid-nineteenth century. Among all farmers in the North in 1860, part-owners were about half as numerous as tenants, but among the Yankee-born farmers they were as common as tenants.[18] We interpret this group as commercially-oriented farmers who were farming on a scale greater than their own financial resources permitted.

Using the data for the reconstructed families, we have also estimated the number of years that the farmer had been resident in the state in which he was located in 1860. This was estimated as the mean of the age of the oldest child born in the state and the youngest child born out of state. If no children were born in state, then our best estimate for period of residency was half the age of the youngest child. If all children were born in the state, we estimate the period of residency as the mean of the age of the oldest child and the father. If there were no children, we assumed the farmer to have lived half his life in the state. This statistic show that Yankees living in the Old Northwest had been resident in their 1860 state of residency an average of 17.5 years, whereas the vast majority of those who remained behind had stayed in their state of birth throughout their lives. The "stayers" held more wealth, both real and personal, than those who had moved. The difference in personal estate was particularly marked, with a 50 percent differential between the groups.

The number of Yankee-born migrants who settled at ever earlier dates generally declines, except for the late 1830s and early 1840s when more than expected seem to have settled in the Old Northwest. In the seven-year period 1844–50, for example, an average of twenty-four families in the sample settled in the Old Northwest and in the seven years from 1830–36, an average of twenty-two families settled in the region, but during the depression from 1837–43, an average of twenty-seven families per year arrived. It is tempting to interpret this as evidence of increased out-migration in the wake of economic distress in the depression of the late 1830s and early 1840s. This would be consistent with the postulates of the "safety valve" hypothesis.

We have also used the data on length of residency in the Old Northwest to see whether there is any trend in wealth based upon length of residence. However, since earlier work has shown a marked life cycle pattern of wealth accumulation among various groups in 1860 and because those who settled earlier will, other things equal, be older than those who came later, we have adjusted individual wealth estimates for the aggregate life cycle effect.[19] This was done by regressing wealth on age and age squared and calculating the residual wealth. The life cycle equation was:

$$\text{Wealth} = -4596.623 + 313.902 \, (\text{age}) - 2.655 \, (\text{age})^2$$
$$(1344.040) \quad (58.283) \quad\quad (0.604)$$
$$n = 1,199 \quad\quad\quad\quad R^2 = 0.055$$

which shows significant life cycle effects although there remains a great deal of unexplained variation. Wealth among Yankee-born farmers in the Old Northwest thus peaked at age 59.[20]

The mean residual wealth values by length of residency are plotted in figure 1. The trend in wealth by date of settlement appears to pivot around the depression of the late 1830s and early 1840s. Those who arrived earlier, especially in the late 1820s and early 1830s, generally did better than expected. Those who came in the 1850s did rather worse. Both periods were periods of great land speculation in the Old Northwest. In the 1820s and early 1830s, the speculation was driven by the opening of new lands in Illinois and Michigan, liberalized land-sale terms, and projected ambitious internal improvements. In the 1850s speculation accompanied the spread of the railroad into the Old Northwest.

This trend in wealth accumulation with longer residency may be interpreted as the returns to migration. This rate averaged about 1 percent a year over the period on the mean total wealth of the typical Yankee-born

FIGURE 1

Average Wealth of Yankee-born Farmers in the Old Northwest by Date of their
Settlement, Adjusted for Life Cycle Accumulation, 1820–1860

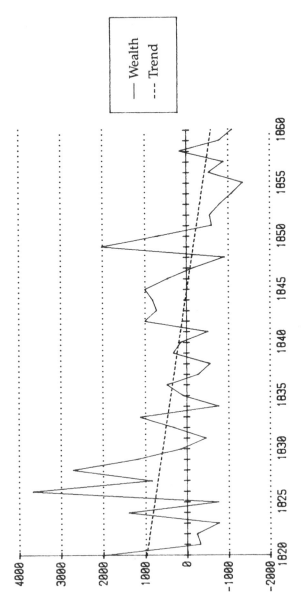

farmer in the Old Northwest, or about forty dollars per year. Based on estimates of the costs of migration in the South made by Schaefer, it would probably take at least one and possibly two decades for a Yankee farm family to recoup the costs of migration to the Old Northwest at this return.[21] Such a long repayment period lends credence to the argument that Yankee farmers migrated westward so that they might pass on working farms (or the capital to buy one) to their sons.

Most studies describing early settlement in the Old Northwest draw a sharp distinction between the Yankee settlers and those from the South. Mathews, for example, said of them, "Many of the Southerners [who settled]...were poor; they had been unable to hold slaves in the South by reason of their poverty, and had come into the Northwest Territory not only to better their condition, but also to avoid a system of which they did not disapprove on principle, but had found unpleasant on account of the social distinctions it produced."[22] The two groups also seem to have had different attitudes and values: "The southerner is perhaps the most hospitable and generous to individuals. He is lavish of his victuals, his liquors, and other personal favors. But the northern man is the most liberal in contributing to whatever is for public benefit."[23] Moreover,

> They differed in speech, in manners and attitudes, often in politics. Yankee food and recipes and household methods were different. The ideas of thrift and shrewdness and addiction to notes, bonds, bookkeeping, and mechanical contraptions were frequently irritating to the easier-going and neighborly Southerner who would lend his oxen but seldom think of renting them. Yankee feelings of superiority were not easily concealed, and at least one pioneer records they became "objects of the deepest animosity to the settlers in Southern Illinois, Indiana, and the South-western States."[24]

Our data can cast some light on how Yankee- and Southern-born settlers in the Old Northwest differed in terms of objective personal and household characteristics (table 4). We also compare the characteristics of the northeastern-born farm heads of household residing in the Old Northwest with those of those born in the Old Northwest and those of foreign-born immigrants. Among the four groups, the Yankee-born were the oldest, the most literate, and the wealthiest in real estate holdings. They were relatively similar, however, to the southerners in their real estate holdings and in their period of residency in the Old Northwest. The southern settlers, however, differed from their Yankee neighbors by having significantly larger families, much lower literacy rates, and by being younger. Indeed, literacy among the Southerners is lower than among the foreign-born. The southern-born farmer, however, contrary to what Mathews claimed, was no poorer than the Yankee-born farmer.

TABLE 4

Personal and Household Characteristics of Yankee-born Farmers in the Old Northwest Compared with Those of Other Farmers in that Region, 1860

Characteristics	Yankee-Born	Old North-westerners	Other Migrants	Immigrants
Age (years)	46.3	33.4*	44.1*	44.1*
Literacy (%)	95.9	91.1*	86.9*	93.0*
Household Size	6.0	5.54*	6.34*	5.75*
Number of Children	2.8	2.8	3.4*	3.1*
Percentage of Tenants	5.9	13.8*	15.2*	6.5*
Percentage of Part-Owners	6.6	8.1*	5.3*	3.9*
Period of Residency (years)	17.1	33.4*	17.8	14.5*
Wealth:				
Real Estate ($)	3045	2352*	2924*	1823*
Personal Estate ($)	780	627*	846	527*

*Significant difference between this mean and that for Yankee-Born at the 5 percent level.
Source: Computed from the Bateman-Foust sample grants.

The data in table 4 also show that those farmers who were born in the Old Northwest were much younger than any of the other farm groups. They also headed smaller households but had about the same number of children as those born in the Northeast. They therefore had less labor available for the farm chores. Immigrants were the same age as these migrants from the South but had a considerably higher literacy rate. On average they had been in the Old Northwest three years less than the northeastern- or southern-born migrants.

Tenancy rates among the native old northwesterners and the southern migrants were more than double those of the other groups. One would have expected that those who had been born in the region should have had better opportunities than those who arrived later, but this was not the case for this group. Tenancy and part-ownership was lowest among immigrants despite their having the lowest mean wealth value for both real and personal estate.

Although all of the groups that we have considered differed from one another in important respects, the two groups that were most similar were the Yankee-born farmer in the Old Northwest and those of his contemporaries who stayed behind. it is these two groups on whom we focus exclusively in the sections that follow dealing with the kind of farm the two groups operated and how the agriculture that they practiced differed.

In the new territories of the Old Northwest, the most common farm size was eighty acres, an area equal to the minimum permitted under the Land Act of 1820 (figure 2). Over 16 percent of all farms in the region had exactly eighty acres. Furthermore, multiples of 2 and 0.5 were also common. Odd-sized farms were fairly infrequent, suggesting that most farms had not been subdivided through transfers, inheritance, or sale since the original

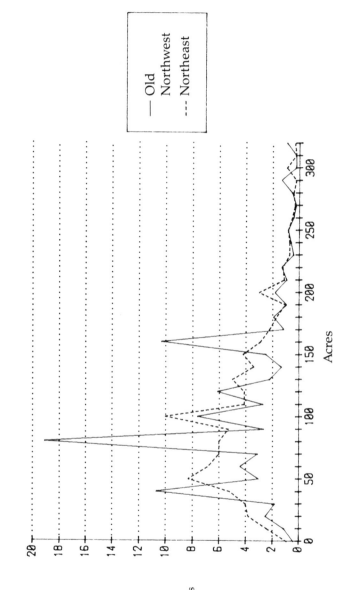

FIGURE 2

Size distribution of Yankee Farms in the Northeast and Old Northwest, 1860

farm was purchased. In the Northeast, on the other hand, the modal farm had one hundred acres and there was a much higher incidence of odd-sized farms.

One often-cited reason for westward migration was the high cost of farm purchases in the Northeast and the much lower costs of buying a similar or larger farm in the West. Although differences between the size distributions and in the size of the modal or mean farm make direct comparisons of means of doubtful value, in table 5 we present the average statistics for farms of one hundred acres in both regions. The cost for the average one hundred-acre farm was virtually identical between the regions. Total costs were within forty-seven dollars of one another, some forth-one dollars of which was due to the value of the farm itself. This differential probably reflects nothing more than the slightly higher percentage of improved to unimproved areas on the northeastern farms. Livestock values were identical. Farms such as these, whether in the Northeast or the Old Northwest, were beyond the reach of a large percent of those who migrated to escape eastern poverty and unemployment.

TABLE 5

Average Farm Costs for a One hundred-acre Farm Operated by a Yankee-born Farmer in the Northeast and Old Northwest, 1860

Item	Northeast	Old Northwest
Cash Value of Farm	$2,848	$2,807
Value of Implements	115	109
Value of Livestock	434	434
TOTAL COST	3,397	3,350

Source: Computed from the Bateman-Foust sample.

The estimate of $3,350 for a one hundred-acre farm in the Old Northwest is broadly consistent with, if somewhat more generous than, those given by contemporaries. A correspondent of the *Wisconsin Farmer*, for example, suggested that such a farm in Wisconsin (with fifty acres improved and fenced) could be purchased for $1,600, and that livestock and implements would cost perhaps another $710.[25] In Illinois, James Caird estimated costs at $2,250 for the land.[26]

The similarity between costs for a one hundred-acre farm in the Northeast or the Old Northwest, however, belies a substantial difference between the costs of the average farm in each region. The average Yankee-operated farm in the Old Northwest was considerably larger than the mode. It had 129 acres, 57 percent of which was in crops (table 6). By contrast, the average farm in the Northeast was ten acres smaller. Nevertheless, the Yankee farm in the Northeast had almost ten acres more in crops than in the Old Northwest and over 70 percent of the land was under cultivation. Despite their smaller size, northeastern farms were generally more valuable than the average farm in the Old Northwest. The average farm operated by Yankees in the East had a market price of $3,753 compared with only $2,968 for their counterparts' typical farm in the Old Northwest.

TABLE 6

Characteristics of Yankee Farms in the Northeast and Old Northwest, 1860

Characteristic	Northeast	Old Northwest
Value of Farm*	$3,753	$2,947
Value of Implements*	136	108
Value of Livestock*	540	445
Improved Acreage (acres)*	84	73
Unimproved Acreage (acres)*	36	56
Improved/Total Acreage*	0.70	0.57

*Significant difference between means at the 5 percent level.
Source: Computed from the Bateman-Foust sample.

Why the difference? The value of a farm depends upon the quantity and quality of the land, buildings and other fixed investments such as fences, ditches, or land clearing that affect the quantity of crops that can be produced. It also depends upon proximity to markets or transportation since this affects the prices received for crops and thus the revenues earned. In general, land further west was more fertile but it was often correspondingly more distant from markets and had fewer improvements.

Why were Yankee farms in the Northeast more valuable? Was this a reflection on the value of farm buildings or land prices? To examine these questions, we have regressed the cash value of the farm on improved and unimproved acreage. The coefficients of improved and unimproved acreage are interpreted as the price per acre for improved and unimproved land. The price for the former includes the capitalized value of clearing, breaking, drainage, and fencing. The unimproved land may also be fenced, but in the less densely settled areas it was probably unfenced. The constant term in the equation reflects farm structures and other factors that affected land value but were not related to acreage. Estimates of this equation can therefore provide some crude breakdown of the census "Cash Value of the Farm," and a basis for comparison between the Northeast and Old Northwest.

Interpreting the constant term in the equations as the value of farm buildings suggests that these Yankee-operated farms must have had fairly substantial structures (table 7). Nine hundred dollars is the highest specific estimate reported by Danhof for farm buildings in the Old Northwest, though he does remark that "larger houses cost as much as $1,000."[27] For a

TABLE 7

The Value of Farm Buildings and Improved and Unimproved Land on
Yankee-Operated Farms in the Northeast and Old Northwest, 1860
(t-statistic)

Region	Farm Buildings ($)	Improved Land ($/acre)	Unimproved Land ($/acre)	R^2
Northeast	1210.43 (18.76)	27.94 (45.85)	5.72 (7.61)	.43
Old Northwest	909.29 (12.44)	20.71 (32.36)	9.52 (13.29)	.59

Source: Computed from the Bateman-Foust sample.

somewhat earlier period, 1843, Solon Robinson estimated the cost of a one-
and-a-half-storey prairie farmhouse in 1843 as $250–300 and a log barn as
$40.[28] Since most contemporary descriptions suggest that barns were fairly
rudimentary and inexpensive structures, costing at most $150 or so, the
constant term suggests that the average Yankee family in the Old Northwest
may have lived in a six- or seven-room house.[29] The $300 premium on farm
structures in the East presumably reflects a locational premium and probably covers the extra farm buildings necessary for the more intensive animal
husbandry practiced by Yankee farmers in the Northeast.

Cropland in the Northeast was significantly more expensive than improved land in the Old Northwest. We interpret this as evidence that scarcity value and proximity to markets must have more than compensated for
its generally lower fertility.[30] Unimproved acreage, on the other hand, was
worth much less in the Northeast than in the Old Northwest. We suspect
that this difference reflects the variations in the potential of this land in the
two regions. In the Old Northwest, where farm-making was still underway,
farmers were clearing new lands and bringing them under the plow. Thus
some proportion of the unimproved land in the Old Northwest could be
upgraded through the farmers' sweat and labor, and converted from $9.50
per acre land into $20.75 an acre land. Moreover, this price for unimproved
land was approximately the same as that being asked on the most desirable
virgin land being offered for sale.[31] Northeastern land, on the other hand,
probably could not be improved. Its value therefore reflects the value of that
land in uses such as a woodlot, production of rough hay, or as range land
for foraging hogs.

Yankee farmers in the Northeast had a much different crop mix than
their contemporaries who had moved westward (table 8). In the East they
kept more cows, an average of 5.34 per farm versus 3.68, but generated
more than twice the income from the dairy than was being earned in the
Old Northwest. This partly reflected the higher prices received for rela-

tively perishable products by farms located closer to markets, but it also reflected superior dairy practice in the Northeast. The dairy, for various reasons, including the comparative profitability of other crops, the lack of suitable transportation for long-distance shipping of perishables, its association with "women's work," and the extensive, land-using nature of American agriculture at this time, was often neglected or relegated to a secondary role.

TABLE 8

Characteristics of Farm Operations by Yankee-Farmers
in the Northeast and Old Northwest, 1859-1860

Characteristic	Northeast	Old Northwest
Number of Cows*	5.34	3.68
Number of Cattle	4.42	5.18
Number of Hogs*	4.21	11.22
Value of Meat	$82.57	$74.06
Value of Home Manufactures	$3.54	$4.77
Value of Dairy Products	$195.91	$87.50
Gross Farm Income*	$1,014.83	$923.86
Income from Wheat*	$42.34	$107.00
Income from Corn*	$78.29	$151.81
Income from Oats*	$59.72	$27.21
Income from Hay*	$214.37	112.92
Gross Farm Income per person*	$186.55	$162.34
Gross Farm Income per improved acre*	$12.13	$12.64

*Significant difference between means at the 5 percent level.
Source: Computed from the Bateman-Foust sample.

Yankees, however, were more appreciative of its market potential in part because they had been forced to develop a cash product suitable for intensive mixed farming on relatively poor but high-priced land sheltered in some way from competition with better, cheaper land farther west. Production of fluid milk for city markets suited this requirement. Farmers distant from the city markets, in western New York for example, tended to specialize in milk for butter and cheese production, either on the farm or in the factories which had begun to develop during the 1850s. In a typical pattern, farmers near cities specialized in fluid milk, often using barn-feeding methods, and those more remote, especially where transportation was poor, produced butter and cheese. Improved transport began to influence New York City and Boston milksheds in a limited way as early as the 1840s as dairies from ten to thirty miles distant shipped milk by rail to the city.[32] Market opportunities also encouraged the formation of large commercial dairies in New York. There, cheese from Herkiner County and butter from Orange and Goshen counties gained reputations sufficient to command premium prices throughout the United States and abroad.[33] Specialized dairy farms with similar economic and physical characteristics existed in New England, and farmers within the milksheds of all large eastern cities frequently concentrated exclusively on fluid milk production.[34] Farther west, specialized dairies were rarer, being found in substantial numbers only in the Western Reserve region of Ohio. Quality generally was poorer than that of eastern products, at least for those shipped over long distances, as reflected in the lower prices accorded western products sold in eastern markets.

On the typical Yankee farm in both regions, the dairy not only met home consumption needs but also seems to have provided a fairly important source of cash income. Fluid milk was supplied to nearby rural nonfarm or urban buyers and butter or cheese were shipped over longer distances with lower risks of spoilage. They became to some milk-producing farmers what liquor was to many who grew corn: a means of converting a product into a less immediately perishable and relatively higher-valued form. "Farmers in the vicinity of crossroads hamlets, county seats, and commercial and industrial centers," says Paul Gates, "found a market for milk...Fresh butter, a standard item in the diet of most families, was always marketable."[35] In the Northeast Yankee farmers earned almost 20 percent of their gross farm income from the dairy. Even in the Old Northwest, Yankees earned 10 percent of their gross income from the dairy, an amount that they probably could not afford to neglect.

Hogs were much more important to Yankee farmers in the Old Northwest than in the Northeast. Relative specialization in hog raising was but one of the adaptations made by farmers in the Old Northwest to relative factor prices.[36] Cheap corn and expensive labor often led to the practice of "hogging down" fields of standing corn and had the virtue of returning the manure to the soil. When fattened, the hogs could then be walked to market—a convenient means of shipping corn in areas of poor roads. In this branch of animal husbandry, farmers in the interior had the advantage over those closer to transportation where field crops were worth more. In the opinion of the *Prairie Farmer*, in the late 1840s it was more profitable to produce two dollar-a-hundred pork at a distance of fifty miles from the market than to grow eighty cent-per-bushel wheat. In 1859–60, since wheat brought about a dollar a bushel, hog farming must have been pushed further into the interior. In the Northeast, however, high grain prices and western competition had made it generally uneconomical for farmers to raise many hogs, and the number of hogs east of Ohio was generally declining.

Although Yankee farmers in the Old Northwest kept three times as many hogs on average as those in the Northeast, hog farming was not a Yankee *forte*. Other groups in the Old Northwest kept many more hogs—southern settlers, for example, kept an average of 20 hogs per farm.[37] Thus, although the Yankee settlers made some adjustments and concessions to the environmental differences in the Old Northwest, some habits and practices died hard.

We also constructed estimates of gross farm income as well as the income from specific crops. Gross farm income is defined as the value of crop production (including estimates of products such as fluid milk, eggs, poultry, and timber that were not counted by the census), net of seed and animal feed, plus an allowance for such items as capital gains on land and livestock and the rental value of the farmhouse.[38] No allowance is made for capital recovery, labor, or home consumption. Crops were valued at farmgate prices constructed from numerous scattered estimates such as price retrospectives published by agricultural experiment stations in Illinois, Indiana, New York, and Wisconsin giving prices received by farmers.[39] These sources are dealt with in more detail elsewhere.[40] Income estimates for specific crops were simply production (net of seed) valued at the appropriate farmgate price.

Because they kept fewer hogs, Yankee farmers in the Old Northwest typically also grew proportionately less corn than other farmers in the region— southerners, for example, earned about 25 percent of their gross revenues from corn. Nevertheless, it remained the single most important source of gross farm income and was more than twice as important to them as it was to farmers in the Northeast. In wheat cultivation Yankee farmers proved themselves much more adaptable. In terms of the proportion of gross revenue earned from wheat, Yankees were much closer to the norm in the Old Northwest and unlike their contemporaries who had stayed behind.

On farms in the Northeast, oats replaced wheat as the main cash grain crop. In part, this reflected urban demand to feed stabled horses, but it was also a response to western competition. Wheat commanded a price that justified hauling considerable distances to markets so that western wheat could be profitably shipped to the East Coast. Oats, on the other hand, were bulkier and less valuable. They could not profitably be hauled any great distance. As a result the market for western oats was segregated from that for eastern oats by the high costs of transportation. The situation was similar for hay, which could be cheaply produced even on worn-out soils in the East but which could not by virtue of its bulk and value/weight ratio be profitably shipped very far.[41] Indeed, hay was the single most important source of income for farmers in the Northeast —earning slightly more even than the dairy—thanks to local urban demands.

Yankee farmers in the East thus specialized in those crops in which they had a comparative advantage by virtue of transportation costs, but those who moved to the West were forced to adapt and produce a different range of crops for market. Those closest to markets produced bulky, relatively low value-to-weight commodities such as oats, hay, and fluid milk. Those at greater distance depended upon more processed products, and those with higher values-to-weight. Nevertheless, they produced a crop mix that was more similar to that of those who stayed behind than that of other groups in the Old Northwest was to that produced by Yankee farmers in the Northeast.

Yankee farmers in both the Northeast and the Old Northwest thus seem to

have responded to market opportunities afforded by a growing nonfarm population and improved transportation by producing that crop mix best suited for
commercial success, especially with respect to satisfying eastern urban demands.
Most farms near urban markets probably always produced surpluses for commercial disposal. Those located at a greater distance were drawn into commercial
production only as transport costs fell. As they fell the area of feasible commercial agricultural production expanded rapidly, bringing farmers on the most distant frontier into competition with those who had already undergone the
transformation to market orientation and who were more favorably located with
respect to markets.

Yankees were in the forefront of this movement toward commercialized agriculture, earning significantly higher gross farm incomes in each region than
other groups. In the Old Northwest, for example, Yankee farms generated average gross farm incomes that were 9 percent higher than earned on farms operated
by southerners, 31 percent higher than that realized by farmers born in the region, and 43 percent more than immigrants. On a per capita basis, the difference
narrows somewhat for immigrants and those born in the Old Northwest; it wid-
ens considerably between southerners and Yankees. This contradicts the *Ohio
Cultivator,* which alleged that Yankee farmers in their desire to produce every-
thing they needed for their own consumption ignored more profitable crop mixes
and as a result made less money than other groups, especially southerners.[42]

By 1860 farmers in the Old Northwest faced a market situation far better than
that which had faced the very earliest settlers. In Ohio, for example, during early
settlement, surpluses were created in advance of adequate marketing facilities.
The thousands of immigrants who flocked to the state each year furnished a sizable market for farm produce, but by the end of their second year of residence
those migrants had in turn become producers and were adding to the surplus.[43]
The problem was that "the land could produce nothing but corn, but as there
was no market for the corn, they made it into whiskey; and, as they could not
sell the whiskey, they drank it."[44]

Physical surpluses of food and feedstuffs were greater in the Old Northwest
than in the Northeast. Assuming an adult diet of 771 pounds of milk (consumed
as milk, butter, or cheese), 200 pounds of meat, and 13.5 bushels of grain (in can
equivalents) and minimal livestock feed allowances, the average Yankee farm in
the Old Northwest had a surplus of food and feed crops (not including hay or
pasturage) of 383 bushels in corn equivalents.[45] In the Northeast the average surplus was much smaller, 175.9 bushels. Indeed, it was only as large as it was because the average was raised by productive agriculture in New Jersey, New York,
and Pennsylvania.

The composition of the regional surpluses, however, differed markedly. The
Northeast produced three times the surplus of dairy products and 50 percent
more meat, but only about one-ninth the surplus in grains. Overall in the Old
Northwest, 13 percent of the Yankee-operated farms would have had deficits of

dairy products, 39 percent would have had deficits of meat, and 31 percent grain deficits. In the Northeast only 3 percent would have been short on dairy products, 37 percent short on meat but 57 percent short on grains. Yankees in both regions must therefore have relied upon some trade to achieve an adequate consumption bundle as well as producing surpluses for market sale.

Although Yankee farms in the Old Northwest produced more than farms in the Northeast, revenues were lower because distance from markets and local competition lowered prices by more than enough to offset the higher production levels. Nevertheless, the bottom 50 percent of Yankee farmers in both regions earned about the same—$750 or less, and the distributions are virtually identical to this income level (figure 3). Beyond $750, however, there were substantially higher proportions of Northeastern farms earning more, such that although 84.5 percent of Yankee farmers in the Old Northwest earned $1,500 or less, in the Northeast the proportion was 81.1 percent. The greater number of very successful and high income earning Yankee farms in the Northeast thus accounts for the higher average farm income in that region. Profitability was, however, higher for Yankee farmers in the Old Northwest. We estimate that they earned $12.64 per acre under the plow compared with $12.13 per acre in the Northeast, and since land values and the average investment in farms in the Old Northwest were lower, the rate of return was higher in the Old Northwest.

Northeasterners who were farmers when the new, more productive western lands were being opened to settlement typically were forced to make serious decisions regarding their economic futures. Because the newly settled land produced most crops more cheaply, the individual family that had been growing such crops found themselves increasingly at a competitive disadvantage. They also found eastern land values rising under such pressures as urbanization and land development. Their choices were relatively limited. They could abandon agriculture, going to work in the developing manufacturing sector, either in urban or rural areas of the northeast, or in the service occupations. Reared in the Jeffersonian tradition, many found those unacceptable and unattractive alternatives. If, however, they wished to cling to their agrarian tradition, only two significant paths faced them: they could shift into producing goods with a low value to weight, or they could switch from field crops altogether toward market gardening, to dairying, or to some similar specialization for which there was a nearby market, one sheltered from western competition by high transport costs or by unpreventable perishability. Or they could move westward to continue as farmers, producing more or less their traditional crops in a new location. This latter group has occupied our attention above.

We should note, however, that not all those northeasterners who had moved to the Old Northwest by 1860 did so to maintain a farm existence. Nor were all pushed from their native region by declining opportunity. Many were attracted to the new region by prospects of becoming more profitable farmers, bigger landowners, or potentially wealthy speculators. And many, before and after 1860,

FIGURE 3

Cumulative Distribution of Gross Farm Income Earned by Yankee Farmers in the Northeast and Old Northwest, 1859–1860.

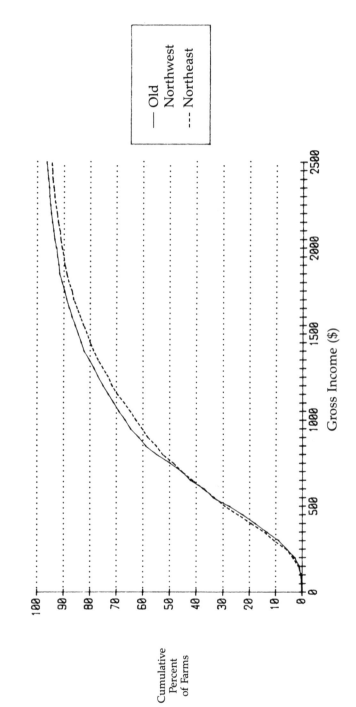

moved westward to participate in the growing nonagricultural sector as entrepreneurs, professionals, or laborers. Still, our focus in this paper primarily has been on those who went west carrying their agricultural heritage, experience, and ambitions along with them.

What can we conclude about this group? The Yankees who moved to the Old Northwest were typically less wealthy than those who remained behind, but in their new region they were the wealthiest. They also had more children in their families than their northeastern "stayer" counterparts, but fewer than other groups who had relocated to the Old Northwest. They were also less likely to have become tenant farmers than other groups, including native northwesterners. Old habits and even relatively new customs died hard, if at all in the migration westward. The Yankee settlers also had substantial investment in their farms and generally produced output levels that would have allowed commercial market trade. Income differences between these two farm groups were, however, similar for most families. Finally, one can observe in the output of potentially commercial and marketable surpluses and in the income data, the emerging tension between farming as the foundation for the yeoman society in the Old Northwest and the commercial integration of agriculture into the system of industrial capitalism.

Notes

1. See, for example, Thomas Hart Benton, *Thirty Years' View*, 2 vols. (New York: D. Appleton and Co., 1854), 1: 133–36, and Robert F. Berkhofer, "Jefferson, the Ordinance of 1784, and the Origins of the American Territorial System," *William and Mary Quarterly*, 3d. ser., 29, 2 (April 1972):231–62, especially n. 1.

2. A different, Jeffersonian, interpretation appears in Jeremy Atack and Fred Bateman, *To Their Own Soil: Agriculture in the Antebellum North* (Ames: Iowa State University Press, 1987).

3. There is a continuing debate over the motivation for migration, especially whether migrants were "pushed" out of their birthplace or "pulled" by irresistible attractions in their new homelands. Most studies imply a combination of the two factors and nowhere is this clearer than in Turner's writings on the frontier where migrants were alternately driven out of the East by onerous working conditions and economic hard times and being lured westward by the prospects of cheap land and economic and social independence. See Frederick Jackson Turner, *The Frontier in American History* (New York: Henry Holt, 1920). See also Ray Billington, *Westward Expansion: A History of the American Frontier* (New York: Macmillan, 1967); T. D. Clark, *Frontier America: The Story of the Westward Movement* (New York: Scribner's, 1959); S. H. Holbrook, *The Yankee Exodus: An Account of Migration from New England* (New York: Macmillan, 1950); Lois K. Mathews, *The Expansion of New England* (Boston: Houghton Mifflin, 1909); Lewis D. Stilwell, "Migration From Vermont (1776–1860)," *Proceedings of the Vermont Historical Society* 5, 2 (1937): 63–246; C. W. Thornthwaite, *Internal Migration in the United States* (Philadelphia: University of Pennsylvania Press, 1934).

4. New England Ballad," *Edinburgh Review* 55 (July 1832), 480. Quoted by R. C. Buley, *The Old Northwest: Pioneer Period 1815–1840*, 2 vols. (Bloomington: Indiana University Press, 1950), 1: 10.

5. Mathews, *Expansion of New England*, 174.

6. Buley, *The Old Northwest*, 1: 47, quoting the *Congressional Globe*, 26 Cong., 2 sess., Appendix 65.

7. Hal S. Barron, *Those Who Stayed Behind* (Cambridge: Cambridge University Press, 1984), 136. This study focuses upon the experiences of residents of Chelsea, Vermont, For a discussion of out-migration from Vermont, see Stilwell, "Migration from Vermont."

8. Most studies dealing with the development of the Old Northwest, or with the development of particular states within the region, devote considerable . coverage to in-migration. See, for example, Buley, *The Old Northwest*, vol. 1, chaps. 1 and 2, and vol. 2, chap. 10; Beverley W. Bond, Jr., *The Civilization of the Old Northwest* (New York: Macmillan, 1934), especially chap. 2. There are also a number of studies dealing with early out-migration. See, for example, Mathews, *Expansion of New England*. Except for Lewis Stilwell's analysis of migration from Vermont, however, the analysis is qualitative rather than quantitative. See Stilwell, "Migration From Vermont."

9. U.S. Census Office. Seventh Census, *Census of 1850*, (Washington, D.C.: Robert Armstrong, 1853), Table 15, p. xxxvi.

10. Ibid.

11. U.S. Census Office. Eighth Census, *Population of the United States in 1860*, (Washington, DC: Government Printing Office, 1864), 616–619.

12. Data collection was funded by the National Science Foundation through GS-27143. The geographic distribution, selection criteria, and the characteristics of the sample are described in Fred Bateman and James D. Foust, "A Sample of Rural Households Selected from the 1860 Manuscript Censuses," *Agricultural History* 48, 1 (January 1970): 75–93.

13. All farms were included in the sample provided they met the following criteria: (1) operated by someone born in Connecticut, Maine, Massachusetts, New Hampshire, New Jersey, New York, Pennsylvania, Rhode Island, or Vermont and listing their occupation as farmer, tenant, agriculturalist, or part-time farmer; and (2) acreage, crops, and farm, implements, and livestock values reported for the farm they operated.

14. Mathews, *Expansion of New England*, 208–9.

15. See, for example, Richard Easterlin, George Alter, and Gretchen Condran, "Farm and Farm Families in Old and New Areas: The Northern States in 1860," *Family and Population in Nineteenth Century America*, Tamara Hareven and Maris Vinovskis, eds. (Princeton: Princeton University Press, 1978), 22–84; and Donald Leet, "Human Fertility and Agricultural Opportunities in Ohio Countries from Frontier to Maturity, 1810–60," *Essays in Nineteenth Century Economic History*, David Klingaman and Richard Vedder, eds. (Athens: Ohio University Press, 1975), 138–58.

16. Allan Bogue also identifies a separate class of "farmers without farms" who gave occupations as farmer on the population schedules and reported a zero real estate value but for whom no farm was located in the agricultural schedules. He argues that these comprised optimistic farm laborers and recent settlers in the process of looking for a suitable farm. See Allan G. Bogue, *From Prairie to Corn Belt: Farming on the Illinois and Iowa Prairies in the Nineteenth Century* (Chicago: University of Chicago Press, 1963), 56–66, especially 63–65. Other researchers have also found different variations and conventions for identifying tenants. See, for example, Frederick A. Bode and Donald E. Ginter, "A Critique of Landholding Variables in the 1860 Census and the Parker-Gallman Sample," *Journal of Interdisciplinary History* 15, 2(1984): 277–95, especially 278–80.

17. This represents a change in terminology (though not group) from that used in Atack and Bateman, *To Their Own Soil*, where they are referred to as "tenants in part." This name change is consistent with the terminology of Gray et al., *Farm Ownership and Tenancy, USDA Yearbook of the Department of Agriculture 1923* and E. A. Goldenweisser and Leon E. Truesdell, *Farm Tenancy in the United States* (Washington, D.C.: Government Printing Office, 1924). This study is a part of the Fourteenth Census: U.S. Department of Commerce. Census Bureau. *Census Monograph IV*.

18. See Jeremy Atack, "Towards a Typology of American Agriculture in the North-

ern United States: Part 1. Tenants and Yeomen in the Nineteenth Century: The Problem of Rising Tenancy," *University of Illinois Bureau of Economic and Business Research Faculty Working Paper No. 1298* (September 1986), for an extended analysis.

19. See Jeremy Atack and Fred Bateman, "Egalitarianism, Inequality, and Age: The Rural North in 1860," *Journal of Economic History* 41, 1 (March 1981): 85–93. Also Jeremy Atack and Fred Bateman, "The 'Egalitarian Ideal' and the Distribution of Wealth in the Northern Agricultural Community: A Backward Look." *Review of Economics and Statistics* 63, 1 (February 1981): 124–29; and Atack and Bateman, *To Their Own Soil*, chap. 6.

20. Wealth is maximized when ∂Wealth/∂Age = 313.902 − 5.31(age) = 0.

21. See Donald Schaefer, "A Model of Migration and Wealth Accumulation: Farmers at the Antebellum Southern Frontier," *Explorations in Economic History* (forthcoming). A contemporary source giving advice to New England migrants bound for Kansas in the 1850s estimated fares from Boston to Kansas City, Missouri, at forty dollars per person aged twelve and older, including one hundred pounds of baggage. Excess baggage was costed at three to four dollars per hundred pounds. See Thomas H. Webb, *Information for Kansas Immigrants* (Boston: Alfred Mudge and Sons for the New England Emigrant Aid Company, 1856), 4–5.

22. Mathews, *Expansion of New England*, 208.

23. Governor Thomas Ford, *A History of Illinois From Its Commencement as a State in 1818 to 1847* (Chicago: S.C. Griggs, 1854), 281.

24. Buley, *The Old Northwest*, 1: 47–48. Embedded quote is from Joseph Gillespie, "Recollections of Early Illinois and her Noted Men," *Fergus' Historical Series*, no. 13 (Chicago, 1880), 6.

25. "The Cost of Buying and Stocking a Farm in Wisconsin," *Wisconsin Farmer* 8 (1856): 440.

26. James Caird, *Prairie Farming in America* (London: Longman, 1859), 89. See also Clarence H. Danhof, "Farm-Making Costs and the 'Safety Valve'": 1850–60, *Journal of Political Economy* 49, 3 (June 1941): 317–59, especially 324–29.

27. Danhof, "Farm-Making Costs," 327, 353–54. Quote is from p. 354

28. *Cultivator* 10 (1843): 37. Quoted by Percy W. Bidwell and John I. Falconer, *History of Agriculture in the Northern United States, 1620–1860* (Washington, D.C.: Carnegie Institution, 1925), 271.

29. See, for example, Danhof, "Farm-Making Costs," n. 106.

30. See Jeremy Atack and Fred Bateman, "Mid-Nineteenth Century Crop Yields and Labor Productivity Growth in American Agriculture," *Technique, Spirit, and Form in the Making of the Modern Economies: Essays in Honor of William N. Parker,* Gary Saxenhouse and Gavin Wright, eds. *Research in Economic History*, suppl. 3 (1984), 214–42 for estimates of the yield differential.

31. The Illinois Central Railroad, for example, realized an average price of $11.50 an acre. See Paul W. Gates, *The Illinois Central Railroad and Its Colonization Work* (Cambridge: Harvard University Press, 1934), 159 and 260–62. See also Danhof "Farm-Making Costs," 331–34, especially nn. 35 and 36.

32. Paul W. Gates, *The Farmers' Age: Agriculture 1815–60* (New York: Holt, Rinehart and Winston, 1960), 239–41. The Erie Railroad was extended into the Orange County dairy region of New York in 1842, shifting some of that region's butter and cheese producers to fluid-milk production.

33. The relationship between urban growth and dairy development in New York state is discussed in detail in Eric Brunger, "Dairying and Urban Development in New York State, 1850–1900," *Agricultural History* 29, 4 (October 1955): 169–74.

34. According to the Ohio Dairyman's Association, as early as 1811 cheese was being transported over relatively long distances into such port cities as New York and New Orleans (Ohio Dairyman's Association, *Report of the Fifth Annual Meeting of the Ohio Dairyman's Association for 1899.* [Columbus: Ohio Dairyman's Association, 1900]). In 1848, according to an Ohio experiment station report, the Western Reserve counties exported more than fifteen million pounds of cheese, most of which went into eastern markets (Ohio Agricultural Experiment Station, *Bulletin 326* [Wooster: Experiment Station Press, July 1918], 87). Fluid milk obviously was less transportable than dairy products, most cities drawing their supplies from within a very small radius. Where conveyed by wagon, 15 miles usually defined the outer boundaries of a city's milkshed. The presence of rail facilities could extend this to as much as 150 miles. For specific discussion of this issue, see New Hampshire Agricultural Experiment Station, *Bulletin 120* (Durham: University of New Hampshire, 1905). Even by 1900 most fluid milk entered urban markets from fairly short distances, ranging from 20–30 miles for Detroit and Cincinnati to about 200 miles for New York City. See Edward G. Ward, "*Milk Transportation: Freight Rates to the Fifteen Largest Cities in the United States,*" U.S. Department of Agriculture, *Division of Statistics, Bulletin 25* (Washington, D.C. Government Printing Office, 1903).

35. Gates, *Farmer' Age,* 236, 241.

36. The following paragraph draws heavily upon Bidwell and Falconer, *Agriculture,* 435–41.

37. Data from the Bateman-Foust sample.

38. See Atack and Bateman, *To Their Own Soil,* especially chap. 13. Capitol gains were very important, especially in the Old Northwest. See Gates, *Farmers Age,* 399, 403; also Atack and Bateman, *To Their Own Soil,* chap. 13.

39. Illinois: L.J. Norton and B.B. Wilson, "Prices of Illinois Farm Products from 1866 to 1929," University of Illinois Agricultural Experiment Station, *Bulletin 351* (Urbana, Ill.: July 1930). Indiana: Howard J. Houk, "A Century of Indiana Farm Prices, 1841–1941," Purdue University Agricultural Experiment Station, *Bulletin 476* (West Lafayette, Ind.: January 1943). New York: S.E. Ronk, "Prices of Farm Products in New York State, 1841 to 1935," Cornell University Agricultural Experiment Station, *Bulletin 643* (Ithaca, N.Y.: March 1936). Wisconsin: W.P. Mortenson, H.H. Erdman, and J.H. Draxler, "Wisconsin Farm Prices—1841 to 1933," Agricultural Experiment Station of the University of Wisconsin, *Research Bulletin 119* (Madison, Wis.: November 1933).

40. Atack and Bateman, *To Their Own Soil,* chap. 13.

41. See Gates, *Farmers Age,* 157, 173.

42. *Ohio Cultivator* 13 (1 August, 1857): 232, quoted by Eugene H. Roseboom, "The Civil War Era, 1850–1873," *The History of the State of Ohio,* Carl Wittke, ed. (Columbus: Ohio State Archaological and Historical Society, 1944), 100.

43. William T. Utter, "The Frontier State, 1803–1825," *History of the State of Ohio,* 146.

44. W.A. Lloyd, J. Falconer, and C. Thorne, "Agriculture in Ohio," *Ohio Agricultural Experiment Station Bulletin No. 326* (Wooster, Oh. 1918), 50.

45. For a discussion of the basis for the human and livestock dietary allowances, see Atack and Bateman, *To Their Own Soil,* especially chap. 12.

6.

LABOR FORCE CHANGES
IN THE OLD NORTHWEST

Eleanor von Ende
Ohio University

Thomas Weiss
University of Kansas and
National Bureau of Economic Research

WHATEVER NAME IS USED to designate the geographic area—the Old Northwest or the more official sounding East North Central—the region has generally been regarded as one of America's great success stories, experiencing change and progress that has been rarely matched elsewhere. In the words of Walter Havighurst, "No other region on earth has been so transformed in one life span."[1] Even in the early years after the passage of the Northwest Ordinance, and certainly in the opening decades of the nineteenth century, one senses that the region and its settlers were infused with an energy and dynamism that set it apart from the rest of America and distinguished it not only from the tradition-bound South but also from the more commercial Northeast. Perhaps not everyone shared the enthusiasm of the most ardent boosters, but they must have possessed that hardy and adventuresome spirit that would eventually carry the region to its industrial heights. To some outsiders, and later scholars, the early years may have been beset by the "turmoil of pioneering," but that was not sufficient to daunt the wave after wave of optimistic migrants. In the traditional story, the region moved on from its frontier era of traders and trappers to become the nation's breadbasket and, later, its industrial heartland, as well as one of the industrial behemoths of the world. Indeed, by one measure the region achieved one of the highest standards of living in the world by 1860.[2]

There is no reason to question the accuracy of such a portrayal of the region's economic history. Events in the last quarter of the twentieth century may raise some doubts about the region's economic machine and its ability to transform itself once again into a cornerstone of the nation's success, but the successes of the nineteenth century were no fiction and suggest that one should not count the region out too quickly. The story of the region's historical success, however, has not been fully and systematically documented. There is no dearth of literature on the subject. Indeed there is a surfeit of many wonderful narrative histories that provide a rich fabric of growth and change in the region. What is lacking is a comprehensive statistical picture of that performance.[3] Although such an empirical description would gloss over or subsume many of the rich and colorful details, it would provide a broader perspective from which to appreciate those features and peculiarities, and it would provide firmer evidence on the region's successes and transformations.

Labor force statistics are one of the key components of any comprehensive, systematic record, and they are essential for any examination of long-term change. Empirical questions about the growth of total or partial factor productivity for the region's economy, for specific sectors, or for comparisons of regional economic performances, all require evidence on the labor input. The more complete and detailed that evidence, the more complex the investigations can be. And the more accurate is that evidence, the more confidence we can have in the results.

Twenty years ago Lebergott produced his estimates of the nineteenth-century American workforce. He gave us a comprehensive picture of the long-term changes in the labor force and provided data that have been used by many other researchers. That evidence showed some industrial and demographic detail but did not present information on the various regions and states of the country. A long-term project now underway is attempting to extend the national series to the regional, and perhaps state, level. The present paper reports on a portion of that work, the evidence for the Old Northwest and, in particular, that for the antebellum period.[4]

OUTLINE OF ESTIMATION METHODS

THE METHODS USED HERE are essentially those laid down by Lebergott to derive estimates of the national labor force. The total labor force is the sum of estimates of the number of workers in five population components: free males aged sixteen and over, free females aged sixteen and over, free males aged ten to fifteen, free females aged ten to fifteen, and slaves aged ten and over. The estimate of the number of workers in each population component was derived as the product of the population in that group times the group-specific participation rate. Although this is the same method used by Lebergott, a key difference here is that the methods are applied at the state level so that the national total is built up from the individual state estimates. Moreover, regional figures can be derived as well.

The population figures used are primarily those obtained from the census volumes for the various years. Those figures were reorganized in certain years in order to obtain the age breakdowns desired. For slaves, it was also necessary to estimate the sex distribution in 1800 and 1810. The participation rates assumed to prevail in the antebellum years for each group were estimated using evidence for the postbellum period, specifically the years 1870 to 1920, along with some census data available for 1850 and 1860. For each state a participation rate was estimated for each of the four free population groups; males aged sixteen and over, females aged sixteen and over, males aged ten to fifteen, and females aged ten to fifteen.[5] In addition, a participation rate of .9 was assumed for slaves aged ten and over. This is the same rate used by earlier researchers, especially Lebergott (1966) and David (1967).[6]

The individual state data for each age-sex group was examined for possible trends, and it was determined that a trend was evident only in the participation rate of females aged sixteen and over. For the other groups, the postbellum means were assumed to have held in the antebellum years as well.

The evidence examined for trends covered the entire population in the age-sex category and so was used to derive an unadjusted level of the antebellum participation rates. Those antebellum estimators were then adjusted to reflect the fact that the antebellum workforce was almost entirely white, and that the foreign-born share of the white population was lower in the years before 1860 than in the postbellum period.

Additional evidence existed for some of the antebellum years, specifically 1820, 1840, 1850, and 1860. The evidence for the first two years did not permit useful disaggregation by age and sex. The latter two did, however, provide valuable information, especially on the numerically largest group, males aged sixteen and over. With some adjustments this evidence enabled us to obtain the adult male workforce in 1850 and 1860. The implied participation rates were combined with the postbellum data to give additional observations on this important group. Perhaps most noteworthy, these antebellum rates confirmed that there was no trend in the adult male participation rate and indicated as well that the changing share of the foreign born had virtually no effect on the particular group's participation rate.

RESULTS

THE ESTIMATES OF THE Old Northwest's labor force and participation rates are presented in table 1, along with statistics for the United States. Both the regional and national series were derived using the same procedures so comparisons can be made without having to be unduly concerned with differences that might be attributable to the estimation methods.[7] For the most part, any bias or error in the regional figure is likely to have an effect on the national series as well, so that their relative positions or changes should not be distorted. Moreover, we think that there are no serious biases in either case, at least not in the sense that these estimates differ in scope or even magnitude from earlier estimates.

First of all, the postbellum figures rest entirely on the census counts of gainful workers, so the figures are closely akin to the series produced by earlier researchers.[8] There are some differences to be sure, arising from the fact that the census counts for 1870, 1890, and 1910 are generally regarded as having some flaws, and attempts to correct those figures have varied. The Miller and Brainerd series are the most divergent as a result of these adjustment procedures. They decided that in spite of some obvious flaws they would use the original census data.[9]

TABLE 1

Labor Force and Participation Rates
(All Ages)

Year	Old Northwest	United States	Old Northwest	United States
1800	12940	1712452	0.254	0.323
1810	65838	2337364	0.242	0.323
1820	197708	3147993	0.249	0.327
1830	368349	4271775	0.251	0.332
1840	787521	5777581	0.269	0.339
1850	1299887	8192457	0.287	0.353
1860	2061135	11290100	0.298	0.360
1870	2739245	12809429	0.300	0.325
1880	3615994	17392099	0.323	0.347
1890	4811957	23546849	0.357	0.376
1900	5887473	28939505	0.368	0.383
Percentage Changes				
1800 to 1860			17.3%	11.5%
1870 to 1900			22.7	17.8
1800 to 1900			44.9	18.6

Source: U.S. Census of Population, 1800 through 1900; Appendix Table 1, and Weiss, 1987.

   See text for a summary description of the methods used to estimate the labor force in the various years. The postbellum figures are essentially census data, with revisions made in the 1870 and 1890 figures. The antebellum figures are primarily the sum of estimates of the number of workers in each major age-sex group, where the estimate for each group is the product of the population times an age-sex specific participation rate. The 1850 and 1860 Censuses provided direct counts of portions of the labor force (free males aged 16 and over in 1850, and free persons aged 16 and over in 1860). For details see Weiss, 1987.

Since the widely-used series by Stanley Lebergott seems to be the prevailing standard, we can use that as a yardstick to judge the reasonableness of our national figures, and indirectly the regional figures. The present figure of 12,809,429 for 1870 is only 1 percent below Lebergott's total for that year, though our 1890 figure is not quite 1 percent above his estimate. The 1910 figures differ slightly more, the present estimate being below Lebergott's by approximately 450,000 workers but still within 2 percent. Thus there is nothing radically different about the present postbellum national series, which is not surprising since the two series are based on the same raw material. Since the region's labor force was estimated in the same manner and with the same data, it must be close to estimates that might be derived by others.[10]

The antebellum labor force figures do not rest as solidly on census counts, and consequently there are more opportunities for estimates of different researchers to diverge. Conceptually, our estimates were carried out at the state level using essentially the same procedures as did Lebergott, so major differences would not likely arise. Minor variations did occur, due primarily to the present use of some evidence that was unavailable to Lebergott, especially some manuscript census sample data for 1860.[11] Our state-by-state approach also contributed to some differences in two ways. First, examination of individual state data made it clear that certain state figures reported in the censuses of 1850 and 1860 were in need of correction.[12] Second, the sex and age specific participation rates used to estimate the number of workers varied by state, and as the importance of a state's population changed over time the present aggregated national figures would reflect this. The minor variations that did arise between our figures and Lebergott's are indeed comforting. With the exception of 1800, the differences are 2.1 percent or less, with the present figures being slightly higher in each year except 1850, in which year our estimates are .7 percent below Lebergott's. Our estimate for 1800 is nearly 10 percent below Lebergott's original figure, but is only .7 percent above Paul David's revision of that estimate.[13] Moreover, the differences appear to be in the right direction, reflecting the greater weight given to those states in the Northeast, such as New York, Pennsylvania, and Massachusetts, which on average had higher participation rates among adult male workers. The differences also reflect variations in the estimates of the number of free female workers aged sixteen and over. Again, as with the postbellum data, the present antebellum figures do not represent a radical revision at the national level, and since the national figures are but the sum of the individual state estimates, the totals for the Old Northwest are certainly comparably accurate.

There is an obvious difference in the levels of participation between the Old Northwest and the nation, the more so in the antebellum period. Of course, the chief source of the discrepancy was the higher participation rate of slaves, especially females and those aged ten to fifteen years, combined with the greater incidence of slavery outside the region. This is seen quite clearly in the sharp narrowing of the aggregate participation rates over the decade of the 1860s. In the antebellum period, the average difference between the region and the nation was around 6 to 8 percentage points, but after the Civil War the two rates differed by only 1 to 2 points. The remaining difference can be attributed to the higher participation of free females aged sixteen and over, especially in the Northeast.

The relative growth of the workforces clearly favors the Old Northwest, which of course reflects largely the filling up of the territory. But even after allowances are made for the growth of population, the territory showed a more rapid increase in the labor force than was true for the nation. In other words, the share of the population in the workforce rose more in the Old

Northwest than for the entire country. In the antebellum years, the region's participation rate increased by 17.3 percent, but the nation's rose by only 11.5 percent. From 1870 to 1900, the increases still favored the Northwest with the region's rate rising by 22.7 percent and the nation's by 17.8 percent.[14] At the end of the century, the participation rate in the Old Northwest stood 45 percent above the 1800 figure, and the U.S. figure was only 18.6 percent higher than that at the beginning of the century.

An obvious implication of this disparity in participation rate changes has to do with relative growth in per capita income. If nothing else differed between the region and the nation, that is, if the course of labor productivity growth and the industrial redistribution of the labor forces had been similar, per capita income in the Old Northwest would have increased more than twice as fast as the national average. A big part of this favorable performance would have been concentrated in the Civil War decade, but the region would have shown some advantage in both the antebellum period, in particular the years 1840 to 1860, and the period after 1870.

These aggregate statistics cannot do justice to the dynamic economy of a frontier area like the Old Northwest, especially in the more tumultuous antebellum period. For one thing, the method of estimation has precluded much change that might have occurred. Although these statistics may capture well the general trend of events, and reflect adequately the performance of the region relative to the nation, some variation has been obscured. The trends and variations that are revealed reflect differences in the aggregate participation rates across states, the changing importance of states in the regional total over time, and changes in the participation rates within states. These latter changes can in turn be traced to differences in the average participation rates of the various population components combined with changes in the composition of the population and to small changes in the participation rates of specific groups.

The variation across states is shown in table 2. In the antebellum years, Ohio dominated the region, and as a consequence the state and regional rates are similar and move in parallel. Over the entire century, the state rate increased by an additional percentage point above the regional change, while the changes in the period prior to the Civil War and in the years afterward were closer. For the most part, the movement of the rates in the other states showed a pattern similar to that in Ohio, but with some lag as they began development at different starting dates. Moreover, in those early years of each state, the populations were made up heavily of males of prime working age so that the overall participation rate was not typical of a more normal population. This is most obvious in Michigan in 1820 and again in Wisconsin in 1840. Subsequently, the relative increase of the other population components with their lower participation rates pulled the overall rate down. Once the newer state digested those early sharp changes in the pop-

TABLE 2

Participation Rates by State

Year	Illinois	Indiana	Michigan	Ohio	Wisconsin	The Region
1800	0.000	0.291	0.000	0.249	0.000	0.254
1810	0.271	0.238	0.355	0.238	0.000	0.242
1820	0.271	0.239	0.403	0.248	0.000	0.249
1830	0.247	0.234	0.334	0.254	0.000	0.251
1840	0.277	0.249	0.302	0.269	0.399	0.269
1850	0.277	0.273	0.306	0.294	0.292	0.287
1860	0.302	0.281	0.321	0.295	0.304	0.298
1870	0.292	0.273	0.341	0.315	0.278	0.300
1880	0.325	0.321	0.348	0.311	0.317	0.323
1890	0.363	0.352	0.365	0.356	0.345	0.357
1900	0.374	0.357	0.374	0.372	0.354	0.368
Percentage Point Changes in the Participation Rates						
1800–1860[a]	.031	.043	−.034	.046	—	.044
1870–1900	.082	.084	.033	.057	.076	.068
1800–1900[b]	.103	.119	.072	.123	.062	.114
Average Participation Rates						
1800–1860	.274	.258	.337	.264	.332	.264
1870–1900	.338	.326	.357	.339	.324	.337

Sources: U.S. Census of Population, 1800 through 1900; Miller and Brainerd, 1957, and Appendix Table 1.

a. The change is measured from 1810 for Illinois and Michigan.
b. The change is measured from the initial date in the series for each state.

ulation structure, the overall participation rate was influenced by the same forces that determined the long-term rise in the older states. The major force was a steady increase in the share of males aged sixteen and over in the population. A second factor was the increase in the participation rate of adult females. By the end of the century, all states experienced noticeable increases from what we might call their initial "normal" participation rate, such that at the close of the period all the state rates are within 2 percentage points of each other. Looking at broader averages, and again with the exceptions of the two more frontier states of Michigan and Wisconsin, the postbellum averages are roughly 7 percentage points above the antebellum figures.[15]

The restrictive nature of the method of estimation shows up in the participation rate behavior of the various population components as shown in table 3. The most obvious thing is the great stability in the adult male participation rate. The rates for 1850 and 1860 differ slightly from the other antebellum years, reflecting the availability of the census data for those years. For 1800 to 1840, the virtual constancy reflects the basic assumption that the best representation of adult male rates is the average of the rates over those years for which we do have evidence. The reasonableness of this assumption seems borne out by the closeness between the rates for 1850 and 1860 and the postbellum figures. Perhaps most importantly, the antebellum census evidence shows that there was no apparent break in the participation rate behavior of this numerically important labor force component in the period before and after the Civil War.[16] The miniscule change in the rate for this group that did occur between 1800 and 1840 reflects the greater importance of Ohio and its somewhat higher than average male participation rate in the earlier years.

TABLE 3

Regional Participation Rates
(By Age Group)

Year	Males 16+	Females 16+	Males 10–15	Females 10–15	Total
1800	0.899	0.030	0.147	0.038	0.254
1810	0.899	0.036	0.146	0.038	0.242
1820	0.898	0.040	0.150	0.038	0.249
1830	0.898	0.047	0.151	0.037	0.251
1840	0.897	0.057	0.150	0.038	0.269
1850	0.906	0.068	0.148	0.038	0.287
1860	0.895	0.081	0.146	0.039	0.298
1870	0.890	0.098	0.118	0.019	0.300
1880	0.884	0.106	0.159	0.033	0.323
1890	0.907	0.146	0.154	0.046	0.357
1900	0.895	0.168	0.153	0.056	0.368
Postbellum Averages					
Northwest	.894	.130	.146	.039	.337
the U.S.	.903	.176	.231	.091	.358

Sources: U.S. Census of Population, 1800 through 1900; Miller and Brainerd, 1957, Table L-3; Weiss, 1987.

The Total participation rate measures the labor force aged 10 and over relative to the population of all ages.

The postbellum averages are reported since the sex-specific values were used to calculate the antebellum workforces for each population component, except females aged 16 and over.

The only group for which there was a clear trend in the participation rate was females aged sixteen and over. A mild trend seems well established in the postbellum period, and it was begun in the earlier years.[17] The extension of such a trend over such a long period is of course a chancy proposition, and since there is virtually no evidence about female participation rates in the antebellum years it is difficult to provide any check on the procedure. There is, however, the data available in the manuscript census schedules for 1860, and a sample of that evidence makes clear that female participation rates in the antebellum period must have been very similar to those of the postbellum period.[18] The sample rates were very close to both the 1870 participation rates, which in almost every state were the lowest in the period 1870 to 1920, and to the values predicted by the estimating equation. Both the 1870 value of .085 and the forecasted (i.e. retrodicted) value of .078 were below the .111 rate derived from the sample data for rural northern households, suggesting that our procedure may be underestimating the number of female workers in the antebellum period.[19]

For workers aged ten to fifteen years, the postbellum statistics indicated that there was no trend in the participation rates for males or females. Consequently, the antebellum rates are at base the mean rates that prevailed in each state in the period 1870 to 1910. However, for these age groups there were substantial differences between the participation rates for native whites and for the foreign born, and so the antebellum rates were adjusted to reflect the changing composition of the population. The rate in each year is simply a weighted average of the rates for the two major nativity groups. As can be seen in the evidence in table 3, the adjustment does not alter the rates much, but given the lower rate for native whites and their higher proportion in the population in earlier years, the overall teenage rate is pushed down slightly.[20]

INDUSTRIAL DISTRIBUTION

THE GROWTH OF POPULATION and the labor force and the increase in the participation rates of the population were not the only substantial changes occurring in the region during the nineteenth century. The industries and occupations in which that labor force was engaged changed dramatically over the course of the century. Unfortunately, our present knowledge of the details of this structural change is woefully inadequate to convey the richness and complexity of this dynamism in the antebellum period. The census records pertaining to industrial and occupational detail do not cover the entire period, and in those years for which statistics are available, the reported evidence is incomplete in one way or another. For the nation Lebergott was able to flesh out these changes by resorting to a number of imaginative procedures and by conducting an extensive search of a wide variety of other documents and sources.[21] At the individual state level, there is surely a great abundance of other sources of information that could eventually be surveyed to provide the detail of change for the Old Northwest and other regions. We have not yet accomplished this herculean task but have made use of the more aggregated census data to sketch out the broad outlines of change for the Old Northwest. For the most part, we have only sorted the labor force into its agricultural and nonagricultural components, although some additional occupational details were acquired in the process.

An important feature of this work is an extensive reevaluation of the census data for the years 1820, 1840, 1850, and 1860. Since these are the only antebellum statistics that provide occupational coverage for substantial portions of the population, they are extremely valuable, and their accuracy is of great concern. Our assessments have made more clear the likely age, sex, and industrial coverage of the 1820 and 1840 censuses, and in turn this knowledge enabled us to revise the reported evidence in appropriate ways and observe which gaps in the coverage needed to be filled.[22]

In table 4 we have presented the data on the agricultural share of the labor force in the states and region of the Old Northwest and have included the national statistics for comparative purposes. Although the figures are based heavily on census information, in each year those reported statistics were revised, modified, and expanded in different ways, and, in a few years, there was not even the census evidence with which to start. As a consequence, the estimates for various years may differ slightly in terms of their reliability. This can be seen readily by looking at the figures for individual states, such as Michigan in 1820 and Wisconsin in 1840, where the anomalous shares may reflect some flaws and biases of the census counts rather than economic reality. Fortunately, these were unimportant members of the region at the time, so that the regional figures are not seriously distorted.[23] More importantly, the reported data for Ohio, Illinois, and Indiana were either more reliable in the original or contained an obvious error that could be easily corrected. As a consequence, the regional figures should give a fairly accurate portrayal of the major changes in the composition of the labor force.

The obvious feature of the evidence is that the region shifted from one that in 1800 was more concentrated in agriculture than the nation to one less devoted to that specialty. Dramatic changes had already taken place before the Civil War. Although the region was still predominantly engaged in agriculture, and more so than the nation, it had experienced a large decline in that sector's importance. Given that it was extremely concentrated in farming in 1800, this could, of course, have been expected, but the decline occurred in the face of additional states and population joining the region. Each of these young additions being at an earlier stage of development would have acted to hold up the farm share of the region's labor force. If we look, instead, at the figures for Ohio, we can see that without these younger states the region might have shown a more rapid decline in the importance of agriculture.[24] After the Civil War, the region moved out of agriculture quickly in comparison with the nation. By 1880 the two were equally farm based, but thereafter the Northwest revealed its greater industrial potential.

The timing of change varied across the states in the region. In part this was due to differences in their dates of origin, but there must have been

TABLE 4

Agricultural Share of the Labor Force

Year	Ill.	Ind.	Mich.	Ohio	Wisc.	The Region	United States
1800		0.884		0.860		0.863	0.768
1810	0.869	0.871	0.622	0.854		0.850	0.762
1820	0.863	0.882	0.524	0.808		0.820	0.788
1830	0.929	0.919	0.739	0.765		0.815	0.706
1840	0.799	0.873	0.883	0.708	0.571	0.771	0.619
1850	0.729	0.732	0.663	0.618	0.622	0.666	0.536
1860	0.628	0.697	0.629	0.578	0.645	0.626	0.526
1870	0.559	0.632	0.517	0.519	0.600	0.557	0.515
1880	0.493	0.591	0.498	0.461	0.537	0.507	0.494
1890	0.354	0.493	0.410	0.354	0.447	0.396	0.406
1900	0.287	0.428	0.381	0.302	0.408	0.342	0.388
Percentage Point Changes							
1800–1840	-0.070	-0.011	0.261	-0.152		-0.092	-0.149
1800–1860	-0.241	-0.187	0.007	-0.282	0.074	-0.237	-0.242
1860–1900	-0.341	-0.269	-0.248	-0.276	-0.237	-0.284	-0.138
1800–1900	-0.582	-0.456	-0.241	-0.558	-0.163	-0.521	-0.380

Sources: Miller and Brainerd, 1957, Table L-4; Weiss, 1986; and Weiss,1987.

The figures for the years 1870 through 1900 are from Miller and Brainerd (1957, Table L-4). For the antebellum years, the figures for the Old Northwest and the constituent states were constructed for this paper, and their derivation is explained in the Appendix and in Weiss (1987). The U.S. figures are from Weiss (1986) and may not be exactly comparable to the state and regional figures as the estimation procedures have been modified somewhat from that earlier effort, and those modified procedures have not yet been carried out for all states. Those U.S. figures are essentially refined measures of the estimates made by Lebergott (1966) so they do represent the current state of our knowledge. There is also some inconsistency between the antebellum and postbellum figures for the Old Northwest region and states due to the different ways in which those workers categorized as laborers, not otherwise specified were allocated to agriculture in 1850 and 1860, as opposed to the years 1870 to 1900.

other forces at work too. Indiana, for example, began its development sooner than all other states except Ohio, yet was still the most heavily agricultural at the end of the century. Ohio, on the other hand, started shifting out of farming sooner than all other states, as would be expected given its early starting date, and it shifted to a greater extent than all the others except Illinois. The latter moved cautiously into nonagricultural activities before the Civil War, but subsequently altered its industrial structure far more rapidly than the region or the nation.

IMPLICATIONS FOR ECONOMIC GROWTH

THE PRECEDING EVIDENCE IS, of course, the stuff of economic growth. Other things being equal, i.e., no change in average worker productivity, increases in the participation rates push up per capita output. Given that output per worker in agriculture in the nineteenth century was on average below that in nonagricultural industries, the shift of the labor force out of agriculture also works to increase output per worker. Of course, we know from the national figures that the most important force pushing up income per capita was the improvement in worker productivity within each industry and sector. Obviously, in a period in which agriculture is the dominant activity, the course of worker productivity in that sector will heavily influence the movement of average productivity and income per capita in the region and nation. Thus, a time series on farm output taken in conjunction with a series on the farm workforce would have an important bearing on the estimation of change in per capita income. Unfortunately, the statistical record for the early years of the century is lacking. Although there are many good accounts of the details of agricultural change and the problems of setting up farms and experimenting with crops and techniques, there is no overall summary series of what that activity produced. For the most part, a systematic account does not begin until 1840.[25] Given the lack of a summary output series, our present analysis is primarily speculative but, we think, somewhat illuminating.

Our method of investigation follows along the lines laid out by Paul David (1967) in his construction of conjectural estimates of real growth before 1840. Growth of per capita income is brought about by the three factors noted above: growth in the participation rate, shifts of the labor force out of agriculture, and increases in worker productivity, especially in agriculture. By making an assumption that worker productivity changed at the same rate in farm and nonfarm activities, we can make some conjectures about the course of growth with a minimum of information.[26] We have confined our conjectures to the antebellum period. The results of our exercise are summarized in tables 5 and 6.

Our input data consist of the labor force figures discussed above, evidence on the course of agricultural productivity taken from David (1967), and evidence on the relative levels of productivity in farming and nonfarming industries taken from Easterlin (1960). Since the evidence on the participation rate change and on the shifts in the composition of the labor force seem fairly solid, we use only one series for each of those but use two different hypothetical views about the growth of agricultural productivity. First, we produce an estimate of growth in per capita income under the assumption that there was no change in worker productivity within either the farm or nonfarm sectors. Our alternative calculation assumes that productivity advanced at the same rate in the region and the nation. Neither of these calculations gives us what we would like, an estimate of the time path of growth in per capita income in the region, but they do give us insight into the relative importance of the different sources of growth and suggest how the region is likely to have performed vis-a-vis the nation.

TABLE 5

Calculated Indexes of Conjectural Growth
Variant A (No Productivity Growth)

	Old Northwest			United States		
Year	Per Capita Income	Part. Rate	Share Effect	Per Capita Income	Part. Rate	Share Effect
1800	0.897	0.944	0.950	0.863	0.953	0.906
1810	0.858	0.900	0.954	0.866	0.953	0.909
1820	0.901	0.926	0.973	0.861	0.965	0.893
1830	0.911	0.933	0.976	0.925	0.979	0.945
1840	1.000	1.000	1.000	1.000	1.000	1.000
1850	1.129	1.067	1.058	1.097	1.041	1.053
1860	1.196	1.108	1.080	1.125	1.062	1.059
Changes in the Indexes						
1800–60	0.299	0.164	0.130	0.262	0.109	0.153
1800–40	0.103	0.056	0.050	0.137	0.047	0.094
1840–60	0.196	0.108	0.080	0.125	0.062	0.059
Percentage Changes in the Indexes						
1800–60	0.333	0.174	0.137	0.304	0.114	0.169
1800–40	0.115	0.059	0.053	0.159	0.049	0.104
1840–60	0.196	0.108	0.080	0.125	0.062	0.059

For sources and notes see Table 6.

In the calculations presented in this table we have assumed that there was no productivity change in either the region or the nation.

As can be seen in the results for Variant A, the two labor force factors, the rise of the participation rate and the shift out of agriculture, would have increased income per capita by roughly equal amounts in the region and the nation over the antebellum period, 33.3 percent in the Old Northwest and 30.4 percent in the U.S. Of the two factors, the change in the participation rate was the more important in the region, accounting for approximately 56 percent of the combined increase, though the shift out of agriculture had a slightly greater impact on the nation as a whole, statistically accounting for 58 percent of the increase. The two major subperiods show somewhat different results. In the earlier period, 1800 to 1840, the labor force changes alone would have raised per capita income in the nation by more than in the region (15.9 percent versus 11.5 percent), but in the years just prior to the Civil War the region had a more favorable increase (19.6 percent versus 12.5 percent). Both factors worked to the advantage of the region in those years, with the rise in the participation rate being still a stronger influence than the industrial shift.

In variant B we have allowed worker productivity change to proceed at the same rate in both the region and the nation. The consequence, of

TABLE 6

Calculated Indexes of Conjectural Growth
Variant B

Year	Old Northwest				United States		
	Output Per Worker	Per Capita Income	Part. Rate	Share Effect	Per Capita Income	Part. Rate	Share Effect
1800	0.824	0.739	0.944	0.950	0.711	0.953	0.906
1810	0.777	0.667	0.900	0.954	0.674	0.953	0.909
1820	0.756	0.681	0.926	0.973	0.651	0.965	0.893
1830	0.884	0.805	0.933	0.976	0.818	0.979	0.945
1840	1.000	1.000	1.000	1.000	1.000	1.000	1.000
1850	1.000	1.128	1.067	1.058	1.096	1.041	1.053
1860	1.207	1.444	1.108	1.080	1.358	1.062	1.059
Changes in the Indexes							
1800–60	0.383	0.705	0.164	0.130	0.647	0.109	0.153
1800–40	0.176	0.261	0.056	0.050	0.289	0.047	0.094
1840–60	0.207	0.444	0.108	0.080	0.358	0.062	0.059
Percentage Changes in the Indexes							
1800–60	0.465	0.954	0.174	0.137	0.910	0.114	0.169
1800–40	0.214	0.353	0.059	0.053	0.406	0.049	0.104
1840–60	0.207	0.444	0.108	0.080	0.358	0.062	0.059

Sources for tables 5 and 6: Tables 1 and 4 above; Appendix table 2 below; Weiss, 1986; David, 1967; and Easterlin, 1975.

The Per Capita Income Index is the product of the other indexes.

The Part. Rate Index is based on the participation rates presented in Table 1.

The Share Effect index combines the effect of the change in the farm share of the labor force with the evidence on the ratio of farm to nonfarm productivity. The farm share values are from table 4 above and from Weiss (1986). For the U.S. the ratio of farm to nonfarm productivity was assumed to be .544 (David, 1967, adjusted in light of revisions made to the farm labor force estimates in Weiss, 1986). The Old Northwest ratio is .615. The farm income per worker was derived by dividing Easterlin's estimates of farm income (1960, table A-1) by the present farm labor force estimates. (Appendix table 2). Nonagricultural income per worker was taken from Easterlin (1960, table A-1, variant B).

The Productivity Index was derived using David's index of farm output (1967, table 6) and revised estimates of the U.S. farm labor force (Weiss, 1986, table 3). We have also assumed that productivity change for the region was equal to the national average.

course, is to show far greater growth in per capita income in both the region and the nation, with the region obviously retaining its advantages due to the labor force changes.[27] The importance of productivity change can be seen by comparing the changes in the indexes of productivity with the changes in the growth index. In both the region and the nation, productivity advance was far more important than either of the labor force factors and greater than the effect of those changes combined; this is true for the whole period as well as for each of the two major subperiods. For the entire period, productivity change was of roughly the same importance in both the region and the nation. However, in the early subperiod, productivity advance was more important in the region than the nation, though in the years 1840 to 1860 it was of greater significance in the nation than the region. Of course, since the rate of productivity advance was assumed to be the same in both locations, this change in the relative importance is nothing more than the obverse of the labor force changes discussed earlier.

The impact of the productivity factor makes it very evident that an improved picture of the course of economic progress in the Old Northwest awaits the construction of a reliable series on agricultural output. We have not produced such a series, but some preliminary work in that direction suggests that the rate of agricultural productivity advance in the region was more rapid than it was in the nation. For one thing, Easterlin's evidence indicates that between 1840 and 1860 farm income per worker increased faster in the Old Northwest than in the nation; 24.4 percent versus 15.3 percent.[28] By extending his output series backward to 1800 on the assumption that the value of nontraded farm output per capita remained constant, we find that output per worker increased by 31 percent between 1800 and 1840 and by 63 percent over the entire antebellum period.[29] Since we have not fully evaluated the evidence, assumptions, and procedures, we have not presented those estimates here. Nonetheless, they do suggest the very real possibility of substantially faster growth in the region than elsewhere and certainly highlight the importance of productivity advance, even in a region where other substantial changes were taking place.

This research has been funded by the National Science Foundation (Grant No. SE8308569). The research reported on here is part of the National Bureau of Economic Research Program on the Development of the American Economy. Any opinions expressed are those of the authors and not those of the National Bureau of Economic Research.

Notes

1. Havighurst (1947, p.8). The same modest view was expressed earlier by Hinsdale (1975, p.386) as well as by more recent scholars.
2. Fogel and Engerman, (1974, pp. 246–48).
3. Recent works by Atack and Bateman (1986) and Sullivan (1986) are attempts to fill this gap.
4. The assessment and revision of the labor force statistics for the census years 1870, 1890, and 1910 are presented in a separate paper (Weiss, 1985).
5. Participation rates were derived using the data from Miller and Brainard (1957) with our adjustments made to the census data for 1910.
6. Easterlin used somewhat different participation rates in constructing his estimates for 1840. In those states in which he adjusted the census data, he assumed a 100 percent rate for male slaves aged twenty-four through fifty-four and a 50 percent rate for male slaves aged ten through twenty-three. Perhaps most importantly, he assumed a zero participation rate for all female slaves, for male slaves aged zero to nine, and for those over the age of fifty-four (1960, p. 129).
7. Of course, at a minimum one must be aware that the Old Northwest figures are not beset with any of the estimation problems that might plague the estimation of the slave workforce and, more importantly, the industrial allocation of that workforce.
8. Early estimates were produced by Whelpton (1922) and Edwards (1940), and these have been refined and extended by Carson (1949), Miller and Brainerd (1957), and Lebergott (1966).
9. Miller and Brainerd conducted extensive tests of the census data and admitted that their "own series indicated that data were affected by changes in census techniques" (p. 404). They chose not to make any adjustments because they feared that their efforts would distort the timing of changes in the labor force composition (pp. 402–404). It would seem, however, that if the changes they observed were produced by vagaries of census enumerations, the failure to adjust would distort their view of the underlying economic forces, especially where it seems clear that the census biases varied by state. For most researchers the issue is not whether to make a correction but how best to accomplish it.
10. One can readily wonder why we bothered to carry out such small revisions. The main reason is that we wished to have revised figures on a state basis, so we had to make some adjustments in any event. Our aggregates are then the sums of the revised state figures, and their closeness to the accepted national figures is comforting. Of course one does not know that the differences will be small before the revisions are executed, and after the fact one is inclined to use them. For a more detailed discussion of the revisions and comparisons with the work of others see Weiss (1985).
11. In addition, some minor revisions were made to Lebergott's original figures in order to rectify some inconsistencies in the execution of the estimation procedure (see Weiss, 1986).

12. See Weiss, 1986b.

13. Lebergott now accepts that his original estimate of the number of workers aged ten to fifteen years in 1800 was too high, and has revised his labor force total downward (1984, p. 66). His revised total is approximately 2 percent below the present estimate.

14. The increases between 1860 and 1900 were 23.5 percent and 6.4 percent for the region and nation respectively. The national rate declined during the decade of the 1860s due to the different participation of free blacks as opposed to slaves. Thus we have reported the 1870 to 1900 change as being more indicative of the changes that were taking place under more normal circumstances.

15. The influence of the adult males' participation in the labor force can be seen by comparing this difference in the average participation rates with the share of free males aged sixteen and over in the total population. That share averaged 26 percent in the antebellum years and 31.9 percent in the postbellum years.

16. The rates presented here incorporate some revisions to the 1850 and 1860 census data for males aged sixteen and over, revisions which made use of the postbellum participation rates. For the Old Northwest, the corrections amounted to only 4,372 workers in 1850 and 178,060 in 1860. The latter is 9.6 percent of the unadjusted figure and was concentrated in Illinois (111,019). For a complete description of these adjustments see Weiss (1986b).

17. For the years 1870 to 1920, the trend in the adult female participation rate in each state was best captured by an equation of the form (ln $PR_i = a_i + B_iT$) where PR is the participation rate of females aged sixteen and over; T is the time trend variable; i is the state. A fuller discussion is presented in Weiss (1987).

18. Fortunately the sample data available that contain the relevant age, sex, and occupational detail, are those for rural northern households, and thus, quite appropriate for the Old Northwest (Bateman and Foust, 1973). For a discussion of the sample see Atack and Bateman (1986).

19. The sample data for Ohio were extremely deviant, indicating that 44 percent of the adult females were in the labor force. If Ohio were excluded from the sample, the North Central mean rate would be .084.

20. In order to construct a weighted average in the years before 1850, we had to first estimate the foreign-born share of the population. This was done using the data on the stock of foreign born in 1850 and 1860, data on the flow of immigrants over the years 1830 to 1860, conjectures on the flow of immigrants during the 1810s and 1820s made by Seybert and Tucker (U.S. Bureau of the Census. *Population* 1800 through 1910, p.xviii), and assumptions about the survival rates of the immigrant stocks and flows (Weiss, 1987). The foreign-born share of the population, which was around 20 percent in the postbellum period, was only 15 percent in 1860 and 11.5 percent in 1850. We estimate that the share was 6.5 percent in 1840 and somewhat smaller in earlier years. Since it seems clear that the foreign-born shares were fairly small in the antebellum years, our adjustment for this factor could not introduce much error into the estimates of the labor force participation rates.

21. Lebergott (1966).

22. It appears that the 1840 census statistics most likely pertain to workers aged ten

and over, including free and slave, as well as male and female, but excluding those in certain industries. Conversely, this means that in those industries that were covered, the census figures measure the total labor force. And, importantly, the covered industries include agriculture. In 1820 it appears that in the covered industries, which again included agriculture, the census figures seem to describe the number of free male workers aged sixteen and over, plus the number of slave workers (male and female) aged ten and over. The details of these assessments are found in Weiss (1986b).

23. The Michigan figure may indeed reflect the realities of the time. In 1820 the territory's population was extremely small (8,896), and the industrial structure was heavily influenced by the activities in Detroit and at Fort Michilimakinac, where in both places trading and trapping took precedent over farming.

24. This ignores the possibility that it was the addition of these states and their agricultural production which enabled Ohio to diversify.

25. Clark (1966) and Kohlmeier (1938) provide some evidence extending back to 1825, with the focus of their work being the trade in grains. We are presently engaged in an effort to extend the series on regional farm output back to 1800, making use of their estimates of the traded grain surpluses and farm output.

26. This assumption about the course of relative productivities is debatable. Paul David made the assumption on the grounds that it would understate the overall rate of growth because it is commonly accepted that productivity growth in nonfarm industries was greater than in farming (1967, p. 185). Gallman has argued that in the early decades of the nineteenth century the nonfarm sector was not predominantly manufacturing, where productivity advance may not have been as rapid (1971, p. 84).

27. In these calculations we have used a regional ratio of farm to nonfarm productivity of .615 taken from Easterlin (1960, p. 98). If we had assumed that the regional ratio was the same as the national (.544), then per capita income for the region would have increased by 105 percent over the period.

28. The percentages reported in the text were derived using Easterlin's agricultural income and the present labor force estimates (1975, p. 110). If instead we also used his regional farm labor force estimates, then income per worker would have increased by 17.9 percent.

29. This estimate rests crucially on the assumption of constancy in the per capita figure and on the accuracy of the estimated value of the grain trade obtained from the work of Kohlmeier (1938) and Clark (1966).

Bibliography

Atack, Jeremy, and Fred Bateman. *To Their Own Soil: Agriculture in the Antebellum North*. Ames: Iowa State University Press, 1986.

Bateman, Fred, and James Foust. "Agricultural and Demographic Records of 21,118 Rural Households." Bloomington: Indiana University, 1973. Data Tape.

Buley, R. Carlyle. *The Old Northwest*. 2 vols. Indianapolis: Indiana Historical Society, 1950.

Carson, Daniel. "Changes in the Industrial Composition of Manpower Since the Civil War." Vol. 11, *Studies in Income and Wealth*. New York: National Bureau of Economic Research, 1949.

Clark, John G. *The Grain Trade of the Old Northwest*. Urbana: University of Illinois Press, 1966.

David, Paul. "The Growth of Real Product in the United States Before 1840: New Evidence, Controlled Conjectures." *Journal of Economic History*, 27, no. 2:151-97.

Davis, James E. *Frontier America, 1800-1840*. Glendale, Calif.: Arthur H. Clark, 1977.

Easterlin, Richard. "Interregional Differences in Per Capita Income, Population, and Total Income, 1840-1950." Vol. 24, *Studies in Income and Wealth*. Princeton: Princeton University Press, 1960.

_____"Farm Production and Income in Old and New Areas at Mid-Century." *Essays in Nineteenth Century Economic History*. Edited by David Klingaman and Richard Vedder. Athens: Ohio University Press, 1975.

Edwards, Alba. *Comparative Occupation Statistics for the United States, 1870-1940*. Sixteenth Census of the United States, population. Washington, D.C., 1943.

Fabricant, Solomon. "The Changing Industrial Distribution of Gainful Workers: Comments on the Decennial Statistics, 1820-1940. Vol. 11, *Studies in Income and Wealth*. New York: National Bureau of Economic Research, 1949.

Fogel, Robert, and Stanley Engerman. *Time on the Cross*. Boston: Little, Brown and Company, 1974.

Gallman, Robert E. "The Statistical Approach: Fundamental Concepts as Applied to History." George Rogers Taylor and Lucius F. Ellsworth, editors. *Approaches to American Economic History*. Charlottesville: University Press of Virginia for the Eleutherian Mills-Hagley Foundation, 1971.

Havighurst, Walter. *Land of Promise*. New York: The Macmillan Company, 1947.

Hinsdale, Burke A. *The Old Northwest*. New York: Arno Press, 1975. A reprint of the 1899 edition published originally by Silver, Burdett and Company.

Klingaman, David, and Richard Vedder, eds. *Essays in Nineteenth Century Economic History*. Athens: Ohio University Press, 1975.

Kohlmeier, A.L. *The Old Northwest as the Keystone in the Arch of American Federal Union*. Bloomington, Ind.: Principia Press, 1938.

Lebergott, Stanley. *Manpower in Economic Growth*. New York: McGraw-Hill, 1964.

_____"Labor Force and Employment, 1800-1960." Vol. 30, *Studies in Income and Wealth*. New York: Columbia University Press, 1966.

Lebergott, Stanley. *The Americans: An Economic Record*. New York: W.W. Norton & Company, Inc., 1984.

Miller, A., and C. Brainerd. "Labor Force Estimates." *Population Redistribution and Economic Growth*. Everett Lee et al. Philadelphia: American Philosophical Society, 1957.

Scheiber, Harry. *Ohio Canal Era: A Case Study of Government and the Economy, 1820–1861*. Athens: Ohio University Press, 1969.

Sullivan, Timothy. "Regional Industrialization, Industrial Structure and the American Midwest, 1850–1880." Paper presented at the Social Science History Association Meetings, St. Louis, Missouri, October 1986. Mimeo.

U.S. Bureau of the Census. *Population*. 1800 through 1910.

_____*Occupations*. 1900.

_____*Occupations*. 1910.

_____ *Population*, 2. 1940.

_____ *Historical Statistics of the United States*. Washington, D.C., 1975.

Utter, William T. *The Frontier State, 1803–1825*. Vol. 2, *The History of the State of Ohio*, Carl Wittke, ed. Columbus: Ohio State Archaeological and Historical Society, 1942.

Weisenburger, Francis P. *The Passing of the Frontier, 1825–1850*. Vol. 3, *The History of the State of Ohio*, Carl Wittke, ed. Columbus: Ohio State Archaeological and Historical Society, 1941.

Weiss, Thomas. "Adjustments to the Census Counts of Population and Labor Force, 1870, 1880, and 1910." Lawrence: University of Kansas, 1985. Mimeo.

_____. "Revised Estimates of the United States Workforce, 1800 to 1860." Vol. 51, *Studies in Income and Wealth*. Chicago: University of Chicago, 1986.

_____. "Assessment and Revision of the Antebellum Census Labor Force Statistics." Lawrence: University of Kansas, 1986b. Mimeo.

_____. "Labor Force Estimates by State and Region, 1800 to 1860." Lawrence: University of Kansas, 1987. Mimeo.

_____. "Demographic Aspects of the Urban Population, 1800 to 1840." *Quantity and Quidity: Essays in Honor of Stanley Lebergott*. Middletown, Conn.: Wesleyan University Press, forthcoming.

Whelpton, P.K. "Occupational Groups in the United States, 1820–1920." *Journal of the American Statistical Association*, September 1926.

APPENDIX

ESTIMATION OF THE ANTEBELLUM AGRICULTURAL LABOR FORCE

THE ESTIMATES OF THE antebellum agricultural labor force were based as much as possible on the existing census statistics. The census accounts are not flawless, suffering from some ambiguities regarding coverage and classification and from some apparent measurement errors. On the other hand, they were collected at specific dates during the antebellum period, so they do represent the contemporary state of affairs and capture some of the economic realities of the time. Moreover, the more egregious errors are quite apparent and can be readily corrected. So, like many before us, we have examined and assessed the census data for 1820, 1840, 1850, and 1860, and made revisions where called for. Since the assessments and revisions of the earlier censuses made use of the evidence in the later ones, the presentation of the estimates proceeds backward in time. The results are summarized in Appendix table 2.

TABLE A-1

Total Labor Force, 1800 to 1860

Year	Illinois	Indiana	Michigan	Ohio	Wisconsin	The Region
1800		1642		11298		12940
1810	3331	5836	1681	54990		65838
1820	14954	35221	3584	143948		197708
1830	38870	80278	10570	238632		368349
1840	131895	170505	64020	408767	12333	787520
1850	235980	269884	121854	583069	89101	1299887
1860	516669	379489	238634	690711	235631	2061135

A summary of the methods of estimation is presented in the preceding text. For a more complete discussion see Weiss (1986 and 1987).

TABLE A-2

Agricultural Labor Force by State, 1800 to 1860

Year	Illinois	Indiana	Michigan	Ohio	Wisconsin	The Region
1800		1451		9717		11168
1810	2894	5083	1045	46934		55956
1820	12898	31053	1879	116339		162170
1830	36110	73745	7808	182453		300116
1840	105337	148806	56522	289568	7047	607279
1850	172083	197523	80767	360425	55380	866176
1860	324691	264398	150011	399537	152056	1290694

The methods used to estimate the agricultural workforce statistics are discussed in the accompanying Appendix.

ESTIMATES FOR 1860

THE CENSUS OF 1860 collected occupational data for free persons (male and female) aged fifteen and over. Examination of the participation rates implied by the reported statistics, along with evidence derived from a sample taken from the manuscript schedules of the census, indicated that some of the state counts were too low. These counts were revised upward using the participation rate data available for the postbellum years, as well as that for 1850. For the Old Northwest states, the census count was increased by 178,059 workers. The largest adjustment was made in Illinois where the original count, with allowance made for female workers, implied that only 68 percent of the males aged sixteen and over were in the workforce. Our adjustment raised the figure by 111,019 workers, or 28 percent. Smaller corrections were made in Indiana (32,328 workers) and Ohio (34,713 workers). These changes in the census totals were distributed by occupation in the same proportion as the unadjusted figures.[1]

The revised occupational statistics were then grouped into industries according to the classification used by Miller and Brainerd (1957, p.382), which in turn primarily followed the classification used by Alba Edwards (1940). In addition to those occupations that could readily be assigned to particular industries, there were a number that would be found in more than one industry. The chief such occupation was laborers, of which there were nearly 1,000,000 reported for the U.S., and 219,000 in the states of the Old Northwest. These were distributed between farm and nonfarm industries in each state in the proportion in which the male population aged sixteen and over was distributed between rural (farm) and urban (nonfarm) locations. This addition of laborers to the farm occupations raised the industry total by 202,256, or approximately 16 percent.[2]

To this revised census farm total we added estimates of the number of agricultural workers who were males aged ten to fifteen years. The number was set equal to 70 percent of the estimated total number of male workers in this age category. The 70 percent was the share derived from the manuscript census sample data for the states of the Old Northwest and is approximately equal to the 75 percent figure used by Lebergott.[3] In the Old Northwest, this addition amounted to only 62,680 or roughly 5 percent of the total farm workforce.[4]

ESTIMATES FOR 1850

THE ESTIMATES FOR 1850 were derived following the same procedures as those used for 1860. The census data were assessed and revised, the occupations allocated to industries, and the number of farm workers among those population groups not covered by the census were then added to the revised census total. The original census figures are remarkably reasonable, especially for the Old Northwest states. The only revision in the region was an increase of 4,372 workers in Wisconsin. The census did report a total of 909,786 laborers for the U.S. and 167,888 in the Old Northwest. Again, a number of these laborers were allocated to farming based on the rural share of the male population aged sixteen and over. The adjustment amounted to 149,505 workers, or 17.3 percent of the final industry total.

The census count of 1850 pertained to only free males aged fifteen and over, so additions were made for females aged sixteen and over, and males aged ten to fifteen years. The former was estimated as 12 percent of the total number of female workers aged 16 and over, and the latter as 70 percent of the total number of workers in that age category. In both cases the percentages were those for the states of the Old Northwest derived from the manuscript census sample of rural households for 1860 (Bateman and Foust, 1973). The additions amounted to 9,247 females (1.1 percent of the industry total) and 36,735 males aged 10 to 15 (4.2 percent of the industry total).

ESTIMATES FOR 1840

THE ESTIMATES OF THE agricultural workforce for 1840 are based almost entirely on the census statistics. The census of 1840 collected and reported some employment statistics, but unfortunately, the count did not cover all industries, and the census did not specify which portions of the population were counted in those industries that were included. There is no reason to think that the census neglected any free workers regardless of sex or age because the census takers were directed to collect the number of persons in each family employed in the covered industries (Wright, 1900, pp. 33 and 143). However, the exact demographic coverage was not spelled out precisely, and whatever the intention of the census superintendent the report appears to have varied from one census district to another.

The census was also vague about the definitions of the industries that were reported. The census published employment statistics for seven industries: mining; agriculture; commerce; manufactures and trades; navigation of the ocean; navigation of canals, lakes, and rivers; and the learned professions and engineers. Which occupations belonged to which industries was apparently left to the discretion of the census marshals. Moreover, the possibility that an industry like manufacturing included fishing and forestry, or that commerce included all professional services, cannot be dismissed.

This double imprecision regarding industrial and demographic coverage made it difficult to decipher exactly which employment statistics are reported. Nonetheless, we think we have been able to determine the age and sex coverage, thereby enhancing the usefulness of the industrial figures that were reported. For the seven industries covered, it appears that the census attempted to count all free workers aged ten and over and included some, but not all, slaves. Given the incompleteness of the slave worker count, the reported figures in the slave states cannot be used without adjustment. In the nonslave states, with some obvious exceptions, the figures appear to be reasonably accurate counts of the number of free workers engaged in the covered industries. Although these statistics do not give us the total labor force in each state, they do provide reliable evidence on the bulk of the workforce, and especially on the agricultural sector.

In summary, the assessment consisted of adjusting the reported census total to include an estimate of those industries that were not covered, primarily personal services and fishing and forestry. From this revised total we deducted our estimate of the number of female workers aged sixteen and over, those workers (male and female) aged ten to fifteen, and slave workers aged ten and over. The residual left after these additions and deductions should be free male workers aged sixteen and over. Since we have very good evidence as to the likely participation rates for this group of adult male workers, we used those rates to judge the reasonableness of the residual figures. There were some states in which this residual was clearly anomalous, but most of those were confined to the South and appear to be due to the difficulties of counting the number of slave workers in the original census and in our adjustments. Outside the South, the residuals seem very reasonable in most states. There were a few extreme deviations (Pennsylvania and New Jersey being much too low, and a few New England states being too high), but, for most, the residuals are very small. For twelve out of the seventeen nonslave states the residual was within 10 percent of the expected value of the adult male participation rate. In the Old Northwest, only Ohio was noticeably low, while Indiana and Michigan were slightly high. The implication of this test is that in order for the residuals to come out so reasonably, the census apparently attempted to count all workers, at least all free workers, aged ten and over. To be sure there were errors and deficiencies that varied across states, but with a few exceptions the reported counts outside the South are good measures of the number of all free workers employed in the covered industries.

We did make adjustments to those few states in which the residual was substantially out of line. In the Old Northwest, only the Ohio count was revised. This was done by examining the ratios of the reported number of workers to the population aged ten and over in each county and correcting any that were noticeably out of line. Four counties had no labor force reported and the revised count was derived by multiplying the population by the mean participation rate for those counties in which there was no suspicion of error (the adjusted state mean). There were thirteen other counties that had low ratios and two that had unusually high ratios. In those counties the subdivisions were examined to see if the county deviance was due to peculiarities in just a few townships. In eight of the thirteen, the ratios were low in every subdivision so the adjusted state mean participation rate was used to produce corrected figures. In the remaining five counties in which the original ratios were too low, and in the two counties with very high ratios, there were some number of subdivisions that appeared to have provided good counts and these ratios were used to correct the counts in the other subdivisions. The adjustment totaled 22,659, still leaving the count somewhat lower than might be expected on the basis of the average adult male participation rates. The revisions were allocated to industries on a county by county basis. Where we had reliable evidence for some subdivisions, that evidence was used to distribute the adjustment; where that was lacking, we used the shares for those counties in which there was no suspicion of error. The farm total was increased by 16,989 workers.[5]

ESTIMATES FOR 1820

THE CENSUS OF 1820 also provided some employment counts, but they, too, suffer from the ambiguity and incompleteness of coverage that plagued the 1840 figures. So, we performed the same tests on the 1820 counts as we had for 1840. In 1820, however, the residuals were most reasonable when the census count was taken to include only free males aged sixteen and over plus slaves aged ten and over. Again, even when restricted to the more likely coverage, the census counts in a few states were anomalous and in need of correction.

For the Old Northwest, corrections were made in Indiana and Michigan. The adjustment in Michigan was quite small, an addition of only 478 workers. An examination of the ratios of workers to population indicated that the counts in Detroit city and Brown county were too low, and that in Oakland county a bit high. Brown and Oakland counties were revised using the adjusted state ratio of workers to population aged sixteen and over, with each industry adjusted proportionately. For Detroit city, a lower ratio of workers to population was used (the unadjusted state mean) since many of its urban workers would have been employed in industries not covered by the census. The agricultural count in particular appeared very low in Detroit; only 1.1 percent of the population reported that they were employed in agriculture when over 17 percent of the people were so employed in St. Louis, a much larger frontier city at the time. The St. Louis data were used to distribute the revised workforce total for Detroit city. A much larger adjustment was made to the Indiana census count. In total the figure was reduced from 64,973 to 34,622; a change of 30,351. Most of this revision is simply a correction of an error in addition in the census count of agricultural workers. In addition, there were six counties that had deviant ratios of workers to population, two of which reported no agricultural workers and four of which showed extremely high ratios. Those with no farm workforce reported were adjusted using the adjusted state average. The others were corrected by using a worker to population ratio 10 percent above the adjusted state mean. The net effect of these adjustments was to lower the farm labor force by 1,509 workers, giving a revised count of free male farm workers aged sixteen and over of 29,565.

To these revised census counts of adult male workers in agriculture we added an estimate of female workers aged sixteen and over and males aged ten to fifteen. Again, we used the information derived from the manuscript census sample for 1860 which showed that 12 percent of the female workers aged sixteen and over and 70 percent of the male workforce aged ten to fifteen were employed in agriculture. For the region, this increased the agricultural workforce by 826 females and 6,574 males.

ESTIMATES FOR 1800 AND 1810

FOR 1800 AND 1810, we used the estimation procedure laid out by Lebergott for 1800.[6] In his approach the adult male farm workforce was derived as a residual of the difference between the total number of male workers and the number of those engaged in navigation, urban, and rural nonfarm occupations. We have made some small modifications. We estimated the number in navigation using a ratio of navigation workers to rural male population aged sixteen and over.[7] The ratios were taken from the census data of 1840 and 1860 and showed remarkable stability in those years. For Ohio, we used a ratio of .009, the value in both 1840 and 1860. For the other states, we used the average of all their ratios in 1840 and 1860 (.0035). For the rural nonfarm estimate, we also used ratios of certain workers to the rural male population aged sixteen and over. For manufacturing and commerce, we used the ratios for Illinois that prevailed in 1820 (.0664 for manufacturing and .0154 for commerce). In 1800 and 1810 the states of importance were Ohio and Indiana. Their ratios for these industries were lower in 1820 than 1840, so they were probably lower again in 1800 and 1810. The 1820 Illinois ratio was below either of the other two, so it seemed like an appropriate proxy to use in earlier years. For those rural workers in forestry, fishing, mining, and construction, we used the same ratio we had derived for Ohio in 1820. The Ohio ratio (.01) fell between the values for Illinois (.013) and Indiana (.006) and seemed appropriate since Ohio was the dominant state, and there seemed little reason to expect any trend in this conglomeration of occupations. For urban workers in 1810, we simply multiplied the urban male population aged sixteen and over by the average male participation rate for Ohio.

The preceding gave us our estimates of male farm workers aged sixteen and over, to which we added separate estimates of females aged sixteen and over, and males aged ten to fifteen. As in other years, we used the data from the 1860 manuscript census sample of rural households and allocated 12 percent of the adult female workforce and 70 percent of the male youths to farming.

The above procedures yielded an estimate for Michigan that implied a farm share far above that which prevailed in 1820 (86.4 percent versus 52.4). Certainly the 1820 data could be in error, but we think that to a large extent it reflects the realities of that early economy with an emphasis on trading and trapping. Indeed, if one deducts the influence of Detroit city and Fort Michillimackinac, the remainder of the state showed a farm share of 80 percent in 1820. Thus we made a separate estimate for Michigan in 1810 by simply multiplying the 1810 rural population by the 1820 ratio of the farm workforce to rural population.

ESTIMATES FOR 1830

FINALLY, THE ESTIMATES FOR 1830 were derived by following a variant of the approach taken by Lebergott. Lebergott estimated his free farm workforce for 1830 using a ratio of the farm workforce to farmers, the latter of which was derived using the ratio of farmers to rural white families that prevailed in other years. We have taken the more expedient approach of estimating the farm workforce in each state on the basis of the ratio of that workforce to the rural population; the ratio being the mean of the ratios for 1820 and 1840.

Notes to the Appendix

1. We also made a minor change in the age coverage; we deducted an estimate of the number of fifteen-year-old workers in order to obtain a count of free workers aged sixteen and over. The deduction was made by multiplying the estimated population fifteen years of age by the participation rate for fifteen-year-olds reported for 1900. The fifteen-year-old population was estimated as a fraction of those aged ten to fourteen years, the fraction being the average for each state for the years 1870 to 1920.

2. This gives a different total than would be derived by strictly following Lebergott's procedure. He chose not to allocate any unclassified laborers to farming in either 1850 or 1860 (1966, pp. 152–53).

3. Lebergott estimated the total number of male workers aged ten to fifteen as 22.6 percent of the population and the number in agriculture as 17 percent of the population, which makes the farm share 75 percent (17/22.6)(1966, p. 152).

4. Obviously the procedure must be modified to account for slave labor when estimating the farm workforce in the South.

5. Again the problem of adjusting the figures to properly take account of the slave workers in farming gives one somewhat less confidence in the revised national totals. It appears, however, that the 1840 farm share of the labor force was probably higher than has heretofore been believed. Our preliminary adjustments indicate that the share may have been as high as 70 percent of the labor force as opposed to 62 or 63 percent as shown in the extant labor force statistics (see Lebergott, 1966, table 1; Weiss, 1986, table 3).

6. Lebergott (1966) made a separate estimate of free white male workers and of free black male workers. Given the small number of free blacks in the Old Northwest, we have treated all male workers alike. Moreover, we have also included those few slaves present with the adult male population and workers.

7. We used the rural population so that there would not be any chance of double-counting these workers as part of the urban workforce. In 1800 this is not a problem at all as there was no urban population.

7.

TOCQUEVILLE'S VIEW OF THE NORTHWEST IN 1835:
Ohio a Generation After Settlement

Lee C. Soltow
Ohio University

*The. . .inhabitant of Ohio, obliged to subsist by his own
exertions regards temporal prosperity as the chief aim of his
existence: and as the country which he occupies presents
inexhaustable resources to his industry, and ever varying lures
to his activity, his acquisitive ardor surpasses the ordinary
limits of cupidity: he is tormented by the desire for wealth, and
he boldly enters upon every path that fortune opens to him.*[1]
—Alexis de Tocqueville, 1835

IN HIS 1798 *ESSAY*, Malthus portrayed a dismal future for mankind because of population pressures on the supply of land. A dramatic exception was the unoccupied land in America, as represented by the potentially great state of Ohio. In 1798 to 1803, its lands held only the promise of future wealth, not its reality. It would be necessary to view the experience of at least one generation in order to amass evidence for predicting society's ability to accumulate wealth in the state. For the first generation of settlers, what was the average growth in wealth holdings? Was one man's wealth much different from another's? Were there significant regional differences in wealthholdings?

This article reports the findings of a study of the distribution of wealth in real estate among Ohioans in 1835. Authorities made a fresh evaluation of all real estate in that year, including the values of the soils, houses, barns, mills, warehouses, distilleries, wharves, and other permanent structures. Each of the 175,000 properties owned by 130,000 persons in the state has been recorded from the tax records by Dr. Gerald Petty of Columbus, who kindly has made these data sets available to me for analysis.

TOCQUEVILLE'S HYPOTHESES

IN THE OPENING SENTENCE of his 1835 masterpiece, *Democracy in America*, Tocqueville stated his findings: "Among the novel objects that attracted my attention during my stay in the United States, nothing struck me more forcibly than the general equality of condition among the people." He found that this level of equality permeated the entire culture and could be found in the economic, political, and social activities and alignments of its populace. Individuals began their lives on American soil under conditions of poverty and previous misfortune. Neither a single individual nor a select few could become dominant because farms were small, at least compared to the grand estates in Europe. Tocqueville felt that Americans held contempt for equality as such, but the dynamism—the fluidity due to frequent changes in the holding of wealth—as well as the absence of primogeniture and entailed estates presumably worked to assure economic equality. On the other hand, he felt that some persons had a "depraved taste for equality." But this fluidity itself may have stimulated the desire of persons in the lower wealth ranks to curtail the activities of those of higher rank. In any case the economic equality of America was fundamental to providing the background for its social and political equality.[2]

What were Tocqueville's views concerning Ohio? It is often difficult to determine whether his discussion of a given principle applied to Europe, to the United States, or more specifically to Ohio. He did travel in Ohio during the years 1831–32 and studied literature concerning the state, particularly its legislation, as late as 1835. He was struck by the degree of administrative direction at the township level. The state governed, but the counties, and especially the townships, administered the laws. In this way no select few could gain control of administration or, presumably, enjoy special privileges. He felt that "executive power is disseminated in a multitude of hands," resulting in an absence of gradation in powers. Such a setting for government would be conducive to disseminating wealth in a broad fashion. It was not that there existed a condition of Utopian equality: Tocqueville found some rich and a few poor even in this sparsely-settled area.

In what sense was Ohio's first generation unique? To be sure, he found that although there was at least some inequality in the state, it was less than that found among previous generations in areas further east. Especially after the colonial period, there was a trend toward decreasing inequality within society. For one thing, the laws of primogeniture had been eliminated. For another, the electoral franchise was broadened so that the voices of ordinary people were heard. Moreover, the relative abundance of land made it possible for the ordinary person to accumulate wealth. Rather than move to Ohio, had individuals remained either in the East or in Europe, "it is probable that, instead of becoming rich landowners, they would have remained humble laborers."[3]

Tocqueville's background was fundamental to his perceptions of Ohio. Why wouldn't a French nobleman be struck by the activities of Ohio's ordinary farmers? The relative status of the French nobility had declined appreciably by the 1830s, as compared to its level before 1789; yet landed estates, the equal of which were not to be found in America, still existed. The landed nobility continued to be a dominant force in many European countries: this institution was completely absent here. In Sweden, for example, the relative distribution of land was substantially more unequal among all landholders than among nonnoble landholders.[4] But even in that country there were no equivalents to France's Versailles and the chateaux of the Loire.

Another aspect of Tocqueville's purview was the degree of poverty in each region and country. Naturally, he gave little attention to the subject in *Democracy in America* since there was so little poverty here. It is difficult to find the word "poor" in his treatise except as he describes the condition of immigrants upon their arrival. Only slavery appeared as a blight on society, and Tocqueville was quite cognizant of differences in activities and in social structure in Kentucky, as compared to Ohio. He had witnessed poverty in Europe, and in 1835 wrote a powerful tract in which he observed that the advanced industrial nations and regions experienced poverty in greater degree than was the case in less-developed areas. In England 17 percent of the population lived on charity; in Portugal the proportion was only 4 percent. In France the departments of the Nord and La Manche provided the same contrast.[5]

Tocqueville's model for Europe was one where development and industrialization brought greater equality among upper classes and greater inequality among lower classes. He tended to stress the greater equality, particularly since the upper classes played such a dominant role in the direction of society, in its government, and in other activities having social and cultural ramifications. He seemed to see no lower classes in America except in the context of the administration of prisons, ostensibly the subject of his investigations while in America.

Just what the young nobleman's overall perception was of inequality in 1835 for countries or regions such as Ohio is difficult to state in terms other than his generalities. Let me attempt to sketch, very broadly, a possible scheme for Tocqueville's thinking by using a lognormal chart. A lognormal curve is one that is found rather frequently to be a reasonable approximation for wealth and income distributions. In such distributions the logarithm of the variate has the properties of a normal or bell-shaped curve. A lognormal chart is one where such a curve plots as a straight line when cast in the form of a cumulative curve, as shown in chart 1.

In a nation that had experienced industrialization, one would find that its landed nobility in the top 1 percent would, at best, maintain its preindustrial income. Those at the very top—the elite nobles above the ninety-ninth percentile in income or wealth—would maintain their positions from their rents. Those above the ninetieth percentile (or somewhere above the eightieth to ninety-fifth) but below the ninety-ninth percentile experienced

CHART 1

Some possible Income Distrubitons about 1835

(Log Normal Probability Paper)

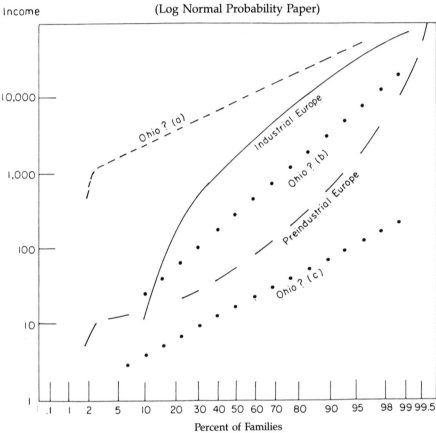

Income

Percent of Families

great gains with the onset of industrialization. This group included the burghers, merchants, manufacturers, and shippers. The industrial revolution also benefitted those from the fiftieth to twentieth percentiles, particularly with factory employment providing income far surpassing the former state of rural poverty, always plagued by seasonal unemployment. It is the bottom group, below the seventeenth percentile, that had difficulty finding employment; this group of destitute did not benefit from the industrial revolution except for the relief support they received from persons who then were relatively better off. The destitute may have been worse off than their counterpart group before industrialization, a subset of the population formerly sheltered on manorial estates.

It is difficult to sketch pre- and post-industrial revolution income distributions. In chart 1 I offer two extremes, possible bounds to configurations that may have been simple straight lines. The two limiting curves cross at the seventeenth and ninety-ninth percentiles, the two intersections suggested by Tocqueville. Persons just below the ninety-ninth percentile level experienced gains relative to their counterpart group before industrialization. The gains were more spectacular at the ninetieth percentile, with the greatest rises occurring at possibly the eightieth or seventieth percentiles. Chart 1 tends to magnify conditions in the two tails of the distribution, as opposed to the ordinary display achieved with a Lorenz curve. Not shown is the condition above the ninety-ninth percentile. It is possible that the curves would change slopes above this, with a new intersection, at an even higher income, a condition indicating great gains due to industrialization for the select few whose wealth was the result of manufacturing. Finally, the two bounds sketched in may be exaggerations of some tendencies. The curvatures shown may overemphasize the conditions that Tocqueville stressed. Perhaps the two curves should have been drawn essentially as straight lines, particularly above the seventeenth percentiles. Perhaps the industrial line should be straight, but the preindustrial line curved, as shown. This latter configuration demonstrates the immense income at the very top, including that of the king.[6] Fortunately these patterns can be tested with data for wealth (if not for income) from various countries, an investigation that is only in the beginning stages.

What bearing do preindustrial and industrial curves have on the situation in Ohio? Probably not much at all, except to highlight the contrasts. Those Ohioans in the lower 16 percent, those lower than one standard deviation below the mean, were, in part, either fresh immigrants from Europe or the young beginning their search for affordable land. Even this subset of Ohioans must have had adequate employment except possibly during the winter. At the other end of the spectrum were the state's rich, a group that could not be differentiated in terms of a noble class. There is no factor within economic history suggesting a strong discontinuity in the spectrum among wealthholders or suggesting there would not have been a rather continuous differentiation. I have no reason for not sketching Ohio's configuration on chart 1 as other than a straight line. The only question is whether the slope of the line would show about as much overall inequality as in Europe (line b) or if there was little spread (lines a or c).

The average level of income in Ohio, as compared to that in Europe, is yet another dimension of inequality. Perhaps its situation was something like that depicted by line *a*. It is a line showing little relative inequality, yet one where an Ohioan at any given percentile had larger income than did someone with his or her counterpart level in Europe. In this case equality in Ohio would provide an admirable model. The rich would be rewarded at levels surpassing those of the rich in Europe, yet the poorest would be at magnificent levels compared to those in Europe. Perhaps Ohio's line might be mid-way between lines *a* and *b*. There would be an intersection with the curve for industrial Europe; Ohioans then would be better off than their counterparts in Europe below, say, the thirtieth percentile, and worse off above that level. Finally, we should not dismiss the fact that such a young state, a region only one generation removed from a time of essentially no white settlement, may have been at a relatively low level, as suggested with line *c*. The passage by Tocqueville quoted at the beginning of this paper is ample proof that he believed Ohioans were being rewarded handsomely for their industry. Incentives were so strong that people were almost obsessed with garnering wealth. Surely our hypothesis must be that Ohio's position was more like that represented by line *a* than by line *c*.

WEALTH DATA

ANY STATISTICAL VERIFICATION OF a hypothesis for Ohio in 1835 demands income data for that year; unfortunately, such a variable is not available. I must resort to the only possible choice—wealth in real estate, even though only half of adult males in Ohio, at best, had such holdings in that year. We must judge conditions as best we can from the limited information available to us. This means that we can make some judgments about those above the median income, although technically there were some in the top half of the income distribution who held no wealth, and some below the median owned small amounts of land. We can study levels of overall inequality and look for discontinuities or bunchings in the upper tail, but for the lower tail of the income distribution, the evidence of poverty is weak.

Even the wealth data are not free from measurement error, and this is particularly true with respect to the collation of properties owned by any given individual throughout the state. The holdings for each person must be derived from a computer run of the 164,962 properties, filed by county and township. Such a run produces a distribution of 151,428 wealthholders when names are collated within townships but not within counties; 138,785 holders when names are collated within counties; and 109,375 when names are collated no matter where they were found within the state. Somewhere between 40 and 60 percent of the state's 250,000 males aged twenty and older in 1835 were property owners. The actual number of owners probably was somewhere between 125,000 and 130,000. Only a genealogical search could come close to a determination of the precise number. Only such a tracing could determine whether the John Smith who owned property in one county was the same John Smith who owned property in another county and that he, indeed, had property holdings in two or more counties. I only know that in the 1830 Ohio census this by far the most common of names was reported 260 times, and that it appeared In fifty-three of the state's seventy-two counties. Results of my study will be reported for the set of 138,785, that is, by not collating for multi-county holdings. This must be done in the absence of a genealogical study of all inhabitants in the state. Thus, I will be understating inequality levels at least a little because perhaps nine thousand persons with common names did own land in more than one county.

Results of sampling for uncommon names of persons provide valuable evidence of statewide holdings of individuals. From the wealth array of the 109,375 I drew a sample of every one hundredth person. Of those 1,094, 462 were not listed in the Ohio 1830 federal census, 323 were listed only once, and the remaining names appeared more than once in that census. The 785 uncommon names showed the following intercounty holdings:

Number of counties in which name was listed	Number of uncommon names
4	2
3	4
2	46
1	733
	785

Thus, about 7 percent of wealthholders held property in more than one county. These data imply that there were 129,000 wealthholders in the state in 1835. In the remainder of this article I will generally present results from the middle distribution of table 1, the group of 138,785 "persons." In the absence of an arduous and overwhelming genealogical study, it is the closest approximation to a wealth distribution that I am able to make.[7]

THE 1835 DISTRIBUTION

INEQUALITY WAS SURPRISINGLY STRONG in Ohio in 1835. We can say this in spite of the collation problem, as the figures in table 1 attest. The Gini coefficient of .64 – .67 is at least as large as that reported previously for acreage

TABLE 1

The Distribution of Wealth In Real Estate In Ohio in 1835

Class limits	Collating names throughout the state	Collating names within counties	Property values in tax list
$100,000 and up	6	—	—
50,000–99,999	18	11	—
20,000–49,999	153	105	56
10,000–19,999	407	305	263
5,000– 9,999	1,130	848	798
2,000– 4,999	4,761	4,183	4,024
1,000– 1,999	9,256	9,767	9,685
500– 999	17,912	21,513	22,956
200– 499	32,293	42,655	48,565
100– 199	20,471	28,135	33,845
50– 99	11,302	15,583	21,050
20– 49	7,285	9,723	14,431
10– 19	2,463	3,346	5,000
5– 9	1,395	1,870	2,987
2– 4	454	653	1,130
1	67	86	172
	109,373	138,785	164,962
Mean	$ 672	530	446
Gini coefficient	.673	.637	.629
Propertyholder proportion, PHP	.427	.542	.644

Source: Tax records, 1835, Ohio Historical Society Library

in Ohio in 1810 and 1825 and for the value of real estate in Ohio in 1850, 1860, and 1870, all with Gini coefficients of .58 – .60.[8] The variation in dollar values in 1835 certainly should have been at least some degree larger than that of variation in acreage in 1825 or, for that matter, in 1835. The value of an acre of land varied substantially throughout the state, with some regions being much more fertile than others. The upshot of price adjustment leads to the argument that inequality in the state very well may have been about the same in 1810, 1825, and 1835; the coefficients for land values of .58 – .60 in 1810 and 1825 would have been at about the 1835 level if acreage could have been adjusted to dollar values. The relative inequality in Ohio real estate in 1835 was similar to that for the United States in 1850. It was less than in other countries, as we shall see. For example, there was more inequality in the distribution for persons owning real estate in Sweden in 1845 than in Ohio in 1835.[9]

INTERNATIONAL COMPARISONS

THE FINDINGS THAT HAVE bearing on the speculations presented in figure 1 are important. First consider the proportions of persons holding real estate, as determined for Ohio and other areas. The approximately 129,000 holders in Ohio represented almost exactly 50 percent of the state's population of adult males; the counterpart measure for Sweden was 26 percent. The ownership level in Scotland in 1830 was only 4–5 percent, and as early as 1775 it was a mere 3 percent.[10] The proportion owning land in England in 1800 was around 10 percent. These levels of ownership or wealth participation have strong bearing on income distribution because rents from the land were a significant portion of income for the owners. Thus, rents were concentrated among an exclusive, small group in Europe. In Ohio rents were more diffusely scattered in incomes above the median and, to a certain extent, below the fiftieth percentile of income. The concentration of land ownership among few or many owners, the spread of acreage among many or few farm tenants, as well as the widespread or limited use of farm laborers provide qualitative and quantitative distinctions that have strong bearing on income distribution. The income lines of chart 1 dropped much more below the seventieth–ninetieth percentile range for Europe as compared to the line for Ohio.

The shape of the wealth distribution itself provides an indication of general equality and inequality of income. It tells whether there are discontinuities or groupings within the wealthholder class. The Ohio distributions provided in table 1 tell us that we should expect Ohio's configuration to plot as a straight line on lognormal probability paper. The class limits of the table form an approximate ratio scale and the frequencies appear as a bell-shaped configuration. The actual plottings provide more explicit confirmation of the fact that Ohio's distribution was remarkably lognormal. The pattern is demonstrated graphically in chart 2, a form that makes provision for those without wealth by considering all adult males on its horizontal axis. The straight line pattern for Ohio breaks down at about the fiftieth percentile since a few people owned small amounts of acreage. A small group representing about 5 percent of adult males (or 10 percent of landowners) had real values of less than fifty dollars. Such a radical change really is not an indication of a significant discontinuity. Some of these relatively landless were persons who lived in the urban sector but who had small plots of land for gardens or for grazing. At worst, they were a poor group representing the lower tail of the distribution for landholders, a group with land values of fifty dollars or less who would have had closer to one hundred dollars had the line been continuously straight.

There is no other discontinuity in the Ohio distribution of wealth. In this sense there is no way to distinguish one group from another. Each wealth range fits smoothly between the ranges above or below it within the straight line sector. It is no wonder that Tocqueville could find no dominant or subdominant group to consider except the poor who had just arrived. Thus, it was natural for him to think in terms of equality when there was no special coterie to describe. This may be one reason why the cultural historian con-

CHART 2

Wealth Distributions in Four Countries 1825–1845

(Log Normal Probability Paper)

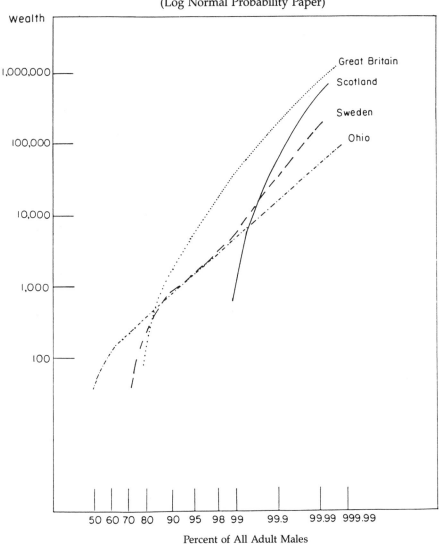

Percent of All Adult Males

centrates on aspects other than income or wealth differentials when describing social conditions of the period in the Northwest. Left unstated is the fact that the slopes of the lines in chart 2 may have been small or large. This aspect will be judged by examining slopes of wealth distributions for other places and times. The discussion of Gini coefficients already presented indicates that the slopes for Ohio were strong.

The distributions presented in chart 2 clearly indicate that inequality was less in Ohio than was the case for the three European countries. This we know from the general slopes of the various configurations—those with the steepest gradients displayed the strongest contrasts between rich and poor landholders. The line for Scotland demonstrates the greatest differentiation, followed by that for Britain, again with curvature in its pattern. Only the Swedish configuration showed some semblance of linearity. The Scottish upward sweep suggests that the data above the 99.99th percentile would display a number of "super rich." The configuration below the 99th percentile demonstrates a tapering similar to that in chart 1 for the industrial pattern. Data for Ireland reveal a shape very similar to that for Scotland.

The estimates presented in chart 2 all lack precision since each measure is not exactly comparable with the Ohio data. Particularly troublesome are the determinations of market values as well as appropriate exchange rates. Data for Scotland pertained only to 1825 county distributions of real estate and did not include collations of significant holdings of 100-or-so great landlords with holdings in more than one county. The wealth distribution for Great Britain is derived from stamp duties issued for probates of wills and testamentary inventories and administrations as well as for inventories not testamentary; the number of adult males aged 20 and older in this case was for the deceased, and wealth was adjusted to the age distribution of the living.[11] The measurement errors involved are small enough that the cumulative distribution lines for the three countries and Ohio all may be placed on the same chart, with the vertical axis being in American dollars in the period around 1835, and the horizontal axis representing the normal probability scale for all adult males in each area.

Chart 2 tells us that the slopes of the European distributions were substantially larger than was the slope for Ohio. In each of the three countries the rich had much greater shares of the total and the poor had smaller shares. This we see since the lines for Europe start in the upper right-hand corner, with values ten times those for Ohio, and drop well below those for Ohio anywhere in the area from the ninety-ninth to eightieth percentiles. The outstanding feature for Ohio in the 1830s was that the wealth of its middle class far exceeded its counterparts' in Europe. It is little wonder that Tocqueville found equality in my state!

The European configurations were not linear in the manner of the Ohio curve. A gradual rise in ownership among the farm population in the last of the nineteenth century or early twentieth century may have been enough to straighten the lines, to buoy up the fiftieth to eightieth percentiles. On the other hand, population increases actually may have depressed the fiftieth to eightieth percentiles when a larger group of farm laborers, farm tenants, and urban laborers appeared. Delicate forces could push the percentiles in this middle group either up or down in this range (relative to those above them). Tocqueville believed they were pushed upward as further democratization took place. In Ohio the middle group was sufficiently strong to raise the sixtieth to eightieth percentiles to form a straight line. It was a line without discontinuity, a line demonstrating no class differentiation.

Yet, the Ohio configuration was not perfect. All adult males might have owned land. Theoretically, the Ohio pattern could have continued as a straight line throughout its entire spectrum to yield a lognormal distribution of wealth in real estate among all families or adult males. Such an extreme would have meant that all males would have owned a farm plot of a few acres or, at least, a city lot. Ohio's straight line portion does project to a value of two dollars at the first percentile, the price of an acre of land in some sections of Ohio at that time.[12]

Property ownership in Ohio would have been more widespread had initial land prices for *new* settlers been lower than they were. The drive for ownership would not have extended to 100 percent of settlers since at least some would have sold their land quickly in order to move elsewhere. Some understanding of what this means is to look at ownership participation in areas of cheap land, a procedure to be followed shortly. Another possibility is to examine real estate ownership today because home ownership in effect has been subsidized by income tax benefits. The 1983 Federal Reserve study provides a distribution of wealth in real estate for the United States that has a slope very similar to the 1835 Ohio curve, with one exception. The U. S. slope continues to 67 percent of families and single individuals, not the 50 percent cutoff for Ohio in 1835.[13]

REGIONAL DIFFERENCES

TOCQUEVILLE'S PERCEPTIONS OF INEQUALITY changes were applied to regions within a country. In a less-developed region there were fewer destitute needing help than in a developed one. This development effect would have been weaker in the case of the United States since poorer persons were likely to move to newly settled areas of plentiful land, where prices would have been lower. A further mitigating factor in the American situation was timing. The more recently settled areas such as Ohio would have been less subject to those lingering colonial institutions whose purpose was to strengthen inequality. For example, the manorial estates in New York and South Carolina survived to a certain degree even though the institutions of primogeniture and entail had been eliminated. It seems that Tocqueville found, in general, less inequality in the Northwest than in other regions of this country.

Would the effects of development or timing appear in an analysis of Ohio's regions? Or would the general level of inequality be about the same throughout the entire state? Certainly a poor man living anywhere in Ohio would have had little reason for not moving if he thought he could better his position materially. There were no strong language or cultural barriers in Ohio such as existed between or within European countries. The proportion of those with little or no estate should not have differed greatly. At least this is the hypothesis to be tested.

Nor would there have been compelling reasons for the rich to be better off because of living in one area rather than in another. New opportunities presented themselves everywhere, and one was free to move without constraint. Some distinction might arise between rural and urban regions since a few bankers, merchants, and traders may have garnered large aggregates of real estate values, particularly in the Cincinnati area. A few farmers owning very desirable soils could have become quite rich relative to others. In a region of greater variability in soil fertility, it is likely that there would have been more inequality in wealthholding than in a region of uniform soils. The data generated by Dr. Petty are an admirable source for studying inequalities on an area basis by studying its four major regions, its 73 counties, along with its townships, numbering somewhere around 1,123 at that time. Studies of inequality will be reported at the township level since there were about 155,000 persons reporting ownership of property in the township tax records. An amazing detail of wealth variability, by area, readily unfolds from this data bank.

First, consider the four quadrants of the state, based on latitude 40°, and longitude 83°30', lines intersecting just east of Columbus. The southern regions were settled earlier; the west generally was more fertile. The 1835 data presented in table 2 demonstrate the fact that land prices in the state varied widely. The average price of land in southwestern Ohio was almost five times that in the southeast, and at least two-thirds again as large as that in the north. Differences in fertility and cultivability provided the basis for substantial inequality between regions. Differentials in wealth, in turn, were associated with differentials in literacy, newspaper circulation, and, to a small degree, school attendance, as shown in table 2. A family or community with three to five or more times the assets of another surely could better afford to support cultural activities, including libraries and schools.

Does it then follow that relative dispersion of wealth varied from quad-

TABLE 2

Regional Indexes of Wealth Distribution in Ohio in 1835

	North-west	South-west	North-east	South-east	All
Propertyholders					
Number	24,353	43,258	60,733	10,441	138,785
Average RE	$ 544	676	475	207	529
Inequality, G_{RE}	.625	.647	.615	.572	.637
Share of top 1%	20%	18	19	13	20
Share of top 10%	52%	52	50	44	52
Males 20 and older	41,383	87,723	101,140	20,267	256,000
Proportion owning					
property (POP)	.588	.493	.600	.515	.542
Wealth average					
Real estate (RE)	$ 284	303	304	105	275
Personal estate (PE)	$ 52	56	42	35	49
Acreage					
Acres per adult male	85	56	72	82	69
Price per acre	$ 3.78	6.16	4.01	1.32	4.32
Percent plowed, 1880	60	60	57	45	58
Census of 1840					
Illiterates per adult	5.8%	7.9	4.9	11.0	6.7
Newspapers per adult[a]	0	108	38	0	42
Students per child					
5-19	35.6%	34.1	42.2	32.3	36.6
Counties 1835, average					
Year of formation	1816	1806	1808	1810	1811
Miles from Cincinnati	123	59	199	142	127

a. times 1,000,000

Sources: The 138,785 owners collated by county of table 1; Annual Report of the Auditor, 1835, Ohio, Laws of Ohio, 1835, insert table; censuses of 1830, 1840, and 1880.

rant to quadrant? Rather amazingly, the answer was essentially "no." In the southeast there was less inequality among real estate holders (G_{RE}) but the proportion of adults owning property (POP) was not as large as that in the north. The southwest did demonstrate a little more inequality in both respects, while the northern quadrants excelled especially in terms of those holding land. The two aspects of inequality can be brought together with an overall measure of inequality, $G_{All} = POP * G_{RE} + (1 - POP)$, a Gini coefficient among all adult males, assuming those without land had zero wealth.

	NW	SW	NE	SE
G_{RE}	.63	.65	.62	.57
POP	.59	.49	.60	.52
G_{All}	.78	.83	.77	.78

In the southwest, with its greater wealth per capita, there definitely was less equality than in the other three regions. Cincinnati's location in the

Chart 3 Tier Chart of Ohio Wealth Distribution in 1835
(Log Normal Probability Paper)

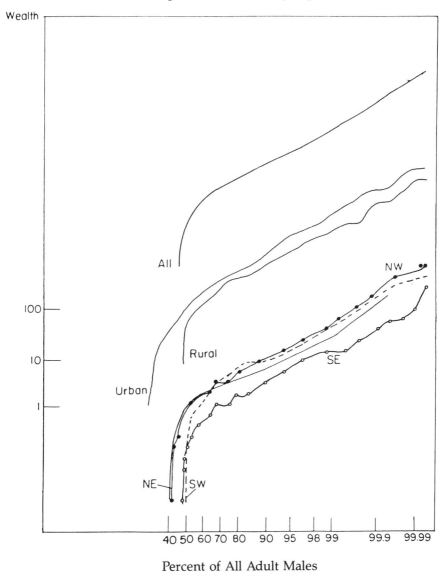

Percent of All Adult Males

southwest quadrant undoubtedly had some effect on the results, an aspect that must be investigated. Yet this region's inequality by no means was overwhelmingly different from elsewhere. The lower portion of chart 3 portrays the essential features of the lognormal distribution in all four regions.

URBANITY

TOCQUEVILLE VIEWED METROPOLITAN AREAS with some alarm. He noted riots in Philadelphia and in New York and felt that the "town population is a future if not present threat to America."[14] One wonders what his general perceptions were about inequality in urban propertyholding in America, and in Ohio, in particular. Large landowners very well may have lived in urban areas, so it is difficult to know whether he felt that inequality above the median income was greater or smaller in urban than in rural areas. To the extent that cities harbored rising middle classes, they were part of the equalization of Tocqueville's model. It was the activities of those below the median income that brought instability, actions associated with the "rabble." He apparently did not feel that property ownership extended very deeply into the income distribution.

Urban and rural distributions have been plotted in the middle section of chart 3. The lines demonstrate that inequality among wealthholders was larger in the urban sector since its slope was larger. Yet an individual at the same percentile in the urban sector had more wealth than did his counterpart in the rural sector; an exception to this statement is in the 60th to 70th percentile range where the two lines touch each other.

Ohio evidence shows that urban wealth was substantial in 1835 compared to rural wealth. Inequality also was reasonable, with greater inequality among wealthholders, but also greater participation in wealthholding in the population.

	Urban	Rural
G_{RE}	.74	.61
POP	.71	.51
G_{All}	.81	.80

Finally, we note that Ohio's four regions exhibit the relative patterns of inequality presented previously, even when classified by urbanity. The southwest had greater relative dispersion of wealth in both sectors. The evidence to this point indicates only mild corroboration, at best, of Tocqueville's model for regions and cities. The area of best soils, the most developed and the wealthiest area had greater inequality of income above the median and below it. But its pattern really was not out of line with that in the other regions, and it pointed to no possible trend in inequality over the long run.

Urban wealth distribution actually suggested that the rural-urban movement could benefit wealth positions and would not increase the plight of the poor.

COUNTIES AND TOWNSHIPS

TOCQUEVILLE OBSERVED THAT THE counties and townships were the centers of decision making in America's northern states. He was impressed with the township's activities—its commissioners, judges, and election officials; each county's coroner, recorder, sheriff, treasurer; and each region's representatives and senators in state government. Central to this direction was the electoral system, including universal suffrage. He had harsh words for the process since, in his view, it led to the choice of mediocre officials. He felt that in this way the poor dictated policy while the rich chose to seclude themselves from governmental activities.

The hypothesis concerning the status of poor and rich in a society with universal suffrage can be tested. Consider Tocqueville's strong statement, "In the United States, where the poor rule, the rich have always something to fear from the abuse of their power."[15] His assertion can be tested at the local level by examining some township records. For my test I chose the first subset available from some remarkable Ohio records for 1835. For Greene Township in Shelby County there is an extant list of its 102 white males aged twenty-one and older, as reported in its quadrennial census of that year. There is also a township list of the forty-six persons who voted in the general election of 1835 for the offices of commissioner, sheriff, representative, etc. The names on the two lists can be matched with the list of the seventy propertyholders in the township. Did the propertyless vote in greater proportions than did the propertyholders?

IN THE TOWNSHIP

	Number owning property	Number of propertyless	Propertyholder proportion
Voters	18	28	.391
Nonvoters	20	36	.357
Totals	38	64	

The chi-square test demonstrated no significant difference in proportions and really suggests that the proportions were the same. In this case the wealthy or at least those with property were participating at the same rate as other groups. A more thorough test would include the holdings of these persons anywhere in the county or state as well as an analysis of voters in other townships in Shelby or other counties.

Many of Tocqueville's grand generalizations demand statistical analyses at the local level. The proportions of persons owning land, the proportions of wealth owned by the top few landowners, are keys to understanding income, consumption, and patterns of saving in the community. In turn, these measure the possibilities of envy, leisure time, and state revenues and taxes, concepts stressed by Tocqueville. The overriding difficulty in endeavoring to quantify these patterns is the fact that there is so much variability between counties and between townships. We shall see that it is dangerous to focus on any given county, township, or village.

The Gini coefficient of inequality is the best general measure of relative inequality, varying from 0.0 if there is perfect equality, to 1.0 if there is perfect inequality. The latter is the case when one person owns all of the real estate in the area. The data of table 3 indicate the enormous range found in the state. Some areas had Gini coefficients of less than .3; others had coefficients of .7 or more. These coefficients translate roughly to the following for all townships: the share of total wealth of the top 1 percent of propertyholders varied between 4 percent and 19 percent; the share of the top 10 percent varied between 23 percent and 57 percent. (These are the ownership proportions using lognormal assumptions and G levels of .3 and .7, as stated in the last two columns of the table.) To generalize about the dispersion of wealth within townships and counties as Tocqueville did was somewhat dangerous. Certainly in some areas of Ohio, inequality was of the same magnitude as that existing in aristocratic strongholds in Europe.

TABLE 3

Gini coefficients of the Distributions of Real Estate Among Holders
in Counties, Townships, and Urban Areas in Ohio in 1835

Gini coefficient	Counties	Townships All 50 or more holders	Villages, towns, and cities	Share of all wealth[a] of top 1%	of top 10%
.90 and up	–	1	1	–	50%	85%
.80–.89	–	8	3	8	30	70
.70–.79	2	52	42	48	19	57
.60–.69	25	157	137	175	13	46
.50–.59	30	351	336	267	8	37
.40–.49	15	323	297	139	6	29
.30–.39	1	157	110	47	4	23
.20–.29	–	34	11	20	2	18
.10–.19	–	15	1	11	1.5	13
.00–.09	–	25	–	46	1	10
Number of areas	73	1,123	938	760		
Average G	.572	.489	.514	.513		
Average number of holders	1,901	136	158	36		

a. The share of wealth is obtained from lognormal tables classified by G; thus, the lognormal table with G = .9 shows the top 10% with 85% of wealth.

Our French nobleman bemoaned the fact that America's equality was synonymous with mediocrity, that it led to low cultural creativity and resulted in a society of drab uniformity in its activities.[16] He failed to understand that equality under conditions of high per capita wealth would produce an educational system paving the way for creative activity. The Ohio school system was to expand greatly in succeeding decades, with the time after the 1830s being the beginning of the take-off period.[17]

Let us look at but one aspect, the relationship between illiteracy and ownership participation at the county level. Consider the regression equation.

$$ILL = .142 - .133 \text{ POP}, \quad N = 73 \text{ counties and } R^2 = .07 \text{ (standard}$$
$$(.057)$$

error in parentheses), and where ILL is the proportion of adult whites who were unable to read and write, as reported by the census of 1840; POP is the ratio of the number of property owners to the population of white males aged twenty and older in 1835. Counties with higher participation had lower illiteracy rates. Wealth allowed greater literacy and would make it possible for cultural participation by a broader mass of society. Importantly, school attendance by children in 1840 was positively related to POP in 1835. This type of equality would ultimately lead to cultural levels of significance for a broad spectrum of Ohio's citizens. Per capita wealth also played its part, being inversely related to illiteracy and positively related to school attendance.

AN OHIO-ILLINOIS MATCH

THE PROPERTY OF OHIOANS in their state in 1835 is but part of an unfolding story of property acquisition. Their wealth in Ohio and in other states in 1850 and 1860 was considerably larger than the figures in table 1 for 1835, an aspect to be reported later using data from a small sample of 139 persons. Yet another dimension involving one hundred thousand to two hundred thousand cases can be derived from matching the names from the set for Ohio in 1835 with the available list of names of persons receiving land grants in Illinois in the period from 1814 to the 1870s. To determine how many Ohio propertyholders undertook the ownership of land to the west is to quantify the spirit of the westward movement. An individual could take steps to acquire land and very possibly to move at least across the state of Indiana, a distance of 150 miles, or double this distance from the middle of Ohio to the middle of Illinois. Such a person or family was, indeed, part of a group that viewed its settlement in Ohio as transient or somewhat temporary. A quantification of owner mobility adds refinement to measures of general mobility of populations. It is an aspect of economic life in America that was generally absent in Europe. Stated otherwise, it was that aspect of life that introduced restlessness, the characteristic described by Tocqueville in the introduction of this paper.

A spectacular example of movement of an individual and his resources from the one state to the other occurred in the case of Michael Sullivant. His father, Lucas Sullivant (1765–1823) was the largest landowner in 1810, owning 41,459 acres, or 1 percent of Ohio's land in private ownership.[18] One of his sons, Michael (1808–79), was listed in 1835 as owning $48,356 in property located in Ohio, enough to place him twenty-sixth among the 109,373 wealth aggregates collated for the state. Sullivant began early to accumulate acreage in Illinois, and ultimately he obtained 64,427 acres from 667 entries for land grants. Apparently he moved to Illinois in the 1850s, having sold all of his properties in Ohio. In the 1870 federal census he is listed in Sullivant Township, Ford County, Illinois, as having one million dollars in real estate and seven hundred thousand dollars in personal estate.

The matching of names from Ohio lists for 109,373 or 138,785 persons with names of 177,712 in Illinois is a process fraught with danger. In the absence of a genealogical study, one never knows whether the matched names are indeed for the same persons. The Sullivant name is unique because of its last letter. In addition, the family was well known, so properties were easy to trace. Such names as Lyman Truman or Timothy Guard probably were unique, and I have included them even though each had very sizeable grants in Illinois and owned very little in Ohio. In other cases the reverse was true; thus, Ambrose White had a value of $17,690 in Ohio and only 160 acres in Illinois. How does one decide when a name is uncommon? I used a rather drastic measure in eliminating common names before matching. If the person or name appeared in more than one county in the Ohio tax list, he or it was deleted from the matched list in creating the subset of uncommon or unique names.

A surprising proportion of propertyholders, 10.5 percent of the 96,106 uncommon names, were found in Illinois. This estimate is not necessarily an overstatement since I required full matching for all letters stated in the name; thus T. Guard in Illinois would not be a match with Timothy Guard in Ohio. A separate check was made using the 785 names reported in Ohio

	OHIO			ILLINOIS	
Value	Number		Acres	Number
$10,000 and up	14		10,000 and up	6
1,000–9,999	958		1,000–9,999	397
100– 999	6,828		100– 999	6,229
10– 99	146		10– 99	3,473
1– 9	184		1– 9	24
	10,130			10,130
Mean	$446			302 acres
Inequality, G	.595			.595

in 1835 not appearing more than once in the 1830 census of Ohio; 10.9 percent of these had received land grants in Illinois.

There was little or no correlation between the size of holdings in the one area and in the other, partly due to the lapse in time involved in the process of resource relocation. Some large owners in the one state owned very little in the other. A significant finding is that the relative dispersion of holdings in the matched samples was similar in both states. In this broad sense, Ohio's inequality was being transferred to Illinois. The range in economic condition had forces helping to create the same relative dispersion in the westward movement within the Northwest Territory. The mean and inequality for Ohio are not out of line with those given in table 1 for all persons, considering the fact that individuals with intercounty holdings have been eliminated.

DEMOGRAPHIC DIMENSIONS

I HAVE ATTEMPTED TO obtain additional detailed information about the future status of a small sample of propertyholders in Ohio from a search of other Ohio records. The 1835 owners can not be classified by age, education, or occupation except as they can be found in the censuses for 1830 and 1840, and particularly for 1850. A sample of 139 wealthholders was drawn by choosing each 1,000th person from the list of county-collated wealthholders, arrayed by wealth. Of the sample of 139 persons, 46 were found in the 1850 census (plus 3 obvious matches with widows or sons). The remaining individuals either died, or moved to other counties in Ohio or to other states, or were missing from the census lists for unknown reasons. The average age of the 46 was 57 in 1850 or 42 in 1835. Death rate data for Massachusetts tell us that about 30 of the 139 had died during the fifteen-year period and that roughly 63 had moved or, at least, were not living in the situs county in 1850.[19] For the sample of 139, perhaps half-again as many propertyholders moved as had remained.

The 1835 owners found in the 1850 census generally demonstrated possession of sizeable wealth and educational achievement. All male heads of families were literate, as were most wives. Children generally attended school, particularly if the parents were native born. Almost all stated their occupation as farmer. Other occupations were: blacksmith, landlord (in a town), coal digger, and cabinet maker. The age and wealth medians give some insight into their material progress.

Age	Number	Real estate median 1835	1850
34–53	18	$230	$1,300
54–70	28	290	1,580
	46	254	1,550

The familiar wealth-age gradient was present in both years. Wealth was clearly larger in 1850 than in 1835, but not by the factor of six, as shown. Real estate in 1850 was defined as the "total wherever owned," but in 1835 values were for real estate owned in a particular county only. Among the forty-six matched names found in 1850, there were eleven with no wealth. There was evidence of property transfer since 1835 owners with no wealth in 1850 were living in households where other members reported wealth. The scatter diagram of wealth in the two years demonstrated a pronounced positive relationship. For example, RE_{50} = \$273 RE_{35}.[39] for the thirty-five cases of persons with property in the two years. Surely propertyholders were experiencing strong increases in capital gains during this period.

ECONOMIC GROWTH

TOCQUEVILLE WAS CORRECT IN perceiving that Americans were enchanted with their record of economic growth, the improvement in their wealth positions over time. This assertion we cannot deny unless, in some way, there was no individual betterment. The results of the small sample just presented surely indicate improvement, but the data lack the authority of a large sample. Per capita growth in real estate grew 1.47 percent a year in Ohio from 1826 to 1835.[20] The demonstration of change can be achieved by matching the acreage of Ohio's tax records for 1810 and 1825 with real estate values in 1835. Individuals living in the state in the earlier period should have held significantly better positions than those who arrived later if, indeed, there had been individual betterment.

The list of uncommon names in 1835, 1825, and 1810 reveals the following averages:

UNCOMMON NAMES

	1835–1810 Match	No match		1835–1825 Match	No match
Number, 1835	2,909	93,194	Number, 1835	14,792	81,311
Mean, 1835	\$ 751	\$ 472	Mean, 1835	\$ 648	\$ 450
Number, 1810	2,909	7,949	Number, 1825	14,792	27,930
Mean, 1810 (acres)	258	273	Mean, 1825 (acres)	223	214
Average annual change					

$$751 = 472 (1.019)^{25} \qquad\qquad 648 = 450 (1.037)^{10}$$

The differences in averages between the matched and unmatched sets really reflect only age differences or residence differences. One person was, say, twenty-five years older than another in 1835 and the age gradient accounted for 1.9 percent a year; his actual betterment for the quarter-century may have been many times greater since the age gradient generally shifted upward each year. The gradient for the 1825–35 set is twice as large, reflecting persons of, say, ages forty and fifty rather than forty and sixty-five. A gradient of 3.7 percent coupled with per capita growth of 1.4 percent a year would bring advancement of 5.1 percent a year. Tocqueville certainly sensed that there would be material advancement for Ohioans.

SUMMARY

WE HAVE SHOWN THAT the distribution of wealth in Ohio in 1835 was far from egalitarian. It had about the same relative dispersion as does real estate among propertyholders in the United States today. Yet, by European standards, there was sufficiently less relative inequality in Ohio to lead to the peripatetic Tocqueville's conclusion that such egalitarianism was oppressive. Was there an inverse-U shape in the pattern of equality as suggested by Tocqueville in describing the distribution as Ohio developed? Apparently not, if one disregards the period prior to white settlement. The study of wealth distributions in Ohio from 1810 to 1870 shows little change, almost constancy. Gini coefficients of inequality for propertyholders remained between .58–.64 throughout the period.

There was a great deal of variation in the extent of ownership participation from county to county, township to township, and city to city, making it dangerous to generalize about local conditions as Tocqueville did. Nevertheless, relative dispersion in each of Ohio's four main quadrants in 1835 displayed the basic pattern of relative spread that existed within the state as a whole. This pattern was repeated further west in the Northwest Territory, as demonstrated by the matching of the names of individuals who transferred assets from Ohio to Illinois. The fact that there was inequality should not detract from the general economic growth of property values in the state. The wealth of the 1830s provided the basis for the development of schools and literacy, the condition necessary for cultural activities to transcend the narrow bounds of creativity predicted by Tocqueville as arising from equality. Surely the cultural activities of all of Ohio's classes, supported by the property values of its broad middle classes could surpass the activities of the few—those cloistered in the narrow group of great landowners in Europe.

Notes

1. Alexis de Tocqueville, *Democracy in America*, The Henry Reeve Text, rev. Francis Bowen, ed. Phillips Bradley (New York: Vintage Books, paperback edition of the 1945 Alfred Knopf edition), 1: 378, for the passage dealing with Ohio.

2. Ibid., 3, 53.

3. Ibid., 293–94, 56.

4. Lee Soltow, "Inequalities on the Eve of Mass Migration: Agricultural Holdings in Sweden and the United States in 1845–1850," *Scandinavian Economic History Review*, vol. 3, forthcoming (1987).

5. Alexis de Tocqueville, "Memoir on Pauperism," *Tocqueville and Beaumont on Social Reform*, Seymour Drescher, ed. and trans. (New York: Harper Torchbooks, 1968), 2–3, 6.

6. Tocqueville's few figures on income suggest the preindustrial curve (*Democracy*, 1: 226).

7. Relative inequality of the 785 state-collated wealth figures (with G = .601) was not much larger than that of the 845 county-collated figures (G = .593).

8. Lee Soltow, "Progress and Mobility Among Ohio Propertyholders, 1810–1825," *Social Science History* 7:4 (Fall 1983): 415.

9. Soltow, "Inequalities on the Eve of Mass Migration."

10. *Parliamentary Papers, 1854–55* 47, pp. 686–88; Lee Soltow, "Wealth Distribution in England and Wales in 1798," 69; Soltow, "Inequalities on the Eve of Mass Migration."

11. Chart 2 data are derived from the following sources: Lee Soltow, "Inequalities on the Eve of Mass Migration." The 232,817 owners of real estate are reported in Riksarkivet, Stockholm, Folder AK 26, Representations Kommitten, "Statistiska Berakningar Uprattade af Representations reformer *1846–1847; General Sammandrag of Statistiska Tabeller, meddelade af Kommiten for behandling af faragan om National representationens ombildning" (Stockholm: Kongl. Boktryckarr, 1846), Part A, pp. 13–27, and Part B, pp. 3–21. The data for Great Britain are for 23,530 persons deceased in 1829, as reported in *Parliamentary Papers, 1830* 25, pp. 243–44, and B. R. Mitchell, *Abstract of British Historical Statistics* (Cambridge: Cambridge University Press, 1962), 8–9, 12–15, 38–43. These death rates were applied to the age cohorts of the distribution of wealth of the living in the United States in 1850. The distribution for the deceased had a mean value a little over 20 percent larger than that for the living for the population of males aged twenty and older.

   Scottish data for 5,752 proprietors in 1825 are from *Parliamentary Papers, 1854–55* 47, pp. 686–87. For a scholarly treatment of distribution in Scotland in an earlier period, see Loretta R. Timperley, *A Directory of Land Ownership in Scotland*, Scottish Record Society, n.s. 5 (Edinburgh: 1976), 1–428; Loretta R. Timperley, "Landownership in Scotland in the Eighteenth Century" (Ph.D diss., University of Edinburgh, 1977), 154, 243–76.

   One Swedish riksdaler banko was converted as 1.59 American dollars, as stated in 1850 in *Senate Executive Documents*, vol. 7, no. 52, p. 178 (February 1853). The British conversion was made with the ratio 4.40/1.2, considering the above mean wealth ratio for deceased and living. The Scottish conversion was made using a rate of L1 Sc = 10 rigsdaler, considering the estimates of John Sinclair in *Statistical Account of Scotland 1791–1799* (Withrington-Grant edition), 1: 142.

12. This projection leads to an overall lognormal distribution of wealth, with a Gini coefficient of .80.

13. This statement must be treated carefully since there were proportionately more individuals in the age group 20–25 in 1835. The *real estate* data were provided to me by the Federal Reserve Board in October, 1986.

14. Tocqueville, *Democracy*, 1: 299–300.

15. Ibid., 1: 257.

16. Ibid., 2: 75–77.

17. Lee Soltow and Edward Stevens, *The Rise of Mass Literacy and the Common School: A Socioeconomic Study of the United States to 1870* (Chicago: University of Chicago Press, 1981), 105.

18. Lee Soltow, "Inequality Amidst Abundance: Land Ownership in Early Nineteenth Century Ohio," *Ohio History*, vol. 88 (Spring 1979): 136–37.

19. U.S. Bureau of the Census, *Historical Statistics of the United States, Colonial Times to 1970*, part 1, Washington, D.C., 1975, p. 63.

20. See Lee Soltow, "The Growth of Wealth in Ohio, 1800–1969," in *Essays in Nineteenth Century Economic History: the Old Northwest*, David C. Klingaman and Richard K. Vedder, eds. (Athens: Ohio University Press, 1975), 196.

8

STRUCTURAL AND IDEOLOGICAL DIMENSIONS OF LITERACY AND EDUCATION IN THE OLD NORTHWEST

Edward W. Stevens, Jr.
Ohio University

The boys and girls who cannot read must go through the world like the man on his journey. They will never know whether they are on the right road or the wrong one.
McGuffey's Newly Revised Eclectic Second Reader, 1853

INTRODUCTION

THIS ESSAY DOCUMENTS SOME of the salient features of educational reform and the structural determinants of illiteracy in the Old Northwest, particularly Ohio, prior to 1850 and the expansion of secondary education. The period preceding the great common school expansion of the fourth and fifth decades of the nineteenth century was one in which educational reformers gradually came to recognize the structural determinants of illiteracy in the United States. It was, moreover, one in which the ideological foundations for the common school revival were secured to a point that made it possible for reformers and legislators to agree on the necessity of mass public education as essential to the survival of a free people. The period preceding these decades was not punctuated by the large scale reform of common schools though the Lancasterian system, for example, showed educators the possibilities for dealing with mass education in an inexpensive and efficient way. A sense of urgency characterized some calls for educational reform, but the process of implementation was gradual and grudgingly given by state legislatures.

In the period immediately following the passage of the Constitution, the United States was a literate nation by comparison to most of Europe. It has been estimated that there was an overall illiteracy rate of 25 percent in the new nation at the opening of the nineteenth century. This overall figure, however, masked large regional and local differences. First there was a north-south vector ranging from high literacy rates in New England to low literacy rates in the southern states. This was overlaid by an urban-rural dichotomy that cut across regions. Large differences existed at the county level also though systematic county level data does not exist until 1840.[1] If we are to judge by signature counts from petitions and wills, there were large differences among various cities and counties in the late colonial period.[2]

Observers of the period were generally impressed with the educational level of Americans. They too noted great local differences, however. Thus La Rochefoucault Liancourt observed in 1795 that the people of Rhode Island were "singularly illiterate," but that most people in Connecticut and Massachusetts could read, write, and do simple arithmetic.[3] In 1796 Henry Lemoine commented of the American people, "They all read and write, and understand arithmetic." He continued: "Almost every little town now furnishes a small circulating library."[4]

In an oration delivered by John Gardiner on 4 July, 1785 in Boston, he spoke of the close relationship between freedom and the advancement of letters and science. His analysis was accompanied by the following proclamation: "In no part of the habitable globe is learning and true *useful* knowledge so universally disseminated as in *our native* country. Who hath seen a native adult that cannot write? Who knows a native of the age of puberty that cannot read the Bible?"[5]

Despite the relatively high literacy rates and the unbounded optimism of some observers, other political and academic leaders worried that levels of education were not sufficient to maintain a free republic, nor to strengthen literary and philosophic institutions to a point where they might provide a continuous source of useful ideas. The ebb and flow of optimism and incessant worry was characteristic of contemporary appraisals of advancement in scientific knowledge and agriculture, also. In both cases it was a matter of achieving a level of literacy necessary to the advancement of practice and theory. In the case of agriculture, the concern was to achieve basic literacy itself.

The basic structural dimensions of the problem of illiteracy—low population density, intergenerational persistence, scarce community resources, and low levels of individual wealth—can be seen in the expressions of contemporary observers of the westward movement. As late as the fifth decade of the nineteenth century, the *Daily Cincinnati Enquirer* ran a serial by Mrs. Sedgwick titled the "Puzzled Housewife" in which a frontier woman struggled with the education of her children. Said the protagonist: "When I know that the material wants of my family are provided for, I devote myself to the intellectual education of my children; and here, far away from schools and masters, pour into their minds the knowledge I acquired in my youth."[6] The problem was recognized also by Edward Everett. In a talk to Boston philanthropists in behalf of Kenyon College (1833), he spoke of the help needed to bring education and prosperity to the West:

> The individual settler can fell the forest, build his log house, reap his crops, and raise up his family, in the round of occupa-

tions pursued by himself; but he cannot, of himself, found or support a school, far less a college; nor can he do as much toward it as a single individual, in other States, where ampler resources and a denser population afford means, cooperation, and encouragement at every turn.[7]

In Illinois, George Forquer, an aspiring politician, also alluded to the problem of low population density. Though a strong supporter of education, his assessment of the condition of education in Illinois in 1832 was sobering. Said Forquer: "I must confess that, until our country becomes more densely populated, and less difference of opinion prevails on this subject, I doubt the practicability of preparing any coercive system of common schools which would be sustained by the people."[8] Without a doubt, the utility of both literacy and literary studies was much in dispute. Said James Hall in the *Western Monthly Magazine (1833)*: "A human being may know how to read, and yet be a very stupid fellow...Reading and writing are not magic arts; of themselves, they are of little value...and thousands of individuals with diplomas in their pockets, are far inferior, in point of common sense and information, to the common run of backwoodsmen."[9]

The realistic appraisals of Forquer and Hall illustrate well the structural obstacles and ideological resistance to the spread of schooling in the new western states. To educational reformers, the feelings of Hall epitomized the anti-intellectualism that threatened political and economic progress. Overcoming the structural difficulties of low population density and inadequate surplus wealth (individual and aggregate) was difficult enough from the standpoint of reform. To deal with anti-intellectualism required a different tact. As will be seen later, educational reformers and editors waged their campaign for expanded common schooling on grounds of utility and national and regional pride. The campaign against illiteracy thus spanned both the structural and ideological dimensions of the problem.

PATTERNS OF ILLITERACY

THE PATTERNS OF ILLITERACY that characterized the settlement of the Old Northwest were probably similar to those in the eastern states 150 years earlier. Certainly this was the case when one compares illiteracy rates among testators in the eastern regions and counties of Maine, New Hampshire, Essex County, Massachusetts, and Hartford County, Connecticut (Fig. 1) with Washington County, Ohio, one of the three largest in the state in the late eighteenth and early nineteenth centuries. (Fig. 2)[10]

The curvilinear pattern of illiteracy was part of what seems to be a common progression in the relationship among initial settlement, population dispersion, and resettlement. Like the highly literate and select group of settlers in the fourth decade of colonial Massachusetts, those coming to

FIGURE 1

Illiteracy Rates (IL) in Essex County, Massachusetts (1640–1681), Hartford County, Connecticut (1635–1729) and in New Hampshire and Maine (1641–1750)

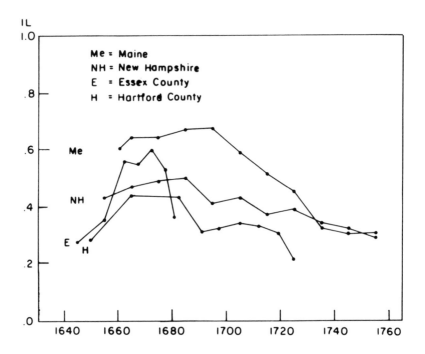

Source: From Lee Soltow and Edward Stevens, *The Rise of Literacy and the Common School in the United States* (Chicago: The University of Chicago Press, 1981), p. 35.

FIGURE 2

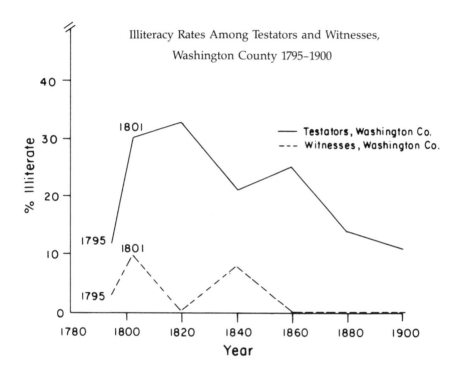

Illiteracy Rates Among Testators and Witnesses,
Washington County 1795–1900

Source: Adapted from Edward Stevens, "Literacy and the Worth of Liberty," *Historical Social Research,* 34 (April, 1985), p. 68.

Washington County in the late 1780s had a higher educational achievement than the general population from which they emigrated. Within one generation, however, the illiteracy rate had almost tripled as population dispersed, migration continued, and new communities formed, but were yet unable to sustain the initially high literacy rate of the original settlers.

As in seventeenth-century New England, the illiteracy rate among testators began to decline over three generations from its initial high point. One must remember, however, that illiteracy rates among testators generally represent educational experiences approximately thirty to forty years previous. The sharp decline in illiteracy rates among testators from 1860 to 1900, for example, represents in large part their educational experiences between 1820 and 1860. A similar trend is apparent in Army enlistment data, where a rapid decline in illiteracy rates is apparent from 1850 to 1890.[11]

By 1850 illiteracy rates among testators were far greater than in the population at large. United States Census figures show an illiteracy rate of 10 percent among whites and 5 percent among free blacks in Washington County in 1850. In the state of Ohio, the rate was 7 percent for whites and 42 percent for free blacks. The statewide illiteracy rate in Ohio in 1850 was 7 percent, but for testators in Washington County the rate was 25 percent. The rapid expansion of schooling from 1835 on no doubt pushed overall illiteracy rates rapidly downward.[12] The age bias of testator data, however, had the effect of biasing illiteracy rates upward by comparison to other data that takes the full range of ages into account. Of course, when only testator data is used, and comparisons are made over generations, then the relative increases or decreases of illiteracy rates are not affected except perhaps by changes in probate procedures.

Illiterate persons were not marginal in terms of economic activity, but they were dependent upon others for understanding the terms of basic financial arrangements. The making of a will was but one of several financial arrangements open to illiterate persons. Historical precedent tells us that the likelihood of those making wills in the lower tail of the wealth distribution was less than in the middle and upper ranges. Nonetheless, the making of a will was a common and intensely personal activity in all wealth categories. Illiteracy did not exclude a person from entering into contractual arrangements, either. There is ample evidence that illiterate persons entered into simple two party contracts, deeding, and mortgaging.[13]

In Washington County, Ohio, the same curvilinear pattern for illiterate participation in deeding is evident as it was with testators (fig. 3). Data for mortgaging does not begin until 1840 but the downward linear pattern of decreasing illiteracy from 1840 on is very close to that for grantors.

Illiteracy rates among grantors and mortgagors were generally lower than among testators, indicating a more selective and probably younger population. From 1840 on there is approximately a 5 to 7 percent difference

FIGURE 3

Illiteracy Rates Among Grantors and Mortgagors,
Washington County, 1790–1900

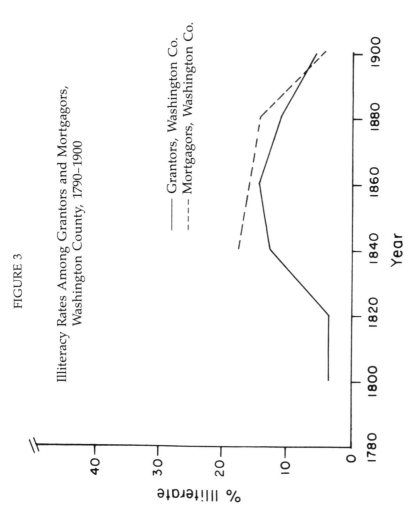

Source: Adapted from Edward Stevens, "Literacy and the Worth of Liberty," *Historical Social Research*, 34 (April, 1985), p. 68.

between illiteracy among testators and that among grantors and mortgagors.[14]

Data from testators, grantors, and mortgagors clearly shows participation by illiterate persons in these important economic activities. That this participation was also accompanied by problems and disadvantages is also evident. Courts frequently heard cases involving the legitimacy of the mark, the testamentary capacity of illiterate persons, the reliability of testimony given by them, questions involving the intent and possible negligence of illiterates, and fraudulent schemes perpetrated upon unsuspecting illiterate persons.[15]

The degree to which illiterates were dependent upon others in basic financial transactions can be gathered from analysis of data from grantors and mortgagors as shown in Table 1.

Table 1

The Dependency of Illiterate Grantors and Mortgagors in Washington County, 1790–1900

Type of Transaction	Percentage of Transactions		
	Single Illiterates	Two or More Illiterates but no Literates	Literates and Illiterates
Deeds	2	2	8
Mortgages	2	4	10

Source: Subsamples of 1924 separate deed transactions and 701 separate mortgage transactions from the sample of 2603 grantors and 1151 mortgagors from Washington County, Ohio.

As I have pointed out elsewhere, the problem was most acute for the single illiterate and those transactions having two or more parties all of whom were illiterate. We must be alert to the fact, however, that the difficulties of the illiterate person affected literate persons also since both parties were presumed to know the substance of the transaction and to have agreed upon its terms.[16]

Illiteracy and Wealth

A number of historical studies of literacy have reported a positive relationship between the dichotomous variable of literacy/illiteracy and levels of wealth.[17] For nineteenth-century United States, Soltow and Stevens have dealt extensively with the relationship of illiteracy to indexes of development, school enrollments, and wealth distributions. County level data from the manuscript censuses of 1840 and 1870, for example, show illiteracy increasing with declines in the proportion of improved acreage, cash value per acre, and capital employed in manufacturing. When school enrollments among children ages five to nineteen in 1860 are cross-classified with the wealth class of parents, increases in enrollment are found to be positively associated with wealth among age classifications ten to fourteen, and fifteen to nineteen. This was true for students of native-born parents and for those of foreign-born parents.

For children ages five to nine, there was little relationship between school enrollment and parental wealth. It would be expected that the differences were greater among older children since by 1860 mass public schooling at the primary level had become a reality. Individual wealth was still associated with literacy even by 1870. Thus, for example, only 3 percent of the illiterate persons were found in the top 10 percent of wealthholders in 1870, and 40 percent of them were found in the bottom 30 percent.[18]

Data from Ohio also show a persistent association between wealth and illiteracy. As will be evident later, they also show that the accouterments of literacy—book ownership and library membership—were related to individual wealth. Table 2 shows the relationship between deed and mortgage values and illiteracy.

Mean values of transactions for literate grantors were consistently higher than for illiterate grantors. Moreover, this difference grew larger from 1820 to 1900. A similar difference existed for literate and illiterate mortgagors. Here, however, there is no indication that the difference increased in the latter part of the nineteenth century. The overall magnitude of the differences between literate and illiterate mortgagors was slightly larger than for grantors, however. Differences between literate and illiterate grantors and mortgagors generally reinforce other findings that literacy and wealth were positively related.

Several explanations for these persistent differences can be offered though no one is probably sufficient to explain all situations. Certainly the influence of parental wealth on school enrollments was one factor. Secondly, it is known that there was a tendency toward intergenerational illiteracy so that it was difficult to break the cycle of illiteracy without some formal intervention.[20] Thus it would be expected that intergenerational illiteracy would persist under conditions where little formal schooling was available. Third, illiteracy cut off access to certain occupations, particularly those associated with upward economic mobility in an expanding urban economy. In the absence of such opportunities, the effects of illiteracy could be expected to continue across generations.

THE DEVELOPMENT OF INSTITUTIONS FOR EDUCATION

The Growth of Schooling

If the data from Washington County are any indication, illiteracy was not a bar to basic financial transactions despite the difficulties involved. Nor was

Table 2

The Mean Value and the Range of Values in Dollars of Deed and Mortgage
Transactions Classified by Year and Illiteracy for Washington County, 1780–1900

Year and Transaction	Value of Transaction				Ratio of Mean Values (IL/LL)
	Literates		Illiterates		
	M	Range	M	Range	
1790					
Deeds	401	32–1,386	—	—	—
Mort.	—	—	—	—	—
1800					
Deeds	396	20–10,000	205	40-800	1.9
Mort.	—	—	—	—	—
1820					
Deeds	380	12–4,500	369	100–1,000	1.02
Mort.	—	—	—	—	—
1840					
Deeds	401	13-4,000	294	15-1,500	1.4
Mort.	581	12-5,200	317	19-2,650	1.8
1860					
Deeds	652	15-8,000	498	20-2,000	1.3
Mort.	528	48-5,000	388	50-2,150	1.4
1880					
Deeds	863	15-8,500	530	20-2,700	1.6
Mort.	595	50-3,200	456	31-1,600	1.3
1900					
Deeds	932	20-13,000	519	25-3,400	1.8
Mort.	868	17-12,000	409	60-800	2.1
1790-1900					
Deeds	627	12-13,000	433	15-3,400	1.4
Mort.	663	12-12,000	381	19-2,650	1.7

Source: Subsample of 1060 deed transactions and 729 mortgage transactions from Washington
County, Ohio. Institutional grantors and "token" considerations of $10 and below are omit-
ted.[19]

the individual economic utility of schooling and literacy a point stressed by
most educational reformers and political leaders in the period prior to the
common school awakening. Yet the very fact of economic and political participation is what made illiteracy a major problem as seen by contemporary
observers. It was a problem that, in the aggregate, was seen in terms of both
utility and morality.

Literacy leading to practical knowledge and an increase in the aggregate
wealth of the nation was on the minds of those interested in the improvement of agriculture and manufacture. To this extent the economics of illiteracy were a concern of reformers in the early nineteenth century. Concern
with the moral dimension of literacy, however, went much deeper and was
rooted in the legacies of the Protestant Reformation and natural law theory.
The former had taken shape within the institutions of New England Puri-

tanism; the latter had persisted in the form of late eighteenth-century constitutional theory. In the late eighteenth and early nineteenth centuries the two had been wedded in the nationalism of the new American republic. The potential incompatibility of this religious/secular dichotomy, however, was not readily apparent in the pan-Protestantism of the early nineteenth century. The gradual emergence of public schooling as the gatekeeper of the national well-being eventually forced these two dimensions apart. Yet it was in this arena also that the debates over the uses of literacy were resolved. Thus by the mid-nineteenth century the purposes of literacy had become the purposes of schooling.

The actions of those who attempted to control the process of schooling and hence the process of becoming literate should be seen within the contexts of nation-building and a fervent evangelical Protestantism. We should bear in mind that these provided a foundation on which reformers could build, and that strategies used by reformers to convince the public that mass literacy was a worthwhile goal depended on these ideological foundations. The economic and political structures necessary to support schooling were thus linked to ideology though not necessarily in a linear, deterministic way.

The structural determinants of literacy and illiteracy were also recognized by common school reformers as important factors to be dealt with in the expansion of public schooling. In fact, their efforts may be seen generally as strategies to intervene and alter these factors so as to control their effects. The details of reform differed from state to state more in rate of implementation than in substance as reformers freely shared their ideas and reinforced one another's efforts.

Westward expansion in the early nineteenth century put added pressure on educational institutions to maintain levels of literacy thought necessary to the stability and progress of a free nation. In these early years of settlement in the Old Northwest, there were frequent expressions of the Jeffersonian ideal of an educated, self-governing population of individual freeholders making decisions in their own and the nation's best interests.

Freedom of the press was an important element in this formula. Religion, morality, and knowledge summed up the traditional ends of education and literacy. These had received official recognition in the Northwest Ordinance and the first Ohio Constitution. There were frequent occasions for orators to fill in the details as they saw fit. The following oration given on 4 July, 1808 in Marietta, Ohio, by Stephen Smith was part of a larger plea for national unity and the advocacy of more internal improvements:

> In order to become good citizens it is necessary that we have
> some general knowledge of the laws by which we are governed,
> that we may know how to obey them...By means of the press,

acting with such vast mechanical powers, knowledge is spreading, and ignorance, superstition and tyranny are sinking before the rising sun of reason...it is through the medium of the press that we expect to derive our information; it is the lever by which the human mind is to be raised to an incalculable height; and we have just reason to expect that our free representation will guard the rights of the press, and that the press in its turn will spread that information among the people which is necessary to preserve the rights of representation, and diffuse energy and enterprise throughout the community.[21]

The concern with education and its relationship to political and moral well-being in Ohio prior to 1820 was concentrated in Cincinnati. Small towns without newspapers had easy access to the editorials of the larger towns, however, because the mailing of newspapers was common.[22] Thus it was not difficult for readers in southeastern Ohio to read the sentiments expressed in the *Western Spy* of Cincinnati—sentiments that described education as a "companion which no misfortune can depress—no clime destroy—no enemy alienate—no despotism enslave." It was education, the piece continued, that kept man from "degradations of passions participated in with brutes" and allowed him to achieve "the dignity of an intelligence derived from God."[23]

At the other end of the state in 1818, the *Cleveland Register* in a reprinted piece on "Independence of Mind" drew its readers' attention to the Jeffersonian principle, "An ignorant unenlightened people...sunk in the shade and degradation of moral and intellectual debasement, can never be FREE." "A general diffusion of knowledge," it continued, "is the only source from which public spirit draws its essence of vitality—the only foundation of rock on which a nation's liberty can rest."[24] This rhetoric of education and freedom once established in the early period of statehood became an important element in the crusade for common school reform that followed.

Prior to the enabling state legislation of 1821 that provided for the "regulation and support of common schools," subscription schools were the most common means of formal education. Many of these were conducted in homes on a rotational basis or in log houses built as schools in more stable communities. Children were often enrolled in subscription schools by circulating subscription lists to local families. The number signing presumably determined whether or not a teacher could afford to conduct school.

Subscription schools varied in duration and size and ranged from those providing very meagre instruction in the basics to those calling themselves academies. Ads appeared frequently for these schools in the early newspapers of the Old Northwest. The few extant subscription lists indicate that fees were set by the quarter, ninety days. Some fees were also pegged to the number and level of subjects in which a child was enrolled. Thus, for example, Mrs. Williams opened a school for young ladies in Cincinnati in 1802 and charged $2.50 per quarter for reading, $3.00 for reading and sewing, and $3.50 for reading, sewing and writing.[25]

Mrs. Williams's school was a more elaborate affair than most in this early period. The records of the Muskingum Academy (1800, 1803) indicate that in these early years thirty cents was the rate for young children in schools in outlying areas or in smaller towns and cities. The approximate rate for older children who presumably took more advanced subjects was forty or fifty cents per quarter. In numerous cases children of the same family would attend on alternate days so that three, for example, might attend for the price of one.[26]

The subscription school run by Andrew Burklew in New Castle Township, Coshocton County, in 1822 cost two dollars per quarter. Burklew's agreement with the subscribers included a rate of two dollars per quarter per child to be paid "in good merchantable wheat, rye, flax, wool, lining or linsey at the common market price delivered at. . .Burklew's own house." The subscribers also agreed to supply firewood. In return, Burklew agreed to "pay due attention to the teaching of the pupils committed to his trust and instruct them in reading and arithmetic according to their abilities."[27]

Both the size of the school and the quality of teaching in academies ranged from the pretentious to the very modest. The number of academies in Ohio continued to grow throughout the first half of the nineteenth century. Figures for incorporated academies in Ohio in the two decades between 1803 and 1820 show only twelve. The decade from 1831 to 1840 showed a fourfold increase (from ten to forty-four) of chartered academies compared to the period 1821–30. Thereafter, the founding of new academies fell rapidly. Essentially the same pattern was repeated in other states though in some the peak period was between 1850 and 1860.[28]

The Campaign for Common Schools in Ohio

At the same time that the number of academies was increasing, the movement for an expanded system of public common schools gained momentum. The two trends were not necessarily in conflict, yet some tension was inevitable in the competition for the limited resources of individuals and community. More pupils attended public schools than academies, but a clear hegemony of the public school idea probably did not occur until shortly before the Civil War.

In the early years of settlement, state officials usually paid their respects to the lofty educational ideals of the Northwest Ordinance. Reluctant legislators, however, did not provide fiscal support. The rule was voluntarism. Ohio's constitutional provision for education was enthusiastic and permissive, but fiscally neutral:

But religion, morality, and knowledge being essentially necessary to good government and the happiness of mankind, schools
and the means of instruction shall forever be encouraged by legislative provision not inconsistent with the rights of conscience.
(Article VIII. 3.)

. . . . .

That no law shall be passed to prevent the poor in the several
Counties and townships within this State from an equal participation in the schools, academies, colleges, and universities
within this State which are endowed, in whole or in part, from
the revenue arising from the donations made by the United
States for the support of schools and colleges; and the doors of
the said schools, academies, and universities shall be open for
the reception of scholars, students, and teachers of every grade
without any distinction or preference whatever contrary to the
intent for which the said donations were made. (Article VIII. 25)[29]

Indiana allowed for a state system extending from township schools to a
state university, but little was done to build the system. Local incentive and
local interests dictated much of what happened with common schooling in
the early nineteenth century. In Indiana this was taken to an extreme when
in 1836 a law made it possible "for any individual citizen to hire a teacher
and draw his share of the school funds for his own children."[30] As late as
1840 the House Committee on Education reported:

We present almost the only example of a State professing to have
in force a system of common school education, which does not
know the amount, or condition of its school funds, the number
of schools and scholars taught, and to receive the distribution of
those funds.[31]

Illinois was probably better off because of a unique enabling act that, in
addition to funds derived from section 16, mandated that 3 percent of the
monies from the sale of public lands within the state be "for the encouragement of learning, of which one-sixth part shall be exclusively bestowed on a
college or university." School lands could be leased by an act of 1819. In
1823 legislation in Illinois provided for the establishment of "a common
school or schools in each of the counties. . . which shall be open and free to
every class of white citizens between the age of five and twenty-one." What
was given by one hand was taken away by another, however, when a law of
1827 declared that "no person [could] be taxed without his consent." This,
in addition to the repeal of a 2 percent appropriation, essentially put state
funding of education back where it was a decade before—in the hands of
subscription schools.[32]

In Ohio school legislation following the general commitment of the

Northwest Ordinance and the state constitution was enabling, but until 1825 had no real force. An act of 1806 provided for the election of trustees and treasurer to deal with section 16 and to "lay off school districts." But this was permissive, not mandatory. In the following years, various bills and recommendations involving the support of schools by a tax on banks, the licensing of teachers, and the "discontinuance of long-term leases of school lands" were defeated by one or both houses of the legislature or simply ignored. In 1827 and 1828, authorization was given to townships to sell school lands.[33]

In the first three decades of the nineteenth century, newspaper editors began to build some pressure for expanded common schooling. In 1818 in Cincinnati and Zanesville, Ohio, for example, they lauded Governor Brown's liberal attitude toward expansion. The column titled "On Education" appearing in the *Zanesville Muskingum Messenger* noted harshly that "legislators, born and educated under a government like ours, who will not endeavor to establish, promulgate and enforce some law for the general dissemination of, at least, what is called common school education, certainly do not deserve the confidence of their constituents."[34]

The following year in the eastern Ohio city of Steubenville, the *Western Herald* also complained, though in a milder tone, of the lack of legislative action and "hoped that our legislature will, at length, devise some practicable system for the education of all youth of the states."[35] Interstate comparisons were a common device used to prod apathetic legislators. The underfunding of Ohio schools, for example, was the subject of an early letter in the *Western Spy and Literary Gazette*:

> While other states in the union are getting to themselves lasting honors by providing the means for encouraging elementary education, we who are in greater need, are shutting our eyes to these noble examples, letting slip the golden opportunity, and suffering the rising generation to make the most gigantic strides toward barbarism that ever people so circumstanced did.[36]

The most important school law in Ohio before the mandatory legislation of 1825 was that passed in 1821 titled "An act to provide for the regulation and support of common schools." This provided for the organization of districts, annual meetings of the school committee and householders of the district, erection of a school house, levying of taxes, and the employment of teachers.[37] Much of the mandatory act of 1825 repeated or carried provisions similar to the 1821 act. In addition it provided for an enumeration of the householders, certificates of good moral character for teachers, school examiners, and a required course of study, including reading, writing, and arithmetic. Of course, other subjects could be taught if a qualified teacher could be found.

Between 1825 and 1837 (the creation of the office of State Superintendent of Schools), much of the educational legislation was concerned with the sale and lease of school lands and the administration of the common school fund. It was also in this period (1829) that exclusionary practices based on racial discrimination received official blessing. Thus in the legislation of 1829 nothing was to be construed as permitting blacks and mulattoes to attend the common schools of the state; nor were they to be taxed for such.[38]

Once reform had been achieved at the state level, the press went out of its way to encourage compliance and to urge local communities to make the most of the opportunities. In the case of the latter, editors commonly reprinted or quoted extensively from governors' messages, legislative acts, or other official reports, a practice that probably had the effect of reinforcing for the local populace the legitimacy of the public common school.

The financial and organizational guidelines established by the state legislature in Ohio in 1821 and 1825 enabled editors to give more attention to local coverage of school affairs and to urge citizens to support the efforts of reform-minded town councilmen and school trustees. Persistently, the increased concern with local school affairs brought a more careful examination of school attendance, teacher quality, and financial support. This, in turn, brought further reforms at the state level when it became obvious to reformers that some localities were unwilling or incapable of resolving these issues.

By the mid-1830s equal educational opportunity was surfacing as an issue for the press and was accompanied by the legislative debate over creating the office of the Superintendent of Common Schools. The gains of the previous decade toward a more systematic and stable structure for common schooling made the issue of opportunity even more critical. Having made the commitment and some investment as well, perhaps it became a case of rising expectations among the reform-minded. The calm acceptance that "access to a common school education is so very cheap and easy," noted by a Cleveland editorial in 1831, was replaced by an increasingly critical evaluation of the inadequacies of schooling.[39]

The creation of an office of state superintendent in 1837 signaled a major move (even though short-lived) toward centralization of control of the educational process. The Lewis Act of 1838 also reflected the emergent common school awakening of the period. By this act a township clerk became a superintendent of common schools within the township. A year later the treasurer of the township was authorized to deal with most school funds. Six months became the minimum school year, and a new, more comprehensive, school fund was created. Following the act of 1838, a statewide property tax was levied for the support of common schools.[40]

Samuel Lewis's first *Annual Report* was a careful summary of the major themes that inspired common school expansion in mid-nineteenth-century United States. Lewis was convinced by his travels in Ohio and neighboring states that the support of schools was widespread and cut across all classes. In short, he was convinced that a consensus existed in support of mass education at the primary level. Said Lewis in an essay on "The Expediency of Adapting Common School Education to the Entire Wants of the Community":

> After traveling more than eight hundred miles in the current year, expressly on this business, and conversing with men of all classes in almost every situation of life, in such a manner as to get at the sentiments of those with whom we conversed, we have found but a single man opposed to public and general provision for education.[41]

Lewis also advocated township high schools. He was sensitive to the issue of location and its relationship to opportunity.[42] By building the school at or near the center of the six-mile-square township, Lewis calculated that two-thirds of the youth would be within two miles of its doors. With very few exceptions, he said, all youth would be within three miles. Lewis argued that youth attending the high school would be ages ten to eighteen so that walking should be no problem. Even if parents did raise this objection, he said, high schools could be arranged "within every four or five mile square." Lewis did not see expense as a valid objection to secondary schooling. Funds for land and building, he thought, could be raised by subscription or a very "light tax." He was careful to note that teachers must be qualified and should be required to pass an examination.[43]

Lewis argued strongly that a high school would be a financial saving to the community. It would cost less than private academies and would be better equipped. The advantage, he said, arose from a more efficient division of labor and a reduction in per student equipment costs. He felt, moreover, that the high school would be a model of good education to be emulated by district schools. This, he noted, would "promote a healthy spirit and action among school officers and teachers."[44]

Though Lewis addressed these mundane matters, he knew, as did other reformers such as Mann of Massachusetts, Barnard of Connecticut, and Pierce of Michigan, that a larger and more ideologically forceful appeal must be made. The minimum criterion was utility. Every child, said Lewis, should receive at least enough education "to make him useful."[45] Like Jefferson before him and a long line of both conservative and progressive educators after him, Lewis saw education as a way of sorting and selecting human resources. His concern was with discovering and developing "an immense amount of human talent." Of special importance were the undiscovered "philosophers, astronomers, chemists and eminent men, in all the different sciences (who) would be found in the next generation of our farmers, mechanics, and all other professions and occupations."[46]

The first state superintendent's office was of a short duration (three years) in Ohio and reflected the conflict between whiggish efforts at centralization and local prerogatives in education. Democratic localism and a niggardly purse at the state level combined to forestall what Michael Katz has called the incipient bureaucracy of mid-nineteenth-century public schooling. Yet most of the structural features as well as their ideological correlates were present by 1840. Legislative precedents had been set for state funding, curriculum content requirements, and the organization of instruction.

By comparison to the post-Civil War decades that brought a much larger commitment of state resources, the events prior to 1840 seemed paltry. By comparison to the first two decades of the nineteenth century, however, contemporary observers must have been struck by the force of state intervention into the educational process. The entire process was incremental, however, and not of epic proportions as sometimes suggested. What heroes there were seem to have been articulate men of uncommon commitment. One must be careful in citing the importance of their precedents to future development, then, not to give a simplistic impression of a linear progression of events the telos of which was greater and greater success. It was a time of backsliding and struggle as well as exhilaration.

THE CONSUMPTION OF PRINTED MATERIAL

THE ASSOCIATION BETWEEN LITERACY and wealth found in the adult population involved in deeding and mortgaging was also evident in behaviors associated with the consumption of print. Here, however, it was a matter of the degree to which these behaviors were determined by wealth rather than the existence of a literacy/illiteracy dichotomy.

Book ownership was clearly a preferred way of investing in culture in Athens and Washington counties, Ohio, in the first half of the nineteenth century. (It must be remembered, however, that a relatively small proportion of individual and family wealth was committed to education and entertainment.) A previous study of estate inventories in these counties has shown that in the years between 1790 and 1859 book ownership as a percentage of estate inventories never fell below 34 percent and ran as high 67 percent. For other entertainment and cultural items the corresponding figures were 2.5 percent and 18.2 percent. On the basis of cultural and entertainment items listed in estate inventories, then, books far outstripped other items (such as musical instruments or art) in popularity. Still, it should be kept in mind that even with books, only 1.2 to 1.4 percent of personal estate values were committed to these items.[47]

Wealth was related to book ownership in two important ways. First, it determined the number of books owned, and second, it affected the types of books owned. As I have indicated elsewhere, "the mean estate values of those owning classical works was more than twice that of the mean for all book owners," so that "wealth and the ownership of classical works showed a strong positive relationship." Other types of books did not show a strong relationship to wealth, and the wealth/classical books relationship was strongest before 1830. To some extent it is likely that the relationship reflected the expense of these works in the first place though it is also possible that classical tastes were cultivated more among the wealthy than those of middle and low wealth.[48]

It is possible to see the effects of wealth on number of books owned by comparing the mean estate values of book owners and nonbook owners, by looking at the percent of book owners above selected wealth percentiles, and by comparing the number of books owned by those above and below median wealth values. The mean estate values for book owners above the median wealth values of Athens and Washington counties was 40 to 50 percent larger than for nonbook owners. For those below the median wealth values, the difference diminished to about 10 percent. Of course book ownership itself was less likely among those below the median wealth values of the two counties. When book ownership is looked at in relation to selected wealth percentiles, it was found that during the period from 1790 to 1859, 59 percent of the book owners were in the upper half of the wealth distribution. The two comparisons suggest that wealth was a determinant of book ownership.[49]

Among book owners themselves, the number of books owned was also related to wealth. Fifty-six percent of the inventories listing books had from one to nine of them. About 37 percent had ten to nineteen books listed. A comparison of book owners below and above the median wealth line shows that about one-third of those below the median wealth line owned only one book. It should be pointed out, however, that the majority of book owners both below and above the median wealth line had invested in three or more books. One may infer that the commitment to print as a cultural form did not usually stop with a token purchase.[50]

Private purchases were not the only type of consumer behavior affected by wealth. A study of social library membership in early Ohio also indicates that wealth played a role in this dimension of the spread of print culture. The social library was a voluntary association usually based on joint stock membership or the payment of a subscription fee. It was a popular though not a public institution in the first part of the nineteenth century in Ohio. Before that time it had been popular in New England so that between 1781 and 1790 fifty-one such libraries had been established in six New England states. In the last two decades of the eighteenth century, this number increased to 325.[51]

In a study of four of these libraries in Ohio between 1812 and 1844, "the men who subscribed to these social libraries were characterized by greater wealth than their neighbors in surrounding counties."[52] Using data from tax duplicates, it was found that the dollar value of acres owned by library members was an average of $2^1/_2$ times as great as that for the counties in which the libraries were located. The figure for personal property was almost two times as great.[53]

Despite the great wealth differences between members and nonmembers, there was a wide range of wealth among members themselves. Moreover, in the years between the second and fifth decades of the nineteenth century, there was a definite leveling of wealth among both members and nonmembers. This occurred more so among library members, however. Thus, although membership was definitely selective in terms of wealth, it is also true that men of very modest means could be members of social libraries. Membership, then, was selective, but not exclusive.[54]

The Press and Education

The absence of systematic data for those subscribing to periodical literature makes it extremely difficult to study patterns of consumption as they relate to wealth in the first half of the nineteenth century. Much of this literature was inexpensive, however, and it is likely that it reached the hands of persons across a wide range of wealth. Paper-covered books (particularly primary school texts and chapbooks), newspapers, and periodic issues such as magazines and almanacs were relatively inexpensive and available after 1830. The trade of Uriah P. James, Cincinnati bookseller and publisher, gives us a good idea of the breadth and prices of his offerings in this era.

James's trade expanded rapidly in the period from 1837 to 1846. Some of this increase was directly attributable to expanded common schooling and the need for school texts. James, however, carried a great variety of items, including religious tracts, almanacs, magazines, dictionaries, travel, biographies, and a few more expensive collected works. An entire series of Picket's school books (speller, grammar, primer, and three readers) was available at trade prices for about $2.50. The primer was about $.03 per copy, and the others went up in price rapidly.[55] Even if the markup doubled the price, $3.00 or $4.00 would probably buy the set at retail. Thus in effect the core of a common school education was available for the equivalent of an investment of about eight or nine days' work of a farm laborer in 1830 and four or five days' work for a common laborer on the Erie Canal in 1840.[56] If the books were shared among the several children in a family (which they usually were), the cost per child was substantially lower. The means to basic literacy thus could cost very little.

Religious tracts were sold at comparable prices as were almanacs and self-improvement books. If we compare Picket's primer to other books sold on the religious market, we see that prices for school books were slightly higher. In 1835, for example, the *Methodist Almanac*, a New York publication, advertised Sunday school books and Youth Library books from $.12 to $.31 per dozen. Small books used for rewards and premiums to school children were between $.15 and $.44 cents per dozen, and juvenile books from $.12 to $.20 per dozen.[57] Publishers of religious tracts developed a systematic and efficient distribution system that was probably the envy of many commmercial publishers.

The religious press literally flooded the market by the 1830s. The Systematic Monthly Distribution Plan was inaugurated by Arthur Tappan of the New York Tract Society. Though the plan initially concentrated on urban residents, its goal, and that of other tract societies, was to put a book or tract in the hands of every American. The Methodist Book Concern implemented similar goals and strategies in Ohio. An invoice of 1826 shows that such inexpensive publications as the *New American Primer, Watson's Apology,* and the *Family Advisor* were available.[58] By 1848 the Concern was printing twenty-seven thousand publications every day that year.[59]

Education for self improvement was an important aspect of developing higher levels of literacy. It would have been difficult, as now, however, to take advantage of the numerous journals and almanacs without having had a sound common school education. Almanacs were relatively inexpensive. Judging from those that did carry prices on their covers, they averaged 12.5 cents per copy in the mid-1820s. In 1844 *Uncle Ben's Farmers' and Mechanics' Ohio Almanac*, printed in Columbus, sold for 6 cents, the editor claiming to have undersold everyone.

The almanac was, in many respects, the secular equivalent of the catechism, tract, and sermon. Its inexpensiveness and its free format made it an item for popular consumption while at the same time freeing editors to deliver any special message. Almanacs certainly educated the common man and continued the famous tradition established by Benjamin Franklin: the almanac is "a proper vehicle for conveying instruction among the common people who bought scarce any other books."[60]

Almanacs were published for virtually every occasion, cause, and audience, including temperance, antimasonry, sectarian groups, antislavery, comedy, partisan politics, and progressive farming. Thus one finds such single-cause almanacs as the *Democratic Harrisonian Almanac* (1840), the *Log Cabin Almanac* (1841), *Allen's Land Bill Almanac* (1846), and those with special appeals such as the *Methodist Almanac* (1835), or *Marryatt's Comic Naval Almanac* (1837). The special messages of these, of course, were in addition to the obvious utility of such things as methods of planting, regional forecasts, medicinal and moral remedies, and simply keeping time by the position of sun and moon when a watch or clock was not available.[61]

The breadth of content in almanacs was as remarkable as it was mundane. In addition to those already mentioned, common features included the names of local, state, and federal officials and representatives, schedules of court sessions, population figures, lists of roads and mileage, significant historical dates, election returns, simple interest tables, and the ever present calendar and zodiac signs. Most of these were immensely useful and perhaps entertaining. Seldom, however, did editors and compilers rest content with these items. Theirs was frequently a larger mission involving public enlightenment and the reform of vicious habits and wayward thoughts.

The range of reading difficulty was great and frequently reflected the level of ambition of the editor to "cultivate" their audiences. When Joseph Ray edited the *Cincinnati (Freeman's, Farmer's) Almanac*, the essays demanded greater attentiveness. When edited by Solomon Thrifty (Samuel Burr) the reading level was easier. An almanac like Charles Egelmann's the *Western Patriot and Canton Almanack* clearly had a more elevated goal than most. Egelmann included extremely difficult essays on the philosophic, spiritual, and moral dimensions of education, the history of Switzerland, and religion and philosophy. Some ran in series from year to year. From 1838 to 1843 his almanacs carried a "to be continued" essay on education. Thus, over a six-year period a seventy-two page essay could be read by those with enough persistence. Egelmann's almanac was clearly considered by him to be an extension of the formal education process.[62]

The educational renaissance of the 1830s and 1840s brought with it numerous journals for diverse audiences, including literary groups, "professional" teachers, those interested in the upgrading of skills among mechanics, and reformers who sought to advance the acceptance of progressive farming techniques. Journals for these groups were a level above newspapers and almanacs both in sophistication and reading difficulty. It would be a mistake to call these journals popular, yet, taken together, they did reach enough people to form what might be called a "critical mass" for future development. Agricultural journals are a case in point.

Encouraging the use of innovative farming techniques had been a persistent problem for agricultural reformers. In an unedited version of what became a well-known essay titled "Essay on the Farmyard," Colonel George Morgan wrote of the difficulty in 1786: "I am aware that common Farmers among us, reject every appearance of expense, I may almost say, of improvement. But I hope the information of Encouragement your Society [Philadelphia Society for the Promotion of Agriculture] propose to lay before the Publick, from time to time, will evince the Necessity of a different conduct."[63]

Similar complaints could be heard much later as agricultural reformers attempted to organize agricultural societies in the new western states. As late as 1845, the *Ohio Cultivator* reported that the exhibitions of the Montgomery County society were poorly attended by the "farmers of the county." Moreover, the expense of the exhibitions was borne by town citizens. The reasons cited were those that plagued these societies from the beginning: "They were aristocratic affairs, in which the common farmer had no place."[64]

The problem of the reluctant farmer and the antipathy to "book-learning" about agriculture persisted. Illiteracy rates were high in areas of low population density, particularly among poorer farmers.[65] It was perhaps this fact that A. Fothergill implicitly realized when in 1811 he lamented the fact that the important science of agriculture "has been uniformly committed to the sole management of the illiterate part of mankind" who "have obstinately pursued a routine of random practice in imitation of their forefathers, without any settled principles."[66] There can be no doubt that in Fothergill's mind both rationality and progress were linked to literacy.

Journals like the *Ohio Farmer and Western Horticulturist*, edited and published semimonthly by Samuel Medary at a price of one dollar per year, contained information of immense importance to the farmer. Virtually every major advance in the physical sciences had implications for agriculture and was treated as such in the farm press. Editors were self-appointed advocates of agricultural reform and popularizers of the experimental methods of science in general. For them, science was the fulcrum of public enlightenment. They were practical, but they were idealists, and between the two there was no conflict.

Farm journals contained a broad spectrum of information: agricultural chemistry, soil analysis, plowing, planting, cultivation, crop rotation, irrigation, farm management, breeding, mechanical innovations, and essays on education, philosophy, religion, and advice to homemakers. Most of the technical information was not found in even advanced school texts. Thus the journals themselves shouldered the major responsibility for the advancement of technical literacy in the population in general.

This was a task made extremely difficult by the fact that most readers had little preparation to deal with such material. Those who had acquired basic literacy in school had the tools, but agricultural journals were written at a level of reading difficulty two to three grade levels above what the "average" student would have achieved. Journals attempted to offset some of this difficulty by printing vocabulary lists of technical terms. No doubt commitment and interest also played a part in overcoming the lack of preparation. Nonetheless, the linkage between preparation in school and demands made upon the reader of farm journals was tenuous.[67]

The success of the book and periodical press in promoting widespread literacy was built, in part, on the same ideological foundations as public common schooling. Yet its foundations were much broader and included responses to virtually every special interest and institution. From missionary activities to higher levels of technical literacy to entertainment, the press responded with entreprenurial zeal. Editors and publishers created markets as well as served them. Thus their efforts helped to institutionalize literacy beyond formal schooling while at the same time serving the expansionist reform of educators.

CONCLUSION

THE GRADUAL DEVELOPMENT OF mass primary education offering basic literacy and the attempts by educational reformers, editors, publishers, and legislators to overcome the structural determinants of illiteracy spanned both symbolic and functional dimensions. Symbolically, literacy was seen as the key to public enlightenment. Ideology provided the rationale for literacy by defining its role in the fortunes of an emerging republic. The role of literacy in political and economic development was seen in terms of its contribution to the stability of free political institutions, the progressive development of new knowledge, and the raising of technical literacy to a point where new knowledge could be applied on a broad scale. In short, literacy provided at least one of the pillars of the republic.[68]

At the functional level, that is, the level of an individual attribute, literacy was related to wealth and occupation. Its relationship to status and political participation is less clear in the early nineteenth century though these matters have not been treated in this essay. Findings for testators, grantors, and mortgagors show that literacy and wealth were positively related. The direction of causation is open to debate, but when coupled with the positive relationship between parental wealth and school enrollments, the implication is that wealth was the determining factor in the early nineteenth century. The direction of this relationship was gradually altered in the post-Civil War period, though, as literacy became increasingly important to upward economic mobility.[69] In either case it may be said that the nineteenth century inequalities in the distribution of basic literacy were positively related to inequalities in the distribution of wealth.

The study of book ownership and social library membership suggests that wealth affected the quality of literacy because it was a factor in determining access to printed material. That it affected access is quite certain, but, in the presence of cheap printed materials, the way it affected quality is more problematic. Almanacs and religious tracts did not demand a high level of literacy. Farm journals and manuals, on the other hand, did. It is very possible that the type of printed material consumed was more a matter of taste and/or utility than of readability. The relationships among availability, wealth, and readability are not clear in the early nineteenth century and deserve far more study by historians of literacy. Without such an effort, the degree and kind of articulation between public schooling and other educational institutions, including the press, remain unclear. At present, it would seem that articulation was ideologically strong, but functionally weak despite the best efforts of educational reformers to the contrary.

Notes

1. Lee Soltow and Edward Stevens, *The Rise of Literacy and the Common School in the United States, A Socioeconomic Analysis to 1870* (Chicago: University of Chicago Press, 1981), 39, 117.

2. Ibid., 35. Kenneth A. Lockridge, *Literacy in Colonial New England* (New York: W. W. Norton, 1974).

3. Duke De La Rochefoucault Liancourt, *Travels through the United States of America* (London, 1799), 277.

4. Henry Lemoine, *Present State of Printing and Bookselling in America*, intro. by Douglas C. McMurtie (Chicago: Private Printing, 1929), 18.

5. As in Brooke Hindle, *The Pursuit of Science in Revolutionary America, 1735–1789* (Chapel Hill: University of North Carolina Press, 1956), 251.

6. Mrs. Sedgwick, "The Puzzled Housewife," *Daily Cincinnati Enquirer*, Cincinnati, Ohio, 12 July 1842, 2:5-6.

7. As in Rush Welter, *The Mind of America, 1820–1860* (New York: Columbia University Press, 1975), 311.

8. R. Carlyle Buley, *The Old Northwest, Pioneer Period, 1815–1840*, (Bloomington: Indiana University Press, 1951), 1:328.

9. Ibid.

10. Excellent discussions of biases in probate data are given in G. B. Nash, "Urban Wealth and Poverty in Pre-Revolutionary America," *Journal of Interdisciplinary History*, 6 (Spring 1976): 545–84. D. S. Smith, "Underregistration and Bias in Probate Records: An Analysis of Data from Eighteenth Century Hingham, Massachusetts," *William and Mary Quarterly* 32 (January 1975): 100–110, and G. L. Main, "The Correction of Biases in Colonial America Probate Records," *Historical Methods Newsletter* 8 (December 1974): 10–28. The rural poor in particular in Washington County are probably underrepresented in the sample simply because severe problems of transportation and communication would have mitigated against their estates being probated. (See Edward W. Stevens, Jr., "Books and Wealth on the Frontier: Athens County and Washington County, Ohio, 1790–1859," *Social Science History* 5 (Fall 1981): 440. See Soltow and Stevens, *Rise of Literacy*, 39 for the mathematical formulation of the relationship between illiteracy and population density.

11. Soltow and Stevens, *Rise of Literacy*, 52.

12. *Seventh Census of the United States,* 1850 (Washington, D.C:. Robert Armstrong, 1853), 208–13, 810, 818, 860.

13. See Edward Stevens, "Illiterate Americans and Nineteenth Century Courts: The Meanings of Literacy," *Literacy in Historical Perspective*, ed. Daniel Resnick (Washington: Library of Congress, 1983); Edward Stevens, "Literacy and the Worth of Liberty," *Historical Social Research* 34 (April 1985): 65–81; and Edward Stevens, *Literacy, Law, and Social Order* (DeKalb: Northern Illinois University Press, 1987).

14. By law in 1795, a recorder's office was established in every county in the territory of Ohio and the conveyance of land within the territory was to be recorded "within twelve months after the execution of such deed or conveyance." The process for recording deeds was described in detail, but for our purposes the important passage is that which provides that "all deeds and conveyances . shall be acknowledged by one of the grantors or bargainers, or proved by one or more of the subscribing witnesses." ("The Laws of the Northwest Territory, 1788–1800." *Law Series,* vol. 1, *Collection of the Illinois State Historical Library,* ed. Theodore Calvin Pease [Springfield, Ill.: Illinois State Historical Library, 1925], 17:99, 197, 199). Details of the sampling procedure may be found in Stevens, "Literacy and the Worth of Liberty," 79 and Stevens, *Literacy, Law,* Appendix I.

15. Stevens, "Illiterate Americans and Nineteenth Century Courts," "Literacy and the Worth of Liberty," and *Literacy, Law.*

16. Stevens, "Literacy and the Worth of Liberty," 70.

17. See, for example, David Cressy, *Literacy and the Social Order: Reading and Writing in Tudor and Stuart England* (Cambridge: Cambridge University Press, 1980); Francois Furet and Jacques Ozouf, *Lire et ecrire* (Paris: aux Editions De Minuit, 1977); Harvey Graff, The Literacy Myth: *Literacy and Social Structure in the Nineteenth-Century City* (New York: Academic Press, 1979); Kenneth Lockridge, *Literacy in Colonial New England* (New York: W. W. Norton and Co., 1974); R. S. Schofield, "Dimensions of Illiteracy, 1750–1850," *Explorations in Economic History* 10 (1973): 437–54; Soltow and Stevens, *Rise of Literacy;* E. G. West, "Literacy and the Industrial Revolution," *Economic History Review* 31 (1978): 369–83.

18. Soltow and Stevens, *Rise of Literacy,* 128–30, 171–73, 178–79.

19. The deeds and mortgages samples from the years 1790–1840 represent 100 percent of those documents filed in the recorder's office. For the years 1860 and 1880, the sample includes 30 percent of the available documents; 15 percent are included for the year 1900. The reduction in proportion for these latter years was a simple matter of practicality stemming from the large number of documents between the years 1860 and 1900.

   Many transactions had more than one grantor or mortgagor. Some had both literate and illiterate persons as cograntors or mortgagors. Because the unit of analysis was the transaction, it was necessary in computing the means for literates and illiterates to count a transaction only once. Thus, for example, a transaction having three grantors, two of whom were literate and one of whom was illiterate, was counted once (not twice) for the literate and once for the illiterate. Likewise, a transaction having two illiterate grantors was counted once (not twice) for the illiterate category.

   Every deed transaction, with the exception of federal land grants, included some "consideration" given in return for land. Generally this consideration represented the value of the transaction. The value of the consideration, however, should not be interpreted as representing the value of the land itself. The value chosen for the upper limit of "token" considerations was ten dollars. Values from one dollar to ten dollars, therefore, were interpreted as only symbolic or having only technical significance.

   When the general pattern of considerations for deed transactions is analyzed, it is seen that the values for Washington County, Ohio, were fairly stable from 1790 to 1840. Thereafter, values increased sharply. This was true for both individual and institutional grantors. From 1840 to 1860 the increase was 53 percent for individual grantors above the ten dollar token consideration level. From 1860 to 1880 the increase was 37 percent. In the period between 1800 and 1900 adjusted values for deeds in Washington County increased approximately 70 percent for individual grantors and 89.5 percent for institutional grantors.

As with grantors, most mortgagors were individuals. The coming of banking and loan associations caused indebtedness to shift dramatically after 1890 from individuals to institutions. In Washington County indebtedness through mortgage increased gradually over the sixty-year period between 1840 and 1900. The average adjusted value of individual mortgage transactions in 1840 was $550 compared to $806 in 1900, a 46.5 percent increase.

20. Soltow and Stevens, *Rise of Literacy*, 185–88.

21. Stephen C. Smith, Oration Delivered at the Request of the Committee of Associated Mechanicks, New Meeting House, 4 July, 1808 (Marietta: Samuel Fairlane, 1808), 11.

22. Soltow and Stevens, *Rise of Literacy*, 331.

23. *Western Spy and Literary Gazette*, Cincinnati, Ohio, 3 October 1819, 2:3.

24. *Cleveland Register*, 15 September 1818, 4:2-3 as in *Annals of Cleveland*, vol. 1, no. 267 (Cleveland, 1938), 109.

25. Buley, *The Old Northwest*, 331.

26. Account of Pupils in Muskingum Academy, 1800, 1803, Manuscript Collection, VFM 21, Ohio Historical Society, Columbus, Ohio.

27. Miriam C. Hunter, *The One Room Schools of Coshocton County, Ohio* (Ann Arbor, Mich: Braun-Brumfield, 1974), 162.

28. See E.A. Miller, "High Schools in Ohio Prior to 1850," *School Review* 28 (June 1920): 454–69; George F. Miller, *The Academy System of the State of New York* (Albany, N.Y., 1922); Edgar W. Knight, *The Academy Movement in the South* (Chapel Hill, 1920); and James Mulhern, *A History of Secondary Education in Pennsylvania* (Philadelphia, 1933).

29. Constitution of Ohio, 1802. In Isaac Franklin Patterson, *The Constitutions of Ohio* (Cleveland: Arthur H. Clark, 1912), 90, 94.

30. Buley, *The Old Northwest*, 362.

31. Ibid., 327, 363.

32. Ibid., 363–64.

33. Ibid., 353.

34. *Zanesville Muskingum Messenger*, Zanesville, Ohio, 19 August 1818, 2:2-3.

35. *Western Herald*, Steubenville, Ohio, 20 February 1819, 2:1.

36. *Western Spy and Literary Gazette*, 24 November 1821, 2:3.

37. United States Commissioner of Education, *Report*, vol 1, 1900–1901 (Washington:Government Printing Office, 1902), 132, 134.

38. Ibid., 134.

39. *Cleveland Herald*, Cleveland, Ohio, 8 December 1831, 2:5 in *Annals of Cleveland*, vols. 12–14, no. 107, p. 195.

40. U.S. Commissioner of Education, *Report*, 138–40.

41. Samuel Lewis, "The Expediency of Adapting Common School Education to the Entire Wants of the Community, *Western Academician and Journal of Education and Science* 1, pt. 2 (1837–38), 526.

42. In his study of the Beverly High School Controversy in Beverly, Massachusetts, Vinovskis has stressed the importance of geography in voting patterns in the abolition of the high school (Maris A. Vinovskis, *The Origins of Public High Schools* [Madison: University of Wisconsin Press, 1985], 86–88, 104–5).

43. Lewis, "Expediency of Adapting Common School Education," 527.

44. Ibid., 528–29.

45. Ibid., 527.

46. Ibid., 528.

47. Edward Stevens, Jr., "Books and Wealth on the Frontier," *Social Science History* 5 (Fall, 1981): 424, 437.

48. Ibid., 431.

49. Ibid., 434.

50. Ibid., 436.

51. Jessee H. Shera, *Foundations of the Public Library: The Origins of the Public Library Movement in New England, 1629–1855* (Chicago: University of Chicago Press, 1949), 54–69.

52. Edward Stevens, "Relationships of Social Library Membership, Wealth, and Literary Culture in Early Ohio," *Journal of Library History* 16 (Fall 1981) :582.

53. Ibid., 283–84.

54. Ibid., 588–90.

55. Uriah P. James, various catalogs. *Uriah P. James Collection*, no. 198, Ohio State Historical Society, Columbus, Ohio.

56. United States Commerce and Bureau of Census, *Historical Statistics of the United States, Colonial Times to 1970* (Washington, D.C: Government Printing Office, 1975), 163–64.

57. *Methodist Almanac*, ed. David Young (New York: Officers of Methodist Episcopal Church, 1835).

58. *Samuel Williams Papers*, Box 15, Folder 1, Collection no. 148, Ohio State Historical Society, Columbus, Ohio.

59. John Tebbel, *A History of Book Publishing in the United States* (New York: R. R. Bowker, 1972), 1:514.

60. Lazer Ziff, *Upon What Pretext?: The Book and Literary History*, The James Russell Wiggins Lecture, American Antiquarian Society, 1985 (Worcester, Mass.: American Antiquarian Society, 1986), 14.

61. Milton Drake, *Almanacs of the United States*, "Preface," (New York: Scarecrow Press, 1962), 1:iv.

62. *Farmer's (Freeman's) Almanac*, ed. Samuel Burr [Solomon Thrifty] (Cincinnati:

Oliver Farnsworth, various dates); *Western Patriot and Canton Almanack*, ed. Charles Egelmann (Canton, Oh: various dates).

63. Draft of Colonel Morgan's "Essay on the Farmyard" submitted to the Philadelphia Society for the Promotion of Agriculture. *Records of the Philadelphia Society for the Promotion of Agriculture*, MS. vol 2, University of Pennsylvania Special Collections. When the essay appeared in the *Columbian Magazine* (October 1786): 77–82, this passage and others that reflect a sobering appraisal of the obstacles to agricultural improvement were deleted.

64. Robert Leslie Jones, "A History of Local Agricultural Societies in Ohio to 1865," *Ohio State Archaeological and Historical Quarterly* 52 (April–June 1943): 127.

65. Soltow and Stevens, *Rise of Literacy*, 39–40, 167–69.

66. A. Fothergill, "On the Application of Chemistry to Agriculture and Rural Economy," *Agricultural Museum* 2 (1811) :119. 67. The articulation of technical literacy and the literacy achieved in the public common schools of the nineteenth century is the subject of a manuscript recently prepared by the author and titled "Functional Literacy and the Common School: The Education of the American Farmer, 1760–1900." A preliminary version of this manuscript was delivered as a paper to the American Educational Research Association Annual Conference on 4 April, 1984 in New Orleans.

68. See Carl F. Kaestle, *Pillars of the Republic, Common Schools and American Society, 1780–1860* (New York: Hill and Wang, 1983).

69. Soltow and Stevens, *Rise of Literacy*, 178–80.

9.

POSTBELLUM BANKING AND FINANCIAL MARKETS IN THE OLD NORTHWEST

Gene Smiley
Marquette University

I

BY THE ONSET OF the Civil War, transportation and communications developments had largely integrated the populated areas of the United States into national markets for most commodities and resources. Though regional differences in various prices continued during the nineteenth century, these local markets were no longer isolated from events occurring in other locations. The financial markets were certainly no exception to this. But those who have examined the postbellum financial markets have found relatively large regional interest rate differentials and have concluded that the slow decline in these regional differentials suggests that some set of factors retarded the process of interest rate equalization in this period.

This study considers the role of the states of the Old Northwest in the postbellum developments in banking and financial markets in the United States.[1] The following section briefly considers banking developments in the states in the Old Northwest from 1870 through 1913. Section three examines the evidence on interest rate convergence during this period, and section four considers the alternative explanations for the observed rate convergence. Finally, section five considers the role of the financial institutions of the Old Northwest in the developments that promoted the movement toward interest rate equalization across the United States.

II

The civil war banking changes ushered in a dual banking system in the United States. The National Currency Act, as amended in 1864, led most state banks to take out a national bank charter or leave banking. By the 1880s the growth of checking accounts in conjunction with the generally much less restrictive capital, lending, and reserve requirements of the states had led to a resurgence of state chartered banking. Private banking was not as deeply affected and experienced a strong resurgence soon after the Civil War. These changes affected the states in the Old Northwest as strongly as they affected other states.[2] Table 1 presents estimates of the number of banks in these states from 1870 through 1913.

TABLE 1

The Number of Banks in The East North Central States, 1870–1913

	YEAR	NATIONAL	STATE	PRIVATE	TRUST	TOTAL
OHIO	1870	132	nd	nd	nd	nd
	1880	166	32	227	0	420
	1890	228	49	264	0	541
	1900	263	164	276	10	713
	1909	374	412	286	19	1091
	1913	379	nd	nd	nd	nd
INDIANA	1870	69	nd	nd	nd	nd
	1880	92	20	113	0	225
	1890	100	45	177	0	322
	1900	116	96	228	12	452
	1909	253	257	204	93	807
	1913	257	nd	nd	nd	nd
MICHIGAN	1870	41	nd	nd	nd	nd
	1880	79	26	140	0	245
	1890	112	106	232	2	452
	1900	81	194	255	3	533
	1909	98	335	249	5	687
	1913	99	nd	nd	nd	nd
ILLINOIS	1870	81	nd	nd	nd	nd
	1880	136	32	321	0	489
	1890	190	50	449	0	689
	1900	227	155	619	0	1001
	1909	418	389	823	42	1672
	1913	461	nd	nd	nd	nd
WISCONSIN	1870	34	17*	45*	nd	[96]**
	1880	35	30	80	0	145
	1890	65	80	110	0	255
	1900	81	137	129	7	354
	1909	129	455	7	11	602
	1913	129	nd	nd	nd	nd

Sources: The number of national banks was calculated from the annual *Reports* of the Comptroller of the Currency for the indicated years. The number of national banks is an average of the number at the call dates given in each year's report. Excluding the starred figures for Wisconsin the numbers of state and private banks and trust companies are taken from George E. Barnett, *State Banks and Trust Companies since the Passage of the National-Bank Act* (Washington: National Monetary Commission, 1911), 248 and 250.

*These figures for Wisconsin are from Richard E. Keehn, "Federal Bank Policy, Bank Market Structure, and Bank Performance: Wisconsin 1863–1914," *Business History Review*, vol. 48 (Spring 1974), 4.

**This estimate of the total number of banks is incomplete since there are no estimates of the number of trust companies, but it is likely that there were no trust companies in 1870.

nd = no data reported.

For the United States as a whole in the postbellum period, the number of state banks grew much faster than the number of national banks and surpassed the number of national banks in 1895. The number of private banks did not grow as fast, and the number peaked in 1903 or 1904 (depending on the series examined) and slowly declined after that date.[3] In general the growth of state and private banks in the Old Northwest was somewhat slower. In Ohio the number of state banks did not surpass the number of national banks until 1906, the same year as there was a peak in the number of private banks. In Indiana the number of state banks exceeded the number of national banks in 1907, and the number of private banks peaked in 1904 and dropped sharply thereafter.

In Michigan the number of national banks grew from 1870 through 1890 and then declined through 1899. This number grew again until 1910 but even then was less than the number of national banks in each year from 1885 through 1893. The number of state banks grew continuously over the 1880–1909 period, and in 1891 the number of state banks exceeded the number of national banks. The number of private banks peaked in 1904 and continued to fall through 1909.

In contrast to the virtual lack of growth of national banks in Michigan, the number of national banks in Illinois grew more rapidly over the entire period, and even in 1909 the number of national banks exceeded the number of state banks. The number of private banks also grew rapidly in Illinois and continued to grow to the end of the period for which we have data.

In Wisconsin the growth rate of national banks over the 1880–1909 period was somewhat more rapid than in any of the other four states. However, since Wisconsin had considerably fewer national banks in 1880, the total number at the end of the period is lower. State bank growth was rapid, and in 1889 the number of state banks surpassed the number of national banks. A 1903 state law effectively legislated private banks out of existence and most converted to state charters. As a result the number of state banks in Wisconsin increased dramatically between 1903 and 1904. From 1877 through 1903 the number of private banks was also growing, though not as rapidly as the number of state banks.

Many analyses have concluded that the resurgence in state banking was due to the postbellum expansion of the use of checking accounts since this allowed nonnational banks to effectively evade the prohibition (via the federal tax) on the issuance and circulation of nonnational banknotes. With the growing use of checking accounts the enticements of lower capital requirements, lower reserve requirements, and less restrictive loan portfolio requirements compared to national banks led to a rapid increase in the number of state banks.

However, John A. James and Eugene Nelson White have both raised questions as to the importance of the ability to issue national banknotes. James found that national banks prior to 1900 issued far fewer national banknotes than they could have because it was not profitable given the alternative of using checking accounts for essentially the same task.[4] White's examination of the determinants of the bank charter decision in 1908–10 found that the ability to issue national banknotes was not an important determinant.[5] By 1877, the year when we first have adequate (though not necessarily good) estimates of the number of private banks, there were a large number of private banks in all of these states. This suggests that overcoming the inability to issue banknotes, a forbidden private bank activity, was not a primary key to the recovery of state-chartered banking.

In these states the capital requirements for state banks, particularly in smaller towns and cities, was lower than for national banks. In Michigan the 1888 law reduced the capital requirement from fifty thousand dollars to twenty-five thousand dollars. In 1891 the required capital for state banks in towns of fewer than three thousand was lowered to fifteen thousand dollars and raised to twenty thousand dollars in 1899. Wisconsin, Indiana, and Ohio required a state bank to have a capital of twenty-five thousand dollars no matter what the size of the community, although Wisconsin lowered this minimum to five thousand dollars for towns of fewer than three thousand population in 1903. In 1905 the law was amended to require ten thousand dollars capital in towns of fewer than three thousand. Illinois required a capital of twenty-five thousand dollars in communities of fewer than three thousand and increased this in steps to two hundred thousand dollars in cities of over fifty thousand population. This was the same as the pre-1900 national bank capital requirements except that national banks in any town or city of fewer than six thousand had to have fifty thousand dollars capital.

These minimums were substantially less than the minimum national bank capital, though the differences were sharply reduced in 1900 when national banks in communities of fewer than three thousand could be established with twenty-five thousand dollars capital. Only Illinois and (after 1896) Wisconsin followed the National Bank Act in requiring that all capital be paid in prior to beginning operation. In Indiana, Michigan, and Ohio only 50 percent of the capital had to be paid in prior to opening the doors of the bank, with the rest of the capital being deposited within a specified time (usually a maximum of two and one-half years).[6] However, not all of the rest of the capital was always paid in within the allotted time. In Wisconsin prior to 1896, state-chartered banks could begin operation when fifteen thousand dollars of the required twenty-five thousand dollars capital was paid in, which often became all the capital ever paid in.[7] The capital requirements for state banks, both in terms of the minimum amount of capital and the amount of capital to be paid in, were the highest in Illinois. This appears to be an important part of the explanation for the relatively slower growth of state banks in Illinois (compared to national banks) and the stronger growth of private banks.

Reserve requirements were lower and/or less restrictive for state-chartered banks. Until 1887 only three states in the United States had explicit reserve requirements for state banks. Ohio required a 20 percent deposit reserve, but the reserves could be held in the form of specified bonds. This was changed to a 15 percent reserve against all deposits, but 60 percent of the demand deposit reserves could be held as balances in other banks and 73.3 percent of the time deposit reserves as balances in other banks. Wisconsin had a 15 percent reserve requirement against all deposits; Michigan required 20 percent on all deposits. In Michigan three-fourths of the reserves could be held in balances in approved banks; in Wisconsin any portion could be held with approved reserve banks. In 1910 Indiana and Illinois still had no reserve requirement for deposits.[8]

Country national banks had to hold at least 40 percent of their 15 percent reserve requirement against deposits in lawful cash (which excluded national banknotes). The remaining 60 percent of the reserves could be held as balances in national banks in reserve or central reserve cities.

There were also fewer restrictions on loan portfolios for state chartered banks. For national banks the largest loan that could be made to any individual or firm was 10 percent of the capital stock. The largest loan a state bank in Michigan could make to an individual or single firm was 10 percent of capital and surplus; this figure was 15 percent in Illinois, 20 percent in Ohio, and 30 percent in Wisconsin. National banks were forbidden to make loans on the security of real estate, though there is evidence that this restriction was legally (and illegally) evaded.[9] In contrast to this, the restrictions on the mortgage lending of state banks in the states of the Old Northwest were considerably weaker. In Michigan the bank's directors had to approve the extent of such loans with a limit of 50 percent of the total assets of the bank. In Wisconsin the limit was 50 percent of the bank's capital, surplus, and deposits. Indiana and Illinois had no explicit restrictions.[10]

The result was that the chartering of a state bank was considerably more attractive than the chartering of a national bank, particularly in the smaller towns or cities.[11] Walter Dunham argued that Michigan's 1888 general bank act was directly responsible for the rapid growth of state banks there. That act provided for the charging off of bad paper within specified periods, bank examinations, and separate savings and commercial departments so that the state banks could make investments as well as commercial loans. According to Dunham this offset the banknote monopoly of national banks. However, one could argue that the dramatic decline of the minimum capital requirements from fifty thousand dollars to twenty-five thousand dollars with the passage of the 1888 act certainly was as important if not a more important factor in the growth of state banks in Michigan.[12]

The importance of real estate lending to state banks can also be illustrated. Until 1902 in Wisconsin and 1908 in Michigan and past 1909 in Illinois, changes in the state banking laws had to be submitted to a general referendum of the population. In the general election of 1898, Wisconsin's population rejected several changes in the state banking laws. The bank examiner believed that the reason for this was that among the proposed changes was one that "would have limited loans on real estate to 33 percent of the total bank resources. This in turn would have forced many banks to liquidate a large portion of their real estate loans."[13]

Illinois was somewhat unusual in that throughout this period the number of national banks exceeded the number of state banks and there were an unusually large number of private banks whose numbers were still growing in 1908 and 1909. Because state-chartered banks in Illinois had capital requirements equal to those of national banks after 1900 (and not much different prior to 1900), private banks remained a more important alternative to national- and state-chartered banks. In addition to this, there was another factor at work in Illinois. Included in the number of private banks are not only those individuals conducting a commercial banking operation, but also all of those individuals who were commercial paper brokers and investment bankers.[14]

As the largest and most important city in the midwest, Chicago became the midwestern center of investment banking. Don Dailey reported that in Chicago in 1902 there were 141 listed private bankers and brokers most of which, he said, could be classified as "security houses." He was able to determine the functions of 91 of these "houses." Four were private commercial banks. Ten were commercial paper houses. Fifty-one were dealers and/or brokers in securities, and 26 were investment security houses and brokers. Of these, nine were branches of New York houses.[15] One of the problems with an assessment of investment banking is that the extensive, detailed data we have available for chartered commercial banking does not exist for investment banking.

Dailey's study did give some rough idea of the growth of investment banking. He found 61 firms that gave the year they were established. Eight of the 61 said they were established prior to 1880. Twelve said they were established between 1880 and 1889, 34 said they were established between 1890 and 1899, and 7 of the 61 indicated that they were established in the 1900–1902 period.[16]

Beyond this we know only the rather broad general picture of investment banking in the Old Northwest in this period. Investment banking in the United States as a whole tended to be concentrated in New York City. In the middle west, investment banking for the smaller, regional firms was concentrated in Chicago. During the great turn of the century merger wave Dailey says, "In the promotion and financing of large consolidations Chicago bankers played practically no part; almost without exception these were undertaken by Eastern houses."[17]

Though investment banking was growing in Chicago, a common concern was that Chicago bankers had little role in initiating new security issues. After the turn of the century, they became increasingly important to the eastern bankers in marketing new security issues initiated by eastern investment houses. In the 1890s Chicago's bond market was still primarily local and most of the large industrial concerns headquartered in Chicago still had their financial markets in New York City.[18]

Until 1903 commercial banks also engaged in investment banking. Fritz Redlich has argued, "There seems to have been only one city besides New York in that commercial banks undertook large scale investment banking operations during the period under investigation, namely Chicago."[19] The legal basis for national banks' investment activities grew out of a clause in the National Currency Act of 1864 that authorized banks to "discount and negotiate 'evidences of debt' in general."[20] This was interpreted to mean that national banks could deal in United States Government obligations, and then extended to include obligations of municipalities and business corporations, though not corporate stock. "For many years the Comptroller of the Currency, going still further, allowed National Banks to participate in the distribution of new securities and generally deal in securities to the extent that the banks were entitled to use them as an investment."[21]

In 1902 the comptroller ruled that national banks were not authorized to engage in broad investment banking activities. In 1903 the First National Bank of Chicago, under the leadership of James B. Forgan, developed what came to be called the "Chicago Plan," whereby affiliated trust and savings banks were chartered that could not be separated from the parent national banks and were under their control. Usually they had the same officers and same banking facilities.[22] This plan was widely copied.

If investment banking in the United States was dominated by New York City, this was even more pronounced with respect to the organized stock exchanges. The two exchanges of that city, the New York Stock Exchange and the New York Curb, dominated all other exchanges in the United States. In the Old Northwest, Chicago also had the largest stock exchange, one that grew out of the Board of Trade. The first Chicago stock exchange was organized in 1865 and closed soon after the end of the Civil War. In 1869 a second stock exchange was chartered but lasted only a few months. In 1879 the Chicago Mining Board was organized, but the activity quickly swung over to railway stocks and the name was changed to the Chicago Stock Board in 1881. A group of dissatisfied brokers formed the Chicago Stock Exchange in early 1882. Although activity was initially brisk, it fell off after 1885. In 1887 the Western Union Telegraph lines were withdrawn and the Board of Trade opened a competing stock exchange.[23]

The Chicago Stock Exchange recovered by relying upon new issues from new and existing local corporations, most importantly meat-packing firms, mail-order houses, and utilities. However, the volume of activity was never more than a small fraction of that on the New York exchanges in this period. In fact, the Chicago Stock Exchange was smaller than the Boston and Philadelphia exchanges until 1919.[24]

The other stock exchanges in the midwest in this period were even smaller than Chicago's exchange. The Cleveland Stock Exchange was organized in 1889 and primarily served firms in northern Ohio. The Cincinnati Stock Exchange was somewhat older, being formally incorporated in 1887. In its early years it specialized in the bonds of public utilities and municipalities. The Detroit Stock Exchange was the last of those created prior to 1914. Seven individuals formed the exchange in July of 1907.[25]

The stock exchanges in the Old Northwest, like Boston, Philadelphia, and the other regional stock exchanges, primarily handled firms whose issues were "originally financed by banking firms located in the region served by the exchange, or have been firms which have had their principal plants or offices in the vicinity of the exchange."[26] The regional exchanges often functioned as a proving (or seasoning) ground for security issues. If successful they frequently moved on the New York Stock Exchange, which provided greater exposure and a larger market.[27]

III

To address the question of how much and how fast interest rates across the United States tended to equalize during the postbellum period, we need appropriate local interest rates. We have good estimates of national bank loan rates by states and reserve cities from 1888 through 1913.[28] Unfortunately the evidence for earlier years in the postbellum era is far scantier. In the 1880 *Report*, the comptroller of the currency presented "commercial paper rates" in several cities in 1880.[29] Some of these rates were a range, such as 6-8 percent, and some were an average rate. For fourteen of those cities, we have estimates of national bank loan rates each year from 1888 through 1913. The dispersion of the rates for those cities was 1.83 percent in 1880. From 1888 through 1891 the rate dispersion for the same cities averaged 1.22 percent, and averaged 0.75 percent from 1911 through 1913.[30] This suggests that if rates prior to 1888 were consistently available, a trend of rate convergence would be found. Since country bank rates generally exceeded city bank rates, the trend of rate convergence for country banks would likely be even more pronounced.[31]

We can more accurately evaluate changes in interest rate variation across the United States from 1888 on. Figure 1 shows the rate dispersions for country banks by state and city banks by city from 1888 through 1913. Oklahoma had no national banks before 1891, and Oklahoma national banks consistently had the highest loan rates in the nation. Therefore, the country bank dispersions were calculated for all states excluding Oklahoma from 1888 through 1913 and including Oklahoma from 1891 through 1913.[32]

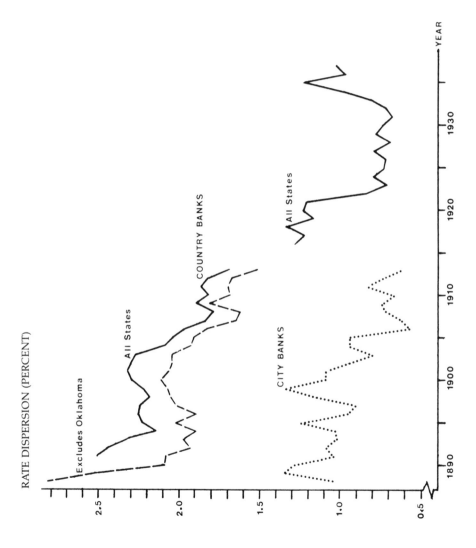

The variation in country bank rates increased in the mid and late 1890s with the depression and recovery of that decade. From the beginning of this period, 1888, through the end, 1913, there is a clear trend of rate convergence. The variation in city bank rates also shows a declining trend and much less variation than country bank rates. At the end of this period, the city bank dispersion was averaging about 0.71 percent.

TABLE 2

Estimated Interest Rates for Country National Banks, 1888–1913.

EAST NORTH CENTRAL STATES					REGIONAL AVERAGES								
YEAR	OH	IN	IL	MI	WI	ENC	NED	MAC	USE	LSE	WNC	MOU	SWT	PCT
1888	7.6	8.1	7.9	7.4	7.8	7.8	6.5	6.4	7.7	10.4	10.9	11.6	13.7	10.9
1889	7.5	8.3	8.0	7.5	7.8	7.8	6.8	6.6	7.9	10.7	10.6	11.2	14.3	10.1
1890	7.2	8.1	7.4	7.2	7.6	7.5	6.5	6.7	7.5	10.4	9.8	11.1	12.0	9.7
1891	6.8	8.2	7.9	7.2	7.2	7.5	6.3	6.1	7.5	9.9	9.2	10.9	13.4	9.4
1892	6.6	7.7	6.9	6.6	6.6	6.9	5.8	6.0	7.2	9.2	8.8	9.8	13.1	8.8
1893	6.6	7.3	6.4	6.1	6.7	6.6	5.7	5.9	7.1	8.8	8.2	9.7	12.8	8.2
1894	6.4	7.3	6.8	6.0	6.6	6.6	5.5	5.6	6.8	9.1	7.9	9.1	11.9	8.5
1895	6.7	7.7	6.6	6.3	6.1	6.7	5.3	5.7	7.2	9.0	7.7	9.4	12.6	8.2
1896	6.2	7.3	6.6	6.4	6.2	6.5	5.4	5.6	7.1	9.6	8.0	9.5	12.0	8.0
1897	6.1	8.0	6.3	6.1	7.1	6.7	5.4	5.7	6.6	9.7	8.1	9.6	11.9	7.7
1898	6.2	7.6	6.5	5.7	6.2	6.4	5.4	5.9	6.8	9.6	8.4	9.3	11.7	8.2
1899	6.2	6.7	6.4	5.4	5.4	6.0	5.7	5.8	6.8	10.1	8.3	9.2	11.7	8.6
1900	6.0	6.7	6.3	6.2	5.8	6.2	6.0	5.8	6.7	9.9	8.2	9.4	11.6	8.8
1901	5.8	6.9	6.1	5.3	5.1	5.8	6.0	5.7	6.8	10.0	7.9	9.3	11.8	7.7
1902	5.4	6.1	5.8	5.2	4.9	5.5	5.3	5.3	6.4	9.0	7.5	9.8	11.3	7.7
1903	5.2	6.2	5.6	5.1	4.7	5.4	5.3	5.5	6.4	9.1	7.4	9.5	11.4	7.8
1904	5.2	5.9	5.6	5.2	5.0	5.4	5.2	5.3	6.2	9.1	7.3	9.0	11.1	7.3
1905	5.2	6.2	5.4	5.0	4.7	5.3	5.2	5.3	6.1	8.6	7.3	8.8	10.7	8.1
1906	5.3	6.2	5.3	5.2	4.9	5.4	5.3	5.2	6.1	8.7	7.4	8.7	10.6	7.3
1907	5.6	5.8	5.5	5.4	4.9	5.5	5.5	5.3	6.0	8.1	7.3	8.8	10.5	7.1
1908	5.5	5.6	5.6	5.5	5.1	5.5	5.3	5.3	6.0	7.9	7.4	8.8	10.3	7.1
1909	6.1	6.0	5.7	5.8	5.5	5.8	5.4	5.6	6.4	8.7	7.7	9.3	10.8	7.8
1910	6.2	6.0	5.9	5.6	6.1	6.0	5.5	5.6	6.8	8.7	7.8	9.3	10.6	8.0
1911	6.3	6.1	6.0	5.8	6.2	6.1	5.5	5.6	6.6	8.7	8.2	9.4	11.0	7.9
1912	6.3	6.5	6.4	6.3	6.4	6.4	5.7	5.9	6.9	8.8	8.7	9.4	11.2	7.7
1913	6.3	6.5	6.3	6.5	6.2	6.4	6.0	6.0	6.8	8.6	8.2	8.9	11.0	7.5

Source: Gene Smiley, "Revised Estimates of Short Term Interest Rates of National Banks for States and Reserve Cities, 1888-1913," Working Paper, Marquette University Economics Department, 1976.

Regions: ENC (East North Central): OH, IN, IL, MI, WI.
NED (New England): ME, VT, NH, MA, CT, RI.
MAC (Middle Atlantic): NY, NJ, PA, DL, MD.
USE (Upper Southeast): VA, WV, NC, KY, TN.
LSE (Lower Southeast): SC, GA, FL, AL, MS, LS, AR.
WNC (West North Central): MS, IA, MO, ND, SD, NE, KA.
MOU (Mountain): MT, WY, CO, ID, UT, NV.
SWT (Southwest): OK, TX, NM, AZ.
PCT (Pacific Coast): WA, OR, CA.

The regional averages are arithmetic averages of the state rates.

Though the variation in country bank rates was falling, the 1.68 percent dispersion at the end of this period indicates that there was still considera-

TABLE 3.

Estimated Interest Rates for City National Banks, 1880–1913.

| YEAR | EAST NORTH CENTRAL CITIES | | | | | | | NEW YORK | ST. LOUIS | SAN FRAN | EAST CITIES | SOUTH and WEST CITIES |
	CINC	CLEV	COLU	INPL	DETR	MILW	CHIC					
1880	6-8	6-8	nd	nd	nd	6-8	4-7	2-3	5-7	8	*	*
1888	6.6	6.4	nd	nd	6.9	5.7	6.9	6.0	7.4	7.7	6.2	7.2
1889	5.8	6.0	nd	nd	7.2	6.6	6.7	5.4	9.0	8.3	6.1	8.2
1890	6.9	5.7	nd	nd	6.6	5.5	7.2	5.9	8.1	8.1	6.0	7.9
1891	6.0	5.8	nd	nd	6.5	5.7	7.6	6.2	6.7	8.1	5.9	7.3
1892	5.1	6.6	nd	nd	6.4	5.7	6.9	5.2	7.7	8.4	5.6	7.2
1893	5.3	5.1	nd	nd	5.8	5.3	5.7	5.0	6.1	8.1	5.4	6.5
1894	5.3	4.7	nd	nd	6.1	5.0	6.2	5.2	6.6	8.1	5.6	6.5
1895	5.1	4.6	nd	nd	6.3	5.1	5.2	4.1	6.1	7.9	5.1	6.6
1896	5.2	4.7	nd	nd	6.1	4.5	5.6	4.7	6.3	7.5	5.4	6.1
1897	5.1	4.5	nd	nd	6.1	4.6	5.4	4.7	5.9	7.5	5.5	6.0
1898	5.1	4.0	nd	nd	6.0	4.0	5.4	3.9	5.9	7.1	5.2	6.3
1899	4.4	4.0	nd	nd	5.7	3.8	5.0	3.6	5.4	7.1	5.5	5.9
1900	4.3	4.1	nd	5.7	5.5	3.8	5.0	4.2	6.2	7.0	5.5	5.7
1901	4.6	4.0	5.5	6.4	5.8	4.0	5.3	3.9	5.2	6.9	5.0	5.4
1902	4.2	3.9	5.1	5.9	5.1	4.5	4.7	4.2	5.8	6.5	4.9	5.6
1903	4.5	4.4	4.9	6.0	5.7	4.3	5.2	5.1	5.4	6.2	5.1	5.8
1904	4.3	4.9	4.6	5.5	5.2	4.8	5.0	5.6	5.1	5.5	5.1	5.7
1905	5.1	4.7	4.8	6.9	5.7	4.0	4.3	3.7	5.5	5.9	4.9	5.4
1906	4.7	5.0	5.6	6.0	5.6	5.1	4.5	4.6	5.2	5.3	5.1	5.5
1907	4.6	5.1	6.1	5.8	6.3	4.6	5.3	5.3	5.4	4.5	5.4	5.1
1908	5.0	4.9	5.7	5.7	6.2	4.3	5.1	5.1	5.9	5.8	5.0	6.2
1909	5.1	5.3	6.0	6.3	6.3	5.1	5.8	5.1	5.0	5.7	5.2	6.2
1910	5.6	4.8	6.5	5.9	6.1	6.3	5.5	5.7	5.9	5.1	5.5	6.2
1911	5.0	5.4	7.0	6.4	6.1	6.1	5.6	5.6	5.8	5.4	5.6	6.9
1912	5.2	6.2	6.9	6.5	6.2	6.3	6.2	5.8	6.4	7.0	5.7	7.0
1913	5.8	6.7	6.8	6.5	6.1	6.4	6.2	5.9	6.3	6.7	5.7	6.8

Source: Gene Smiley, "Revised Estimates of Short Term Interest Rates of National Banks for States and Reserve Cities, 1888–1913," Working Paper, Marquette University Economics Department, 1976. The 1880 rates are commercial paper rates as reported by the Comptroller of the Currency in the 1880 *Report* (Washington: U.S.G.P.O.), p. 7.

CINC: Cincinnati. CLEV: Cleveland. COLU: Columbus, Ohio. INPL: Indianapolis. CHIC: Chicago. DETR: Detroit. MILW: Milwaukee. SAN FRAN: San Francisco. EAST CITIES: Boston, Albany, Philadelphia, Pittsburgh, Baltimore, Washington, D.C. SOUTH AND WEST CITIES: New Orleans, Louisville, Kansas City (MO), St. Joseph, Omaha. The rates for the East cities and South and West cities are arithmetic averages of the city rates.

nd: no data reported.

*The reported rates for Boston and Baltimore were 5 percent (an average), 3 to 5 percent for Philadelphia, 7 percent for Washington, 4 to 6 percent for New Orleans, 6 to 7 percent for Louisville, and 10 percent for Omaha. Other rates were Richmond 7, Charleston 7-8, Savannah 8, St. Paul 8-10, Selma 9, Atlanta 10, and Denver 10-15 percent.

ble variation in country bank rates around the United States. To provide a
somewhat longer perspective on these trends, figure 1 also shows the dispersion of country national bank rates from 1916 through 1937.[33] As can be
seen, rate variation continued to decline after 1913. Following the short,
but severe, depression of 1920–21, rate dispersion fell sharply and during
the 1920s was about the same level as was the dispersions of city bank rates
during the 1908–13 period.

Tables 2 and 3 present estimated interest rates for country and city national banks in the Old Northwest and regional averages for the Old Northwest as well the other regions of the United States. Though country bank
rates in the Old Northwest were somewhat higher than country bank rates
in the Northeast (New England and Middle Atlantic states) in the late 1880s
and 1890s, by the turn of the century they were very similar. Rates of country banks in the upper southeastern states were nearly as close to northeastern rates as those of the Old Northwest. As one moved further south
and/or west, country bank rates rose sharply. They were highest in the
mountain states in the west and in the states of the Southwest. Though
country bank rates elsewhere dropped relatively sharply by 1913, rates for
the southwestern states—particularly Oklahoma—remained much higher.

The city bank rates, shown in table 3, were lower and more alike.[34] In
each state the city national bank rates were usually lower than the country
national bank rates. This was particularly so in the southern and western
states where country bank rates were considerably higher than in the Old
Northwest and Northeast. Excluding New York City and Chicago, a comparison of average city rates in the East and Old Northwest indicates that
they were very similar, with rates in the Old Northwest slightly lower than
in the East from 1894 through 1904. By the beginning of the 1890s, it appears that the city banks of the East and Old Northwest were operating in
one money market.

Tables 4 and 5 present additional information on country bank interest
rate convergence during the period. Table 4 presents country national bank
interest rate dispersions for sets of states. The New England and Middle Atlantic states were the older and most developed areas, and the financial
center of the United States, New York City, was located there. The country
bank rate dispersions were first calculated for the set of states (set A) in the
Northeast. Set B included the Old Northwest, and set C added in the states
of the Upper Southeast. Set D included the lower southeastern states and
the West North Central states. Set E included all of the other states (Southwest, Mountain, Pacific Coast) except Oklahoma, which had no national
banks prior to 1891. Set F was calculated for 1891 through 1913 and included
Oklahoma.

When only the states in the northeastern quarter of the United States are
considered (the NED, MAC, ENC, and USE regions) the rate dispersions

TABLE 4

Short Term Interest Rate Dispersions for Country National Banks
by State for Sets of States, 1888–1913.

YEAR	SET A	SET B	SET C	SET D	SET E	SET F
1888	0.38	0.72	0.77	2.29	2.82	—
1889	0.32	0.63	0.70	2.08	2.51	—
1890	0.43	0.60	0.62	1.82	2.09	—
1891	0.32	0.72	0.77	1.68	2.08	2.51
1892	0.44	0.65	0.76	1.58	1.93	2.44
1893	0.33	0.53	0.67	1.43	1.97	2.32
1894	0.21	0.60	0.68	1.56	1.89	2.14
1895	0.50	0.77	0.91	1.53	2.02	2.23
1896	0.38	0.62	0.80	1.73	1.89	2.25
1897	0.37	0.77	0.75	1.83	2.01	2.24
1898	0.50	0.66	0.73	1.86	2.05	2.18
1899	0.46	0.51	0.66	1.93	2.07	2.22
1900	0.42	0.41	0.53	1.94	2.11	2.29
1901	0.58	0.60	0.66	1.92	2.06	2.32
1902	0.27	0.34	0.57	1.71	2.04	2.30
1903	0.45	0.47	0.64	1.70	2.04	2.27
1904	0.36	0.35	0.52	1.60	1.92	2.08
1905	0.76	0.69	0.73	1.54	1.91	2.03
1906	0.72	0.64	0.69	1.59	1.87	1.96
1907	0.50	0.44	0.52	1.30	1.64	1.83
1908	0.39	0.34	0.47	1.27	1.62	1.78
1909	0.51	0.45	0.54	1.45	1.81	1.89
1910	0.43	0.42	0.61	1.42	1.68	1.81
1911	0.49	0.48	0.56	1.45	1.69	1.86
1912	0.28	0.36	0.54	1.49	1.67	1.82
1913	0.47	0.43	0.52	1.30	1.51	1.68

Source: Calculated from Gene Smiley, "Revised Estimates of Short Term Interest Rates of National Banks for States and Reserve Cities, 1888–1913," Working Paper, Marquette University, 1976. The sets of state country national banks are:
SET A: States in the NED and MAC regions.
SET B: States in the NED, MAC, and ENC regions.
SET C: States in the NED, MAC, ENC, and USE regions.
SET D: States in the NED, MAC, ENC, USE, LSE, and WNC regions.
SET E: All states excluding Oklahoma.
SET F: All states.
For the regional definitions see table 2. The dispersions are the estimated standard deviations of the interest rates.

are relatively low and much the same whether state sets A, B, or C are considered. The rate dispersions rise sharply when the lower southeastern and midwestern states are included, and rise further when the rest of the states are considered.

The trends of these rate dispersions are more easily seen in table 5, where trend coefficients for each of these sets of states for the 1888–1913 and 1900–1913 periods have been calculated. For the New England and Middle Atlantic states there is no trend of rate convergence or divergence in these periods. Very similar trends are seen whether just the Old Northwest

TABLE 5

Rate Dispersion Trends for Sets of States, 1888–1913

	1888–1913			1900–1913		
	CONST.	YEAR	R²/F	CONST.	YEAR	R²/F
SET A	–9.85	0.005	0.11	6.04	–0.003	0.01
		(1.71)	2.94		(–0.30)	0.09
SET B	23.16	–0.012*	0.44	9.84	–0.005	0.03
		(–4.35)	18.92		(–0.65)	0.43
SET C	18.98	–0.010*	0.46	11.36	–0.006	0.10
		(–4.50)	20.21		(–1.14)	1.31
SET D	42.77	–0.022*	0.43	81.97	–0.042*	0.69
		(–4.26)	18.13		(–5.19)	26.97
SET E	54.55	–0.028*	0.61	82.53	–0.042*	0.85
		(–6.10)	37.17		(–8.26)	68.18

	1891–1913			1900–1913		
	CONST.	YEAR	R²/F	CONST.	YEAR	R²/F
SET F	61.04	–0.031*	0.80	96.64	–0.050*	0.87
		(–9.17)	84.05		(–9.06)	81.99

Source: The rate dispersions in Table 8. For definitions of sets of states see Table 4.

*Significantly different from zero at the one percent level.

t-values are in parentheses.

states are included or the Old Northwest and Upper Southeast states included. Over the 1888–1913 period, the dispersion of the rates fell about .1 of 1 percent per year. Since there is no trend for the 1900–1913 period, the majority of this decline occurred during the 1890s. Including the lower southeastern and West North Central States, the rate dispersion fell 2.2 of 1 percent per year from 1888 through 1913, and for all of the states except Oklahoma the rate dispersion fell 2.8 of 1 percent per year over this period. For both state sets D and E, the 1900–1913 decline was 4.2 of 1 percent per year, indicating that rates in the more southern and western areas of the United States fell relatively faster after 1900. When Oklahoma is included (set F), not only are the rate dispersions larger—as would be expected since Oklahoma had the highest rates in the United States—but they also fell more rapidly, particularly after 1900.

The evidence on rate convergence can be summarized as follows. By 1890 city national bank rates in the Northeast (NED, MAC, and ENC) were essentially equal and city bank rates across the United States varied much less than country bank rates. Though country bank rates in the northeastern quarter of the United States (NED, MAC, ENC, AND LSE) were similar at the beginning of this period, rates in the Old Northwest and upper southeastern states were somewhat higher than in the New England and Middle Atlantic states. For the ENC and USE states, rates converged during the 1890s, and for these twenty-one states there was no rate dispersion trend after 1900 nor were the dispersions significantly different for different combinations of the twenty-one states. The rate convergence for the rest of the states was slower, with the stronger convergence trend after 1900, and the variation in rates (though declining over time) was larger the more southerly and westerly the states included.[35]

IV

Though the country bank rate differentials were declining prior to the creation of the Federal Reserve System, substantial differences remained in 1913. A number of contemporary (and later) observers explained this by a "disinclination of capital to migrate" and particularly blamed the prohibitions on branch banking.[36] Lance Davis's studies have led the way in the recent reconsiderations of the postbellum American capital market.[37]

In his studies Davis contended that the convergence of regional rates between 1870 and 1914 was due to the development of "the direct solicitation of interregional funds, by commercial bank rediscounting, and, most important, by the evolution of a national market for commercial paper." In the long-term market, Davis relied on the extant evidence on mortgage interest rates in various regions. He concluded that long-term (mortgage) rates were converging, but "the movement toward a national long-term capital market did not proceed as far or as fast as the movement toward the short term market." Rather than any single development playing a major role, as the commercial paper house did in the money market developments, he concluded, "The growth of life insurance companies, the development of the mortgage banking business, and the evolution of a national securities market all appear to have made some contribution."[38]

These assessments did not go unchallenged. In a 1969 study, Richard Sylla proposed that the observed convergence of regional bank loan rates was due to a dramatic decline in bank entry barriers.[39] He contended that prior to 1900 high capital requirements and mortgage loan restrictions restrained bank creation in the countryside leaving bankers in monopoly positions where they could restrict loan output so as to charge loan rates that were higher than opportunity cost rates. Since country national bankers could not make mortgage loans, this led to a flow of funds from the countryside into the cities to finance industrial development.

Sylla further argued that the growth of nonnational banks was retarded by their inability to issue banknotes. The Gold Standard Act of 1900 dramatically lowered capital requirements for national banks in the smallest communities (less than three thousand population) and made the issuance of national banknotes much more profitable. According to Sylla the rapid growth of national banks after 1900 reduced the monopoly power of country banks leading to a relative increase in their lending and a relative decline in the loan rates they charged.

In 1976 John A. James published two papers that also contended that the regional interest differentials were the result of differential amounts of monopoly power.[40] However, James argued that the (differing amounts of) monopoly power primarily arose from entry barriers for state and private banks. As these barriers were reduced, the increased number of banks reduced the differential amounts of monopoly power and reduced the regional interest rate differences.

James constructed a model of portfolio selection for banks in imperfectly competitive markets. Estimating this model for the country banks of each state and the city banks of each reserve city over the 1893–1911 period, he found that the monopoly power (MP) coefficients were significantly different from zero for thirty of the forty-eight states and District of Columbia, and sixteen of the twenty-eight reserve cities. However, in the western states, where the rates were initially the highest and subsequently fell the most, only four of the twelve states had monopoly power coefficients significantly different from zero.[41]

James contended, "Cross-section regressions for selected dates indicate. . .that local banking market structure or monopoly power was quite important in accounting for interstate variation in country bank interest rates."[42] In the companion paper, he examined the sources of the monopoly power. His conclusion was that the monopoly power arose from entry barriers into state-chartered banking rather than entry barriers into nationally-chartered banking. The explanation for the reduction in monopoly power lay in the passage of general bank incorporation laws in the mid-1880s in many states, as well as lowered state bank capital requirements in many of those states. This "stimulated the rapid growth of state banks after the mid-1880s."[43]

In his 1965 paper, "The Investment Market," Lance Davis used the phrase, "the evolution of a national market," which it was possible to interpret to mean that functionally independent regional capital markets had evolved into an interdependent national capital market over the 1870–1914 period as barriers to capital mobility were reduced.[44] John James had also suggested that local markets, particularly in the western states, were extremely segmented and there was not an integrated national money market.[45] George Stigler, in a classic 1967 paper, criticized Davis's study since he interpreted Davis's work to suggest that the lack of regional interest rate equality denied the existence of a national market.[46]

Marie Sushka and W. Brian Barrett extended this criticism in a 1984 paper. Noting that, "a national or integrated market does not require identical prices, but instead the existence of a behavioral relationship among markets," their examination led them to conclude that at least by the 1870s banking, short-term, and long-term financial markets formed a well integrated market, and these relationships between financial markets changed little during the 1871–1914 period.[47]

To analyze regional rate differentials and rate convergence, Sushka and Barrett constructed a model of a profit-maximizing bank that had monopoly power in its local loan market, but was a price taker in the securities market and in purchasing bank liabilities from the public. The model led them to conclude that the demand for loans, and thus the quantity of loans outstanding at banks, was a function of the loan rate and the competing rate in the securities market.[48] Their statistical examination showed that the regional loan demand changed between 1884 and 1885 for each region, and the index of stock market yields was the only rate that was significantly positive in the 1885–1914 period for all regions (except the Middle Atlantic states).[49]

Sushka and Barrett used this model to test the Davis, Sylla, and James hypotheses for the narrowing of the regional rate differentials, and all three explanations were rejected. They concluded that the narrowing of regional loan-rate differentials was due to the increasing elasticity of the corporate loan demand when the New York Stock Exchange became an alternative source of financing in 1885 with the opening of its department of unlisted securities.[50]

All of these studies have received criticism. James as well as Sushka and Barrett have argued that the empirical evidence does not support Davis's hypothesis of the role of the commercial paper market, and they both note that interest rate differentials were narrowing during the decade of the 1890s, thus refuting the main contention of Sylla.[51] On the basis of the evidence for the state of Wisconsin during the 1870–1900 period, Richard Keehn found little support for the market power hypothesis of Sylla and James.[52] Smiley has criticized James's monopoly power proxy and its significance by noting that the cross-section time series estimate of the banks per capita variable (monopoly power proxy) explained little of the variations in interest rates across states.[53] The Sushka and Barrett hypothesis has also been criticized.[54]

There are several unresolved issues. The contention is that national and state banks' loan, reserve, and, particularly, capital requirements left the banks in the very small cities and towns in relatively isolated, monopolistic positions. Country banks that would have possessed this monopoly power would have reduced their local lending, purchased more securities in the national securities market, and kept the rates they paid on deposits relatively low. There would, of course, have been no need for the monopoly country bank to borrow from its city correspondents, except in rare circumstances. Implicitly it has to be assumed the local borrowers and local depositors, having no alternative to turn to, had to pay the higher loan rates and accept the lower savings rates on their deposits.

However, it is not clear why the monopoly power of the local banks should have increased in moving south and/or west away from the eastern financial centers. Smiley found that, controlling for other variables, state country bank interest rates systematically rose as the distance from New York City increased. He also found that there was no significantly positive relationship between the share of securities in the loans and securities portfolio and the state country national bank interest rate in any years other than 1892 through 1896, 1898, and 1900 in the 1888–1913 period.[55]

The evidence also indicates a positive relationship between loan rates and deposit rates across the United States.[56] Even though the data available understate the interbank borrowing, there is evidence that this was quite common and was more important for the banks in the higher rate areas.[57] For example, in 1890 the comptroller of the currency criticized the practice of banks in high rate areas soliciting funds from individuals and institutions in low rate areas.[58] In Wisconsin the legislature considered this so important that it was written into the 1903 banking law. Anderson reports, "If the commissioner found that a bank was continually borrowing for the purpose of reloaning, he could require it to repay such liabilities. Banks were not to issue certificates of deposit for the purpose of borrowing money."[59]

Finally, most of these studies do not address the question of why significant regional differences in loan rates still existed on the eve of the opening of the Federal Reserve System, and why the differentials continued to decline through the early 1920s when they (apparently) stabilized at much lower levels.[60]

This is not to deny that some monopoly power existed. But Richard Keehn has argued that the regional and statewide measures used are inappropriate to adequately measure "the impact of local monopoly power on bank performance" because "most nineteenth-century banks operated in loan markets considerably smaller than an entire state."[61] The suggestion is that monopoly power (as indicated by higher than opportunity cost returns on bank investment rather than simply negatively-sloped loan-demand curves) was a characteristic of particular individual banks as determined by the circumstances of time and place rather than the general condition for all country banks in all areas.

The crucial characteristic of the monopoly power explanation is that the borrowers in a community did not turn to nonlocal lenders, and nonlocal lenders did not enter each of those local markets where the banks were charging relatively high loan rates and lend at lower rates. No matter how severely the entry barriers (capital requirements) limited bank entry into the local markets, the banks would not have been able to extract any monopoly profits if nonlocal lenders and local borrowers had been highly mobile. This is the fundamental source of the more inelastic demand curve presumably facing the monopolistic local banks, and to explain it we must consider the costs of transferring capital between localities.[62]

Capital owners will transfer capital up to the point where, in equilibrium, the difference in interest rates (and rates of return on capital) between the sending and receiving regions is equal to the costs of making the transaction. Richard Keehn suggests that these "transfer costs" include "transaction, information, communication, and transportation costs."[63]

John James concluded that differential risk premia "cannot be considered as a general explanation of interstate variation in interest rates." His measure of risk was the variance of the loan loss rate.[64] But this measure requires that the loss rate on loans in the various localities be known. The problem in the interregional transfer of capital was obtaining the information necessary to assess these risks. General loss rates in, say, the South or in Kansas, Nebraska, or the Pacific Coast states were not the relevant data. Interregional loans were made for specific purposes, in specific locations, to specific individuals or firms, and at specific times, and it was this detailed and continuing information flow that was necessary to determine whether to make the interregional loans and thus capital transfers.[65]

This makes it easier to understand the emphasis that contemporary observers placed upon the prohibitions against branch banking. Nationwide branch banking, such as prevailed in Canada at the time, was a relatively low-cost means of transferring loanable funds to those locations and borrowers where it would provide the greatest benefits. In this manner it tended to equalize risk-adjusted interest rates. What contemporary observers, such as Breckenridge and Sprague, understood was that in the absence of nationwide branch banking interregional lending entailed much higher transfer costs. Their discussions centered on branch banking, development of the commercial paper market, interbank borrowing, and bankers' balances, because to them it was obvious that it was much less costly for the suppliers of loanable funds or for specialized middlemen (e.g., commercial paper brokers) to handle the interregional transactions than for the individual borrowers to do this.

Lance Davis emphasized the institutional changes that arose from the disequilibrium that development created. The argument is that institutional changes arose out of the attempts to capture potential profits external to any of the existing transactions.[66]

In the late nineteenth century, the rapid geographic spread of the country and the continuing changes in the nature and locations of economic activity created substantial variations in prices. The high costs of transferring capital through the unit banking system created potential profits to capture if new lower cost arrangements were innovated to facilitate the transfer of capital. The process was not one of removing (or reducing) some monopoly barriers so that a more socially efficient equilibrium could be achieved for that given institutional structure; the process was one of developing the institutional structure.

Sprague, Breckenridge, and others argued that branch banking could have sharply lowered these transfer costs. Considering the various short- and long- term financial instruments and transactions, it is not self evident that national branch banking was the only solution, though it was certainly considered an important one, and the Canadian experience with nation-wide branch banking in this era provided support for these views.

Oliver Lockhart argued that sufficient capital mobility to "approximately equalize interest rates throughout the country" could be achieved by inter-bank borrowing as well as branch banking. And he suggested that as the branch banking debates were taking place in the post-1893 period, inter-bank borrowing was already expanding to promote this interest rate equali-zation.[67]

There were a number of methods by which banks borrowed from (gener-ally) their correspondent banks.[68] Of these methods the only ones readily identifiable were rediscounting with recourse and borrowings under the category of bills payable.[69] The other borrowings left no telltale record. Banks attempted, where possible, to conceal their borrowings due to a "general prejudice" against it since customers disliked having their notes sent out of the bank. In addition, Lockhart suggests that businessmen may have feared that the bank would not always be able to accommodate them, as well as a general worry that a borrowing bank was on the edge of insol-vency.[70] Lockhart indicates country banks borrowed more than city banks, and state banks borrowed more both relatively and absolutely than national banks.[71] New York City banks made one-third of all interbank loans, and the banks of the three central reserve cities made three-fifths of all interbank loans.[72]

At about the time Lockhart was writing, Walter McAvoy was writing about the importance of the commercial paper house and how it had tended to equalize and lower interest rates.[73] Somewhat later, Albert O. Greef and Margaret Myers reinforced this view of the role of the commer-cial paper houses.[74] In 1965 Lance Davis estimated regional interest rates in the period, found they were tending to converge, and from his study con-cluded that the commercial paper market played the primary role in this.

The developing commercial paper market was, in a sense, the demand shift that Sushka and Barrett discussed. It occurred not by having the indi-vidual firms or businessmen go to the banks in the cities and the East to borrow, but by the development of specialized commercial paper brokers and houses who could handle these interregional transfers at lower transfer costs. And this was a process of development over a period of time as the entrepreneurs (the commercial paper brokers) discovered the potentially profitable opportunities.

The developments in the long-term capital market are usually considered separately, though there is an element of artificiality in this separation. Commercial banks were the important intermediaries in the short-term commercial loan markets and the open market for commercial paper. But these banks made mortgage loans (directly and indirectly),[75] and purchased bonds and other long-term securities of railroads, state and local governments, utilities, and other private firms. And until 1903 national banks engaged in investment banking.

E. G. Moulton pointed out that a considerable amount of commercial bank lending for firm investment also took place since bankers often established a "line of credit" based roughly upon a firm's "quick" assets. The loan could then be used for fixed capital as well as working capital. Moulton estimated that the percentage of noncollateral loans used to create fixed capital was 20 percent, based on his "investigations extending over a period of several years."[76]

In the mortgage market, mortgage brokers appeared in the late 1860s and 1870s. These brokers began specializing at searching out western mortgages to place with eastern investors, and the innovations resulted in full-fledged mortgage banks by the 1880s. Davis points out that these did not survive the droughts of the 1880s and depression of the 1890s as farmers were pushed into bankruptcy. Life insurance companies were moving into this market in the 1900–1921 period and moving eastern savings to the western mortgage markets.[77]

Innovations that brought about reductions in transfer costs were also taking place in the securities markets. By the 1870s a national market for U.S. government securities and railroad stocks and bonds existed, but not for most other types of securities. As Navin and Sears have noted, until around 1890 the Boston Stock Exchange was the most important industrial stock exchange in the country.[78] But, slowly, other regional securities markets were emerging. The Old Northwest securities markets were briefly discussed above, and there were others such as those in San Francisco, Philadelphia, Baltimore, Los Angeles, New Orleans, Pittsburgh, St. Louis, and Washington. Except for Boston, Philadelphia, and Baltimore, most of these were organized in the 1880s and 1890s.[79]

As entrepreneurs innovated methods of lowering the costs of transferring the ownership of industrial securities in regional markets, the same forces were working in the national securities market, the New York Stock Exchange. The trust movement of the 1880s placed on the market an increasing number of trust certificates of these new, large firms. The growing number of these exchanges led the New York Stock Exchange to establish its "unlisted department" in 1885. As Navin and Sears pointed out, it was not until the early 1890s that "the Boston Stock Exchange lost its preeminence in industrial securities, and New York stepped into a position of leadership from which it has never receded."[80] Davis noted that it was 1914 before manufacturing securities were given equal status with government and transport issues as security for stock market loans.[81]

We propose then, that the regional interest rate differentials arose as a result of the rapid industrial development and rapid geographic growth into relatively capital poor and resource rich areas of the United States. This growth combined with the prohibitions on branch banking raised the capital transfer costs. The possibilities of profits from greater capital reallocation led to the innovation of new institutional relationships that lowered the costs of transferring capital and promoted regional interest rate equalization. The continued geographic expansion through the 1890s partially offset the tendency toward interest rate equalization arising from the capital market innovations.

These innovations in the capital markets of this era were numerous and complex and continued to occur over an extended period of time. By their nature they often did not leave the trail of data that would allow the more precise (quantifiable) evaluation of their contributions. They are not as dramatic and conveniently precise as a decline in monopoly power due to a decline in bank capital requirements or the 1885 creation of a department of unlisted securities on the New York Stock Exchange. But we cannot ignore or minimize the importance of these changes due to our inability to more precisely measure them. By 1914, when the Federal Reserve System began operation, these capital market innovations had reduced country bank rate differentials, but significant differences still remained. The city bank differences, which were initially much lower, had dropped to very low levels by 1914.

The development of the capital market innovations did not end in 1900 or 1914. Rather, they continued. Walter McAvoy, writing in 1922, pointed out that commercial paper houses and the commercial paper market had continued to develop and expand up to the time he wrote his paper. He estimated, "The volume of paper handled by the commercial paper houses in 1921 was equal to nearly 10 per cent of the loans made by the national banks of the country in that year."[82] Thus, McAvoy explained the continued trend of rate convergence by the continued development of the commercial paper market.

Oliver Lockhart argued that the rise of interbank lending in the 1869–1914 period had partially compensated for the lack of branch banking. But, it had not done so completely since the unit banking system "gave us a great number of small banks whose paper could not feed a broad discount market." He argued that it was the creation of the Federal Reserve System that led to the resolution of the problem of interbank borrowing and promoted the continued rate convergence.[83]

Finally, Lance Davis argued that developments in the formal securities markets had established a national market by the 1920s and most of the "potential external profits" from the mobilization of long-term finance had been eliminated.[84] In the short-term market, Davis suggested that the developments were insufficient to lower the transfer costs enough to eliminate rate differentials. He suggests that the growth of national firms "capable of borrowing in one market and using the funds in another" finally provided the "interregional competition" that the unit banking system was unable to provide.[85]

V

What was the role of the Old Northwest in these postbellum financial innovations that promoted the regional reallocations of capital and the tendency toward regional interest rate equalization?

In general the New England, Middle Atlantic, and, to a much lesser extent, Pacific Coast states were the areas from which capital was reallocated in the 1880–1920 period.[86] Albert Greef's work suggests that by the 1870s commercial paper dealers were operating in the larger cities of the Old Northwest, and Lance Davis suggests that the dealers then spread into the countryside, integrating the more rural banks into the market.[87] Though country national bank rates in the Old Northwest were somewhat higher than the rates in the New England and Middle Atlantic states until the turn of the century, they are essentially the same after that. This suggests that by 1900 the Old Northwest had become a capital exporting region along with the Northeast. Although speaking of the development of Chicago as a financial center, Melchior Palyi came to a similar conclusion: "The major development began when the city started on its own capital exports on a substantial scale. Before the late 1890's it was overwhelmingly a capital importer and an intermediary in the transfer of capital from the East."[88]

The roles of intermediaries in the complex regional reallocations of capital taking place during the postbellum period were important because they lowered the costs of these transfers. There is historical evidence that illustrates the complexity of these intermediary relationships between banks. The records of the Plankinton Bank in Milwaukee from 1887 to 1893 were preserved, and Theodore Anderson has examined these.

Upon opening its doors for business, the bank received a flood of letters from banks asking to serve as its correspondent. Banks in Cincinnati, Cleveland, Chicago, San Francisco, and many other cities offered to collect checks for the Plankinton Bank and pay interest on (usually some minimum amount of) balances deposited. The interest rate on balances ranged from 2 to 3 percent, and in some cases a higher rate was paid the larger the balance maintained. The fees and terms of check collection and shipment of excess balances varied by region and bank. Anderson points out the competitive nature of this process and implies that these services were provided at well below cost by the correspondent banks.[89] This is consistent with Brian Gendreau's recent analysis that the implicit return on banker's balances was at least as high as on loans due to the costly nature of the correspondent bank's check clearing and bill collection services.[90]

Anderson's examination also indicates the complexity of the process of interbank lending. The National Bank of the Republic in New York was one of the Plankinton's correspondents and discounted the Plankinton's paper. At one point the bank's president, John Jay Knox, indicated that he was unable to discount some mining paper because his bank "had, at the request of its correspondent banks, made numerous loans to the customers of those correspondents." He did say that in about two months he might be interested in purchasing some of the notes the Plankinton held of "M. A. Hanna and Company, which had an excellent financial reputation."[91]

At the same time, the Plankinton Bank was discounting for the smaller banks for which it was a city correspondent. In response to a letter from the Plankinton, the president of the Seymour Bank of Seymour, Wisconsin, wrote that at that time he did not need any notes discounted, ". . . but I may be glad to have some of your help in carrying a few of my best customers. They will want about $8,000 during the winter and spring at 8 per cent interest, out of which I want you to allow me 1 per cent, leaving 7 per cent for you."[92]

Clearly these kinds of relationships were common during the period and continued to grow in the following years. Slowly, and in a complex and costly process, the financial markets were redirecting short-term funds from the eastern areas toward the western and southern areas through the correspondent banking relationships.

By the 1890s Chicago was the second largest city in the United States, the major financial center of the central part of the U.S., and one of the three central reserve cities. Consequently, its financial development and markets have been examined in much greater detail than for any other state or city in the Old Northwest.[93] The records of the First National Bank of Chicago were preserved, and F. Cyril James examined these. In 1864, 41 national and 6 state and private banks had opened correspondent balances with the First National Bank, and it had opened accounts with two Boston, one Philadelphia, and five New York City banks. By 1873, 80 national banks in fifteen states had accounts with the First National Bank. Chicago banks' correspondent balances had increased 50 percent since 1870. By 1880, 154 national banks and 288 state and private banks had correspondent balances with the First National Bank. Though the bulk of the banks were located in the East and West North Central states, many other states were represented.[94]

James reports that by the end of the 1870s an increasing number of country banks in the central and western states were withdrawing their correspondent balances from New York City in order to place them in Chicago. From 1876 to 1886, Chicago's correspondent balances increased 250 percent. Through the late 1870s, Chicago banks had depended on New York City banks for funds, "customarily borrowing from their reserve agents by the rediscount or pledge of commercial paper." By 1880 Chicago banks were beginning to lend some "surplus" funds in the New York call-money market.[95]

Palyi reports that the estimated number of banker's balances accounts in Chicago rose from less than four hundred in 1868 to more than thirteen hundred in 1878 to over twenty-four hundred in 1889.[96] In 1890 the comptroller reported that 94 percent of the national banks had correspondent balances in New York City banks, and 31 percent of the national banks had correspondent balances in Chicago banks.[97] When Chicago's second largest bank, the National Bank of Illinois, failed on 21 December 1896, 350 banks were carrying accounts with it.[98]

The correspondent balances were important since they were the cornerstone of interbank relations. Interbank rediscountings and borrowings were often a ratio of the borrowing bank's average balances with its correspondent, and borrowing through correspondent banks was much less costly than borrowing through other banks. The correspondent banks purchased and sold commercial paper and other securities for their country bank clients. As the evidence shows, while country banks were rediscounting or borrowing from their larger city correspondents, these city banks were often simultaneously borrowing from Chicago, New York City, or banks in a few other large eastern cities.

Chicago's reliance—and perforce the whole array of correspondent bank relationships working through Chicago—upon New York City's eastern money market did not end when Chicago became a central reserve city. The balances of Chicago banks in New York City banks were not diminished a "single penny," despite the fact that such balances could no longer be counted as part of the legally required reserve." Such balances were the basis for the rediscounting and borrowing that the New York City banks allowed their correspondents. Thus James points out, "Chicago herself still looked to New York for assistance." This was in the early 1890s at exactly the time that, as he notes, banks throughout the southwest as well as northwest were looking to Chicago banks "for the extra funds necessary to meet the normal demands of business."[99]

These examples can do no more than hint at the complex, multilevel process by which correspondent banking relationships developed to facilitate—even if in a still rather costly manner—interregional flows of funds. The correspondent banking relationships provided smaller country banks with a wide variety of costly services. Watkins noted, "The advice given as to business conditions and types of investment was a matter of great importance to the smaller banker, who was often lacking in the facilities or ability to make his own analysis."[100] Watkins also pointed out that the larger city banks such as in New York City, Boston, Chicago, St. Louis, and Kansas City were more willing to make loans to firms in other regions than they would have been because "current credit information was to be had partly through correspondents located in the same section as the borrower. This was even true in part of commercial paper bought through brokers."[101] Clearly interbank borrowing and lending, directly and through the correspondent banking arrangements, and the commercial paper brokers were continuing developments that facilitated the widespread dissemination of costly information and lowered the costs of transferring capital.

In the long-term capital market, the institutions of the Midwest were also playing an increasingly important role. In the decades prior to the First World War, Howard Preston reported that Iowa mortgage dealers were selling Iowa mortgages to savings banks in Illinois, Wisconsin, Vermont, New Hampshire, and Iowa.[102] In the two decades prior to World War I, the growing number of life insurance companies located in the Old Northwest were playing an increasingly important role in purchasing western mortgages.[103]

According to Preston the growing volume of state, local, and municipal securities from Iowa were primarily sold outside the state, mainly to investment houses in Chicago which then took over the role of distributing the securities.[104] Investment banking in Chicago specialized to some extent in the origination and distribution of state and local government and public utility issues. The bond market in Chicago was still primarily local at the close of the nineteenth century, but this was beginning to change. By the end of the 1890s, the First National Bank's bond department was becoming very important in the distribution of securities originated by eastern investment houses. The First National Bank sold the securities it purchased to its correspondent banks throughout the western states. By 1904 five of the largest Chicago banks were actively involved in distributing new securities.[105] As noted earlier Fritz Redlich argued that Chicago was the only city besides New York City in which commercial banks undertook large-scale investment banking operations.[106] The First National Bank also led the way in developing methods whereby national banks could still, in practice, participate in investment banking after the comptroller's ruling against this in 1902. Thus, the banks and investment houses of the Old Northwest were playing an important role in the distribution of securities issued by large firms all across the United States.

However, this activity remained centered in New York City, and this centralization was even more extreme in the case of the formal markets for the exchange of new and existing securities. The New York Stock Exchange was a national exchange and by 1900 was expanding to become the national industrial stock exchange. The regional stock exchanges in the Old Northwest (as well as other regions) that were developing in the 1880s concentrated on local issues that were smaller and/or did not have national reputation. As Bunting and Kamm have pointed out, some of the firms listed on regional exchanges proved to be more successful and their securities were moved to the New York Stock Exchange which, as James E. Walter pointed out, provided much more prestige and exposure.[107]

From this evidence we can conclude that the banking and financial institutions of the Old Northwest played an important role in the developments occurring in the national short-term and long-term capital markets in the postbellum period. In the process of innovating new institutional relationships and intermediaries to lower the costs of transferring capital between regions (and between shifting agricultural, commercial, and industrial demands) the banks of the Old Northwest played an important role. Because these states were older and economically more advanced than other southern and western areas, they made an earlier transition from an area importing capital from the New England and Middle Atlantic regions to one also exporting capital to other southern and western regions.

The banks in the cities became relatively more important. This was especially true of Chicago, which became the "second" city in the United States. By virtue of its position, size, and importance it became the regional financial center for the entire central portion of the United States stretching from the Mississippi River to the Rocky Mountains. But the other reserve cities of the region—Cincinnati, Cleveland, Detroit, Milwaukee, and later Columbus and Indianapolis—also played important, though lesser, roles.

Short-term commercial paper was less "personal" in nature, and the lower costs of information about the borrowers led to a broader open market for these notes. The commercial loans of the banks to their commercial and industrial borrowers were much more personal in nature and entailed greater information costs. As a result these were exchanged through the complex and intricate correspondent banking relationships rather than through a broad open market. Though farm mortgages were long term in nature, they required costly personal knowledge of each of the relatively small borrowers and so lacked broad open markets. The long-term securities—stocks and bonds—of the larger corporations became the mainstays of the securities market. The best of these lent themselves to a national market, and for reasons of historical development New York City became the center of the national securities market. The securities markets of the Old Northwest were regional and limited in scope. Though their role of providing a market to exchange the securities of the smaller regional firms was important, they were clearly subsidiary to the national long-term securities market.

Though the banks of the Old Northwest played an important role in these capital market processes and developments, no individual bank or banks of an individual city played a crucial role. The process of the interregional reallocation of capital through the capital markets was a complex process requiring the participation of many banks in many regions at many levels. Though the role of the Old Northwest banks switched from capital importer to capital exporter, it is extremely doubtful whether, in some counterfactual sense, the interregional capital reallocation would not have occurred if the Old Northwest banks had not participated. Market processes would still have been innovated to promote the transfers as long as potential benefits existed.

Notes

1. Antebellum banking developments in the Old Northwest have been examined elsewhere. See Donald R. Adams, Jr., "The Role of Banks In the Economic Development of the Old Northwest," *Essays in Nineteenth Century Economic History: The Old Northwest,* David C. Klingaman and Richard K. Vedder, eds., (Athens: Ohio University Press, 1975).

2. Though a number of state banking histories for the antebellum period exist there are fewer for the postbellum period. For Wisconsin, Leonard Krueger's study concentrates somewhat more on the antebellum period; Theodore Anderson's book provides more coverage of the postbellum years and the twentieth century (Theodore A. Anderson, *A Century of Banking in Wisconsin* [Madison: State Historical Society of Wisconsin, 1954]; Leonard B. Krueger, *History of Commercial Banking in Wisconsin* [Madison: University of Wisconsin Press, 1933]). For Illinois, volume 1 of Francis Murray Huston's study covers banking developments, though, as one would suspect, considerable emphasis is placed on developments in Chicago (Francis Murray Huston, *Financing an Empire: A History of Banking in Illinois,* 3 volumes [Chicago: The S. J. Clarke Publishing Company, 1926]). Chicago banking developments are covered thoroughly in F. Cyril James's two volume work, and the development of the outlying Chicago banks is briefly covered in E. N. Baty's study (F. Cyril James, *The Growth of Chicago Banks,* 2 volumes [New York: Harper and Brothers, 1938]; E. N. Baty, *The Story of the Outlying Banks of Chicago Chicago:* [Chicago and Cook County Bankers Association, 1924]. There are no studies of postbellum banking in Indiana. Though the title of Logan Esarey's study indicates that it extends to 1873, it does not extend past the Civil War. (Logan Esarey, "State Banking in Indiana, 1814–1873," *Indiana University Studies: Contributions to Knowledge Made by Instructors and Advanced Students of the University* (Bloomington, Ind.: Published by the University, 1913] 1:219–305). I was unable to locate any studies of postbellum banking in Ohio. There are two studies of postbellum banking in Michigan. T. N. Hinchman's 1887 study is primarily on the antebellum era though it does extend up to 1887. W. L. Dunham's 1929 study is superficial and primarily a promotional effort (W. L. Dunham, *Banking and Industry in Michigan* [Detroit 1929]; T. N. Hinchman, *Banks and Banking in Michigan* [Detroit: M. Graham, 1887]). There is a 1932 study of banking in Detroit, but it concentrates almost exclusively on the period from 1918 through 1932 (G. Walter Woodworth, *The Detroit Money Market,* Michigan Business Studies, vol. 5, no. 2 [Ann Arbor: University of Michigan, 1932]).

3. Eugene Nelson White, *The Regulation and Reform of the American Banking System,* 1900–1929 (Princeton: Princeton University Press, 1983), tables 1.1 and 1.5, pp. 12–13, 37.

4. John A. James, "The Conundrum of the Low Issue of National Bank Notes," *Journal of Political Economy,* vol. 84, no. 2 (April 1976): 359–67.

5. Eugene Nelson White, "The Membership Problem of the National Banking System," *Exploration in Economic History,* vol. 19, no. 2 (April 1982): 121. Also

see White, *Regulation and Reform*, 51. White's study is the most recent examination of the charter decision. The original classic study of this was by George E. Barnett, *State Banks and Trust Companies since the Passage of the National-Bank Act* (Washington: National Monetary Commission, 1911). Richard E. Sylla's earlier study argues for the same conclusion, though he stresses that the inability of state banks to issue bank notes was relatively more important prior to 1880 (Richard E. Sylla, *The American Capital Market, 1846–1914: A Study of the Effects of Public Policy on Economic Development* [New York: Arno Press, 1975], 56, 67–70).

6. The information on capital requirements comes from Barnett, *State Banks*, chap. 2, and White, *Regulation and Reform*, 14–23.

7. Anderson, *A Century of Banking*, 88.

8. White, *Regulation and Reform*, table 1.4, pp. 30–31. There are some minor differences between the reserve requirements reported in White and those reported by Barnett, *State Banks*, chap. 5.

9. See Richard H. Keehn and Gene Smiley, "Mortgage Lending by National Banks, 1870–1914," *Business History Review*, vol. 51, no. 4 (Winter 1977): 474–91.

10. White, *Regulation and Reform*, 23–25. Barnett, *State Banks*, chap. 4.

11. Branch banking was a minor factor in two states. Until the legislature prohibited it in 1909, there was a small, but growing, amount of city branch banking in Wisconsin. In 1900 there were two city branch banks operated by state banks. By 1909 five state banks were operating seven branches (Anderson, *A Century of Banking*, 126). State banks in Detroit had established branches in 1871, 1889, and 1896. In 1909 a ruling by the Michigan attorney general said that branches were legal. This gave a clear advantage to state banks, particularly in Detroit, until the McFadden Act of the late 1920s allowed national banks to establish branches if state law allowed this.

12. Dunham, *Banking and Industry*, 76–79.

13. Anderson, *A Century of Banking*, 90.

14. This probably explains why Barnett found from five to seven private banks in Wisconsin from 1906 through 1909, even though Wisconsin legislated private commercial banks out of existence. The number likely represents individuals in (one would surmise) Milwaukee engaged in commercial paper operations and/or investment banking.

15. Don M. Dailey, *Investment Banking in Chicago* (Urbana: Bureau of Business and Economic Research, University of Illinois, 1931), 7–9. Reprinted in Vincent P. Carosso, Advisory Editor, *The Chicago Securities Market* (New York: Arno Press, 1975).

16. Dailey, *Investment Banking*, 8.

17. Ibid., 9.

18. James, *Chicago Banks*, 2; 697–99. Melchior Palyi, *The Chicago Credit Market* (Chicago: University of Chicago Press, 1937), 64.

19. Fritz Redlich, *The Molding of American Banking, Men and Ideas: Part II* (New York: Hafner Publishing Company, 1951), 391.

20. Ibid., 389.

21. Ibid., 389.

22. Ibid., 393. Vincent P. Carosso, *Investment Banking in America: A History* (Cambridge: Harvard University Press, 1970), 96–97. James, *Chicago Banks*, 2; 693–95.

23. Wallace Rice, *The Chicago Stock Exchange: A History* (Chicago: The Committee on Library of the Chicago Stock Exchange, 1928), 28–29; reprinted in Carosso, ed., *The Chicago Securities Market*. Jacob O. Kamm, *The Decentralization of Securities Exchanges* (Boston: Meador Publishing Company, 1942), 102–104.

24. Rice, *Chicago Stock Exchange*, 44.

25. Kamm, *Decentralization*, 104–8.

26. Ibid., 96

27. Ibid., 21. The point was also made by David Bunting. See David Bunting, "Organized Securities Markets and the Development of Big Business," a paper presented at the Western Economic Association annual meetings, San Francisco, 26 June, 1976.

28. There are three sets of similar estimates of national bank interest rates during the postbellum period. The first was developed by Lance E. Davis and published in 1965 (Lance E. Davis, "The Investment Market, 1870–1914: The Evolution of a National Market," *Journal of Economic History*, vol. 25 [September 1965]: 355–93). The second set, developed by Gene Smiley, was presented in a 1975 article and is a refined version of Davis's set (Gene Smiley, "Interest Rate Movement in the United States, 1888–1913," *Journal of Economic History*, vol. 35 [September 1975]: 591–620). The set was revised in 1976. Gene Smiley, "Revised Estimates of Short Term Interest Rates of National Banks for States and Reserve Cities, 1888–1913," Working Paper, Marquette University Department of Economics, (1976). The third set, also a refined version of Davis' rates, was developed and presented by John A. James in several papers in 1976 (John A. James, "Banking Market Structure, Risk, and the Pattern of Local Interest Rates in the United States, 1893–1911," *Review of Economics and Statistics*, vol. 58 [November 1976]: 453–62; John A. James, "The Development of the National Money Market, 1893–1911," *Journal of Economic History*, vol. 36 [December 1976]: 878–97; John A. James, *Money and Capital Markets in Postbellum America* [Princeton: Princeton University Press, 1978]).

29. Comptroller of the Currency, *Report* (Washington, D.C: Government Printing Office, 1880), 7.

30. The cities were Cincinnati, Cleveland, Milwaukee, Chicago, New York City, St. Louis, San Francisco, Boston, Baltimore, Philadelphia, Washington, D.C., New Orleans, Louisville, and Omaha. The rate dispersion is the sample standard deviation of the rates. For 1880 three calculations were made. Since a range of rates was reported for some cities and an average rate for others, a calculation was made using the upper rate where there was a range, a calculation made using the lower rate for ranges, and a calculation where all ranges were averaged to produce an average rate. For 1880 those dispersions were: (high) 1.77 percent, (low) 2.03 percent, and (averaged) 1.83 percent. The dispersions for those cities in later years were: 1888, 1.01; 1889, 1.38; 1890, 1.36; 1891, 1.14; 1911, 0.82; 1912, 0.78; and 1913, 0.66 percent. The dispersion measure employed here is the sample standard deviation of the rates rather than the coeffi-

cient of variation. The relative dispersion measure should be used where variations in absolute prices are considered, and an absolute dispersion measure used where variations in relative prices, such as interest rates, are being considered. James contended that a dispersion measure is inappropriate since it focuses on rate convergence from above and below toward some "mean" rate; rather, rates should be compared to the rate in the most developed market, the East. A dispersion measure is appropriate if the rate differentials lead to a reallocation of capital. James's proposed measure would be appropriate if the reason for the rate differentials was differing degrees of monopoly power in segmented markets. Reducing the monopoly power would lower rates in the higher rate areas, but not change rates in the lower rate areas.

31. Lance Davis did present estimates of "net rates of return," which extended back to 1869. He suggested that these could proxy interest rates. However, the ability of net rates of return to approximate interest rates has been questioned both on the basis of the types of data used in their construction and on the basis of evidence of the correlation between the net rates of return and acceptable interest rate estimates from 1888 through 1913. Several other studies have used Davis's net rate of return. For the criticisms see Gene Smiley, "Interest Rate Movement," 593–94, no. 6. These criticisms were elaborated on in Gene Smiley, "Banking Structure and the National Capital Market, 1869–1914: A Comment," *Journal of Economic History*, vol. 45 (September 1985): 653–59. Also see Marie Elizabeth Sushka and W. Brian Barrett, "Banking Structure and the National Capital Market, 1869–1914," *Journal of Economic History*, vol. 44, (June 1984): 463–77; and Marie Elizabeth Sushka and W. Brian Barrett, "Banking Structure and the National Capital Market, 1869–1914: A Reply," *Journal of Economic History*, vol. 45 (September 1985): 661–65. Jeffrey Williamson also used Davis's net rates as interest rate proxies. See Jeffrey G. Williamson, *Late Nineteenth-Century American Development* (New York: Cambridge University Press, 1974), chap. 6.

32. The rates were taken from Smiley, "Revised Estimates." To provide a consistent set of state rates, the rates for reserve cities created during the years after 1888 were added to the country bank rates using weights of the shares of all loans and discounts of national banks in the state. The city banks' dispersions are calculated for the nineteen reserve cities existing in 1888.

33. The rates for 1916 through 1937 are from Gene Smiley, "State and City Loan Rate Estimates, 1916–1940," Working Paper, Marquette University Department of Economics, 1981. They were presented in Gene Smiley, "Regional Variation in Bank Loan Rates In the Interwar Years," *Journal of Economic History*, vol. 41 (December 1981): 889–901.

34. Except for Columbus, Ohio, and Indianapolis, Indiana, only rates for reserve cities that existed throughout the 1888–1913 period are reported. Though a few reserve cities in the East and South were created, there were many created in the midwestern and western states.

35. This statement has to be qualified. The three Pacific Coast states had country bank rates which were not quite as high as other MOU and SWT states and declined more during the period.

36. See the following studies: R. M. Breckenridge "Discount Rates in the United States," *Political Science Quarterly,* vol. 13 (March 1898): 142; Oliver M. W. Sprague, "Branch Banking in the United States," *Quarterly Journal of Economics,* vol. 17 (February 1903); 245; Oliver C. Lockhart, "The Development of Interbank Borrowing in the National Banking System, 1869–1914," *Journal of Political Economy,* pt. 1, vol. 29 (February 1921): 138–60; pt. 2, vol. 29 (March 1921): 222–40 (Lockhart's statement can be found on pp. 239–40); Margaret G. Myers, *The New York Money Market: Vol. 1. Origins and Development* (New York: Columbia University Press, 1931), 233; Richard H. Keehn, "Federal Bank Policy, Bank Market Structure, and Bank Performance: Wisconsin, 1863–1914," *Business History Review,* vol. 48 (Spring 1974): 8; White, *Regulation and Reform,* 3. The more recent explanations for the regional interest rate differentials are considered below. Some other reasons have been advanced. In 1931 Keith Powlison argued that banks in the older, more developed areas generated lower profits because they were lending in more stable, diversified markets (Keith Powlison, *Profits of the National Banks* [Boston: R.G. Badger, 1931] 83). More recently, Hugh Rockoff has argued that regional interest rate differentials were associated with variations in regional bank failure rates (Hugh Rockoff, "Regional Interest Rates and Bank Failures, 1870–1914," *Explorations in Economic History,* vol. 14 [January 1977], 90–95). Jeffrey G. Williamson argued that the differentials were demand driven as disequilibrating changes in regional demands and lagged adjustments slowed interest rate convergence (Jeffrey G. Williamson, *Late Nineteenth Century American Development: A General Equilibrium History* [New York: Cambridge University Press, 1974], chap. 6).

37. Davis, "The Investment Market," 370. See also Lance E. Davis, "Capital Mobility and American Growth," chap. 22, in Robert W. Fogel and Stanley L. Engerman, eds., *The Reinterpretation of American Economic History* (New York: Harper and Row, 1971); and Lance E. Davis and Douglass C. North, *Institutional Change and American Economic Growth* (New York: Cambridge University Press, 1971).

38. Davis, "The Investment Market," 370, 380.

39. Richard E. Sylla, "Federal Policy, Banking Market Structure, and Capital Mobilization in the United States, 1863–1913," *Journal of Economic History,* vol. 29 (December 1969): 657–86. See also, Richard E. Sylla, "The United States, 1863–1913," chap. 8, in Rondo Cameron, ed., *Banking and Economic Development: Some Lessons Of History* (New York: Oxford University Press, 1972), and Sylla, *American Capital Market.*

40. James, "Banking Market Structure"; and James, "The Development of the National Money Market." See also James, *Money and Capital Markets.*

41. James stated that "almost all of the estimated MP [monopoly power] coefficient for country banks reported in table 1 are negative and most are highly significant" (James, "Banking Market Structure," 458–59). If one cannot reject the hypothesis that the coefficient is actually zero, then the negative sign means nothing. The term "most are highly significant" is rather ambiguous. For country banks 30 of the 49 MP coefficients were significantly different from zero at the 1, 2, 5, or 10 percent levels. Of the 30, 16 were significant at the 1, 2, or 5

percent levels, and 13 at the 10 percent level. A common interpretation of the 10 percent level would be that this indicates a "marginally significant" coefficient. Adopting this interpretation then, only 17 of the 49 MP country bank coefficients were "highly significant," 13 of the 49 were "marginally significant," and 19 were not significantly different from zero, hardly strong support for the monopoly power thesis. In the twelve western states, where rates were the highest and fell the most, the four significant coefficients were significant only at the 10 percent level.

42. James, "The Development of the National Money Market," 888. These cross-section regressions for selected dates were not reported in either paper, nor in the monograph.

43. Ibid., 895.

44. It is not clear that Davis meant that regional capital markets were functionally independent, rather than referring to those institutional changes that made capital flows easier and promoted a tendency toward interest rate equalization. Most of his 1965 paper, "The Investment Market," was devoted to discussing the institutional changes that occurred. This was made clearer in the chapter on financial markets in Davis and North, *Institutional Change and American Economic Growth*. There the discussion is not on the elimination of the segmentation of regional capital markets, but on the profit motivated "arrangemental innovations" that lowered transactions costs and thus a tendency toward interest rate equalization by a reallocation of capital.

45. James, "Banking Market Structure," 461, 459.

46. George Stigler, "Imperfections in the Capital Market," *Journal of Political Economy*, vol. 75 (June 1967): 287–92.

47. Sushka and Barrett, "Banking Structure," 465, 467.

48. Ibid., 469–71.

49. Ibid., 472–73. The other rates they tested were the New York City loan rate, the commercial paper rate, and bond yields. The only rate that significantly affected the regional demands over the entire period of 1875–1914 was the New York City loan rate.

50. Ibid., 473–77. It would be very surprising to find (as they did) that the opening of this New York Stock Exchange department immediately made all of the regional loan demands much more elastic.

51. James, "The Development of the National Money Market," 884–88. Sushka and Barrett, "Banking Structure," 473–76.

52. Keehn, "Federal Bank Policy," 3–11. Richard H. Keehn, "Market Power and Bank Lending: Some Evidence from Wisconsin, 1870–1900"; *Journal of Economic History*, vol. 40 (March 1980): 52.

53. Gene Smiley, "Interest Rate Convergence in the United States, 1888–1913," *MidSouth Journal of Economics*, vol. 8 (September 1984), Appendix B, p. 184.

54. Smiley, "Banking Structure...Comment." See also Sushka and Barrett, "Banking Structure...Reply." The most extensive review and critical examination of these studies of this topic through 1977 is Richard E. Sylla, "Financial Intermediaries In Economic History: Quantitative Research on the Seminal

Hypotheses of Lance Davis and Alexander Gerschenkron," 43–80, *Recent Developments in the Study of Business and Economics History: Essays in Memory of Herman E. Krooss, Research in Economic History,* Robert E. Gallman, ed., Supplement 1 (Greenwich, Conn.: Jai Press, 1977).

55. Smiley, "Interest Rate Convergence," 179–82. In the cross-sectional regressions of each year, the distance coefficient declined over time and was not significantly different from zero in 1912 and 1913.

56. The comptroller published data on estimated average rates of interest on loans and average rates of interest on deposits for country banks by state (as well as city banks by city) for 1889, 1894, and 1899 (in the 1899 *Report*), in 1902, and in 1910. Examination of this data indicates a consistent positive relationship between loan rates and deposit rates (controlling for other variables). See The Comptroller of the Currency, *Reports,* (1899) pp. 484–97, (1902), pp. 252–79, and (1910), pp. 766–76.

57. For discussions of interbank borrowing in this period, see Lockhart, "The Development of Interbank Borrowing." Also refer to Leonard L. Watkins, *Bankers' Balances* (Chicago: A. W. Shaw Co., 1929).

58. The Comptroller of the Currency, *Report,* vol. 1 (1890), 14.

59. Anderson, *A Century of Banking in Wisconsin,* 94.

60. The continued decline can hardly be attributed to continued declines in monopoly power due to bank entry. The number of national and state banks grew 71.5 percent from 1885 to 1895, 58.6 percent from 1895 to 1905, 65.4 percent from 1905 to 1915, and 7.4 percent from 1915 to 1925 (Calculated from White, *Regulation and Reform,* tables 1.1 and 3.1, pp. 12–13 and 132).

61. Keehn, "Market Power and Bank Lending," 46.

62. It should be noted that the creation of the National Banking System with its relatively high bank capital requirements did not create interest rate differentials where none had previously existed. The dramatic and rapid geographical expansion of the United States in the postbellum period did this. One of the best brief discussions of this can be found in Davis and North, *Institutional Change and American Economic Growth,* chap. 6, particularly pages 105–08.

63. Keehn, "Federal Bank Policy," 21.

64. James, "Banking Market Structure," xx. If the interregional loan was made to a specific bank, then the costs of acquiring all of the relevant information were reduced, and, through portfolio diversification by the borrowing bank, the probability of losses for the lending bank (or investor) on the interregional loan were reduced.

65. This is roughly consistent with the distinction Davis made between "uncertainty" and "risk." Davis argued that there were continuing differentials in "net rates of return" (after deductions for losses), so it "must have become obvious that western loans were not 'all that much' riskier." (Davis, "The Investment Market," 358). An individual lender, in, say, Boston was not concerned with the general level of the net return or the loss rate in, say, the Plains states. The lender would be concerned with the specific individual or firm who was requesting the loan, the uses of the money that would be lent, the credit condi-

tion and history of the borrower, the conditions in the area, and so forth. All of this specific information on circumstances, time, and place was necessary to even assess the risks.

66. Davis, "The Investment Market." Davis and North, *Institutional Change and American Economic Growth*, chap. 6.

67. Lockhart, "The Development of Interbank Borrowing," 138.

68. Ibid., 141–43. Banks in higher rate areas could sell certificates of deposit to banks in lower rate areas, though the comptroller discouraged this. Banks could rediscount notes and bills with their correspondent banks, and they could borrow directly—amounts that would then be listed under "bills payable." They often borrowed by overdrafts on their correspondent balances, and they often hid other borrowings in the "other liabilities" category even though the regulators disliked this. A bank's officers or directors could borrow from a correspondent bank using their own personal credit and deposit the amount in their bank. Other subterfuges were also employed. The borrowings were discussed in a more practical manner in Edgar G. Alcorn, *The Duties and Liabilities of Bank Directors*, 3d. ed. (Indianapolis: U.S. Bank Note Co., 1915), 146, and in William H. Kniffin, Jr., *The Practical Work of A Bank*, 5th ed. (New York: The Bankers Publishing Co., 1919), 273.

69. If a bank rediscounted without recourse, then they, in effect, sold the note outright and there would be offsetting changes in the asset side of the ledger. There would be no entry on the liabilities side (in "notes and bills rediscounted" or "bills payable") to indicate the rediscounting.

70. Lockhart, "The Development of Interbank Borrowing," 145–46.

71. Ibid., 139, n. 1.

72. Ibid., 236.

73. Walter McAvoy, "The Economic Importance of the Commercial Paper House," *Journal of Political Economy*, vol. 30 (1922): 78–87.

74. Albert O. Greef, *The Commercial Paper House in the United States* (Cambridge: Harvard University Press, 1938). Myers, *New York Money Market*.

75. See Keehn and Smiley, "Mortgage Lending by National Banks," for a discussion of this.

76. H. G. Moulton, "Commercial Banking and Capital Formation," *Journal of Political Economy*, pts. 1, 2, 3, 4, IV, vol. 26 (May, June, July, and November 1918), 484–508, 638–63, 705–31, and 849–81. The quote is from p. 648. In general, these points are made in the discussion on pp. 638–58. Commercial paper was often valued by banks because it was paid off at maturity with no obligation to renew it, unlike commercial loans. In this sense commercial paper was considerably more liquid than commercial loans.

77. Davis and North, *Institutional Change and American Economic Growth*, chap. 6, particularly pp. 118–27.

78. Thomas R. Navin and Marian V. Sears, "The Rise of a Market for Industrial Securities, 1887–1902," *Business History Review*, vol. 34 (June 1955); 110.

79. Kamm, *The Decentralization of Securities Exchanges*, chap. 5.

80. Navin and Sears, "The Rise of a Market for Industrial Securities," 115.

81. Davis and North, *Institutional Change and American Economic Growth*, 127.

82. McAvoy, "The Economic Importance of the Commercial Paper House," 79.

83. Lockhart, "The Development of Interbank Borrowing," 239–40.

84. Davis and North, *Institutional Change and American Economic Growth*, 127.

85. Ibid., 117.

86. Richard A. Easterlin's estimates of interregional capital movements between 1880 and 1920 suggest a strong movement out of these two regions into the other regions (except for the Pacific Coast states—mainly California). E. S. Lee, A. R. Miller, C. P. Brainerd, and R. A. Easterlin, *Population Redistribution and Economic Growth in the United States, 1870–1950* (Philadelphia: American Philosophical Society, 1957), 1; 729–33, vol. 2:179–81.

87. Greef, *Commercial Paper House*, chap. 11, especially pp. 38–51. Davis, "The Investment Market," 372–73. Davis and North, *Institutional Change and American Economic Growth*, 117–18.

88. Palyi, *Chicago Credit Market*, 227.

89. Anderson, *A Century of Banking*, 68–70.

90. Brian Gendreau, "The Implicit Return on Bankers' Balances," *Journal of Money, Credit, and Banking*, vol. 15 (November 1983), 411–24.

91. Anderson, *A Century of Banking*, 70–71. If the National Bank of the Republic in New York purchased the notes without recourse, then no telltale evidence of the transaction would appear in either bank's balance sheets to note the interbank lending. Knox's specific reference to the notes of the Hanna Company indicates the importance of information as to the nature of and reputation of the *firm* in interregional lending and suggests that these types of transactions were rather common practice.

92. Ibid., 71.

93. For example, see Baty, *Story of the Outlying Banks of Chicago*; Dailey, *Investment Banking in Chicago*; Huston, *Financing an Empire*; James, *Growth of Chicago Banks*; Palyi, *Chicago Credit Market*; and, Rice, *Chicago Stock Exchange*.

94. James, *Growth of Chicago Banks*, 346, 444–45, 488–89.

95. Ibid., 490.

96. Palyi, *Chicago Credit Market*, 210–11.

97. Ibid., 215.

98. James, *Growth of Chicago Banks*, 673.

99. Ibid., 536.

100. Watkins, *Bankers' Balances*, 209.

101. Ibid., 242.

102. Howard Preston, *History of Banking in Iowa* (Iowa City: The State Historical Society of Iowa, 1922), 283.

103. See Davis and North, *Institutional Change and American Economic Growth*, chap. 6 for a discussion of this. The Northwestern Mutual Life Insurance Company

of Milwaukee was one of the country's larger life insurance companies in this period. This company's role in the purchase of western mortgages is discussed in Harold F. Williamson and Orange O. Smalley, *Norhtwestern Mutual Life: A Century of Trusteeship* (Evanston, Ill.: Northwestern University Press, 1957), 127–28. See also Lester Zartman, *Investments of Life Insurance Companies* (New York: H. Holt, 1906).

104. Preston, *History of Banking In Iowa*, 325–26.
105. James, *Growth of Chicago Banks*, 697–99.
106. Redlich, *Molding of American Banking*, 2:391.
107. See Bunting, "Organized Securities Markets," 17; Kamm, *Decentralization*, 21; and James E. Walter, *The Role of Regional Security Exchanges* (Berkeley: University of California Press, 1957), 46.

10
RIVER TRANSPORTATION AND THE OLD NORTHWEST TERRITORY

Gary M. Walton
University of California, Davis

INTRODUCTION

AMERICANS HAVE A LONG history of revealed hunger for tradition, and we are widely known for our events of instant tradition. It should, therefore, come as no surprise that Ohio University, the first institution of higher learning in the Old Northwest, should celebrate the bicentennial of the founding of the Old Northwest Territory and its statutory underpinnings, the land ordinances of 1785 and 1787.

On the other hand, it should be made clear that in business terms we are celebrating a poor year; one of the best things to be said for 1787 is that it was probably better than 1786. The nation was straining to pull itself up from the depths of the maritime depression that engulfed the entire American seaboard and its commercial hinterlands. A host of farm foreclosures propelled debtor mobs and uprisings on the frontier, culminating in Shay's attack on Springfield, Massachusetts, on 25 January, 1787, but the militia ended Shay's Rebellion within days. The Annapolis Convention of 1786, which focused on commercial problems and the related need to amend the Articles of Confederation, went nowhere, and progress on these and other issues awaited the larger body of delegates assembled at the Constitutional Convention in Philadelphia in May 1787.

Aside from the hope inspired by the Philadelphia gathering, 1787 provided little worthy of celebration except for Congress's handling of the western lands. By special act of Congress, the Ohio Company had been given permission to purchase a million and a half acres at nine cents per acre in the Northwest Territory. This was a far cry from the minimum one dollar per acre price set by the 1785 Ordinance which together with its 640-acre minimum stipulation discouraged settlement. At the urging of the Ohio Company, Congress addressed the matter of governmental status and political organization in the territories. The principal components of the 1787 Ordinance were the exclusion of slavery north of the Ohio River; the division of the territory into not less than three nor more than five states; from an initial government of three judges, a secretary, and a governor, all appointed by the president, a legislative body could be elected and a non-voting member sent to Congress when five thousand male inhabitants were resident; and, most important, when a territory had sixty thousand inhabitants it would be admitted as a state "on an equal footing with the original states in all respects whatever." Such progressive "colonial" measures were almost without precedent in world history, and the State of Virginia must be given substantial credit for ceding its western territories to Congress with the equal footing clause as a condition.

In short, the Northwest Ordinances of 1787 and 1785 were instrumental in shifting community property with its "tragedy of the commons" characteristics into secure private holdings and in fostering free enterprise in the Jeffersonian tradition. These ordinances will be forever remembered and glorified in academic circles for their positive political effects.[1]

The ultimate relaxation of sales conditions, especially the minimum acreage requirements and credit restrictions, along with the Louisiana Purchase of 1803, which provided secure navigation rights through New Orleans, were further important factors propelling settlement in the Old Northwest. On 20 July, 1803, Frankfort, Kentucky's newspaper, the *Guardian of Freedom*, trumpeted that the new rights of navigation on the Mississippi insured "a perpetual union of the states, and lasting prosperity to the the Western Country." Indeed, as in other stories of historical settlement, the crucial linkages between cheap water transport, land settlement and population growth, and commercial enterprise and economic growth are evident here. The history of the Old Northwest is deeply rooted in its original avenues of commerce, the rivers, and in commercial activities stimulated there by favorable prices for its produce.

PRICES, PEOPLE AND ACRES

THE IMPORTANCE OF ECONOMIC opportunities to western settlement has been stressed repeatedly, but the first to provide a link between prices and settlement for the Northwest Territory was George Rogers Taylor. His spotlight was on the boom year 1805: "The extremely low prices of 1802 and 1803 had improved in 1804 and had reached in 1805 the highest level to be attained before the War of 1812. The year following saw slightly lower levels; and in 1807 the downward trend was clearly evident."[2] He further notes that "In the decade before the War the amount of public land sold in the territory north of the Ohio River reached its highest point in 1805, (619,000). In 1806 sales continued high (473,000 acres), but in no other year did they reach the 400,000 mark."[3] Though the population of Cincinnati increased 28 percent in the years 1800–1805, it more than doubled between 1805 and 1807, and the *Scioto Gazette* of Chillicothe reported in 1805 that immigration exceeded "all reasonable bounds of calculation."[4]

Writing on the period immediately following, Douglass C. North has provided us with systematic evidence on the relationship between land sales in the western states and prices of key staples. Figure 1 portrays his evidence for land sales in the principal corn- and wheat-producing states. The boom decades of 1810–20, the 1830s, and the 1850s are evident.

FIGURE 1

Corn and Wheat Prices and U.S. Public Land Sales in Ohio, Illinois, Indiana, Michigan, Iowa, Wisconsin, and Missouri, 1815–1860.

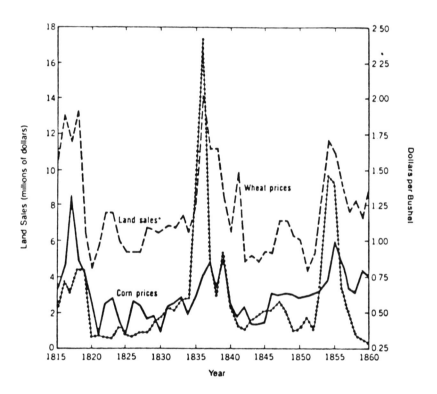

Source: North (1961):137

Table 1 provides population estimates by decade for these same states and aggregates for the five states formed from the Old Northwest Territory.

TABLE 1

Population in Northwestern States and Total U.S., 1790–1860
(in 000's)

Region/year	1790	1800	1810	1820	1830	1840	1850	1860
Ohio	—	45.4	230.8	581.3	937.9	1,519.5	1,980.3	2,339.5
Indiana	—	5.6	24.5	147.2	343.0	685.9	988.4	1,350.4
Illinois	—	—	12.3	55.2	157.4	476.2	851.5	1,712.0
Michigan	—	—	4.8	8.8	31.6	212.3	397.7	749.1
Wisconsin	—	—	—	—	—	30.9	305.4	775.9
Totals for states of the Northwest Territory	—	51.0	272.4	792.5	1,469.9	2,924.8	4,523.3	6,926.9
States of the Northwest Territory as % of U.S.	—	1.0	3.7	8.2	11.4	17.1	19.5	22.0
Iowa	—	—	—	—	—	43.1	192.2	674.9
Missouri	—	—	20.8	66.6	140.5	383.7	682.0	1,182.0
Subtotal	—	51.0	293.2	859.1	1,610.4	3,351.6	5,397.5	8,783.8
Total U.S.	3,929.0	5,297.0	7,239.9	9,633.8	12,866.0	17,069.5	23,191.9	31,443.3
Northwest Territory plus Iowa and Missouri as % of U.S.	—	1.0	3.8	8.9	12.5	19.6	23.3	27.9

Sources: Derived from Serial Set 2030, House Executive Document 133, pp. 50–152, except for estimates for 1790 and 1800 which are from Nettels (p. 178)

The percentage changes for each decade for these five states from 1810 to 1860 averaged 192 percent, 85 percent, 99 percent, 55 percent, and 53 percent. Clearly the data reveal differences among the states and the typical slowing up consistent with more complete stages of development. The key surges are clear, however, and the Northwest's population grew rapidly relative to the nation, especially in the boom decades 1810–19, 1830–39, and 1850–59. On the eve of the Civil War, 22 percent of the people in the U.S. lived in states formed from the Old Northwest Territory.

Some critics have argued that land sales in these boom periods were dominated by pervasive speculation.[5] Much land was actually being put into use, however, as shown in Table 2. In the states of the Northwest region plus Iowa and Missouri, for which the data are most reliable, the surges in improved acres are striking: 23.5 percent, 6.5 percent, 7.1 percent, 5.4 percent, and 7.8 percent in each decade respectively from 1810 to 1860. Conse-

TABLE 2

Acres of Improved Land[a] in Selected States in the Northwest, 1810–60
(in 000's)

State	1810	1820	1830	1840	1850	1860
Ohio	225,675	2,892,456	4,665,000	7,558,750	9,851,493	12,665,587
Michigan	—	—	—	—	1,929,110	3,419,861
Indiana	125,530	751,445	1,751,409	3,485,729	5,046,543	8,161,717
Illinois	72,692	325,272	931,860	2,818,373	5,039,545	13,251,473
Missouri	89,805	286,870	605,117	1,653,001	2,938,425	6,246,871
Iowa	—	—	—	184,969	824,682	3,780,253
Wisconsin	—	—	—	105,930	1,045,499	8,746,036

[a]The source states that "by 'Improved Land' is meant cleared land used for grazing, grass, or tillage, or lying fallow."

Source: National Ship-Canal Convention. Serial set 1476, vol. 4, House Misc. Doc. (unnumbered), 688.

quently, advances in corn and wheat prices coincided with surges in population and improved acres in these primary corn- and wheat-producing states.

Such supply responses did not occur coincidentally in isolated markets. As transportation developments more solidly linked the interior to the seaboard and abroad, the Northwest evolved into an important segment of the national and international economy. Although economic unification on a national scale was far from complete in the early nineteenth century, considerable progress had been achieved fairly early in the commodity markets. As Thomas Berry's analysis of regional price movements graphically shows, a strong linkage was forged between the East and West during the period:

> In such first-magnitude movements as those of 1793–1797 and 1810–1817 there was a lag measuring somewhat more than a year in length.... Taking a later interval (1816–1860) weighted general indices of monthly prices in New York, New Orleans, and Cincinnati show agreement with each other to a surprising degree.... Cincinnati prices lagged the greater part of a year in their decline in 1819–1820, but they were only three or four months behind the seaboard markets in the turning-point of 1839 and reacted simultaneously at the time of the panic of 1857.[6]

A viable transportation system was the key to improving market linkages between the interior and the seaboard and abroad. First, advances on the rivers, and in later decades the canals and finally the rails, brought about tremendous cost reductions, to the benefit of both producers and consumers of items shipped. For example, wholesale prices of wheat and corn in Cincinnati were just under 50 percent of wholesale prices in Philadelphia or New York in 1816–20, but they were around 70 percent of these in the late 1850s. For flour, mess pork, and lard, western wholesale prices as a percentage of eastern prices moved from around 60 percent to over 90 percent during this forty-year period.[7] With shippers and other middlemen taking a smaller cut, western producers received higher net prices and consumers paid less. For good reasons, then, transportation improvements were the focus of widespread concern.

THE COMMERCIAL GATEWAYS

RECOGNITION OF THE IMPORTANCE of river transportation to the West is eloquently stated by a contemporary of the period, James H. Lanman (1841):

> Steam navigation colonized the west! It furnished a motive for settlement and production by the hands of eastern men, because it brought the western territory nearer to the east by nine tenths of the distance....Steam is crowding our eastern cities with western flour and western merchants, and lading the western steamboats with eastern emigrants and eastern merchandise. It has advanced the career of national colonization and national production, at least a century![8]

Indeed, Buley's classic thirteen hundred-page study of the Old Northwest begins with the words:

> It was spring at Pittsburgh, wet and cold, but nevertheless, spring. The muddy waters of the Monongahela joined the clear and more rapid current of the Allegheny, and westward between the wooded hills stretched the broad Ohio, *La Belle Riviere* of the French, for a thousand miles an open and inviting pathway to the West. The thriving young city of about 5,000 people was stirring with the bustle of commerce and industry, for the western traffic was booming, and Pittsburgh was the gateway to the West.[9]

In fact, during the antebellum period there were three gateways that linked the interior, north and south, with the rest of the nation and the outside world. The route to the northern gateway ran eastward from the Great Lakes, either down the St. Lawrence River or along the Hudson or Mohawk river valleys, the latter being the more popular route, with New York's ice-free port as its eastern terminus. The northeastern gateway linked Pittsburgh and Wheeling on the Ohio River to Philadelphia and Baltimore on the east coast. The third gateway, at New Orleans, was the main southern entrepôt.

The major development on the northern gateway was the opening of the

Erie Canal in 1825. This was followed by the building of the Welland Canal, by improvements in the St. Lawrence Seaway system, and finally, by the completion of the New York Central and the New York and Erie railroads in 1852.

The northeastern gateway generated a keen rivalry between Pittsburgh and Wheeling on the one end and Philadelphia and Baltimore on the other and justified the extension of the National Road to Wheeling in 1817. The opening of the Pennsylvania Turnpike to Pittsburgh quickly followed. The Pennsylvania Canal system, tenaciously linking Pittsburgh and Philadelphia, was opened in 1834, but its anticipated competitor, the Chesapeake and Ohio canal system, was never finished. The railroad extended the rivalry, however, and the Pennsylvania and the Baltimore and Ohio railroads reached Pittsburgh and Wheeling within months of each other in 1853.

The major event on the southern gateway was the development of steamboat services on the Mississippi after 1811. Improvements in ocean travel were also important and permitted the establishment of regular packet lines running between New York and New Orleans by the early 1820s.

A breakdown of the absolute amounts of shipments through each gateway from the interior, given in figure 2, crudely reveal the relative importance of each gateway. The southern gateway was dominant throughout most of the period, and until the late 1830s the southern gateway accounted for over 80 percent of these shipments. Thereafter, its position was steadily eroded, and by the end of the period it serviced slightly less than one-half of the total.

Prior to the opening of the Erie Canal in 1825, the northern gateway had handled virtually no outbound traffic, as most of the canal's early freight still originated in western New York. Therefore, the immediate impact of the new waterway on shipments from the states of the Northwest was small. By the late 1830s, however, the picture had changed radically, and by 1860 the development of feeder systems and other improvements had enabled the northern route to edge past the southern gateway in volume of shipments from the interior. As indicated in figure 2, this relative growth occurred primarily in the last two decades of the period.

The northeastern gateway played only a minor role in the carriage of shipments from the interior, never accounting for more than 7 percent of the total and generally for less than 5 percent.

Unfortunately, very little quantitative information is available on the inbound trade, largely due to the odd-sized, unstandardized nature of the goods shipped, since manufactures of various shapes and sizes were an important part of the total. Nevertheless, the total volume of inbound shipments was small compared to outbound tonnage.

Despite the range of error in accounting for the inbound trade, it is quite clear that when both inbound and outbound shipments are taken together

FIGURE 2

Freight shipments from the interior by Western gateways, 1810–60.

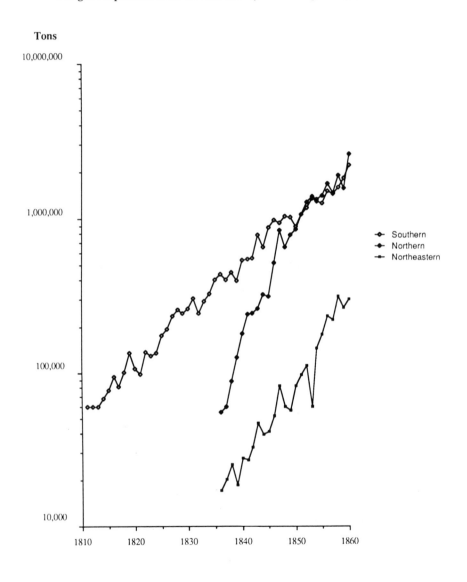

Source: Haites, Mak, and Walton (1975), p. 124, 125, 127.

the southern gateway dominated most of the antebellum period. Prior to 1845 it received more incoming cargo than passed through the other two gateways combined. It is this finding that urges an emphasis on the importance of the river system in the West. In the pre-1845 period, the main commercial link between the West and the seaboard and abroad was through New Orleans, and it was by river that goods moved inland to and from the southern gateway.

A consideration of trade flows among the western subregions and within these regions does not alter this general conclusion. Because only scattered pieces of information exist on these trade flows it is not possible to assess accurately the aggregate magnitudes of such movements. However, among the western subregions and states this traffic was carried primarily by two major components, both of them water systems. The Great Lakes system formed one route and the rivers—the Mississippi, the Missouri, the Ohio, and others—comprised the other. Canals, such as the Welland, which connected Lake Ontario to the other Great Lakes, and the Louisville and Portland canal around the falls on the Ohio River, were important complements to these systems. But even the relatively successful Ohio Canal, linking the Ohio River to Lake Erie, was relegated to the role of feeder. Similarly, the railroads did not change the West's general reliance on these two components in the antebellum period, except perhaps in the final few years. Wagon and overland transport were of moderate importance for short hauls, but more distant overland freighting was impractical until the advent of the railroad. Consequently, when trade within the interior is considered in addition to trade from and into the interior, the river system remains an important and probably dominant element of the overall commerce of the West.

As the evidence shows, however, the preeminence of the river routes and the southern gateway was being displaced in the last two decades of the antebellum period. First the canals in the 1830s and then the railroads in the 1850s brought about a redirection of traffic from a predominantly southern orientation to an east-west routing.[10] Starting in the Ohio Valley and the northwestern grain regions, these developments slowed the rate of growth of river commerce.

Nevertheless, despite its relative decline the southern route did not suffer in absolute terms. The spread of railroads, roads, and canals, in combination with developments of the Great Lakes, more closely bound together the Northwest and provided an alternative to New Orleans as a link to the East and abroad. But the resulting alterations in trade patterns and redirection of interregional traffic was more than offset by the growth of river trade, especially in the South. Shipping activity on the western rivers continued to increase throughout the entire antebellum period, despite the displacement effect of the iron horse.

As emphasized by Albert Fishlow, the major influence of the railroad came after the outbreak of hostilities: "Almost all the trade emanating from or destined for the South was quite independent of developments in the railroad sector, in part because the overland connections between that region and the others were poorest, but more fundamentally because competitive water routes represented barriers so formidable that integration would have made little difference and hence received little attention."[11]

Moreover, improvements in river transportation maintained it as the superior medium throughout much of the West, despite attempts by canal promoters in some areas to lessen their dependence on the river. In the case of Cincinnati, which played a pivotal role in the direction of traffic to the East and South, Harry Scheiber notes, "Despite the availability of both the railroad and the canal route to the lake, most of Cincinnati's export trade remained southern in orientation. As late as 1850 fully 90 percent of Cincinnati flour exports and 85 percent of whiskey were shipped to the South or New Orleans."[12]

Finally, the total amount of freight and number of passengers carried in 1849 by western river steamboats was 3.32 billion freight-ton miles and 1.1 billion passenger miles.[13] In that one year, western river steamboats carried about 1 billion freight-ton miles more and only about 700 million passenger miles less than the amounts carried by railroads in the *entire* United States in one year a *whole decade later.*[14]

In short, the western rivers were the dominant medium of trade throughout most of the antebellum period and formed a vigorous part of the transportation network right up to the eve of the war itself. It was undoubtedly these considerations that led Hunter to assert, "The rivers formed the backbone of the transportation system of the West prior to the Civil War."[15]

PRODUCTIVITY SURGES ON THE RIVERS

SPECTACULAR PRODUCTIVITY GAINS in river transportation were the key sources of strength to that "backbone," and the details of that story have been spelled out elsewhere.[16] Briefly summarized, steamboat productivity from 1815 to 1860 advanced at an annual compounded rate of 4.9 percent or 4.1 percent, according to two alternative measures.[17] Either estimate indicates an impressive rate of increase, especially in comparison with other important transportation media, such as canals, ocean shipping, and railroads. The available evidence suggests that the increase of steamboat productivity on western rivers between 1815 and 1860 exceeded that of any other major transportation medium over any equal time in the nineteenth century. For instance, the annual rate of advance of total factor productivity in U.S. railroads from 1839 to 1910 was approximately 3.5 percent (5.4 percent 1839–59).[18] Similarly, productivity change in ocean shipping from 1814 to 1860 has been measured at 3.5 percent,[19] and the fall in real rates in the last half of the nineteenth century, when steam replaced sail, was less than during that earlier period.[20] Productivity studies for canals during the nineteenth century have not been undertaken, but it is doubtful that canal productivity increased significantly and it may even have declined.[21]

The advance of steamboat productivity was not steady, however, and the great surge occurred before 1850. From the periods of 1815–19 to 1846–50 these rates were, respectively, 6 percent and 5 percent, according to the two measures. From 1846–50 to 1856–60 they were 1.4 percent and 1.3 percent, respectively. Despite the exceptionally high rate of productivity change, the steamboat industry did exhibit typical features of industry growth and retardation. Most of the productivity advance occurred early and then gave way to a noticeable slowing up. Attainment of maturity was apparent by mid-century.

The impressive rise in steamboat productivity and its consequent reduction in freight and travel costs dominate the story of western river transportation during the antebellum period. The advent of the steamboat quickly eclipsed the keelboat from operations on major trunk routes. Prior to 1817 all upriver commerce had been carried by large keelboats,[22] whereas by 1821 it is reported that steamboats "have almost entirely superseded the use of Barges, which were formerly the largest boats in use."[23]

In contrast, flatboating not only survived on the trunk routes but even expanded in the face of the stiff competition generated by the newer technology. For instance, some 1,287 flatboats had arrived at New Orleans in 1816. Thirty years later the number of arrivals increased to a peak of 2,794.

The contrasting fate of the two older craft is explained in part by the differential impact of the steamboat on upstream and on downstream rates. Successful keelboat operations depended primarily on upstream revenues, with nearly five-sixths of total revenues being earned on that passage, and it was on the upstream rates that the steamboat had its most dramatic effects. Keelboating predictably retreated to the more remote areas as steamboating services spread throughout the river system. Keelboating probably experienced some productivity-raising improvements such as the practice on the tributaries of towing keelboats by steamboat. But these were only minor advances and their overall effects were small.

The case of flatboating, however, was quite different, and the survival and expansion of this common old technology occurred despite the fact that flatboats retained all their simple crude physical characteristics. Furthermore, there were no technical advances in their handling or navigation.

Flatboating productivity advanced, nevertheless, and from 1815 to 1860, total factor productivity increased at an annual compound rate of 4.4 percent or 3.8 percent, depending on the measure. However, these broad averages obscure the fact that like steamboating, most of this productivity advance occurred before the mid-1840s. For instance, by the two measures, flatboat productivity grew at an annual rate of 7.4 percent or 5.1 percent between 1815–19 and 1835–39, and at 1.6 percent or 2.6 percent thereafter. The earlier rates, which were more than twice as high as in the later periods, are impressive, especially when it is recalled that neither a significant change in the physical characteristics of the boats nor any breakthrough in the techniques of their navigation occurred during this period. Indeed, over the entire period 1815–60, the rate of productivity advance for flatboats was only slightly less than that for steamboats.

SOURCES OF PRODUCTIVITY CHANGE

THE REMARKABLE SURVIVAL AND expansion of flatboating on the western rivers is largely explained by externalities. Flatboating reaped a bountiful, if indirect, harvest from the new steamboat technology, from improvements in steamboating and from river improvements. First, the steamboat reduced the opportunity costs of labor by shortening return passage times and by lessening the hardships of the upriver trek. Second, it created inducements for repeated trips and therefore for acquiring new flatboat skills. This, in conjunction with river improvements, led to the use of larger flatboats, which further economized on labor for crews did not grow in proportion to boat size. Because of these improvements, flatboats were enabled to maintain an active role on the western rivers until the very brink of the Civil War.

The persistence of old technologies is often explained by the durability of capital. As long as earnings exceed the variable costs of operations, rents accrue to capital, justifying continued use. Consequently, new technologies do not always immediately replace old techniques, and a great deal of time often passes before innovations spread throughout an industry.

It is apparent, however, that this explanation does not apply here. Each flatboat voyage typically required a new boat, and investments would certainly have dried up unless expected revenues on each voyage exceeded costs for the crew, other variable expenses, and the new vessel. A more likely thesis is that old technologies may hold on stubbornly, either because they continue to improve independently or, as in this case, primarily because they benefit from external improvements. The frequent practice of scholars to concentrate on the new and to ignore the old reinforces the repeated, but often misleading, perspective of technological change as a series of sharp discontinuities in the historical record.

Moreover, the story of improved steamboat productivity was not simply one of technical advances. Freight rates per one hundred pounds on the upstream New Orleans-Louisville route, in 1820 constant dollars, fell from $3.12 to $2.00 between 1815 and 1820, and then fell to $.28 by 1860. Downstream, the freight costs in constant 1820 dollars changed from $.62 to $.75 between 1815 and 1820, and then fell to $.36 by 1860. It is noteworthy that because of much higher volume and utilization downstream, rates became higher that way than upstream, but also noteworthy is the fact that the decline in costs that came after the introduction of steam power (circa 1820) was greater both in absolute and in relative terms than the cost reduction from introducing steam power. The introduction of steam power was obviously of great importance, but most of the reduction of costs came from subsequent improvements after the introduction of steam.

For the most part, these later improvements and sources of productivity advance comprised a whole accumulation of minor alterations instead of any few major changes. They came primarily from learning by doing and include basic changes in the physical characteristics of the steamboats and in their handling and timing of operations. The vessels were restructured from seagoing-styled vessels to low draft hulls suitable for shallow waters, and drafts were further reduced by converting to lighter construction and equipment. Consequently, their carrying capacity and payload tons delivered per voyage increased threefold. Clearing the rivers of snags and other river improvements plus these physical changes lengthened the typical season of operations by 50 percent and quadrupled the number of yearly round trips of steamboats (1810–60).

Historical writings on steamboats have considerably overemphasized the importance of increased speeds. For example, consider Kirkland's stress: "They quickened their speeds. Whereas in 1815 it had taken twenty-five days for the voyage from New Orleans to Louisville, the pre-bellum record, made in 1853, was four days, nine hours, and thirty minutes. These record breakers traveled day and night and averaged nearly fourteen miles an hour. Most customary were trips of four and a half to six days. *While speed increased, fares decreased.*"[24]

Increased speeds, however, accounted for only about one-third of the increase in round trips per year per vessel. The longer operational period and reductions in cargo collection times together accounted for two-thirds of this efficiency gain. In general, they were not the result of new knowledge about basic principles, but a restructuring of known principles of design and energy, and many men shared in these improvements. As stated so ably by Hunter:

> The story is not, for the most part, one enlivened by great feats of creative genius, by startling inventions or revolutionary ideas. Rather it is one of plodding progress in which invention in the formal sense counted far less than a multitude of minor improvements, adjustments, and adaptations. The heroes of the piece

were not so much such men as Watt, Nasmyth, and Mausdlay, Fulton, Evans, and Shreve—although the role of such men was important—but the anonymous and unheroic craftsmen, shop foremen, and master mechanics in whose hands rested the daily job of making things go and making them go a little better.[25]

Finally, the steamboat brought an impressive surge of productivity to inland water transportation. The evidence on price convergence between the interior and the seaboard revealed in Berry's classic study and on the rapid growth of population in the West question Ransom's conclusions: "The Old Northwest at the outset of the canal era was a largely unsettled region"[26] and

> Life on a farm in the Old Northwest in the heyday of the "canal era" remained essentially an isolated, rural existence. It took the introduction of the railroad with its ability to move people and goods rapidly, together with the telegraph's revolutionary impact on the speed of information, to transform the Old Northwest into the young industrial society of the Civil War period. And canals, which had provided the initial impetus to the settlement of this vast region, were quietly retired amid the bustle of a new and very different era.[27]

The story of productivity on the rivers both for steamboats and flatboats suggests far greater developments and conditions of enterprise and commerce than Ransom's words convey. Steamboating on the rivers, not canals, was the "initial impetus" to settling the western regions and the states of the Old Northwest Territory, and the steamboat was the key that unlocked the interior.

Notes

1. Carroll and Faulk (1976), 87–88; Hughes (1983), 99–101; Jensen (1958); Vedder (1976), 85; and Walton and Robertson (1983), 186–90.
2. Taylor (1931), 99–101.
3. Ibid, 30.
4. Ibid, 30.
5. See, for instance, Albro Martin's review of David H. Fischer's *Historian's Fallacies, Toward a Logic of Historical Thought* (New York: Harper and Row, 1971), *Journal of Economic History* 32, no. 4 (December 1972): 968–70; and Peter Temin, *The Jacksonian Economy* (New York: W. W. Norton and Co., 1969), 93–112.
6. Berry (1943), 97–99.
7. This information is derived from Cole (1938) and Berry (1943) as noted in Haites, Mak, and Walton (1975), 126.
8. *Hunt's Merchant Magazine*, 6:124.
9. Buley (1962), 1.
10. For excellent treatment of different aspects of this redirection of trade and from different perspectives see Fishlow (1964), 352–64; Kohlmeier (1938); Scheiber (1969), chap. 12; and Clark (1966), 221–36.
11. Fishlow (1965), 288.
12. Scheiber (1969), 255.
13. Serial Set 619, Senate Exec. Doc. 42, 114.
14. Fishlow (1965), 337.
15. Hunter (1933–34), 23.
16. Haites, Mak, and Walton (1975), chaps. 5 and 6.
17. The productivity assessments are based on two measures of change in total factor productivity. The first compares the rate of growth of output (ton miles of freight and passengers carried, weighted by revenue shares) to a weighted index of the rate of growth of labor, capital, and other inputs. The second measure compares the rate of growth of output prices (a weighted index of freight rates and passenger fares) to the rate of growth of a weighted index of prices paid to the factors of production, the labor, capital, and other inputs.
18. Fishlow (1966), 583–646.
19. North (1968), 953–70; it should be noted that his measure using deflated ocean freight rates from periods of war to peace probably overstates the true productivity increase, because ocean rates were unusually sensitive to international conflicts.
20. North (1966), 109–10.
21. The significance of these productivity increases or rate reductions, of course, also depends on the volumes shipped. More meaningful comparisons require an analysis of total cost savings.

22. Hall (1848), 13.
23. Serial set 78, House Doc. 35, 22.
24. Kirkland (1969), 142.
25. Hunter (1949), 121.
26. See Ransom in Klingaman and Vedder (eds.) (1975), 263.
27. Ibid., 264.

Bibliography

Baldwin, Leland D. *The Keelboat Age on Western Waters.* Pittsburgh: University of Pittsburgh Press, 1941.

Berry, Thomas S. *Western Prices before 1861.* Vol. 74, Harvard Economic Studies. Cambridge: Harvard University Press, 1943.

Buley, R. C. *The Old Northwest, 1815–1840.* Bloomington, Indiana: Indiana University Press, 1962.

Carroll, John Alexander, and Odie B. Faulk. *Home of the Brave: A Patriot's Guide to American History.* New Rochelle, N. Y.: Arlington House, 1976.

Clark, John G. *The Grain Trade in the Old Northwest.* Urbana: University of Illinois Press, 1966.

Cole, A. H. *Wholesale Commodity Prices in the United States, 1700–1861.* Cambridge: Harvard University Press, 1938.

Fishlow, Albert. "Antebellum Interregional Trade Reconsidered." *American Economic Review* 54 (May 1964): 352–64.

_____*American Railroads and the Transformation of the Ante-Bellum Economy.* Cambridge: Harvard University Press, 1965.

_____"Productivity and Technological Change in the Railroad Sector, 1840–1910." *Output, Employment and Productivity in the United States after 1800.* N.B.E.R.: New York, 1966.

Hall, James. *The West: Its Commerce and Navigation.* Cincinnati: H. W. Derby and Co., 1848.

Haites, Erik F., James Mak, and Gary M. Walton. *Western River Transportation: The Era of Early Internal Development, 1810–1860.* Baltimore: Johns Hopkins University Press, 1975.

Hughes, Jonathan. *American Economic History.* Glenview, Ill.: Scott, Foresman and Co., 1983.

Hunt, Freeman, ed. *Merchants' Magazine and Commercial Review.* (Title varies.) Also known as *Hunt's Merchants Magazine.* 63 vols. New York: July 1839–December 1870.

Hunter, Louis C. *Steamboats on the Western Rivers.* Cambridge: Harvard University Press, 1949.

Hunter, Louis C. *Studies in the Economic History of the Ohio Valley.* vol. 19, nos. 1–2. *Smith College Studies in History.* Northampton, Mass.: Department of History of Smith College, 1933–1934.

Jensen, Merrill. *The New Nation A History of the United States During Confederation, 1781–1789.* New York: Alfred A. Knopf, 1958.

Kirkland, Edward C. *A History of American Economic Life.* New York: Appleton-Century-Crofts, 1969.

Klingaman, David C. and Richard K. Vedder., (eds.) *Essays in Nineteenth Century Economic History.* Athens, Ohio: Ohio University Press, 1975.

Kohlmeier, Albert L. *The Old Northwest as the Keystone of the Arch of Federal Union.* Bloomington, Ind.: Principia Press, 1938.

National Ship-Canal Convention. *Proceedings of the National Ship-Canal Convention, Held at the City of Chicago, June 2 and 3, 1863.* Chicago, 1863.

Nettels, Curtis P. *The Emergence of a National Economy, 1775–1815.* New York: Holt, Rinehart and Winston, 1962.

North, Douglass C. *The Economic Growth of the United States, 1790–1860.* Englewood Cliffs, N. J.: Prentice Hall, 1961.

_____*Growth and Welfare in the American Past.* Englewood Cliffs, N. J.: Prentice Hall, 1966

_____"Sources of Productivity Change in Ocean Shipping, 1600–1850." *Journal of Political Economy* 76, no. 5. (September–October 1968): 953–70

Ransom, Roger L. "Public Investment and the Opening of the Old North-West." *Essays in Nineteenth Century Economic History,* Klingaman, David C., and Richard K. Vedder, eds. Athens, Ohio: Ohio University Press, 1975.

Scheiber, Harry N. "The Ohio Mississippi Flatboat Trade: Some Reconsiderations." *The Frontier in American Development: Essays in Honor of Paul Wallace Gates,* David M. Ellis, ed. Ithaca: Cornell University Press, 1969.

_____(ed.) *The Old Northwest.* Lincoln: University of Nebraska Press (1969).

Taylor, George R. "Agrarian Discontent in the Mississippi Valley Preceding the War of 1812." *Journal of Political Economy* 39 (1931), reprinted in *The Old Northwest: Studies in Regional History 1887–1910,* Harry N. Scheiber, ed. Lincoln: University of Nebraska Press, 1969.

_____*The Transportation Revolution 1815–1860.* New York: Holt, Rinehart and Winston, 1957.

U.S. Congress, House. *Navigation of the Mississippi River.* Henry M. Shreve. House Doc. 11, 20 Cong., 1 Sess, 1827, Serial Set No. 170.

_____"Annual Report of the Work Done in Improving the Navigation of the Ohio and Mississippi Rivers," *Message from the President to the Two Houses of Congress,* House Doc. No. 2, 22 Cong., 1 Sess. (1831) Serial Set 216.

_____Department of the Treasury. *The Statistics and History of the Steam Marine of the U.S.* Senate Exec. Doc. 42, 32 Cong. 1 sess., 1852, Serial Set No. 619.

Vedder, Richard K. *The American Economy in Historical Perspective.* Wadsworth Publishing, 1976.

Walton, Gary M., and Ross M. Robertson. *History of the American Economy* (Fifth Edition). New York: Harcourt Brace Jovanovich, 1983.

11.

NATIVE ORIGINS OF MODERN INDUSTRY
Heavy Industrialization in the Old Northwest before 1900

William N. Parker
Yale University

BY 1840 IN THE settled portions of the Old Northwest, in farming villages and at transport junctions along rivers, small craft shops and manufactories lay woven in repeating patterns across the regularly ordered lines and tiers of the sections and townships of the agrarian landscape. Along the Miami River up from Cincinnati, in tiny spots along the canals and lower lake shores where later large cities would grow, slightly denser clusters had appeared. At the great territory's eastern end, a small and scattered charcoal iron production had grown up and at a few points where the vast Appalachian coalfield surfaced in the hills in Ohio, coal was mined.[1] Beginning in 1828 production had risen to two million tons by the end of the Civil War.

With these few and scattered exceptions, the industry of the vast farming area to the Mississippi was light industry, nearly all of it, like the village industry of New England, combining a few tools and materials with some skilled labor and local raw materials—flour milling, saw milling, tanning, shoe making, butchering and meat packing, brewing and distilling, blacksmithing, harness and carriage making and repair, boat building for the lake and river trade. Where the countryside, and with it the towns, grew a bit more prosperous—a thin prosperity, punctuated by speculative booms and breaks—some complex manufactures and services appeared. Printers, barbers, hotel keepers, bankers, lawyers, ministers, professors, doctors, dentists, and politicians set up shop. Pianos, furniture, china, bricks, even steam engines for the river boats found facilities and markets.[2]

All such craft activities filled in readily alongside the main business of the small towns, i.e., simply "business"—buying and selling, arranging land transfers, lending and financing farmers' crops, their production and their movement. As settlement spread across to the Mississippi and the canals and railroads gave huge stimulus to agricultural production, the volume of such transactions was multiplied. The easy drift of the corn, barrelled pork and beef, and timber southward along the rivers began to turn to the East, for at least the northern two-thirds of the area within reach of a direct rail and water link with the seaboard cities.[3] But this linkage did not stimulate local industry; indeed it brought in the competitively cheap manufacturers of New England, New York, Pennsylvania, and Britain. This, along with the lack of water power, kept local industry scattered and of small-scale through the Civil War. Unlike the eastern seaboard, the Old

Northwest did not industrialize under the easy guidance of experienced merchants; it had no textile phase and no putting-out system. The flatness of the terrain made it a stranger to the water wheel; horse power on the farms, steam power on boats and trains and steam and manpower in the mills pulled it into the age of electricity and the diesel engine. Flatness, indeed, was the defining feature of the geography—that and the richness of the soil and its ability to sustain high yields in corn and the major North European crops.

So matters might have stood throughout the nineteenth century. Chicago would have developed solely as a rail junction; Milwaukee, Toledo, and Cleveland would have been simply—as they were in good part in any case—the processing points or exit ports for grain and meat. In the absence of the bituminous coals south and southwest of Pittsburgh, the ores of the Mesabi, Marquette, and other ranges in the upper lakes, and the system of cheap transport that ran between them and among the developing heavy industries—fuel-using, steel-making, steel-using—the midwestern area east of the Mississippi after 1860 would have remained like that to the west, almost entirely a land of farmers, grain merchants, ranchers, meat processors—a market for eastern and European manufactures. But by 1860 Pittsburgh, with several secondary smaller sites in southeastern Ohio, had become a significant coal and iron producing area. The famous Connellsville seam of coking coal, discovered in the 1840s, came into full exploitation after 1860.[4] The steel inventions of the 1850s and 1860s raised even higher the profits and the expectations. Oil, discovered in a salt well, was taken up by New Haven capitalists who hired Colonel Drake to dig the first drilled well in 1859, and the ensuing oil rush around Oil City added to the wealth, the excitement and the rail net of the area between Pittsburgh and Lake Erie.[5] Already in the 1850s Michigan ore was being brought in by lake and canal shipping; the opening of the iron ranges in the Lake Superior country, one after another, to the giant Mesabi deposits in the early 1890s capped the opportunity.[6] On so rich a resource base, with such ready means of cheap access, it was a simple matter for the heavy industry complex to unfold out from Pittsburgh from 1880 on, with lake shipping and rail connections to serve both eastern and middlewestern markets, first in the coal mining area itself and between there and the lake shore, according to the strictest locational principles, then after 1900 under Lake Michigan midway between the coal and ore to serve the markets west and south of Chicago and the lakes.

Accompanying the development in basic fuels and metals, as early as 1880 machinery and heavy engineering plants grew up to service and supply the mines, the railroads, and one another, as well as the iron and steel mills, creating small cities in the Mahoning and Cuyahoga valleys between Pittsburgh and Cleveland and along the lower lake shore.[7] At the same time coal, oil, and electricity broke the Midwest's power bottleneck for light industry, and as the population and market thickened and the demand in growing cities multiplied, metal—fabricating plants, machinery, and tools in familiar succession developed in competition to Yankee and British imports. Thus the industrial region below the lakes by 1900 had become nearly self-sufficient in all but the most specialized equipment, and exported basic metals, and light and heavy manufactures in large volume.

SUPPLIES OF LABOR

THE LABOR, SKILLS, AND machinery required for the industrial growth were of many varieties, and technical skills were needed to operate equipment and control chemical processes, to adapt imported techniques to local conditions and ultimately to develop innovations to be fed out into the world's streams of new technology. Across all the lower states of the Old Northwest, the railroads had already created their body of machinists and repairmen, and the rapid spread of mechanical harvesting after 1860 acquainted more and more farm boys with machinery. Skilled industrial labor—millwrights, carriage makers, blacksmiths, carpenters, machinists—came in from the Northeast or directly from Great Britain or Germany, finding occupation in the growing market towns and transport junctions of the region. With the growth of agricultural wealth and the appearance of local industrial opportunities for manufactures on the scale of the small factory, the demand for such semiskilled industrial labor increased, and the supply from both farms and village industry grew by steady increments. But the rather strict locational requirements for the new heavy industries meant that such labor could not be used on the scattered patterns of a semiindustrialized agricultural region. It had to move into mining regions and nearby sites of steel and heavy engineering establishments, and into shops and merchandising centers located economically to serve the new laboring population attracted there. Heavy industry with its massive fuel and metal requirements could not move out across the farming region as light industry had done. Labor must move into the industrial locations.

Across the entire northeastern portion of the Old Northwest, below the lakes, the generation of young men and women growing up on the farms faced a particularly difficult choice. The unsettled frontier had moved beyond the Mississippi. In 1860 half the American population lived to the west of a north-south line passing through south central Ohio near Chillicothe; and half of that western population lived north of the east-west parallel through that same point.[8] Land in the Old Northwest was still available, especially in the upper and colder states and elsewhere as ranching gave place to grain and grain to a more labor-intensive mixed corn-hog, or hay-dairy farming. But the farm population was used to taking up western lands by a series of small leaps, from one tier of counties to the next, so that family ties might not be completely broken. Westward movement from the long-settled regions to Wisconsin or Minnesota under new conditions of soil and climate and into new patterns of cropping was a more serious leap. The move to the treeless plains from Kansas to the Dakotas where knowledge of new tools, new seeds, new insects, a new climate had to be acquired posed obstacles that must have seemed insuperable for many, even the very young. Still ample supplies of settlers pressed on to take up these lands, and in the 1860s and 1870s the stream was augmented by the great trek of the Scandinavian peoples across the same climatic belt to take up grain farming and dairying in the upper Midwest, while some Czechs, Hungarians, and Ukrainians joined the mass of Yankee and southern migrants to the Plains and semiarid regions. But there remained still a natural increase of the lower midwestern farm population to stay behind and to move at some point—and for many discontented farm youths, very early in their careers—off the farm.[9]

Nearly all these internal migrants were literate in English, knew arithmetic and had been exposed to the elements of Anglo-Saxon culture in its American version, as absorbed in the public rural schoolhouse, the rural church, the farmhouse, the country store and the courthouse. The women had formidable skills of housekeeping and family management, and the men generally knew something of carpentry, construction, animal care, and simple machinery. The move off the farm was almost certainly generally not far—to a growing village, to the county seat and commercial center, to a job in a warehouse, or in apprenticeship to a building or machinist trade. But midwestern farmers, however hard they worked, however menial and physically demanding many of their tasks, were not simple laborers. The strong entrepreneurial streak, a taste for business, for gambling on land and crops, which might have been absorbed as a boy observed his father, was not lost when the boy moved off the farm. He might work at the feed and seed store, or take up selling fertilizer or machinery or insurance on commission. The land grant colleges, endowed by the Morrill Act of 1863, did not have any significant effect until after the states began to assume major responsibility.[10] After 1890 a certain number of farm youth even went on through a secondary education to agricultural colleges, teacher training schools, and the state university. The culture and its formal institutions provided access to the professions—dentistry, the ministry, law; the sector servicing agriculture, and so servicing itself as well, provided employment, and by the 1890s women from farms, or more likely from the first generation off the farm, having long since professionalized school teaching, began to enter the clerical occupations.

The move from farm to city in the Midwest was thus not sudden, drastic, or complete. The youth might live at first in rooming houses or with an established relative; soon after marriage it was possible to rent, then to buy from a developer a new house with a bit of land. Women's work was lighter with more opportunity for social activity, but gardens and home food processing were common. Even in 1900 a substantial number of dairy cattle, pigs and chickens were urban or village residents. The isolation of the countryside itself was broken a bit by the interurban electric cars that spread over the area after 1890.[11]

The supplies of labor—labor skills and labor power—from these domestic sources might have filled to completion the array of labor needs of the Midwest's growing industrial cities. In the earlier industrializations in Europe, factory labor was drawn from the surrounding countryside. Numbers of Irish peasants were brought across the Irish Channel to Liverpool and other British industrial cities,[12] but otherwise the English Industrial Revolution and its counterparts before the 1840s in North France, Belgium, the Rhine Valley, and New England rested on local and largely rural labor. But the industrializations after 1850, in the German Ruhr, the American Midwest and in North Italy differed from the earlier, gentler transformations in three respects. First, they did not have easy access to a rural industrial work force already specialized in industrial work. Second, a significant part of the work required was heavy work, sheer labor power—digging, lifting, pushing, handling coal, metals, and heavy machines. It was no more strenuous than farm work, but it was not the work of an auxiliary labor force. Third, the demand for such labor seemed to come all in a rush.[13] It was a demand for the heavy work of initial capital formation, for building rail lines, erecting heavy equipment, extending mines, creating canals and docks. North Italy drew on South Italy for this labor; the Ruhr drew on East Prussia and Poland. These were not tasks for farmer-business men accustomed to light machinery and generous supplies of horsepower, but for miners, smelters, and a laboring peasantry inured to a life of heavy toil.

Earlier in New York and Ohio, when canals and rail lines were to be built, some local labor had appeared along the routes, but the bulk of the digging and hauling had been done by teams of Irish migrants who followed the line. Now the building of plants and cities south of the Great Lakes gave rise to a similar burst of demand. After 1915 such demands, and demands for factory operatives as well, were supplied to the Midwest from the southern hills. With the shut-off of immigration particularly from eastern and southern Europe by the Act of 1923, these were the only sources of supply. But southern black farm labor became unstuck only during World War I; before that, uncertainties as to its reception in the North and the immobilizing forces of ignorance, poverty, and fear in the South inhibited such mobility. Swelling rural populations in Europe had already created the push for the rural migration of Germans and Scandinavians, and the rural-urban migration of Irish to the Northeast, and later of central and eastern

Europeans and Italians. However it was not until the mid-1890s when heavy industrialization was well under way that the forces of expulsion from eastern Europe and the pull of industrial job opportunities around the lower shores of Lake Michigan and Lake Erie tilted the balance, and streams of laboring immigrants began to arrive.[14] As in the East Coast cities, the migrations had a cumulative quality. Once an ethnic group had gained a beachhead in a section of Buffalo, Pittsburgh, Cleveland, Detroit, Chicago, news traveling back through intimate channels attracted more migrants from the same region, often from the same village or town. The reverse flow of earnings to finance the voyage for others became a visible factor in some small nations' balances of payments. And the presence of countrymen in a community, with church and social circles established, vastly reduced the appearance of risk and strangeness which was for non-English-speaking nationalities the greatest barrier. Ultimately, first Pittsburgh, then Chicago, then the eastern lake cities acquired an urban industrial population layered much as in the cities of the Northeast.

But before the "new immigration" had begun to arrive in large streams, the industrial areas of the Old Northwest had already established the institutional frame, the behavioral characteristics, the fundamental values of an Anglo-Saxon business culture. The new arrivals were not settlers taking up land, trades, and offices, recreating a variant on the societies of Pennsylvania, New York, and New England. That had already been done: indeed a bloody civil war had been fought in defense of its existence and its right to expand West. The new ethnic groups were splintered, too, among themselves even where as a group they constituted a majority, and within each a certain class structure became evident. Language, religion, church schools, endogamy, and the settlement in neighborhoods gave them an integrity even as from one generation to the next their wealth and the variety of their occupations increased. They furnished labor power, working long hours at as low a wage as the market required, and their net effect was to advance the industrialization perhaps several decades beyond the point that a rate based only on the native population could have reached.

URBAN GROWTH

THE CREATION OF TOWNS from crossroad villages and modern cities by the use of the immigrants, with the supplement of foreign born labor, was not as hard or novel a job as it might have first appeared to be.[15] Cities yield economies of scale and of transport, but have themselves no clearly defined minimal size. They can grow as needed, can be created piecemeal block by block, neighborhood by neighborhood. Such physical planning as Midwest cities required was enforced by the arrangement of the plots of land in squares—the descendant of the original land surveys. The cities—

particularly in northeastern Ohio—were the work of small business men, small-time developers, bankers, contractors, politicians—all types well known and widely disseminated on the frontier and across the thoroughly commercialized rural economy. The tasks were those of moving earth and piling up brick and stone, which had been farm tasks as well.

This is not to say that urban growth, life, and activities were not the object of ambivalent attitudes on the part of farmers and the folk in the country town. Country preachers looked on them as places of sin and corruption. Farmers and rural businessmen distrusted their concentrated wealth, and particularly the power of their financial networks, dominated as they were from the East. The loss of sons and daughters to the city was a frequent complaint, and cities were associated in the Populists' demonology with the East, with gold and monopoly. But even for Populists on the western plains, cities were markets, and the doorway to markets. And for small-town Republicans and small business men, they were large-scale magnifications of their own lives and efforts.

The antagonism between town and country, which carried back in Europe to class antagonisms between lord and peasant, and between King and nobility, running like a scarlet thread through European political and economic history, barely appeared in the Midwest. There was never any question of the industrial development being shut off by inadequate market response in the countryside. Farm and city were at the ends of a harmoniously functioning hierarchy of development. A technology of civic services and urban organization—streets, gas works, water mains, trolley lines—could be modeled on the cities of the East and of Europe, and there were enough easterners and Germans in the cities to transfer and develop the technology.

Populists and fundamentalist preachers could not obliterate the lure of the city because it was in fact the lure of a new frontier. At least after the first wave of trappers, hunters, and Indian fighters, American farm and village life, though individualistic in its economy, existed in neighborhoods. Rivalry, friendly or unfriendly, and the 'booster' spirit were alive and vigorous within it and these impulses toward wealth, pride, and local superiority were easily transmitted from the small town to the agglomerations of larger scale. The growth began in the Ohio River towns, in Pittsburgh and Cincinnati, as early as 1800. The canals as they supplemented the rivers and the railroads after 1840 as they criss-crossed the farming areas created more locations for processing and small manufactures, culminating in Chicago—the New York of the Midwest. The cities of the mining and smelting districts, of the heavy equipment and engineering plants, grew out of such collecting and shipping points, along the Ohio and all the small rivers between Pittsburgh and Cleveland in northeastern Ohio.

In the half a hundred or so growing cities, mills and plants, roundhouses and port facilities could be located. Stores, shops, office and public buildings—the downtown areas—were set up. In the residential areas from far down in the working-classes areas to those of the well-to-do, new sections appeared in the square patterns of the rectangular survey, houses along standard designs, with front and back yards, on the model of the small town. Tram cars, after 1880 extended these middle class homes into new belts of farmland and caused extensive subdivision along their routes. By 1900 the structures of physical and tangible social capital had been established into which the immigrants of the twentieth century—Italians and the central and east Europeans, and the southern Blacks and hill people—could be crowded.

MOTIVATION AND SOCIAL CONTROL

HISTORY, RELIGION, AND POLITICAL theory had combined to instill in the Midwesterner the doctrines of the equality of man and the supreme worth of human ingenuity and labor. The history derived not only from the famous frontier, but also from the experience of the succeeding generations of agrarian life. Rural development was a group effort, as well as an individual one, and the man who did not work at it, making use of the opportunities that came his way, put the issue of the whole risky enterprise in doubt. All labor yielded wealth and so commanded respect, but skill, ingenuity, or brains, in handling physical materials or in managing assets and transactions—all qualities that could make labor yield new wealth, commanded admiration. It has often been observed that the Midwesterner did not worship wealth, but something called success of which wealth was the tangible token. Unlike the situation in societies based on the aristocratic principle, wealth seemed to lose rather than gain respectability as it passed from the original accumulation to the second and third generation.

The haunting echoes of Puritan theology in such a set of values—derived though it was from the experiences of the frontier community—are inescapable.[16] All men are born equal: equally free and equally ignorant of their destiny. Whether they are equal in sin or in innocence is less important than the fact of their equality and their ostensibly equal access to grace. In seventeenth-century New England, the signs of grace were not wealth, but visible sainthood, the bearing, disposition, virtue, and radiance that came from a godly public life and a sincere private faith in the goodness and justice of God. In that theology assurance of salvation was never given. A man stood, in Milton's words, "as ever in my great Taskmaster's eye", and far from causing believers to despair, this uncertainty drove a Christian to try even harder and without remission. Of course, nineteenth-century midwestern Protestants admitted the existence of luck, as seventeenth-century Calvinists believed in the doctrine of election, but in both faiths, life was lived with an objective in view. Whether sainthood or more riches, the goal was open to all men to be reached for and it was attainable, if at all, only by a lifetime of work, activity, intelligence, and striving. In midwestern America the opportunity to acquire wealth seemed suddenly to have opened wide, and its acquisition, if not an indication of saintliness, nevertheless earned a man an equivalent or even a superior renown.

This ethic, whether called Puritan or pragmatic, animated activity within the structures of midwestern social life-families, small towns, schools, social clubs, and business enterprises. It caused men to employ readily the capitalist forms of economy that were at hand—private property ownership, banks and financial instruments, free wage labor, contracts and markets. But form—even the forms of government and public order—were not long allowed, as the phrase went, "to stand in the way of progress." Every social form and practice was measured by the iron test: Does it work? And the units of measurement, it was widely agreed, were dollars and cents.

The ethic was derived in equal parts, not only from the frontier and from God, but also from Thomas Jefferson. There was in it an ingredient from eighteenth-century Republican rationalistic humanism that could save so driven and greedy a society from the ultimate self-defeating idiocy of destroying its own human capital. Both children and immigrants had to be socialized and motivated and, if not wholly coopted into the social enterprise, at least induced or obliged to pull their own weight and not to dissent. For this, two liberal institutions were at work: compulsory education and the system of law, justice, and open opportunity. Schools and law were the institutions which gave stability and continuity to a mobile population and a rapidly expanding social and economic organism. But to speak of their function in nourishing and perpetuating the conditions of industrial growth is not to denigrate the integrity of their own peculiar objectives: education and justice. Both schools and courts were the locus of a formidable cadre of skilled professionals commanding respect for their own sake as well as for the economic ends they served. They served those ends so well indeed because they were never wholly coopted within them.

The midwest, in short, although becoming wealthy in an economy of free and enthusiastic enterprise preserved the elements of a liberal society. Education and justice, subject as they might be to corruption and transitory public pressures, still preserved a human face, and by means far more effective than physical force gave hope to the stream of immigrants and to the succeeding generations of youth. To greater or lesser degrees, it 'middle-westernized' them.

The effect on the quantity and flexibility of labor supply was significant. Off farms the indigenous population still was guided by the rural ideals of work, self-improvement, and achievement, settling at some point into the routines of an increasingly structured business civilization, carrying out white-collar jobs and specialized professions as required. The immigrant population as it grew up in ethnic neighborhoods developed an increasing political influence. At the local level, the heritage of the Northwest Ordinance—schools, courts, and ballots— allowed new institutions such as the Catholic Church, the Democratic Party, and local labor unions to break through the small-town oligarchies of wealth, virtue, and Protestant uniformity. The location of urban government within the sovereignty of the state legislature insured the maintenance of rural norms. But any group was free to run its own affairs, to seek a job, to send its children to a recognized school, and to aspire to rising incomes.

The semifeudal class consciousness instilled in the immigrants from Europe was shed, and a new one, based on the conditions of industrial society, was acquired only slowly and with great uncertainty. Local labor unions organized in the skilled trades to establish monopolies in local markets, but in the great and growing new industries, organizations of unskilled or semiskilled labor broke against the internal divisions in the labor force and were floated away after 1900 on the flood of new arrivals. Labor as such was respected and laboring men seeking their fair shares in the system were not stopped from group action. But when labor put on a political face of its own, particularly when the demands threatened property, public order, and the inviolability of contracts, all the pressures of law and public opinion that had preserved and regulated the bourgeois life of the small town were brought down upon its head.

Selig Perlman, the great and sensitive historian of American labor wrote,[17]

> Briefly, if the century-long experience of American labor as an organized movement holds any great lesson at all, that lesson is that under no circumstances can labor here afford to arouse the fears of the great middle class for the safety of private property as a basic institution. Labor needs the support of public opinion, meaning the middle class, both rural and urban, in order to make headway with its program of curtailing, by legislation and by trade unionism, the abuses which attend the employer's unrestricted exercise of his property rights. But any suspicion that labor might harbor a design to do away altogether with private property, instead of merely regulating its use, immediately throws the public into an alliance with the anti-union employers.

THE SCALE OF THE REGION

BETWEEN 1830 AND 1880, the midwestern farm region from the Alleghenies to the Rockies expanded in size and in volume and variety of output. The growing industrial districts of the Old Northwest—both those that shipped and processed the farm output and those that supplied its inputs—the items of farm capital and farm consumption—grew as well, and with the swelling size of the whole mass of production and trade, efficiency, income, wealth and thence markets and production further increased. Initially after 1860 there was the simple substitution of regional products for British and East Coast imports. Since agricultural exports remained at high volume, such substitution presumably made the region richer in holdings of external assets and less dependent on eastern capital. Demand on farms was high, but more important was the share of income going to labor in the industrial population itself. Much deep research is needed to get at the determinants of the wage rates in all the markets and for all the varieties of labor. Somehow, a division of income between spending and saving was created which, when supplemented by the financial flows from local banks and the East, was satisfactory for continued growth. The concern for adequate market outlets is evident in the great emphasis by mail order firms and shop-front stores alike as well as by great firms, on selling. Salesmanship became notoriously the hallmark of the Midwesterner.[18]

The heady spiral of solidly based growth in supplies and in demand gave to the Midwest's economy and culture in the late 19th Century a vigor, a zest, an optimism and self-assurance which made further accomplishment easy and growth apparently endless. The stimulus raised the value of time even as the good living and cheap protein diet increased physical energies; never perhaps in the history of the world have nominally free and prosperous farmers, businessmen, and laborers worked so hard, such long hours, so energetically and with such visible reward.[19] The Northeast had been "cabinned, cribbed and confined," by valleys and hillsides, by peculiar beliefs, by history and class structures; the South by the foul blight of slavery and racial prejudice, an ill-motivated work force, and an idle and ignorant aristocracy. From 1880 to 1930, the Midwest *was* America. Its vision of itself, its self-confidence, had a physical basis—in rich resources and the fortunate self-reinforcing efficiencies of a production scale easily won over a flat terrain and by the homogeneous culture of what radicals suspiciously called market capitalism and bourgeois democracy. Midwesterners, if ever exposed to these phrases, put them in quotation marks and could hardly repeat them without a pang of bad conscience as if even the very use of such terms were a betrayal of the only form of economy or society worth mentioning anywhere on earth or in history. The complement of expanding agriculture and expanding mines, transport, and manufactures, and of a correspondingly expanding internal demand made the midwestern economy a large operation. It had to be large if it were to exist at all, and its size and success rested not only on physical sources but on the optimism generated by the prospect of continued expansion. Import substitution and prosperous farms and cities could provide the expanding markets, but like resources, these sources of growth contained in themselves a tendency to exhaustion and self-limitation. Eventually, creative technological changes and a closer attachment to the world markets would be needed to support the demand and supply conditions that a growing output would require.[20]

ECONOMIES IN PLANTS AND FIRMS

IN THE WORLD'S INDUSTRIAL regions, economies of scale appeared at many points in the organization after 1870. In some branches of production, the economies were external to the individual firm and so offered no problem to the growth of a competitive economy. In agriculture, for example, the productivity advantage to the Midwest of the huge volume of its production —the falling costs in cheap storage, transport, handling and processing facilities, and its input industries, especially machinery—were notable. But in individual plants,too, economies of scale and systematic operation also appeared; and in the organization of such industries—transportation, smelting, continuous processing and assembly—the large corporation made its appearance. Whether cost advantages alone made such economic monsters able to out-compete their smaller rivals, or whether they made their way in the world like village bullies, by threats and shows of market power, they became a fact, and established themselves by 1900 in many major industries, not only railroads, where their cost advantages were obvious, but also in steel, meat packing, farm machinery, oil refining, and within a decade of 1900, automobiles. Many industries where large firms offered no special advantages came to be organized in unstable, and after 1890, occasionally illegal, producer combinations—the "trusts" and monopolies on regional or national scale.[21]

Large plants and large firms faced a serious and novel problem of internal organization. The family farm had had the problem of control of its family members. Sons had to work in the field and daughters in the farm kitchen. The sexual division of labor was clear and unequivocal and enforced by individuals' images of roles, of sexuality, and of self-worth. Affection, discipline, the promise of reward, and finally habit confirmed the countryside in its system of labor management. In small shops, proprietorships and partnerships, the system of semifilial apprenticeship sometimes worked though much less extensively than in the more stable societies of the East and of Europe. The independence and individualism of the indigenous labor force, its mobility and restlessness, were notable. But as firms and plants grew larger, more formal systems of control were required. The competitive advantages of size—whether real or merely financial—were evidently great enough to sustain such organizations, if the labor could be obtained, organized, and controlled.

Here then, was a dilemma. How would a society of small-scale units, competitive farming, and industry organize itself to encompass the presence of giant intruders on its markets and the enforcement of semimilitary systems of internal control, of bosses and workers within them? Other industrializations—in Germany, for instance, and in Japan—counted on feudalism or militarism, or the habits of ancient bureaucracies to provide the answer. Workers lined up like peasants on the estate or soldiers in the army to march into the factory. To a degree, the American workers, native and immigrant, fell into this pattern with surprising readiness. The problem of worker discipline was no harder to solve, nor, until the 1930s, was its solution any more controversial, than the problem of the market discipline to be enforced on the large enterprises themselves.

Shop management began, in fact, as in the early textile mills in England and Rhode Island, by an adaptation of the system of piece rates or subcontracting to homes or small-scale shops. In the steel- and metal-working industries, a portion of the labor was contracted for by the firm through master mechanics who brought in their own staff on contract. The mill then was not a monolithic, centralized structure but a network of small units. The difficulties with the system were many, not only in the relation of subcontractors to workers, but in the independence of the subcontractors themselves, particularly where as master workmen they were few enough to organize in unions and go out on strike. Centralization of control promised to yield higher profit once a firm was organized and its workers had given up other options in order to join it. As the political possibility of centralized management came in view, the inducements to employers to enforce it were raised by the researches into industrial management developed by Taylor.[22] The importance of Taylorism has never been measured, and his methods represent an ideal type of technocratic efficiency that lends itself to caricature. But the simultaneous discovery of efficiency independently in many locations created the typical midwestern factory system—not differing greatly from that of the Waltham system in New England textiles. Productivity was strikingly increased by such methods, and this was the easier to do in that expanding markets allowed productivity gains to be translated into more, rather than fewer, jobs.

The result was not only productivity gains, but an increased authority of management over workers and a clear division of labor and function between the two. How could a society that was based on individual freedom produce such a result? The answer, once again, lies in the "Puritan" component of the midwestern culture's concept of freedom and the individual. Puritanism was characterized by two elements relevant in this context: the individual's faith in himself, his responsibility only to himself and to God; and the respect for the logic of the natural world, for science as the revelation jointly with the Bible of the hand of God. Individual drive and an engineering mentality created a society with an attenuated sensitivity to the human condition, to weak and erring mortality, to the sins and inefficiencies of the flesh.[23] *Fordism*, as the system of efficient factory management came to be called, was its culmination. But it was a system applicable not only to workers on the factory floor but to all phases of corporate operation —inventory management, buying, selling, and finance. It represented a triumph of the accounting mentality over unbridled human creativity. In the Puritan and liberal views, human freedom was derived from and exercised in a world and a society of laws, not of men. Freedom in society is the willing acceptance of an orderly and impersonal discipline. Why should this not be true in a factory or a corporation? But where markets were wide and homogeneous, products simple and capable of production *en masse*, and workers available and malleable, the midwest system, which in its origins in New England has been called the American system, passed the supreme test of its own devising: it produced immediate, tangible, measurable results.

PROBLEMS OF MARKET ORGANIZATION

AN ANALOGOUS PROBLEM WAS created by large firms externally on the markets for products, materials, and labor. Agricultural producers were as numberless as the sands of the sea and sold their goods through channels in which no one could much influence the prices received. Above them in the chain of distribution stood meat and grain dealers, elevator operators, the flour mill and the slaughterhouse, and the railroad, canal, and lake shippers. These were fewer in number, and in any given year could drive bargains from which a farmer, with crops planted or even harvested and animals on the hoof, found it hard to escape. Tiny pockets of monopoly, local shakedowns, appeared everywhere in the system of marketing; where a farmer tried to escape by changing his crop mix, or seeking out a rival dealer or shipper, they reappeared somewhere else. But each handler or processor of a crop on its way to market found himself in a similar situation at the next level. For shipments beyond a very local market, there were competitors, and this layering built up to the great regional centers at Omaha, Minneapolis, and the lake ports, notably Chicago. Here the titles to commodity shipments were bought and sold, pieces of paper changed hands, complicated futures and forward transactions were accomplished and prices fluctuated hour by hour with expectations—sometimes based on information about the future course of supply and demand.[24] Agriculture, then, though honeycombed with tiny and transient local monopolies, was taken as a whole as a textbook model of what economists far away in the East and in Europe described as perfect competition.

The sturdy though delicate web of markets and commodity prices that connected farms to distant markets was partly the creation of steam transport on land and sea that had really reduced the costs of hauling freight over land, and over both land and water had increased the range and speed, reliability, and predictability of shipments. The telegraph and cable set the capstone on the system enabling market information to be diffused instantaneously over wide areas and so extending the range of arbitrage and potential competition. But the railroad also furnished brutal instances of local monopoly power at every station it served. The high fixed costs of a new railroad and the undeniable cost economies of extensive and systematic operation gave railroads local market power; hence the railroads from the 1870s on provided the Midwest with the first incentives to producers' combinations.[25] The opportunity was not missed by politicians, and it served as a target for the zeal of civic-minded idealists. Railroads first brought out in a substantial way the reforming streak in midwesterners, among farmers, businessmen, and professional men, and among liberal ministers and their heirs: the teachers and professors of the moral—now increasingly called "social"—sciences. Railroad regulation at the state level was followed in cities by regulation of the "natural monopolies" of franchised public utilities. The movement, which owed much to German-derived social democracy in Wisconsin, spread rapidly, if often not very effectively, and showed that private property and laissez-faire were no sacred cows if they created monopoly, allowed discrimination among users, and resulted in the misallocation of productive resources.

Manufacturing industry stood midway between the extremes of agriculture's competitive organization and the public utilities' natural or state-created monopoly. Here, as in commodity distribution, in artisan shops and small plants using local materials and serving local markets, pockets of monopoly could exist. Usually, however, without heavy fixed costs or some rare aptitudes or skills, a producer pricing too far above costs found himself undercut. Competition came less in the anonymous, faceless form it exhibited on commodity markets and more often in specific rivalry among a few shops or producers. Here the incentive to combination was always present; in the skilled trades as we have seen, local unions formed. Still, new labor and new entrepreneurs constantly undermined the effectiveness of such combinations.

But the Midwest's industrial burst after 1880 was built on scale economies of large regional markets. In some of the industries where it occurred, optimal plant size was far greater than that of a local shop or smithy, and the large plants serving the wide market tended for reasons of transport cost minimization described above, to be located near one another. The industries had high capital costs, too, and acute needs for outside financing in large lumps. And since finance and all successful asset management is built on the insurance principle of diversifying risks, its pecuniary economies of scale were themselves very great, though many devices developed later for spreading these among small investors, banks, and funds.

So from 1880 on, large plants, large collections of plants, large firms, large producer combinations, large networks of centralized financial control grew up—organizations in which physical cost saving, the benefits of a superior stability, continuous throughput, were inextricably intertwined with the bargaining power of the large customer or the large supplier. It was a system in which within firms many market relations were internalized, and the tests of the market bargaining were supplanted by internal accounting controls and by the internal power politics of the large organization in which routine could enforce discipline and measurement could rationalize routine.

The movement to industrial concentration was the Midwest's thorniest problem—the one most at odds with its proclaimed ideology, while at the same time it seemed to be a source of its industrial strength. Once again, pragmatism furnished the test. So long as the system, supplemented by bursts of "reform" and half-hearted "trust busting," worked, so long as industrial expansion went forward, so long as the national product rose and a vast majority shared in its rise, democracy asked for nothing more. It did not seek to know whether the growth came in the face of the abundant opportunities offered by large markets and ingenious technical change, because of the system of production organization and distribution, or in spite of it, or what hidden operating costs or social inequities its dynamic operation concealed.

THE DAWN OF MODERN TIMES

MIDWESTERN SMALL TOWN SOCIETY by 1900 had created then a gigantic industrial structure across the northeastern edge of the vast region of small farms, rail junctions, and crossroads towns. At the foundation was a drive to produce, and in producing to get rich—not for wealth, not for comfort, not even for power, but simply for the use of talents and energies, simply not to waste the greatest opportunity in the world on the part of common men to increase their earnings by tending to their job and on the part of an uncommon or lucky few to create little empires as energies, wit, luck, or fate might dispose. Deep in the folds of this single-minded culture lay the discipline needed to create, tolerate, and enforce efficient command structures within corporations, and to threaten to overtop even large corporations by state or federal regulation where the ingrained rush toward monopoly ran counter to the social purpose. That purpose was not so much to allow society to acquire wealth as to leave open opportunities for individuals to engage in its further acquisition.

In this way, effective though surely not ideal, through the doorway that lay along the line between Pittsburgh, Cleveland, and Chicago came American industrial prosperity in the Republican half-century before 1930. Here, too, originated many of those transformations of the Midwest's underlying layers of civilization that gave the region and the country a second further expansion and a drastic cultural transformation in the four liberal Democratic decades that followed. Then the spotlight of industrial opportunity shifted from this immense heartland region of farms and furnaces and the response appeared in the American periphery—toward the continent's sea-coasts, in the already densely industrialized Northeast, the stubbornly agrarian rural South, and the ranching and lumbering regions of the Far West and the Pacific rim.

Since 1950, under the name of *Americanization,* this whole body of agrarian and industrial activity with its accompanying organization and ethos has blended with native cultural traditions in the wider streams of world history. No doubt it would betray an excessively narrow perspective to trace it all back to the Connecticut Puritans who first settled Cleveland. But if so, then the conclusion appears that the human needs that modernization appears to satisfy—much as an occasional new social historian may profess to despise them—appear not to be confined to the settlers and immigrants of the Old Northwest, but to constitute, in one form or another, a portion of the universal aspirations of man and womankind.

Author's Note: This essay marks the beginning and not I hope, the end, of a cycle of research on this history. The topics so lightly treated here, and many more, demand sharper definition so as to isolate significant issues. Ultimately, one would like to develop a feel for the relative weights of the factors (such as religion, schooling, resources, entrepreneurship, markets, scale economies) in the development. Only such an Olympian view would allow the construction of counterfactuals (e.g., how fast would the development have proceeded had the eastern European immigrants not come in?) The effort is like the race of Achilles and the tortoise. The goal of full understanding is never reached, but each new research may narrow the distance.

The present manuscript began as a vastly overambitious effort to survey the route and to test my own intuitions on the subject. It was written in first overextended draft under rather odd circumstances in a foreign country at a distance from books and students and with no other pressing occupation. The intuitions exploited were derived from growing up (through high school) in Columbus and from studying in later life similar heavy industrial developments in Britain, Germany, France, Belgium, the light industrial development in New England, and the Old Northwest's agrarian expansion before 1860 and its resultant agrarian civilization and economy.

It is particularly deficient through the superficiality of my knowledge of labor history, urban history, and many topics that greatly engage young historians of the 1980s. The effort is made here to look forward toward the

twentieth century from the eyes of the 1870s, not backward with the eyes of
the 1970s, or even the 1930s. But there is good reason for beginning in history at the beginning; chronological order is the historian's only monopoly,
with all the surprises and distortions it creates. The Republican business
society that ran America until 1930 underwent shattering changes in the
four decades of depression, war, and liberalism. But it would be hard to argue that its vitality and expansive power in transformed form are played
out in the world of the 1980s.

The sources for the history are not well organized for easy access. Good
collections of state documents, business publications, and social studies exist at the several state universities and in the state and local historical societies' libraries, and a few state histories of varying usefulness have been
written. Even business histories, as catalogued in the Harvard Business
School bibliographies[26] are not as abundant as one would expect. No good
bibliography of the materials for a regional economic history has been un-
covered. Except for Father Hogan's work on steel, virtually no recent secondary studies appear to exist for the histories of individual trades or
industries. For some reason only the cotton textile industries, in the United
States, north and south, and the New England machinery industry have
been much favored by historians. The utilization of the moderately abundant quantitative materials in the state and federal censuses is no better. I
could find no studies of internal migration from farms to nearby towns and
cities to estimate the sources and size of the streams.

Two areas somewhat better endowed with scholarship are the history of
the immigrants and the labor movement in the cities and large plants and
stories of a few of the great entrepreneurs and politicians, notably for this
period Carnegie, McKinley, Hanna, Rockefeller and the early days of Henry
Ford. This emphasis in the historiography since 1930 reflects a creditable
concern with the central struggle of big capital with labor in the mid-
twentieth century, and the nineteenth century and early twentieth century
problem of assimilating both into the structures and ethos of American capitalism. The less sensational history of how those structures and institutions developed on the basis of a native culture has been ignored.

One need only compare these works with the rich and sophisticated
studies of the New England mills, the libraries on the South, the tales of the
ranching and mining frontiers in the West to realize the poverty of the central region's literature. To explore the reasons for this would take us far beyond the scope of this note. Perhaps the Midwest has been the norm
against which other regions have been seen. Among most of us modern
scholars, it is not norms but aberrations that seem intriguing. The dearth of
economic studies in Midwest industrialization is thus, in a sense, a confirmation of the final thesis in this paper.

Notes

Middle Western heavy industrialization after 1870 clusters at three foci: Pittsburgh, Chicago, and northeastern Ohio (Cleveland and the counties and small cities in its orbit). This essay centers on the evidence of, and reasons for, industrial growth in the counties in northern and northeastern Ohio before the moderately heavy immigration from eastern Europe after 1895. Pittsburgh lies outside the Old Northwest, and in fact shows many features of the eastern industrial areas in Pennsylvania. Chicago's development is early, strong, but based before 1895 on light manufacturing and food processing (farm machinery and stockyards) and on railroad transshipments. Both these agglomerations are prominent, even dominant, parts of midwestern industrialization but must be omitted here to allow the story to develop around the lower shore of Lake Erie, the lands in northern Ohio first settled predominantly by New Englanders and still called by the name given them when they formed part of Connecticut's original land grant: the Western Reserve. Relevant census statistics on the growth of manufacturing and population, by region of origin, are given in the Appendix.

I am indebted for research assistance to Margaret Levenstein and Maria Choi, for typing to Jeanne Boyce, to the Department of Economics of Yale University for a grant-in-aid, and to the Department of Economics of Ohio University for encouragement and further support.

1. The Ohio coal field and its exploitation in 1880–1900 are described in Ohio State Inspector of Mines, Annual Reports, see esp. sixth Annual Report for 1880 (Columbus, 1881), 13–25 and 57–60. The geology of the Hocking Valley field and the iron works in the Hanging Rock region beginning in 1827 are described in Hunt (1880). Eavenson (1938) appears to have combed the early literature for references to coal mines in the Pittsburgh bed on both sides of the Ohio River (pp. 6–25, 27–30). Production figures for the Ohio fields from 1828 are estimated in Ray (1914). The *Iron Manufacturer's Guide* lists about thirty charcoal furnaces in northeastern Ohio and 50 in southeastern and southern Ohio (Leslie [1859], 109–22). These are small charcoal or raw coal furnaces, and the numbers include furnaces started as early as 1809 and abandoned by 1859. Eavenson's (1942) exhaustive discussion covers western Pennsylvania from 1783 to 1885 (pp. 155–203); Ohio (pp. 264–274); and the Illinois areas shipping to St. Louis and Chicago in the 1840s, (286–92). Eavenson also annual coal production figures, by county, from 1806–85 for each state.

2. Danhof (1969); Weisenburger (1941), 56–118.

3. Kohlmeier (1938).

4. Temin (1964), 79, 94.

5. Giddens (1938), 59; Martens (1971), 21–58.

6. Temin (1964), 92–93; basic references are Wirth (1937), esp. Chap. 1; Walker (1979); Whitaker (1931); Swineford (1882); and for the Cuyuna Range, the Works Progress Administration Historical Records Project (1940).

7. Williamson and Myers (1955) gives an excellent account of one of the largest of these, the Bucyrus Erie Company.

8. Paullin (1932), Plate 80A.

9. A careful quantitative study remains to be done to trace the diaspora of this farm youth, particularly after 1870, when the agricultural land of the three lower states of the Old Northwest had become thoroughly settled. The statements here were surmises based on logic, impressionistic examination of census records, farm journals, and the popular literature. Content analysis of the farm press, on the lines of Louis Galambos's efforts on other issues, might yield some results. (Galambos, 1975)

10. Eddy (1956), Chaps. 4, 5.

11. Hilton and Due (1960).

12. Jeffrey Williamson's recent article contains an interesting new treatment of the role of the Irish migrants in the English Industrial Revolution ([1986], 693–720).

13. Gerschenkron (1962), 5–52, 353–67.

14. The literature on immigration does not seem to give much detailed help on the matter. It appears that the labor force before 1895, if not off the farms, was English-speaking with admixture of Germans, especially in skilled categories and some Italian labor. Critical to the process in its earlier phase was the arrival of many Scandinavian immigrants to the ore-mining regions of Lake Superior from the 1870s on (Karni, Kamps and Ollila [1975], 55–69, by M. E. Kamp). In the Mesabi range towns in 1905, foreign born constituted 55.4 percent of the population, mostly Finns, Italians, and central Europeans. Gates ([1951] 95–109) gives interesting figures for the Michigan copper area far to the north after 1845. In the Pittsburgh and Western Pennsylvania area generally, with its immense expansion, the 'new' immigration began earlier. Data are given in Appendix, tables 2, 3. The great study of Kuznets, Thomas, and others (1957–64) bases estimates by state for net immigration between censal intervals from estimates of birth and death rates and natural increase of native and foreign born compared to census totals. The relevant tables show that in the migration of foreign-born white males, decade net totals (in hundreds) are:

	1870–80	1880–90	1890–1900	1900–1910	1910–20
Ohio	414	711	541	1479	1087
Indiana	128	159	181	381	124
Illinois	639	1760	1413	2392	1014
Michigan	781	1027	439	902	1434

Kuznets and Thomas, vol. I. (1957), spp. Table P-1.

15. Some new material exists in the city histories of Akron and Cleveland that I have examined at Yale University Library. Lane (1892) gives material, together with the usual biographical sketches of notables, for the years to 1892, when Akron's great growth from twenty-five thousand in 1890 to over two hundred thousand in 1920 began. See thereafter City Plan for Akron (Nolen, 1919),

Centennial History (1925), Nichols (1929). For Cleveland, see Robinson (1877) and Orth's gigantic history (vol. 1) and hagiography (vol. 2), as well as the intelligently done sketches of the city's earlier cultural life and growth in the nineteenth century (Benton, 3 parts, 1943–46) to the Civil War. These works were evidently subscription literature promoted by the editor-publisher and partially paid for by the 'representative men' themselves. They are hardly a scientific sample.

In this section I have also utilized the minidescriptions of each city in these states contained in the Tenth Census: 1880 (Population).

16. These observations are based on reading, and reflection on reading, done for a sketch of New England's early industrialization (Parker, 1987). See references there cited.

17. Perlman (1928), 160–161.

18. The history of the traveling salesman is a long one going back to the Yankee peddlers of the early nineteenth century, the sales forces of large commission houses, and the integration of them into the sales agencies or distributors of manufacturing firms, insurance companies, and the like (See Chandler, [1977], Chap. 9). Current research by Olivier Zunz is underway on the shift by Dupont from selling through local agents to a cadre in the field of specialized agents operating out of branch offices and moving from one to another. In rural areas the Agricultural Extension system, organized under the Smith Lever Act of 1914, represents a similar organization distributing knowledge of crops and practices. A peculiarly midwestern development, which spread elsewhere, is the mail-order house beginning after the introduction of rural free delivery on the farms (Fuller [1964], 249–54). With wider mail service came growth of an advertising industry with advertisements in periodical literature. With highways and cities in the twentieth century came billboards, and with radio and television the commercial. The salesman is a folk type in the popular literature from George Ade's *Fables In Slang* to Arthur Miller's *Death of a Salesman*.

19. For an interesting discussion of a lengthening of the workday as a source of increased output, often paraded as increased productivity, see the recent paper by Clark (1986) on Europe. For the Midwest, I found evidence of a longer average day in some earlier research that measured man hours in farm operations relative to the farm labor force employed. See also the interesting remarks of Danhof (Danhof [1969], 141–144) on economizing time.

The shift from horse to tractor between 1920 and 1940 must have relieved the pressures that the time constraints in the presence of abundant land and market pressures and opportunities presented. But that shift itself, by releasing one-quarter or more of cropland from hay and oats further raised the strain on farmers to work more land, even as it speeded up operations.

20. Technological change is an aspect of midwestern industrial development not examined in this essay. A plausible hypothesis is that fundamental scientific research was undervalued and neglected for engineering and inventive activity with a quicker pay-off. The temptation for private and public agencies and popular attitudes to favor a shallow and shortsighted pragmatism is great where resources and markets are ample and vigorous growth occurs on a very limited

technological basis. The possibility has never been examined for the Midwest, but the discussion of England's nineteenth- and twentieth-century development vis-à-vis the continent may be to the point. See an allusion to the problem of technological diffusion and technological creativity in an earlier treatment of the European experience (Parker; [1979] 78–79).

21. The most recent, and one of the most judicious of the long list of reexaminations of the 'trust problem' is by Naomi Lamoreaux (1986). The whole history is now undergoing painful reassessment stimulated by the massive researches of Alfred D. Chandler (1962, 1977). Chandler's work addressed not to the trust problem (horizontal combination) directly, but to the extensions of vertical integration forward into marketing and distribution. The lower costs achieved in this way by a steadier and more assured throughput from raw materials to final consumer derive from economies of scale and systematic operation in the production activities and appear in every case to rest on the spreading of fixed costs of heavy and expensive equipment.

22. I have greatly relied here on (and perhaps misused) the essays of the labor historian, David Montgomery (1979, esp. chaps. 1, 2) and some of the abundant literature on work organization and on Frederick Taylor and 'Taylorism', cited there. On New England, see Ware (1931, Chap. 4).

23. See note 16, above.

24. A valuable recent examination of the development commodity futures markets is made by Jeffrey Williams ([1986], and especially in chaps. 4 and 5 of his Yale dissertation [1980]) of the same title. An instance of the 'fine tuning' of the market to relative costs of sailing ships and steam in lake shipping in the 1850s and 1860s is given in a thorough and seldom cited dissertation by Donald Dohrman (1976).

25. The older literature is still best represented by W. Z. Ripley's classic books on rates, regulation, finance, and organization (1912, 1913).

26. Daniells (1957 and supplements).

BIBLIOGRAPHY

Pre-1880; Resources; General

Barron, Hal S. *Those Who Stayed Behind: Rural Society in Nineteenth-Century New England*, Cambridge: Cambridge University Press,1984.

Conzen, Michael P. *Frontier Farming in an Urban Shadow*, Madison: State Historical Society of Wisconsin, 1971.

Chaddock, Robert E. "Ohio Before 1850" *Studies in History Economics and Public Law*, New York: Columbia University Press, 1908.

Danhof, Clarence H. *Change in Agriculture*, Cambridge: Harvard University Press, 1969.

Eavenson, Howard N. *The First Century and a Quarter of American Coal Industry*, Pittsburgh: By the author, 1942.

Eavenson, Howard N. *The Pittsburgh Coal Bed*, New York: The American Institute of Mining and Metallurgical Engineers, 1938.

Gates, William B. *Michigan Copper and Boston Dollars*, Cambridge: Harvard University Press, 1951.

Giddens, Paul H. *The Birth of the Oil Industry*, New York: Macmillan, 1938.

Hogan, William T. *Economic History of the Iron and Steel Industry in the United States, 3 vols.* Lexington, Mass: D. C. Heath and Co. 1971,

Hunt, T. Sterry, *The Hocking Valley: Its Coals, Iron-Ores, Blast Furnaces, and Railroads*, Boston: S. E. Cassino, 1881.

Jordan, Philip D. *Ohio Comes of Age: 1873-1900*, vol. 5, Columbus: Ohio State Archaeological and Historical Society, 1943.

Kohlmeier, A. L. *The Old Northwest as the Keystone in the Arch of the Federal Union*, Bloomington, Ind.: Principia Press, 1938.

Lesley, J. P. *Iron Manufacturer's Guide*, New York: John Wiley, London: Trubner and Co., 1859.

Martens, Charles D. *The Oil City*, Oil City: First Seneca Bank and Trust Co., 1971.

Ohio, State of, Inspector of Mines, *6th Annual Report for the Year 1880*, Columbus: G. J. Brand and Co., 1881.

Parker, William N. "From Northwest to Mid-west: Social Bases of a Regional History." *Essays in Nineteenth Century Economic History: The Old Northwest*, D. C. Klingaman and R. K. Vedder, eds. Athens: Ohio University Press, 1975.

Ray, Frank A. *Ohio Coal Supply and Its Exhaustion*, Columbus: The Ohio State University Bulletin, vol. 18, no. 32: College of Engineering, Bulletin No. 12, 1914.

Saward, Frederick W. *Saward's Annual*, New York: Saward's Journal, 1920.

Scheiber, Harry N. *Ohio Canal Era: A Case Study of Government and the Economy, 1820–1861*, Athens: Ohio University Press, 1969.

Swank, James M. *History of the Manufacture of Iron In All Ages*, Philadelphia: By the author, 1884.

Swineford, A. P. *Annual Review of the Iron Mining and Other Industries of the Upper Peninsula*, Mining Journal, 1882.

Temin, Peter, *Iron and Steel in Nineteenth-Century America An Economic Inquiry*, Cambridge: Massachussets Institute of Technology Press, 1964.

Walker, David A. *Iron Frontier*, St. Paul: Minnesota Historical Society Press, 1979.

Walsh, Margaret, *The Manufacturing Frontier: Pioneer Industry in Antebellum Wisconsin, 1830-1860*, Madison: State Historical Society of Wisconsin, 1972.

Whitaker, Joe R. *Negaunee, Michigan: An Urban Center Dominated by Iron Mining*, Chicago: University of Chicago Libraries, 1931.

Wirth, Fremont, *The Discovery and Exploitation of the Minnesota Iron Lands*, Cedar Rapids: Torch Press, 1937.

Works Progress Administration, The Minnesota Records Survey Project (WPA), *The Cuyuna Range, A History of a Minnesota Iron Mining District*, St. Paul, 1940.

Labor

Barton, Josef J. *Peasants and Strangers*, Cambridge: Harvard University Press, 1975.

Bodnar, John, *Immigration and Industrialization*, Pittsburgh: University of Pittsburgh Press, 1977.

Brody, David, *Workers in Industrial America*, New York, Oxford: Oxford University Press, 1980.

Eddy, Edward D., Jr. *Colleges for Our Land and Time*, New York: Harper Brothers, 1956.

Fenton, Edwin, *Immigrants and Unions, A Case Study*, New York: Arno Press (A New York Times Company), 1975.

Galambos, Louis, *The Public Image of Big Business in America, 1880-1940*, Baltimore: Johns Hopkins University Press, 1975.

Gerschenkron, A. *Economic Backwardness in Historical Perspective*, New York: Praeger, 1962.

Hilton, George W., and John F. Due, *The Electric Interurban Railways in America*, Stanford: Stanford University Press, 1960.

Hoerder, Dirk (ed.), *American Labor and Immigration History, 1877-1920s: Recent European Research*, Urbana, Chicago, London: University of Illinois Press, 1983.

Hutchinson, E. P. *Immigrants and Their Children*, New York: John Wiley & Sons, Inc., London: Chapman and Hall, Ltd., 1956.

Karni, Michael G., Matti E. Kamps, Douglas J. Ollila, Jr. *The Finnish Experience in the Western Great Lakes Regions: New Perspectives*, Turku, Finland: Institute for Migration, 1975.

Kolehmainen, John I. *A History of The Finns in Ohio, Western Pennsylvania and West Virginia*. Ohio Finnish-American Historical Society, 1977.

Kuznets, S. S., D. S. Thomas, et al, *Population Redistribution and Economic Growth, United States, 1890-1950,* 3 vols. Philadelphia: American Philosophical Society, 1957-1964.

Paullin, Charles O. *Atlas of the Historical Geography of the United States,* Carnegie Institution of Washington, 1932.

Weisenberger, Francis P. "The Passing of the Frontier, 1829-1850" in Carl Wittke, ed., *The History of the state of Ohio,* vol. 3. Columbus: Ohio State Archaelogical Society, 1944.

Williamson, Harold J., and Kenneth H. Myers, *Designed for Digging,* Evanston, Ill: Northwestern University Press, 1955.

Williamson, Jeffrey G. "The Impact of the Irish on British Labor Markets." *Journal of Economic History,* 44:3 (September 1986).

Urban Growth

Cleveland, Past and Present; Its Representative Men, Maurice Joblin, 1869.

Allen, Hugh, *Rubber's Home Town.* New York: Stratford House, 1949.

Benton, Elbert J., *Cultural Story of an American City.* Cleveland: Western Reserve Historical Society, 3 vols., 1943-1946.

Conzen, Kathleen N. *Immigrant Milwaukee 1836–1860,* Cambridge, London: Harvard University Press, 1976.

Conzen, Michael P. "The American Urban System in the Nineteenth Century", *Geography and the Urban Environment Progress in Research and Applications,* vol. 4, John Wiley and Sons, 1981.

Conzen, Michael P. "The Maturing Urban System in the United States, 1840-1910." *Annals of the Association of American Geographers,* vol. 67, no. 1, March 1977.

Cronon, William J. "To Be the Central City: Chicago, 1848-1857." *Chicago History* 10-3, Fall 1981.

The General Committee of The City's First Centennial Celebration, *A Centennial History of Akron,* Summit County Historical Society, 1925.

Jacobs, Jane, *The Economy of Cities,* New York: Random House, 1969.

Lane, Samuel A. *Fifty Years and Over of Akron and Summit County,* Akron, Ohio: Beacon Job Department, 1892.

Memorial Record of the County of Cuyahoga and City of Cleveland, Ohio, Chicago: Lewis Publishing Co., 1894.

Nichols, Kenneth, *Yesterday's Akron,* Miami, Florida: E. A. Seeman Publishing, 1975.

Nolen, John, *City Plan for Akron,* Akron: Akron Chamber of Commerce, 1919.

Orth, Samuel P. *A History of Cleveland, Ohio,* 2 vols. Chicago-Cleveland: S. J. Clarke Publishing Co., 1910,

Pred, Allan, *The Spatial Dynamics of U. S. Urban-Industrial Growth, 1800-1914,* Cambridge, London: The Massachussets Institute of Technology Press, 1966.

Pred, Allan, *Urban Growth and City Systems in the U. S., 1840-1860,* Cambridge, London: Harvard University Press, 1980.

Robinson, W. Scott ed., *History of the City of Cleveland*, Cleveland: Robinson and Cockett—Sunday World, 1887.

Wade, Richard C. *The Urban Frontier*, Cambridge: Harvard University Press, 1959.

Motivation and Social Control

Akron Board of Education, *Annual Reports*, 1871, 1874, 1879, 1882, 1920-21, 1922.

Akron Chamber of Commerce, *Report on the Schools of Akron*, July 1917.

Bodnar, John, *The Transplanted*, Bloomington: Indiana University Press, 1985.

Bodnar, John, *Worker's World*, Baltimore and London: Johns Hopkins University Press, 1982.

Danhof, Clarence H. *Change in Agriculture: The Northern United States, 1820-1870*, Cambridge: Harvard University Press, 1969.

Duff, William A. *History of North Central Ohio, embracing Richland, Ashland, Wayne, Medina, Lorain, Huron and Knox Counties*, Topeka, Indianapolis: Historical Publishing Co., 1931, 3 vols.

Federal Writers' Project of Ohio (WPA), *Guide to Tuscarawas County*, The New Philadelphia Chamber of Commerce, 1939.

The First Centennial History and Atlas of Tuscarawas County, Ohio, New Philadelphia, Ohio: Edwin S. Rhodes, 1908.

Freyer, Tony A. *Forums of Order: The Federal Courts and Business in American History*, Greenwich, Conn.: Ai Jai Press, 1979.

Frohman, Charles E. *A History of Sandusky and Erie County*, Columbus: Ohio Historical Society, 1965.

Galambos, Louis, *The Public Image of Big Business in America, 1880-1940*, Baltimore: Johns Hopkins University Press, 1975.

Hinsdale, B. A. "The Sale of the Western Reserve", Ohio Archaeological and Historical Society, *Quarterly*, Columbus: for the Society, vol. 2, no. 4, March 1889,

Ingham, W. A. *Women of Cleveland and Their Work*, Cleveland: W. A. Ingham, 1893.

Jones, Alfred Winslow, *Life, Liberty, and Property*, Philadelphia, New York and London: J. B. Lippincott Co. 1941.

Knepper, George W. *An Ohio Portrait*, Columbus: Ohio Historical Society, 1976.

Parker, William N. "New England's Early Industrialization" *Quantity and Quiddity: Essays in Honor of Stanley Lebergott*, P. Kilby, ed. Middletown: Wesleyan University Press, 1987.

Perlman, Selig, *A Theory of the Labor Movement*, New York: Macmillan, 1928.

Richardson, J. M. *A Brief History of Tuscarawas County, Ohio*, Canal Dover, Ohio: Bixier Printing Co., 1896.

Stephenson, Charles and Robert Acher, eds. *Life and Labor: Dimensions of American Working-Class History*, Albany: State University of New York Press, 1986.

Williams, R. Y. *Illinois Miners' and Mechanics' Institutes*, Urbana: University of Illinois, Bulletin No. 1-3.

Scale and Productivity

Bradley, Joseph F. *The Role of Trade Associations and Professional Business Societies in America*, Pennsylvania: Pennsylvania University Press, 1965.

Burke, Peter, ed. *The New Cambridge Modern History*, vol. 13. *Companion Volume*, Cambridge: Cambridge University Press, 1979.

Chandler, Alfred D., Jr. *The Visible Hand: The Managerial Revolution in American Business*, Cambridge: Harvard University Press, 1977.

Davis, Edward, *The Future of the Lake Superior District as an Iron-Ore Producer*, vol. 23, no. 18. Minneapolis: Minnesota School of Mines, Experiment Station, 22 May, 1920,

Dohrmann, Donald Ray, *Screw Propulsion in American Lake and Coastal Steam Navigation, 1840-1860*, Dissertation, Yale University, 1976.

Fuller, Wayne E. *RFD: The Changing Face of Rural America*, Bloomington: Indiana University Press, 1964.

Funck, R. and J. B. Parr, (eds.), *The Analysis of Regional Structure: Essays in Honor of August Losch*, London: Pion Limited, 1978.

Meyer, David R., "Emergence of the American Manufacturing Belt: An Interpretation," *Journal of Historical Geography* 9, 2 (1983),

Parker, William N. "Industry" *The New Cambridge Modern History*, P. Burke, ed. Vol. 13. Cambridge: Cambridge University Press, 1979.

Plants and Firms

Chandler, Alfred D., Jr. *Strategy and Structure*, Cambridge: Massachusetts Institute of Technology Press, 1962.

Chandler Alfred D., Jr. *The Visible Hand: The Managerial Revolution in American Business*, Cambridge: Harvard University Press, 1977.

Daniells, Lorna M. *Studies in Enterprise*, a selected bibliography of American and Canadian company histories, Boston: Baker Library, 1957, and Supplements, 1959-64, esp. Sec. 3: H, J, L.

Diamond, Sigmund, *The Nation Transformed: The Creation of an Industrial Society*, New York: George Braziller, 1963.

Giddens, Paul H. *Standard Oil Company of Indiana: Oil Pioneer of the Middle West*, New York: Appleton-Century Crofts, 1955.

Hurst, James Willard, *The Legitimacy of the Business Corporation in the Law of the United States, 1780-1970*, Charlottesville: The University Press of Virginia, 1970.

Lamoreaux, Naomi R., *The Great Merger Movement in American Business, 1895-1904*, Cambridge: Cambridge University Press, 1985.

Ware, Caroline F. *The Early New England Cotton Manufacture*, Boston: Houghton-Mifflin, 1931.

Williamson, Harold J. and Kenneth H. Myers, II, *Designed for Digging*, Evanston, Ill.: Northwestern University Press, 1955.

Market Organization

Davis, Lance E., and Douglass C. North, *Institutional Change and American Economic Growth*, Cambridge: Cambridge University Press, 1971.

Lamoreaux, Naomi R. "The Competitive Behavior of Small Versus Large Firms: The American Steel Industry in the Late 19th Century," *Business and Economic History*, 2d. ser., 9, 1980.

Massey, Henry R. *Combination in the Mining Industry: A Study of Concentration in Lake Superior, Iron Ore Production*, In *Studies in History, Economics and Public Law* 23, no. 3, New York: Columbia University Press, 1905.

Montgomery, David, *Workers' Control in America: Studies in the History of Work, Technology, and Labor Struggles*, Cambridge: Cambridge University Press, 1979.

Nadworny, Milton J. *Scientific Management and the Unions, 1900-1932: A Historical Analysis*, Cambridge: Harvard University Press, 1955.

Ripley, William Z. *Railroads: Rates and Regulation*, New York: Longmans, Green, 1913.

———*Railroads: Finance and Organization*, New York: Longmans, Green, 1912.

Williams, Jeffrey, *The Economic Function of Futures Markets*, Cambridge: Cambridge University Press, 1986.

APPENDIX

TABLE I:

MANUFACTURING IN THE OLD NORTHWEST, BY STATES AND MAJOR MANUFACTURING DISTRICTS, 1870-1910.

CHART KEY: a = Manufacturing employment (10^3)
b = Manufacturing output, gross value (10^6)
c = Wages (10^6)

COUNTY OR STATE		1870	1880	1890	1900	1910
Six State	a	397.7	553.7	1143.5	1278.7	1891.2
Area	b	802.6	1266.3	2495.5	3450.6	5621.0
	c	137.5	194.2	538.3	572.7	1147.5
Ohio	a	137.2	183.6	331.5	345.9	523.0
	b	269.7	348.3	641.7	832.4	1437.9
	c	49.1	62.1	158.8	154.0	317.6
Northeast[1]	a	26.7	79.7	94.4	125.0	
	b	67.5	101.2	204.9	323.2	
	c	11.3	17.3	50.8	59.3	
Southwest	a	46.2	76.1	143.8	120.0	
& Central[2]	b	107.6	148.0	276.9	288.1	
	c	21.1	27.4	70.4	52.7	
East[3]	a	5.0	8.2	14.4	18.6	
	b	8.9	13.1	26.8	49.4	
	c	1.8	3.1	6.9	9.1	
Illinois	a	83.0	144.7	312.2	395.1	561.0
	b	205.6	414.9	908.6	1259.7	1919.9
	c	31.1	37.4	171.5	191.5	364.8
Chicago	a	31.1	81.6	212.3	269.7	
Area[4]	b	92.5	253.9	668.0	905.7	
	c	13.0	35.6	125.0	134.7	
Michigan	a	63.7	77.6	163.9	162.4	271.1
	b	118.4	150.7	277.9	356.9	685.1
	c	21.1	25.3	66.3	66.5	
Detroit	a	1.9	18.6	41.1	52.2	
Area[5]	b	3.7	33.5	82.1	111.9	
	c	.5	7.2	20.1		
Indiana	a	58.6	69.5	124.3	156.0	218.3
	b	108.6	148.0	226.8	378.1	579.1
	c	18.4	22.0	51.7	66.8	121.8
Gary	a	.3	.3	2.3	6.4	
Area[6]	b	.3	3.5	23.0	46.1	
	c	.03	.09	1.2	3.2	
Wisconsin	a	43.9	57.1	132.0	142.1	213.4
	b	77.2	128.3	248.5	360.8	590.3
	c	13.6	18.8	51.8	58.4	119.6

COUNTY OR STATE		1870	1880	1890	1900	1910
Milwaukee[7]	a	8.4	21.3	43.8	53.5	
	b	18.8	44.5	98.6	140.3	
	c	3.4	7.1	20.8	22.6	
Minnesota	a	11.3	21.2	79.6	77.2	104.4
	b	23.1	76.1	192.0	262.7	409.4
	c	4.1	8.6	38.2	35.5	69.9
Minneapolis -St. Paul[8]	a	4.2	6.1	38.2	33.4	
	b	8.4	42.5	121.7	152.1	
	c	1.9	5.0	27.2	21.0	

[1]Mahoning, Trumbull, Stark, Summit, Cuyahoga, Lorain, Lucas, and Richland Counties.
[2]Butler, Hamilton, Montgomery, Franklin, and Clark Counties.
[3]Belmont, Jefferson, and Columbiana Counties.
[4]Cook County
[5]Wayne County
[6]Lake County
[7]Milwaukee County
[8]Hennepin and Ramsey Counties

TABLE II:

WESTERN PENNSYLVANIA, MANUFACTURING EMPLOYMENT

AND GROSS OUTPUT, 1870-1910

CHART KEY: a = employment (10^3)
b = output; gross dollar value ($\$10^6$)

REGION		1870	1880	1890	1900
13 county	a	58.6	18.7	153.3	215.9
Area[1]	b	142.1	171.0	366.8	668.6
	c	28.1	33.4	86.2	114.8
Pittsburg	a	34.2	49.2	97.7	128.4
Area[2]	b	8.8	105.3	244.5	433.8
	c	18.5	22.4	57.3	69.3

[1]Allegheny, Beaver, Blair, Cambria, Elk, Erie, Fayette, Lawrence, McKean, Mercer, Venanga, Washington, Westmoreland Counties.
[2]Allegheny County.
SOURCES FOR TABLES I AND II
Ninth—Thirteenth Censuses of the United States
1870 - Volume 3, Table 9
1880 - Volume 2, Table 4
1890 - Volume 6, Table 6
1900 - Volume 8, Table 6
1910 - Volume 8, Table 4

TABLE III:
OLD NORTHWEST: POPULATION BY ORIGIN, STATES
AND MAJOR MANUFACTURING DISTRICTS, 1870-1910

CHART KEY: a = Population (10³)
b = Foreign born (10³)
c = Foreign born, excluding Ireland, Great Britain, and Germany (10³)

COUNTY OR STATE		1870	1880	1890	1900	1910
Six State	a	8736.4	11987.4	14773.7	17737.1	20326.4
Area	b	1822.4	2184.3	2978.6	3130.5	3610.2
	c	372.8	480.3	865.0	1746.4	1932.4
Ohio	a	2665.3	3198.1	3672.3	4157.6	4767.1
	b	372.5	394.9	459.3	458.7	597.2
	c	36.6	42.9	63.2	111.2	295.5
Northeast[1]	a	398.4	532.0	727.4	975.0	1354.1
	b	101.2	128.5	186.3	224.2	349.8
	c	9.7	12.0	38.5	75.4	198.1
Southwest	a	459.4	563.3	700.5	819.9	982.8
and Central[2]	b	120.5	116.5	124.3	106.8	110.4
	c	7.0	4.5	7.7	11.2	36.0
East[3]	a	107.2	131.2	155.8	173.9	219.2
	b	9.6	10.7	14.7	16.4	33.6
	c	.4	1.3	1.7	5.3	23.0
Illinois	a	1712.0	3077.8	3826.4	4821.6	5638.6
	b	515.2	583.6	842.3	966.7	1202.6
	c	89.0	120.6	244.8	380.6	659.6
Chicago	a	145.0	350.0	607.5	1191.0	1838.7
Area[4]	b	166.8	242.4	482.6	624.7	842.7
	c	27.0	120.6	163.3	380.6	492.3
Michigan	a	1184.1	1636.9	2093.9	2421.0	2810.2
	b	268.0	388.5	543.9	541.7	595.5
	c	72.2	52.3	119.7	148.0	358.9
Detroit	a	119.0	166.4	257.1	348.8	531.6
Area[5]	b	46.6	60.1	96.0	112.3	171.6
	c	2.8	3.5	11.5	21.9	55.6
Indiana	a	1680.6	1978.3	2192.4	2516.5	2700.9
	b	141.5	144.2	146.2	142.1	159.3
	c	16.4	17.4	30.5	30.5	65.4
Gary Area[6]	a	12.3	15.1	23.9	37.9	82.9
	b	3.4	4.0	6.9	9.4	30.4
	c	.4	.4	1.5	3.5	22.9
Wisconsin	a	1054.7	1315.5	1686.9	2069.0	2333.9
	b	364.5	405.4	519.2	516.0	512.6
	c	86.5	114.1	159.5	189.8	192.9

COUNTY OR STATE		1870	1880	1890	1900	1910
Milwaukee[7]	a	89.9	138.5	236.1	330.0	433.2
	b	42.2	55.0	91.9	102.6	129.2
	c	3.9	3.4	18.4	29.3	46.3
Minnesota	a	439.7	780.8	1301.8	1751.4	2075.7
	b	160.7	267.7	467.4	505.3	543.0
	c	72.1	133.0	257.3	300.2	360.1
Minneapolis	a	54.7	112.9	325.1	398.9	557.2
St. Paul[8]	b	31.1	62.7	174.4	210.2	299.3
	c	4.9	11.2	63.0	65.0	99.0
13 County Area	a	732.0	953.5	1298.4	1731.0	2318.0
in Western	b	131.7	152.5	253.6	338.4	551.5
Pennsylvania[9]c	6.1	8.5	53.0	147.6	371.7	
Pittsburgh	a	262.2	355.9	552.0	775.1	1018.5
Area[10]	b	75.9	88.7	153.1	191.5	271.4
	c	4.1	4.3	26.3	71.3	161.0

[1]Mahoning, Trumbull, Stark, Summit, Cuyahoga, Lorain, Lucas, and Richland Counties.
[2]Butler, Hamilton, Montgomery, Franklin, and Clark Counties.
[3]Belmont, Jefferson, and Columbiana Counties.
[4]Cook County
[5]Wayne County
[6]Lake County
[7]Milwaukee County
[8]Hennepin and Ramsey Counties.
[9]Allegheny, Beaver, Blair, Cambria, Elk, Erie, Fayette, Lawrence, McKean, Mercer, Venanga, Washington, Westmoreland counties.
[10]Allegheny County
SOURCES FOR TABLE III
Ninth—Thirteenth Censuses of the United States
1870 - Volume 1, Tables 6 and 7
1880 - Volume 1, Tables 10, 13, and 14
1890 - Volume 1 (Part 1), Tables 15, 32, and 33
1900 - Volume 1 (Part 1), Tables 18, 22, 33, 34
1910 - Volume 2, Table 1

12

THE NATURE OF MIDWEST MANUFACTURING IN 1890

David C. Klingaman
Ohio University

I

APPROXIMATELY ONE HUNDRED YEARS after the Ordinance of 1787 provided for the organization of the Northwest Territory, the Eleventh Census of the United States reported that the population of the United States was slightly over 60 million people. About 13.5 million of them lived in the states of Ohio, Indiana, Illinois, Michigan, and Wisconsin. The five most populous cities there were Chicago, Cincinnati, Cleveland, Detroit, and Milwaukee. All together, these cities had a population of just over 2 million. Among the nation's cities, Chicago was second in population, Cincinnati was ninth, Cleveland was tenth, Detroit was fifteenth, and Milwaukee was sixteenth. Of these five cities, only Cincinnati was an old manufacturing and commercial center; the other four had risen to economic prominence since the Civil War. The spread of manufacturing activity from the eastern seaboard into the Midwest took place largely after 1850 and correlated with the growth in midwest population. Between 1850 and 1890, the population of the United States nearly tripled. The Midwest's population grew a little faster than that, and the city of Chicago experienced a phenomenal increase from 60,000 people in 1850 to 1 million in 1890.

An interesting page in the 1900 census of manufactures is a map prepared by the geographer of the census that shows for each census year the geographic center of manufacturing in the United States, based upon gross value of output. Between 1850 and 1900 the degrees of latitude remain unchanged but, of course, the degrees of longitude of the geographic center shifted west. The degrees of westward drift for each decade are given below[1]:

1850–1860	1° 53′ 41″
1860–1870	0° 07′ 08″
1870–1880	0° 28′ 02″
1880–1890	1° 40′ 37″
1890–1900	0° 44′ 30″

This data would tend to confirm the belief that the spread of manufacturing westward was not a smooth transition. Over the period 1850–90, there seem to have been two decades of relatively slow expansion of industrial-

275

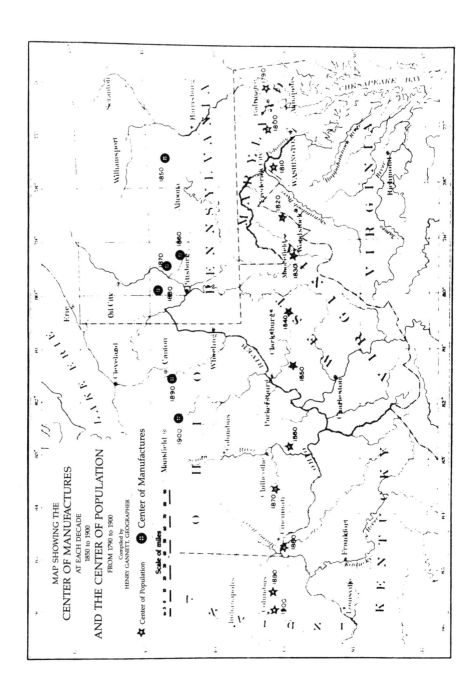

ization into the West separating two decades of fast expansion. The 1850s were a time of strong shifting of population and manufacturing industries into the western states. The period 1860–80 exhibited much slower movement, particularly the Civil War decade. Then the 1880s witnessed another lunge westward of manufacturing activity. During the time that the geographic center of manufacturing marched from central Pennsylvania in 1850 to Canton, Ohio, in 1890, an industrial region to rival that of the Northeast had emerged.

This paper is a descriptive account of manufacturing in the Midwest around 1890. The Midwest is defined here as Ohio, Indiana, Illinois, Michigan, and Wisconsin. One can use the published census volumes to quantify the value added in manufacturing by geographic location and by type of industry. The leading occupations of men and women can be identified in order to disclose how people made a living one hundred years ago. To get this information, it is necessary to rely on the published census volumes with their aggregate data because the manuscript census returns of individual firms were destroyed in a fire many years ago.[2] The Eleventh Census of the United States, taken during the census year of 1889–90, is the primary source material for this study.

The development of raw material supplies and the emergence of a fine railroad network with Chicago as its hub joined with the other sources of economic growth to double the Midwest's share of national value added and employment in manufacturing between 1850 and 1890. The proportion of national value added in manufacturing produced in the midwest region would continue slowly and irregularly upward for another fifty or sixty years, probably peaking during the 1940s in excess of 30 percent. But the

TABLE 1

Midwest Share of National Manufacturing Value
Added and of Employment, 1850-1900

Year	Percentage of National Value Added in Manufacturing	Percentage of National Employment in Manufacturing
1850	11.4	9.7
1860	13.5	12.1
1870	18.2	18.8
1880	20.6	19.5
1890	23.8	22.4
1900	24.3	22.6

Source: *Report on Manufacturing in the United States at the Eleventh Census: 1890*, Part I, GPO, 1895, Table 1. *Abstract of the Twelfth Census*, GPO, 1902, Table 164.

Notes: Ohio, Indiana, Illinois, Michigan, and Wisconsin are hereafter referred to as the Midwest.

major increase in the Midwest's relative importance in the national economy had been made before 1890. In 1850, 55 percent of all the manufacturing jobs in the United States were in just three states: Massachusetts, New York, and Pennsylvania. Ohio, the West's manufacturing outpost of the time, had barely more than fifty thousand manufacturing jobs, less than 10 percent as many as did the three northeastern states.[3] The changing relative importance of Midwest manufacturing is indicated in table 1. By 1890, out of 5.2 million people employed nationally in manufacturing jobs, roughly 2.6 million were in nine northeastern states and 1.1 million were in the Midwest. About four-fifths of these midwestern manufacturing jobs were in Ohio and Illinois.[4]

TABLE 2

Manufacturing Value Added of Cities in 1890
(Millions of Dollars)

Top Five Cities in the Midwest	
Chicago	223
Cincinnati	86
Cleveland	42
Milwaukee	36
Detroit	32
Top Five Cities Elsewhere in the U.S.	
New York	461
Philadelphia	222
St. Louis	89
Boston	83
Baltimore	56

Source: Census Reports, Volume VII, *Twelfth Census, Manufactures*, Part I, Washington, 1902, pp. ccxlviii-ccliv.

Notes: Industries classed as "hand trades" in the Twelfth Census, such as blacksmithing, custom work and repairing, carpentry, masonry, painting and plumbing are not counted in this table as manufacturing output. Including the hand trades would raise the value added of Chicago (from 223) to 255, Cincinnati to 104, Cleveland to 48, Milwaukee to 42, Detroit to 36, New York to 535, Philadelphia to 266, St. Louis to 107, Boston to 105, and Baltimore to 68. See reference source of footnote 13 for the specific industries which the census classified as hand trades.

The significance of urban manufacturing is indicated in Table 2. This table gives the manufacturing value added in the five most important cities of the Midwest and the same for the five most important cities outside of the Midwest. The dominance of Chicago, New York, and Philadelphia is manifest. The relative importance of Cincinnati may surprise. The Queen City equalled Boston and St. Louis and exceeded Baltimore in the output of manufactured goods, as measured by value added.[5]

II

The ten leading manufacturing industries of the United States according to the 1860 census of manufactures were cotton goods, lumber, boots and shoes, flour, men's clothing, iron, machinery, woolens, carriages and wagons, and leather. Cotton goods and lumber products were tied for first and had a value added about double that of leather, the tenth ranked industry. Measured by total employment, the three dominant manufacturing industries in 1860 were boots and shoes, cotton goods, and men's clothing. Each of these industries employed between 115,000 and 123,000 thousand workers.[6] The top industries of 1890 are shown in table 3. Production of various kinds of machinery is now tied with lumber products as the first-ranked industry. Three industries that are new to the top ten are: printers of books, periodicals, newspapers, and jobs; beer and ale; and wholesale slaughtering and meat packing. Cotton goods, flour and meal, and boots and shoes experienced a relative decline in importance after 1860. Though also still important industries in an absolute sense, woolen goods, carriages and wagons, and leather products are no longer among the top ten industries.

TABLE 3

U.S.: Top Ten Industries in 1890
By Value Added
(Millions of Dollars)

Lumber Mill and Planing Mill Products	251
Foundry and Machine Shop Products	242
Printing and Publishing	206
Men's Clothing	199
Iron and Steel	136
Malt Liquor	119
Cotton Goods	113
Boots and Shoes	102
Slaughtering and Meat Packing, Wholesale	82
Flour and Grist Mill Products	80

Sources: *Report on Manufacturing Industries in the United States at the Eleventh Census: 1890,* Part I (Government Printing Office, 1895), 47, 73–78.

Notes: Assuming that USA total value added in manufacturing (including hand-trades) was $4,210 million, the ten industries above comprised 36 percent of national value added.

The value added of the principal industries of the five midwestern states is given in Appendix A. Ohio's leading industry in 1890 was machinery: stoves, steam engines for boilers, equipment for lumber, flour, and paper mills, breweries, mines, and so forth. Ohio had over nine hundred foundry and machine shops and was the nation's third largest producer. Although malt and distilled liquor was Ohio's second ranked industry in value added, it was not an important source of manufacturing employment. After the foundry and machine shops, the iron and steel firms employed the most manufacturing workers. At this time Pennsylvania accounted for slightly more than half of the over 18 million tons of all forms of iron and steel produced in the United States. Ohio was second with about 2.5 million tons, followed by Illinois with 1.6 million tons.[7] The introduction of coke as a fuel in blast furnaces and the greater use of Lake Superior ores had gradually switched the iron industry into western Pennsylvania and beyond. The exceptional quality of the Connellsville coal for making coke had attracted the blast furnaces from eastern Pennsylvania where the reliance was on anthracite coal. The rolling mills and steel plants moved west with the blast furnaces, and Allegheny County became the dominant steel region in the late nineteenth century. The steel mills of northeastern Ohio drew their fuel supply from the Connellsville area southeast of Pittsburgh on the Youghiogheny River and from West Virginia. Northeastern Ohio, e.g., Cleveland and Youngstown, also had the advantage of being located between the iron mines of Lake Superior and the coal fields of Pennsylvania. From Ohio, iron production had skipped to Illinois, mainly to the Chicago area. There was an excellent market for iron products in Chicago and farther west. Chicago also had cheap access to the Lake Superior ores; the fuel came mostly from Connellsville and West Virginia.

Other important Ohio industries were lumber milling, printing, men's clothing, carriages and wagons, and agricultural implements. The twelve industries shown in table A-1 include about 45 percent of the approximately $300 million of total state value added in manufacturing. Although not counted in this study as manufacturing output, Ohio was an important producer of coal and petroleum. In 1887 the state accounted for nearly one-third of the national output of coal and almost one-fifth of aggregate petroleum output.[8]

Indiana's manufacturing value added was about one-third of that of Ohio. The state was surprisingly slow to industrialize. The top industries of Indiana were lumber, liquor, machines, flour and grist mill products, carriages and wagons, and furniture. The value added of the ten industries noted in table A-2 account for about 45 percent of the state's industrial production.

In Illinois the three dominant industries in terms of both value added and employment were wholesale slaughtering and meat packing, foundry and machine shops, and men's clothing. Illinois had eighty-one establishments and nearly eighteen thousand people employed in slaughtering and meat packing. The state produced almost 40 percent of the nation's total value added in that industry. The wholesale slaughtering and meat packing industry seems to have begun in Cincinnati in the 1820s and moved westward with the cattle and hog populations. In addition the development of the refrigerator car had altered the difference between the costs of shipping livestock and dressed meat sufficiently to induce packers to move their plants nearer to the stocking, raising, and feeding operations. The location of these latter operations depended principally on the location of abundant supplies of corn and hay. One-fourth of the national production of farm machinery originated in Illinois, and Illinois was fast pulling ahead of New York and Ohio in this important industry. Manufacturers of agricultural implements were probably forced to shift nearer to the market because of the high cost of freight charges on product shipments that used relatively large amounts of space in railroad cars. Manufacturing locations in Illinois also had the advantage of being nearer to the essential raw materials, i.e., hardwood lumber and iron. Illinois was also the leading state in the production of distilled liquor and railroad cars. These and other industries in table A-3 cover approximately 46 percent of the state's $380 million of manufacturing value added.

The industries of Michigan and Wisconsin are shown in tables A-4 and A-5. Lumber and planing mill products made up the most important industry in Indiana, Michigan, and Wisconsin. In Michigan there were more than two thousand mills employing over fifty thousand workers. The vast pine and hardwood forests were the state's most valuable natural resource. In both states, the value added by the industries shown in the tables cover about 55 percent of total state manufacturing value added.

III

This section focuses on manufacturing in the cities. The value added in the principal industries of the five midwest cities are given in tables 4-A through 4-E. In table B (Appendix) there is similar coverage of New York, Philadelphia, Boston, Baltimore, and St. Louis. Table 2 showed the aggre-

TABLE 4-A

Chicago's Leading Industries in 1890
(Value Added in Thousands of Dollars)

Slaughtering and Meat Packing, Wholesale	29,379
Printing and Publishing: Books, Jobs,	
Newspapers and Periodicals	19,518
Foundry and Machine Shop Products	16,353
Men's Clothing	14,956
Liquor, Malt and Distilled	13,887
Furniture	7,503
Lumber Planing Mill Products	7,408
Agricultural Implements	6,890
Steam Railroad Cars	5,928
Iron and Steel	5,101

Sources: *Compendium of the Eleventh Census of the United States*, Part 2 (Washington, D.C.: Government Printing Office, 1894), table 2 in manufacturers in 165 cities.

gate manufacturing value added for these ten cities. At this point we are interested in looking at the value added by particular industries.

In Chicago the dominant industry was slaughtering and meat packing. In 1889 Chicago received 3.1 million head of cattle and shipped out about 1 million head in the form of dressed beef and canned meat.[9] The city accounted for one-third of the nation's output. More capital was invested in this industry than any other; foundry and machine shops was second. However, so diversified was the Chicago economy that only about one-eighth of the city's total manufacturing value added was comprised of products of the slaughter houses and meat packing plants. Next in importance was printing and publishing (Chicago was probably second to Manhattan). After that came machinery, men's clothing, liquor, furniture, planing mill products, farm equipment, railroad cars, and iron and steel. Chicago tied with Philadelphia as the number one location for foundry and machine shops in the nation. Indeed, the five midwest cities accounted for about 30 percent of the national foundry and machine shop production. In farm machinery Chicago accounted for 15 percent of national output; by 1900, the city would have 25 percent. Other significant industries not mentioned in table 4-A are heating and illuminating gas, brick and stone, women's clothing, and bakery goods.[10]

Cincinnati had a thriving liquor business, about two-thirds distilled and one-third malt. However, there were only a few more than two thousand people employed in that industry. By far the most important industry in terms of employment in Cincinnati was the manufacture of clothing for men. The city had over four hundred shops that hired nearly fifteen thousand men and women. Next came foundry and machine shop products, printing, carriages and wagons, boots and shoes, furniture, cigars and cigarettes, lumber, and slaughtering and meat packing. Cincinnati was the old-

TABLE 4-B

Cincinnati's Leading Industries in 1890
(Value Added in Thousands of Dollars)

Liquors, Distilled and Malt	14,105
Men's Clothing	9,487
Foundry and Machine Shop Products	5,953
Printing and Publishing, Books, Jobs, Newspapers, Periodicals	4,315
Carriages and Wagons	3,841
Boots and Shoes	2,873
Furniture	2,761
Tobacco, Cigars, and Cigarettes	2,095
Lumber Mill Products	1,948
Slaughtering and Meat Packing	1,162

Sources: *Compendium of the Eleventh Census of the United States,* Part 2, (Washington, D.C.: Government Printing Office, 1894), table 2 in manufacturers in 165 cities.

est manufacturing center in the Old Northwest and, although the city was experiencing a relative decline around 1890, was still able to account for roughly one-third of Ohio's manufacturing output. The industries of Cincinnati given in table 4-B make up about 46 percent of the city's total value added.

Cleveland was a younger, faster-growing city than Cincinnati and was oriented more toward heavy industry. The city produced about 16 percent of the state's value added, and the industries shown in table 4-C comprise about 44 percent of total city value added. The foundry and machine shops and the steel mills were the most important industries by far in terms of value added and in number of workers employed. Cleveland was also the core of Ohio's oil refining and ship building business.

Milwaukee accounted for 40 percent of Wisconsin's value added, and the industries in table 4-D cover about 40 percent of the city's total value added. Milwaukee's malt liquor production exceeded that of either Chicago or Cincinnati. Chicago, despite its substantial production, imported beer from Milwaukee.[11] Leather firms were relatively important in Milwaukee and produced such items as saddles, harnesses, belts, trunks and valises.

TABLE 4-C

Cleveland's Leading Industries in 1890
(Value Added in Thousands of Dollars)

Foundry and Machine Shop Products	6,279
Iron and Steel	4,982
Printing and Publishing	2,326
Petroleum Refining	2,220
Malt Liquors	2,114
Ship Building	1,579
Clothing, Men's and Women's	1,544

Sources: *Compendium of the Eleventh Census of the United States*, Part 2, (Washington, D.C.: Government Printing Office, 1894), table 2 manufacturers in 165 cities.

TABLE 4-D

Milwaukee's Leading Industries in 1890
(Value Added in Thousands of Dollars)

Malt Liquors	7,243
Foundry and Machine Shop Products	3,014
Leather, Tanned and Curried	1,717
Tobacco Products	1,636
Printing and Publishing	1,564
Men's Clothing	1,441

Sources: *Compendium of the Eleventh Census of the United States*, Part 2, (Washington, D.C.: Government Printing Office, 1894), table 2 in manufacturers in 165 cities.

TABLE 4-E

Detroit's Leading Industries in 1890
(Value Added in Thousands of Dollars).

Foundry and Machine Shop Products	4,275
Tobacco Products	3,751
Railroad Cars	2,927
Printing and Publishing	2,161
Chemicals	1,890
Lumber Products	1,431
Malt Liquors	1,001
Men's Clothing	914
Iron and Steel	782

Sources: *Compendium of the Eleventh Census of the United States,* Part 2 (Washington, D.C.: Government Printing Office, 1894), table 2 in manufacturers in 165 cities.

Machine shop products made up the major industry of Detroit, both in terms of value added and in number of workers. These firms produced items needed for farms, homes, and industries, such as tools, machine parts, stoves, pipes, and household utensils. The second leading industry in Detroit consisted of cigars, cigarettes, chewing tobacco, and snuff. This was also a relatively important industry in Cincinnati and Milwaukee. The production of steam railroad cars was the second leading industry in Detroit in terms of employment. Chicago, however, was the main producer of railroad cars. The printing of books, periodicals, and odd jobs was an important industry in all of the cities.

Many smaller cities were significant manufacturing cities. For example, Peoria was tops in distilled liquor production and Springfield, Ohio, rivaled Chicago as a manufacturing point for farm equipment. Ranked top to bottom by total value added in midwest manufacturing in 1890 were: Peoria, Indianapolis, Columbus, Dayton, Grand Rapids, Toledo, Terre Haute, Canton, Akron, Evansville, and Youngstown. Next in line came Springfield, Saginaw, Quincy, South Bend, Joliet, and Fort Wayne.

Table B (Appendix) gives data on the principal industries of New York, Philadelphia, Boston, Baltimore, and St. Louis. The industrial structure of these cities was similar to that of the midwestern cities. All had an important machinery industry; clothing and malt liquor production were also common to all of the cities. New York was particularly dominant in women's garments. New York, Boston, and St. Louis had a strong printing industry, and New York, Baltimore, and St. Louis had an important tobacco goods industry. Brick and stone production was relatively more important than it was in the midwestern cities. Two important businesses in Philadelphia were carpets and rugs and hosiery and knit goods. Baltimore had a significant fruit and vegetable canning industry.

Among these various industries, one would expect the optimal scale of plant to be of different sizes. Firms in the Chicago area were larger than the typical firm in most other parts of the country. This probably reflects a different geographic mix of industries. For example, the most efficient size of a wholesale meat packing or farm machinery plant was larger than one producing clothing. In Chicago the average value added per firm in 1890 was $41,500, whereas a simple four-city average for Cincinnati, Cleveland, Milwaukee, and Detroit was $27,200. A simple four-city average of New York, Philadelphia, Boston, and Baltimore was only $20,800. Average capital invested per firm and the average number of workers per firm were also relatively high in Chicago. For example, Chicago businesses had more than twice as much capital per firm as did firms in the four large eastern cities. Capital is defined here as fixed investment in land, buildings, and machines plus what the census calls "live" capital: raw materials on hand, goods in process, finished inventories on hand, cash, and bills receivable. However, a census "firm" means an establishment owned by the same individual or corporation that is located in the same city and that engages in manufacture in the same industry. For example, two foundry and machine shops in Chicago with a common owner were counted by the census takers as a single firm. Hence, the value added per firm here is not the same as value added per plant, i.e., a firm can consist of two or more plants. In the largest 164 cities of the United States, the average capital investment per firm was $31,100; it was also roughly that in New York, Philadelphia, Boston and Baltimore. In Chicago it was $63,600. And Cleveland, Milwaukee, and Detroit had an average capital investment of $44,800. (Cincinnati, however, was only $25,400, perhaps because there was not much heavy industry located in Cincinnati; the city had many comparatively small men's-clothing factories.[12]) It should be noted that these firms referred to do not include businesses the census refers to as "hand-trades," e.g., carpentering, masonry, painting, paper-hanging, dress-making, cabinet-making, blacksmithing, plumbing, plastering, repairing things, and so forth.[13]

The foundry and machine shop industry was the leading industry in the United States and was important both in the Midwest and in the East. An interregional comparison of firm size in the same industry seemed warranted. I looked at the only twelve Midwest cities that had a gross output of machine shop products in excess of one million dollars and compared their mean value added per firm with that of the only thirty-nine cities in the East also having more than one million dollars of gross output. The result was that the two sets of cities had a nearly identical average value added per firm ($60,000). The average capital invested and number of employees per firm were also comparable. These results would not be inconsistent with the notion that the larger midwestern firms were the result of optimal scale of plant differences that were inherent in differences in the industrial structure of the two regions. However, foundry and machine shop firms in the main five Midwest cities (Chicago, Cleveland, Cincinnati, Detroit, Milwaukee) were larger than the machine shop firms of Baltimore, Boston, Brooklyn, New York, and Philadelphia. The Midwest's five-city simple average of value added per firm was $66,000 versus an average of $45,000 in the five eastern cities. The simple five-city average of employees per firm and of capital per firm were decidedly higher in the Midwest, too. The five Midwest cities had about sixty-seven employees per machine shop firm compared to forty-one employees per firm in the five large eastern cities. The Midwest's five-city average capital per firm was $93,500 versus $62,700 in the five-city East.

Further research seems desirable to discover if significantly different technologies were embodied in the industry's newer plants. Perhaps a shift in the range of economies of scale was manifested faster in the more recently built Chicago firms. Another possible explanation of why machine shops were bigger in the Midwest's large cities than they were in the East's large cities has to do with the kind of products they were making. A different product mix could dictate a different optimal plant size. For example, midwestern firms may have concentrated more in metal-working machines but firms in the large eastern cities may have produced relatively more cast iron stoves and cookware.

IV

Next, consider the people who worked in 1890; in effect, how did they make a living? The numbers and proportions of male workers in the United States and Midwest that were employed in the twenty most important occupations are given in table 5. By far, the major occupation was that of a farmer, planter, or overseer. Including farm laborers, jobs directly in agriculture occupied approximately 40 percent of the male workers. The percentage of the United States male and female working population who were employed under the census classification of "manufacturing and mechanical" jobs was about 22 percent in 1890. For the five midwestern states, the figure was 23 percent. In the nine South Atlantic states, about 13 percent of the total working population was so employed. In the more industrialized northeastern nine states, about 36 percent of the employees worked in the manufacturing and mechanical sector of our economy. About 83 percent of these United States workers were males.[14] About half of them were in construction work and hand-trade occupations such as carpenters, painters, masons, blacksmiths, and tailors. Most worked outside at a moving job site or in very small shops. If by a manufacturing job one means work inside a larger building producing a tangible good, it seems likely that, at most, one-eighth of the males who worked were to be found in those kinds of jobs. Most men worked in agriculture, construction, trade, and transportation.

In the late nineteenth century, the relative shift of labor was not so much from farming jobs to manufacturing jobs as it was from agriculture to working in the distributive and service industries. The midwest male occupation distribution resembled that of the national average. There were slight differences. For example, midwestern males were somewhat less apt to be agricultural laborers, bookkeepers, clerks, salesmen, servants, and boot and shoe makers and somewhat more likely to be farmers, nonagricultural laborers, and lumber and steel mill employees. Table 5 captures slightly over three-fourths of the aggregate number of males who worked in the United States during the census year 1889–1890. If one uses the census classifica-

TABLE 5

Top Twenty Male Occupations in the USA Compared
To the Five Midwest States, 1890

OCCUPATIONS	U.S. (THOUSANDS OF PERSONS)	PERCENTAGE OF U.S. WORKERS	MIDWEST (THOUSANDS OF PERSONS)	PERCENTAGE OF MIDWEST WORKERS
ALL OCCUPATIONS	18,821	(100)	4,040	(100)
Farmers, Planters, Oversees	5,055	26.9	1,139	28.2
Agricultural Laborers	2,557	13.6	448	11.1
Non-Agricultural Laborers	1,859	9.9	450	11.1
Bookkeepers, Clerks, Salesmen	843	4.5	127	3.1
Merchants and Dealers	666	3.5	155	3.8
Carpenters	611	3.2	147	3.6
Steam Railroad Employees	461	2.4	102	2.5
Draymen, Hackmen, Teamsters	368	2.0	76	1.9
Miners	349	1.9	74	1.8
Servants	244	1.3	33	0.8
Painters, Glaziers, Varnishers	220	1.2	56	1.4
Blacksmiths	205	1.1	53	1.3
Boot and Shoemakers and Repairers	179	1.0	26	0.6
Machinists	177	0.9	41	1.0
Masons	159	0.8	41	1.0
Iron and Steel Workers	143	0.8	55	1.4
Saw and Planing Mill Employees	133	0.7	45	1.1
Tailors	122	0.6	27	0.7
Printers, Lithographers, Pressmen, etc.	112	0.6	26	0.6
Butchers	105	0.6	26	0.6

Source: *Report on Population at the Eleventh Census: 1890*, Part 2 (Washington, D.C.: Government Printing Office, 1897), ci-ciii, and table 116.

Notes: Midwestern states are Ohio, Indiana, Illinois, Michigan, and Wisconsin.

tion of "manufacturing and mechanical pursuits," then the leading occupations in that classification were, in order, carpentry, painting and plastering, and varnishing (as one occupation), blacksmithing, boot and shoe making and repairing, machinist, masonry, iron and steel, saw and planing-mill work, tailoring, printing (broadly construed), butchering, and officials of manufacturing establishments. Carpentry employed 611,000 men; manufacturing officials (ranked twelfth) employed 101,000 men. So important were carpenter jobs in the economy that painting, plastering, and varnishing (ranked second) accounted for only a little over one-third as many jobs as did carpentry.

It is interesting that the occupations of 1890 were not much different than they were in 1850. Among free males in 1850, the leading (top to bottom) manufacturing and mechanical jobs were held by carpenters, boot and shoe makers and repairers, blacksmiths, masons, plasterers, tailors, various mill and factory operatives (only 50,000), coopers, cabinet and chair makers, painters, millers, wheelwrights, machinists, and harness and saddle makers and repairers. Iron and steel workers jumped from 16,000 in 1850 to 141,000 in 1890. There was also a surge of employment in the various printing occupations. Other occupations that advanced were painting and varnishing and machinist work. Occupations exhibiting relative declines were cooperage, wheelwrights, and boot and shoe making and repairing.[15]

The occupations of women were dramatically different from those of men. For women, clerical jobs were just beginning to emerge as an important source of employment. Table 6 shows the numbers and proportion of females in the leading occupations of the Midwest and the United States. The fifteen occupations cover about nine-tenths of all female workers in the nation. Fully one-third of working women were servants, including waitresses and housekeepers. Among white working women whose parents were both born in the United States, one in four was a servant. Among foreign-born white working women, one in two was a servant. In the Midwest 40 percent of all working women were servants of various kinds. The next largest occupation was that of dressmaker, milliner, and seamstress. About one out of eight working women in the United States and nearly one out of five in the Midwest did this kind of hand work for a living. Nationally, agricultural labor employed about 11 percent of the women who worked. However, these people were overwhelmingly southern blacks. In the Midwest farm labor as an occupation was not an important one for women, though that of farmer was, with 6 percent of the female jobs. Nearly 10 percent of working women in the Midwest were schoolteachers. Other principal occupations of midwestern women were bookkeeper, clerk, and typist (as one occupation), laundress, textile mill operatives, and tailors. Many women also worked as musicians and music teachers, nurses and midwives, and boarding and lodging-house keepers.

TABLE 6

Top Fifteen Female Occupations in the U.S. Compared
To the Five Midwest States, 1890

OCCUPATIONS	U.S. (THOUSANDS OF PERSONS)	PERCENTAGE OF U.S. WORKERS	MIDWEST (THOUSANDS OF PERSONS)	PERCENTAGE OF MIDWEST WORKERS
ALL OCCUPATIONS	3,914	(100)	646	(100)
Servants, Waiters, Housekeepers	1,303	33.3	258	40.0
Dressmakers, Milliners, Seamstresses	494	12.6	117	18.1
Agricultural Laborers	447	11.4	3	0.5
Professors and Teachers	246	6.3	61	9.4
Farmers, Planters, Overseers	226	5.8	39	6.0
Laundresses	217	5.5	18	2.8
Bookkeepers, Clerks, Saleswomen, Steno-graphers, Typists	172	4.4	41	6.3
Cotton Mill Operatives	93	2.4	(a)	(a)
Tailors	64	1.6	16	2.5
Non-Agricultural Laborers	55	1.4	4	0.6
Mill and Factory Operatives	42	1.1	(a)	(a)
Nurses and Midwives	41	1.0	7	1.1
Musicians and Music Teachers	35	0.9	9	1.4
Boot and Shoemakers and Repairers	34	0.9	3	0.5
Boarding and Lodging Housekeepers	33	0.8	7	1.1

Source: *Report on Population at the Eleventh Census: 1890*, Part 2 (Washington, D.C.: Government Printing Office, 1897), ci-ciii, and table 116.

Note: (a) State totals put cotton, woolen, and textile mill workers into one category: 11,000 workers (1.7%).

Consider next the occupations of people who worked only in the cities. Table C-1 (Appendix) gives the percentage of male workers employed in various occupations in the five midwestern cities and in four leading eastern cities. The fifteen occupations cover 60 percent of all of the workers in the Midwest cities and about 55 percent of those in four cities of the East. The eastern cities are New York, Philadelphia, Boston, and Baltimore. The occupation distribution in the two sets of cities is certainly similar. Common laborers of various kinds make up 15.5 percent of midwestern urban workers and 9.7 percent of eastern urban workers. The second-ranked occupation was that of bookkeepers and clerks. The merchant occupation was third in both sets of cities but was relatively more important in the East (7.8 percent versus 5.7 percent of the labor force). Carpenters, steelworkers, machinists, and railroad workers were relatively more important occupations in the Midwest, though teamsters, salesmen, tailors, and servants were relatively more important in the East.

The principal occupations of urban women in the midwestern and eastern cities are given in table C-2 (Appendix). In the Midwest cities, approximately 30 percent of female workers were servants of various kinds. Another 20 percent were dressmakers, hat-makers, and seamstresses. Tailors and clerk-copyists each accounted for about 5 percent of the female working population. Next came teachers, laundresses, sales clerks, and textile workers. In the eastern cities, woman did basically the same kind of work that was done by working women in the Midwest. The working woman in the East was somewhat more likely than her midwestern counterpart to be a servant, dressmaker or seamstress, laundress, saleswoman, or textile worker. She was somewhat less likely to be a tailor, clerk or copyist, and school teacher. As in the case of males, however, one is impressed with how similar were the East and Midwest occupation distributions.

Many of these working men and women were immigrants. In the five midwestern states, the percentage of the whole population who were immigrants varied from 6.7 percent in Indiana to 30.7 percent in Wisconsin; the average for the region was 18.6 percent. This was a few percentage points less than it was for the northeastern states but well above the southern states where the percentage of the population that was foreign born was well under 5 percent. In the United States, 17.6 percent of the white males and 15.6 percent of the white females were immigrants. (In the Midwest 98 percent of the population was white; for example, only eight thousand black people lived in Chicago out of a population of one million.[16]) In the five Midwest cities, the proportion of the population that was immigrants ranged from 25 percent in Cincinnati to around 40 percent in the other four cities. However, the labor force was composed of a higher proportion of foreign born than was the whole population. This was particularly true in cities. In Chicago, Detroit, Cleveland, and Milwaukee, slightly over one-half of the male labor force was foreign born. In certain occupations the percentage was especially high. Among males in Chicago, 88 percent of the tailors, 78 percent of the laborers, and 71 percent of the carpenters were immigrants. On the other hand, 18 percent of the lawyers, 26 percent of the bankers, and 29 percent of the physicians were foreign born. Overall, the leading country of origin was Germany, followed by Ireland and either the Scandinavian countries or Great Britain. About 4 percent of the Chicago male work force was illiterate, and 9 percent of them spoke no English. For common laborers in Chicago, 12 percent were illiterate and 22 percent spoke no English.

Nearly half of the female workers were foreign-born, and 62 percent were 24 or younger. Of the working women, very few were married; in the Midwest fewer than 2 percent were married (6.5 percent in Chicago).[17] Labor force participation rates for women were entirely different in 1890 than they are today. In 1890 women who were in their late teens and early twenties were the most likely to work; around 30 percent of women in that age group worked outside their homes. The vast majority were single; when a woman married she usually dropped out of the labor force. Among women between the ages of 25 and 34, only 17 percent worked. Today, the figure would be roughly 65 percent.[18] Less than one in every fifty white married women was in the labor force in 1890. Currently, more than one in every two are in the labor force.

V

The remarkable growth of the Midwest in the last half of the nineteenth century was not lost upon the 1900 census writers. After pointing out that Ohio, Indiana, and Illinois had increased their share of the national gross value of manufacturing from 14.4 percent in 1850 to 30.7 percent in 1900, they wrote, "No where else in the world has there been so rapid a transformation of the occupations of the population."[19] They went on to say, "These establishments were often on a very large scale, and modern in equipment and construction, utilizing the latest improvements in machinery and methods."[20] Illinois, in particular, stands out as a veritable powerhouse of economic energy. By 1900 the state ranked third in population, second in gross value of farm output, and third in gross and net value of manufacturing output. By value of gross manufacturing output, the rank of Illinois among all states advanced from fifteenth in 1850 to eighth in 1860 to sixth in 1870 to fourth in 1880 and to third in 1890. About this, the writers of the census volume remarked, "This is the most notable and rapid advance in position which has occurred in industrial history."[21] It may still be that today.

Notes

1. Census Reports, vol. 7, Twelfth Census of the United States, in *Manufactures*, pt. 1, (Washington, 1902), clxxi.

2. The 1880 census is the last available census in which researchers can utilize firm-by-firm data for the nineteenth century. The 1880 manufacturing census is currently the subject of a large-scale investigation by Jeremy Atack and Fred Bateman.

3. Census Office, Report on Manufacturing Industries in the United States at the Eleventh Census, pt. 1, in *Totals for States and Industries* (Washington, D.C.: Government Printing Office, 1895), 5–7.

4. Bureau of the Census, *Occupations at the Twelfth Census* (Washington, D.C.: Government Printing Office, 1904), c.

5. The value-added concept is being used in the ordinary way as the difference between the value of gross output during the year and the cost of materials used during the year *(Report on Manufacturing in the United States at the Eleventh Census: 1890*, pt. 1, (Washington, D.C.: Government Printing Office, 1895), 28–29).

6. U.S. Bureau of the Census, *Census of the United States: 1860*, vol. 3 (Washington, D.C.: Government Printing Office, 861), 733–42.

7. *Report on Manufacturing at the Eleventh Census: 1890*, pt. 3, p. 386.

8. The Misc. Documents of the House of Representatives for the Second Session of Fiftieth Congress, 1888–1889 (Washington, D.C.: Government Printing Office, 1889), 171, 437.

9. *Reports of Committees of the Senate of the United States, 1889-90*, Report No. 829 (Washington, D.C.: Government Printing Office, 1890), 3–4.

10. Construction was a very important industry in all of the cities but is not counted here as manufacturing.

11. Bessie Louise Pierce, *A History of Chicago*, (New York: Alfred A. Knopf, 1957), 3:148.

12. Twelfth Census, *Manufactures*, pt. 1, ccxlviii–ccliv, ccxli.

13. Twelfth Census, *Manufactures*, pt. 1, p. xxxvii

14. *Report on Population at the Eleventh Census: 1890*, pt. 2 (Washington, D.C.: Government Printing Office, 1897), 302–3.

15. Ibid., cv–cviii.

16. Bureau of the Census, *Immigrants and Their Children 1920*, Niles Carpenter, Census Monographs, 7, (Washington, D.C.: Government Printing Office, 1927), 308–9. *Report on Population*, pt. 2 (Washington, D.C.: Government Printing Office, 1897), table 118. *Report on Population*, pt. 2, (Washington, D.C.: Government Printing Office, 1895), table 85.

17. *Report on Population*, 1897, table 118.

18. Bureau of the Census, *Statistical Abstract of the United States: 1986*, 106th edition (Washington, D.C., 1985), 24, 392; Bureau of the Census, Special Reports, *Occupations at the Twelfth Census*, cxviii.

19. Twelfth Census of the United States, vol. 7, *Manufactures,* pt. 1, p. clxxvi.

20. Ibid.

21. Ibid., clxxxi.

APPENDIX A

TABLE A-1

Ohio: Leading Industries in 1890
By Value Added
(Thousands of Dollars)

Foundry and Machine Shop Products	24,285
Liquor, Malt and Distilled	20,126
Iron and Steel	18,551
Lumber Mill Products	12,795
Printing and Publishing Books, Jobs, Newspapers and Periodicals	12,693
Men's Clothing	10,668
Carriages and Wagons	9,345
Agricultural Implements	8,679
Tobacco Products	8,400
Flour and Grist Mill Products	6,050
Furniture	5,376

Source: *Report on Manufacturing in the United States at the Eleventh Census: 1890*, Part 1 (Washington, D.C.: Government Printing Office, 1895), 546–55.

TABLE A-2

Indiana: Leading Industries in 1890
By Value Added
(Thousands of Dollars)

Lumber Products	11,716
Liquor, Malt and Distilled	7,823
Foundry and Machine Shop Products	5,523
Flour and Grist Mill Products	4,636
Carriages and Wagons	4,578
Furniture	3,841
Printing and Publishing	3,506
Slaughtering and Meat Packing	3,489
Agricultural Implements	3,450
Railroad Cars	2,149

Source: *Report on Manufacturing in the United States at the Eleventh Census: 1890*, Part 1 (Washington, D.C.: Government Printing Office, 1895), 400–405.

TABLE A-3

Illinois: Leading Industries in 1890
By Value Added
(Thousands of Dollars)

Distilled Liquors	48,079
Slaughtering and Meatpacking	31,387
Printing and Publishing	23,222
Foundry and Machine Shop Products	21,584
Men's Clothing	15,427
Agricultural Implements	14,507
Lumber Mill Products	10,953
Malt Liquors	9,036
Iron and Steel	8,177
Railroad Cars	7,204

Source: *Report on Manufacturing in the United States at the Eleventh Census: 1890*, Part 1 (Washington, D.C.: Government Printing Office, 1895), 386–96.

TABLE A-4

Michigan: Leading Industries in 1890
By Value Added
(Thousands of Dollars)

Lumber Products	37,561
Foundry and Machine Shop Products	7,872
Flour and Grist Mill Products	3,316
Railroad Cars	3,070
Carriages and Wagons	2,920
Ship Building	2,410
Agricultural Implements	2,307
Men's Clothing	2,223
Chemicals	2,161
Malt Liquor	1,981
Iron and Steel	1,697

Sources: *Report on Manufacturing in the United States at the Eleventh Census: 1890*, Part 1 (Washington, D.C.: Government Printing Office, 1895), 464–71.

TABLE A-5

Wisconsin: Leading Industries in 1890
By Value Added
(Thousands of Dollars)

Lumber Products	26,877
Malt Liquor	9,364
Flour and Grist Mill Products	3,088
Agricultural Implements	3,055
Printing and Publishing	2,872
Carriages and Wagons	2,430
Leather	2,422
Tobacco Products	2,128
Furniture	1,888
Iron and Steel	

Sources: *Report on Manufacturing in the United States at the Eleventh Census: 1890*, Part 1 (Washington, D.C.: Government Printing Office, 1895), 628–35.

APPENDIX B

TABLE B

Value Added in the Six Leading Industries of
Five Large Cities in 1890
(Thousands of Dollars)

	New York	Philadelphia	Boston	Baltimore	St. Louis
Foundry and Machine Shops	12,675	17,580	5,367	2,924	6,749
Men's Clothing	28,925	9,782	8,718	6,910	2,966
Printing and Publishing	42,215		9,486		6,062
Malt Liquor	15,740	6,813	2,822	2,209	9,897
Tobacco Products	20,893			3,384	14,290
Women's Clothing	18,868				
Masonry—Bricks and Stone		13,106	4,500	4,913	4,564
Hosiery and Knit Goods		7,223			
Carpets and Rugs		8,931			
Lumber Planing Mill Products			7,408		
Canned Fruits and Vegetables				2,209	

Sources: *Compendium of Eleventh Census of the United States,* Part 2, *Manufactures,* (Washington, D.C.: Government Printing Office, 1984), table 2.

APPENDIX C

TABLE C-1

Distribution of Principal Male
Occupations in Cities in 1890

	MIDWEST CITIES (PERCENT OF ALL MALE WORKERS)	EASTERN CITIES (PERCENT OF ALL MALE WORKERS)
Laborers	15.5	9.7
Bookkeepers and Clerks	8.1	8.6
Merchants	5.7	7.8
Carpenters	5.1	3.1
Draymen, Hackmen, Teamsters	3.8	4.7
Iron and Steel Workers	3.0	1.5
Railroad Workers	2.8	1.7
Painters and Varnishers	2.6	2.3
Machinists	2.4	1.8
Tailors	2.2	3.5
Salesmen	2.1	2.8
Servants and Waiters	2.1	3.0
Printers, Lithographers, Pressmen	1.9	2.1
Manufacturers and Publishers	1.6	1.7
Blacksmiths	1.4	1.2

Sourcs: *Report on Population at the Eleventh Census: 1890,* Part 2 (Washington, D.C.: Government Printing Office, 1897), table 118.

Note: Midwest cities are Chicago, Cincinnati, Cleveland, Milwaukee, and Detroit. Eastern cities are New York, Philadelphia, Boston, and Baltimore.

TABLE C-2

Distribution of Principal Female
Occupations in Cities in 1890

	MIDWEST CITIES (PERCENT OF ALL FEMALE WORKERS)	EASTERN CITIES (PERCENT OF ALL FEMALE WORKERS)
Servants and Waitresses	29.0	32.8
Dressmakers, Milliners, Seamstresses	19.6	23.0
Tailors	5.7	3.6
Clerks and Copyists	4.8	1.7
Teachers	3.7	2.9
Laundresses	2.8	5.0
Saleswomen	2.8	4.8
Textile Workers	1.4	6.8

Source: *Report on Population at the Eleventh Census: 1890,* Part 2 (Washington, D.C.: Government Printing Office, 1897), table 118.

Note: Midwest cities are Chicago, Cincinnati, Cleveland, Milwaukee, and Detroit. Eastern cities are New York, Philadelphia, Boston and Baltimore.

13.

ECONOMIC GROWTH AND DECLINE IN THE OLD NORTHWEST

Richard Vedder and Lowell Gallaway
Ohio University

THE ECONOMIC HISTORY OF the five states comprising the Old Northwest since the region's beginning with the Ordinance of 1787 can be divided into two equal periods. The first century after the ordinance can be called the Century of Growth; the second century, from the 1880s to the present, might be characterized as the Century of Maturity and Relative Decline.

Going a bit further, each period can be subdivided into two eras of roughly equal length, giving us four half-century periods since the passage of the Northwest Ordinance. The first half century, from 1787 to roughly 1840, might be called the Age of Extensive Growth—when population, incomes, and output were all growing rapidly, and probably in nearly equal amounts. The second half century, from about 1840 to about 1880 or 1890, was the Age of Intensive Growth—when output in the region rose sharply in relation to population and in relation to the rest of the nation and world. This is when the five states developed their regional economic preeminence, at a time when the nation was developing its prominence among the countries of the world.

The third stage, from the 1880s to around 1930, was the Age of Maturation—when the region continued to develop and prosper, but when the relative economic importance of the area had shown signs of stabilizing. The fourth stage, the Age of Stagnation, present since the 1930s, has been characterized by continued growth in output and incomes, but a growth at slower rates than in the past and slower than other regions. It has been an era of relative economic decline.

The first part of this paper documents these assertions about economic changes within the region. Several alternative measures of economic vitality are described. The second part, in some respects more speculative than the first, explores various hypotheses about the reasons for regional decline. Appropriately, given this volume's commemoration of the Northwest Ordinance, special attention is placed on the role of the changing institutional and legal framework. Even more speculative is our concluding discussion about the possible existence of an Age of Gentrification, a Renaissance, in the third century.

I. THE ECONOMIC VITALITY OF THE REGION:
EMPIRICAL EVIDENCE

WE HAVE CHOSEN THREE indicators of regional economic vitality to use in our assessment of the changing economic performance of the Old Northwest, now known as the East North Central states, over time: growth in personal income per capita (or some close variant thereof), the rate of unemployment, and the rate of net migration. Per capita income growth is the most broadly used measure of economic growth; the unemployment rate is perhaps the most widely observed macroeconomic statistic, measuring job opportunities; and net migration is probably the ultimate measure of a region's attractiveness to the citizenry.

Income Growth in the East North Central States, 1840–1985

Income data are not available for the first half century of regional growth following the Northwest Ordinance. Reliable information on total and per capita income may be found only beginning in 1840 (table 1). The table emphasizes per capita income and its change over time, comparing the region with the United States as a whole. The basic per capita income estimates for the nineteenth century developed by Richard Easterlin are spliced with United States Department of Commerce data beginning in 1929.[1] To deflate nominal values to real values, the Gross National Product price deflator is used, with 1982 = 100. Earlier values of the deflator (1889 to 1929) were converted from 1958 to a 1982 base by the authors. From 1840 to 1889, the consumer price index was used to deflate; prices changed relatively little with any index used.[2] The region's share of total U.S. personal income was calculated from these data sources. It is reported in the last column of table 1.

Starting with the last column, the data show the enormous growth in the relative importance of the East North Central region during the second half century, from 1840 to 1880. At the time of the centenary of the Northwest Ordinance (in 1887), the region's share of total income was near its historic high. In the region's third half century, or to about 1930, the share of national income dipped very slightly, actually falling in the late nineteenth century but rising again in the first three decades of the twentieth. In the fifty-five years after 1930, the region's relative income share underwent a sharp decline, with the fall being far sharper after 1960 than before.

Although the total income data clearly show a rise in the region's relative importance in its first century and a decline during its second, it is important not to lose sight of the extraordinary absolute growth occurring over time, with real per capita income rising over twenty-one times from 1840 to 1985, an annual real per capita increase of 2.13 percent a year. The average resident of the region in 1985 earned income in two and one-half weeks what it took his 1840 ancestor to earn in a year.

TABLE 1

Growth in Income Per Capita, East North Central States and United States, 1840–1985

Year	Old Northwest		United States		E. N.C.	E.N.C.
	Real Per Cap. Income★	Annual Growth Rate†	Real Per Cap. Income★	Annual Growth Rate†	Inc/Cap. As % of U.S.	Personal Inc. As % Of U.S.‡
1840	$ 565	–	$ 799	–	67.8%	12.24%
1880	1,294	2.09%	1,206	1.03%	107.4	24.14
1900	1,712	1.41	1,612	1.46	106.2	22.42
1929	5,500§	4.11§	4,829§	3.86§	113.9	23.63
1940	5,408	-0.15	4,554	-0.53	118.7	22.73
1950	6,971	2.57	6,259	3.23	115.2	22.48
1960	7,553	0.81	7,172	1.37	105.3	21.73
1970	9,726	2.56	9,388	2.73	103.6	20.66
1980	11,336	1.54	11,078	1.67	102.3	18.81
1985	11,961	1.08	12,064	1.72	99.1	17.33

★ In 1982 dollars. The GNP price deflator index is used after 1889; before that the consumer price index is used to calculate real personal income values.

† From previous date listed in table.
‡ On a total, not per capita, personal income basis.

§ Data not strictly comparable to previous years, so the 1900-29 growth rate may be overstated.

SOURCES: 1840–1900, Richard A. Easterlin, "Interregional Differences in Per Capita Income, Population, and Total Income, 1840–1950," in William Parker, ed. *Trends in the American Economy in the Nineteenth Century*, vol. 24, Studies in Income and Wealth (Princeton: Princeton University Press for the NBER, 1960); U.S. Department of Commerce, *Statistical Abstract of the United States*, various editions; *Survey of Current Business*, April 1986.

The enormous recorded intensive growth from 1840 to 1880 is more extraordinary than the 2.09 percent growth rate recorded in the table for several reasons. First, relative to the nation as a whole, the region stood out during a time the nation was undergoing a "take off." Regional growth per capita was double the national average. The region went from substantially below the national average in income to well above it, in less than two generations. Second, per capita growth rates of 1 percent a year were considered high in this first century after the original industrial revolution in England, and in the first half century of the American industrial revolution. To record a 2 percent growth rate was the nineteenth-century equivalent of the near double-digit growth rates recorded in some rapidly developing nations in Asia today. Third, the evidence is that most of the region's relative growth occurred in the two decades from 1860 to 1880; in part, this reflected the devastating impact of the Civil War on the South (that region showed no growth from 1860 to 1880), but in part probably reflected an acceleration in real income growth within the five states.[3]

The data suggest some slowing in the torrid pace of growth in the last two decades of the nineteenth century, with the regional trend being similar to the national one. If the data are to be believed, the first three decades of the twentieth century were the Golden Age of both the region and the nation, with the Old Northwest outshining the country as a whole, recording real per capita annual growth of over 4 percent per annum over three decades, a record that was unparalleled at that time and is impressive, even by today's standards. Because two data sets (the Easterlin and Commerce Department) are spliced together during this era, it is possible the true growth rate is overstated, but it is hard to believe the true rate was much under 3 percent (for it to be so, the Easterlin data would have to be very seriously understated). Moreover, any data distortions probably are national in scope, so the recorded regional superiority in per capita income growth over the nation as a whole is probably reasonably accurate.

An argument can be made for dating the region's relative economic decline from either the 1930s or the 1940s. In the 1930s economic growth came to an abrupt halt (income actually declined very slightly) after three decades of extraordinary advance. On the other hand, the region's problems in the thirties were a consequence of the Great Depression, and the region actually suffered slightly less than the country as a whole.

In 1940 regional income per capita was more than 18 percent above the national average. Since the "national average" includes the East North Central States, per capita income in the five states averaged more than 22 percent above the income levels in the forty-three other states. By this measure the region was at its peak of relative economic superiority. In every time period after 1940, economic growth in the East North Central states fell below the national average. Growth in the region was robust in the forties— but less so than for the nation as a whole. Growth slowed both regionally and nationally in the fifties, but was particularly anemic in the Old Northwest, which lost almost two-thirds of its per capita income superiority over the nation as a whole within the single decade. Economic growth in the sixties was brisk, but a bit less so than for the nation in general. The slowdown in growth nationally in the seventies was duplicated regionally, with regional growth again falling below national standards.

In 1982 something happened that had not occurred since the early 1860s—income per capita in the Old Northwest region fell below the national average. Although national growth during the early eighties was slightly higher than during the seventies, in the Old Northwest the growth rate slowed significantly, falling far below the national average. The region's relative economic superiority that had lasted for about 120 years had ended. Though the loss in relative economic status in the early eighties was unusually pronounced, commentators during that period, blaming the decline on problems unique to those years, lost sight of the fact that the decline had been going on for four decades before the eighties began. The Midwest did not decline in a day.

Intraregional Income Patterns

The data describing regional income patterns mask very important divergences in economic growth patterns within the area, as table 2 indicates. In the first century and a half of the region's post-Ordinance history, substantial income differentials existed between the five states, and those differentials were growing over time. The Wisconsin figure for 1840 is highly suspect, since the region was very sparsely settled. Aside from Wisconsin, interstate differentials in 1840 were modest. In 1929 by contrast, income per capita in Illinois was more than 55 percent higher than in neighboring Indiana. Since 1929, those income differentials have narrowed dramatically, and Illinois had only a 17 percent higher per capita income than Indiana in 1985 (still the lowest income state in the region). More than two-thirds of the differential had been eliminated by 1985.

TABLE 2

Economic Growth of the Five East North Central States, 1840–1985

State	Income Per Capita:*			Annual Growth +		State As % of U.S.‡		
	1840	1929	1985	1840–1929	1929–85	1840	1929	1985
Ohio	$590	$5,356	$11,640	2.60%	1.40%	73.8%	110.9%	96.5%
Illinois	577	6,568	12,912	2.87	1.21	72.2	136.0	107.0
Indiana	504	4,212	11,010	2.50	1.73	63.1	87.2	91.3
Michigan	541	5,438	11,926	2.72	1.41	67.7	112.6	98.9
Wisconsin	983	4,685	11,554	1.83	1.62	123.0	97.0	95.8
Region	565	5,500	11,961	2.68	1.40	70.7	113.9	99.1
U.S.	799	4,829	12,064	2.11	1.65	100.0	100.0	100.0

*Personal Income in 1982 dollars; see text for price deflators used.
+In per capita real income during period. ‡With respect to personal income per capita.
SOURCES: See previous table, text; authors' calculations.

The two states whose performance most closely resembled the average for the region as a whole in both time periods were Ohio and Michigan. Illinois was the fastest growing state in the period of regional ascendancy and leadership (1840–1929), but the slowest growing state during the era of relative stagnation, with its growth rate declining by well over half. In 1929 Illinois' income per capita was an extraordinary 36 percent above the national average, making it one of the richest geographic areas in the world. By 1985, however, its income was only 7 percent above the national average on a per capita basis. By contrast, Indiana and Wisconsin, relatively slower growing states during the age of ascendancy (although still growing rapidly), have had above average growth rates for the region in the post-1929 period. Indiana, in fact, has outperformed the nation, and Wisconsin nearly matched the nation's performance.

The slowdown in economic growth after 1929 was not only relative to other states, but also relative to the region's own earlier history. At a time when growth rates for the planet as a whole were almost certainly generally rising, the growth rate of the U.S. fell modestly while the region's growth declined dramatically.

These changing patterns after 1929 are not surprising and are consistent with both economic theory and historical patterns elsewhere within the nation. Economic theory suggests resources tend to migrate to areas of highest returns, which tends to lower returns in those areas and raise them in the area of out-migration. Paul Samuelson has called this the "factor price equalization theorem."[4] Thus wages tend to fall relatively over time in the high wage areas, and rise in the low wage ones. Over time the higher income areas in the North and East have lost ground to the lower income areas, particularly in the South, for this reason.

Within the Old Northwest, then, it is not surprising that relatively poor Indiana and Wisconsin have grown faster than more prosperous Illinois, Michigan, and Ohio. It is also not surprising that the region as a whole has lost its economic superiority. Economic theory suggests that further decline in relative incomes, however, should lead to an out-migration of resources (which has already occurred to a considerable extent) that eventually may put a halt to the decline.[5]

Trends in Unemployment

Although there are gaps in the income data, the data on unemployment are even more sparse, indeed virtually nonexistent for the first century of the region's settled history. Data for the second century suggest that regional unemployment has varied considerably, that it has had a recent tendency to rise, and that on the whole it has exceeded that for the nation (see table 3). Regarding the latter point, in every period observed, the regional unemployment rate exceeded the national rate. The earlier (1890 and 1930) data are based on but two observations and may thus not be typical of early twentieth-century experience. It is interesting to note, however, that regional unemployment was about 15-25 percent above national norms during 1890, 1930, and 1978–82. In years of generally high unemployment, regional unemployment has tended to rise well above the national average. It would appear that this is not merely a recent phenomenon.

This raises the possibility that the "natural" rate of unemployment in the Old Northwest states is and has long been somewhat above the natural rate for the rest of the nation. Within the region unemployment was consistently above the regional (and national) average in Michigan; Wisconsin was consistently below the regional norm. Possible reasons for these variations in unemployment trends will be explored in the second section of the paper.

TABLE 3

Unemployment Rates in the Old Northwest and the United States, 1890–1982

State or Area	Average Rate of Unemployment:				
	1890★	1930	1958–62†	1968–72†	1978–82†
Ohio	9.44	8.20	6.16	3.94	8.36
Indiana	9.96	6.90	6.04	4.28	8.61
Illinois	6.93	8.88	5.30	3.88	7.94
Michigan	9.50	10.22	9.18	6.38	10.98
Wisconsin	8.10	5.67	4.44	4.32	7.06
E.N.C. STATES	8.64	8.36	6.33	4.76	8.69
UNITED STATES	7.50	6.53	6.04	4.70	7.26

★ Proportion of the labor force that had been unemployed for four or more months during the preceding year. Not strictly comparable to the other unemployment data.

† The mean of the annual unemployment rates for the five years.

SOURCES: Eleventh Census, *Report of the Population of the United States, Part II* (Washington, D.C.: Government Printing Office, 1897); Fifteenth Census, vol. 2, *General Report* (Washington, D.C.: Government Printing Office, 1932); and *Manpower Report of the President*, various years.

More comprehensive examination of the modern unemployment data suggests the average rate of unemployment in the East North Central states is above the national average, although there are important periods (e. g., the 1970s) where this was not true. Over the twenty-six year period 1960-85, however, unemployment averaged higher in the Old Northwest states than in the United States as a whole.

Migration in the Old Northwest

By "voting with their feet," people demonstrate their locational preferences. The evidence, in table 4, is that there was on balance a net inflow of persons into the East North Central States until 1960. In absolute numbers that inflow peaked in the first two decades of this century, although relative to the region's (or United States') population, the inflow in the early nineteenth century was of greater magnitude. Still, for 160 years the region's attractions drew more people into it than the detractions led people to leave. The post–1960 exodus was both historically unprecedented in the region's history and of an absolute magnitude that was extraordinary. *Net out-migration from the East North Central States from 1960 to 1984 nearly equaled net in-migration from 1900 to 1960, so for the century as a whole there has been virtually no in-migration to the Old Northwest.*

Looking at the absolute in-flows of migration, it appears that there were two peaks: the first came in the generation or two before the Civil War, followed by a decline in the late nineteenth century. The second comes in the first two decades of the twentieth century. The initial wave is associated

TABLE 4

Net Migration in the Five East North Central States, 1800–1984†

Period	Ohio	Ind.	Ill.	Mich.	Wisc.	Region	Migr. As % Of Total Popul.*
1800–20	413	128	38	3	0	582	1141.1%
1820–40	329	311	321	190	22	1173	137.5
1840–60	−351	−31	725	362	633	1338	37.7
1860–80	−146	−34	442	465	202	929	10.2
1880–1900	120	−53	510	234	185	996	5.7
1900–20	707	−38	479	582	47	1777	6.7
1920–40	158	10	353	567	−29	1059	3.1
1940–60	652	158	199	491	−137	1364	3.4
1960–84	−1334	−369	−953	−920	−166	−3742	−7.2

†In-migration minus out-migration; includes immigration; in thousands.

*Migration divided by population at beginning of indicated period.

SOURCES: 1800–1870, authors' estimates. See our "Migration and the Old Northwest" in David C. Klingaman and Richard K. Vedder, eds., *Essays in Nineteenth Century Economic History: The Old Northwest* (Athens: Ohio University Press, 1975), 162–64; 1870–1950, U.S. Department of Commerce, *Historical Statistics of the United States, Colonial Times to 1970* (Washington, D.C.: Government Printing Office, 1975), 93; 1950–84, U.S. Department Commerce, *Statistical Abstract of the United States*, various editions.

with the settlement of the land and might, accordingly, be considered an agricultural phenomenon. By contrast, the second surge in immigration is associated with the region's growing industrialization.

Migration patterns were not uniform across the region. Two states, Illinois and Michigan, had rather sustained in-migration from 1820 to 1960. Both Wisconsin's and Indiana's in-migration was highly concentrated in one generation, Indiana's between 1820 and 1840 and Wisconsin's in the last two decades before the Civil War. Both states witnessed net out-migration before the recent (post–1960) exodus, with Wisconsin having out-migration after 1920, whereas Indiana had it between 1840 and 1920. In absolute terms Ohio's greatest in-migration occurs early in the twentieth century, as does Michigan's; the industrial wave was in absolute terms greater than the agricultural wave. That is not true, however, for the other states.

The massive post–1960 out-migration had already started earlier in Wisconsin and has been less pronounced in that state than elsewhere. It has been particularly severe in Ohio, totalling some 13.7 percent of the 1960 population level, but has been of sizable magnitude in Illinois and Michigan as well, and somewhat less so in Indiana.

WHAT EXPLAINS THE RISE AND FALL OF THE OLD NORTHWEST'S ECONOMY?

IT IS EASIER TO identify the region's rise and comparative "fall" than to explain it. Economic development is a complex process, and any short explanation of its determinants is likely to be inadequate, particularly any unicausal type of explanation. With that cautionary note, let us suggest three types of broad causal explanations that may offer some insight into the changes in the region's economic fortunes. The first might be termed the "market forces" or "convergence" approach, the second could be called the "institutional forces" or "distributional coalitions" approach, and the third explanation might be termed the "structuralist" approach.

According to the market approach, factors of production are rewarded according to their contribution to output, and the quantity of output depends on the availability of resources (whether they be natural, human, capital, or entrepreneurial in character). During the settlement process in the nineteenth century, particularly before 1840, income in the region was relatively low, simply because capital resources were meager. By the late nineteenth century, the passage of time had allowed the region to accumulate a good stock of capital, in part through in-migration of capital, which when combined with superior natural resources (some of the best farmland in the world, along with quantities of such critical industrial minerals as coal and iron), labor, and low cost transportation (due to its being bordered by major rivers and the Great Lakes, and having a hospitable terrain for cheap land transportation), allowed the region to grow rapidly and to specialize and enjoy the gains from trade.[6] This gave the region a superiority over other areas with fewer abundant natural resources, a more costly transportation network, and the like. This superiority evolved and was maintained during the period from roughly 1840 to the 1920s or 1930s.

The region's slowing down after 1940 reflects a movement of resources to other areas. As wage rates were pushed up in the East North Central states during the industrialization of the late nineteenth and early twentieth centuries, labor became relatively costly, and profit-maximizing entrepreneurs increasingly moved capital resources South and West. Similarly, the high wages of the area attracted migrants, from all over the country and the world until about 1960, enhancing the supply of labor but lowering the capital-labor ratio and thereby tending to eliminate some of the economic superiority that had developed earlier. Migration served to eliminate much, possibly all, of the region's economic advantage.[7]

The "institutional forces" or "distributional coalitions" approach argues that institutional developments that favored economic growth in the region's first century, such as the Northwest Ordinance of 1787, were followed by other institutional changes that retarded growth in the second century. Following from Mancur Olson's pathbreaking analysis, "distributional coalitions," or special interest groups, organize and manage to derive benefits for themselves that on balance impose a cost on society.[8] These groups often use the powers of the state to redirect resources in their direction, taking advantage of the fact that where benefits are obtainable they are concentrated in relatively few hands. Given that the cost of these benefits is disbursed among many taxpayers, the few beneficiaries will lobby vigorously for them while those paying the cost are "rationally ignorant" of the process, since the cost per individual is quite small.[9]

Distributional coalitions might include business trade associations, groups seeking government transfer payments (e.g., welfare rights organizations), governmental agencies and their employees, churches, and so forth. Probably the best example and possibly the most important such coalition is the labor union, which attempts to obtain higher wage incomes for its members (but not necessarily society as a whole) through a variety of means, including the use of the strike weapon.

It takes time to organize such coalitions, and Olson hypothesizes that the older an area in terms of its current arrangements for collective action, the more likely the existence of coalitions. For example, over long time periods, special interest groups have the opportunity to win transfers from public funds; older governments tend to also be bigger, stifling efficient private activity to a relatively great extent. Empirical evidence is available that is consistent with this view.[10] According to this approach, the East North Central states moved from being a relatively "new" to being a relatively "old" region sometime in the early twentieth century, and thus began to be hobbled by labor unions and big government.

The third category of explanation for sluggish growth is that the region's output of goods and services became excessively concentrated in forms of economic activity for which product demand was sluggish or for which world trade conditions had led to low prices and poor terms of trade. In the nineteenth and early twentieth centuries, the argument was that areas with a high agricultural concentration tended to lag behind the highgrowth industrial areas. In the late twentieth century, the argument is that highly industrialized areas have a natural tendency to lag behind areas with more emphasis on the service industries or high technology industry.

Testing Three Explanations for Regional Stagnation

Each of the three explanations for stagnation—market forces/convergence, institutional forces/distributional coalitions, or structural forces—can be measured and then related to measures of economic vitality, such as changes in real income per capita. Unfortunately, data limitations restrict our analysis to the period since 1929, although that still allows observation over the span of the more than half century in which the region moved from relatively high growth and economic preeminence through an era of lesser growth and importance.

The convergence hypothesis is very simple to test. It suggests that low wage (and thus income) areas should have grown faster because of a migration of resources that lowered labor supply in those areas and increased them in relatively high income areas. Elsewhere we have demonstrated that migrants indeed responded to interstate income differentials.[11] Did this lead to a convergence of income levels between the forty-eight contiguous states? The answer is yes. The coefficient of variation on per capita income for the forty-eight states fell from .366 in 1929 to .151 in 1985, a decline of 58.9 percent. To examine this phenomenon further, we simply regressed per capita income in 1929, Y_{29}, against real per capita income growth, 1929-85, G, and obtained[12]:

$$(1) \quad G = 414.2901 - .3404 \, Y_{29}, \qquad \bar{R}^2 = .78,$$
$$(24.079 \quad (12.947)$$

where the numbers in parentheses are t-values. The relationship between income at the beginning of the period and subsequent growth is strongly negative and statistically significant, and the single explanatory variable accounts for over three-fourths of the variation in growth. Introduction of a dummy variable for the five East North Central states does not alter things, and that variable is not statistically significant; we cannot conclude that the region's relative income decline occurred for some reason uniquely peculiar to the area.

A model testing the distributional coalitions hypothesis is harder to define. Olson suggested that a useful proxy for the magnitude of such coalitions in an area is the years elapsed since statehood, termed A below, a measure of the age of a state. A problem exists for the southern states that were in a sense reborn after the Civil War. That conflict destroyed many existing institutions (and coalitions). Therefore, a dummy variable is introduced for the affected southern states (1 = southern state; 0 = other state).

One distributional coalition can be measured directly, namely labor unions. The big growth of unions came in the thirties and forties, so it would be appropriate to use a measure of union membership after this growth but still before the middle of the period so the measured impact on end period income is not spurious. We used union membership as a percent of nonagricultural employment in 1953, U.[13]

Finally, distributional coalitions use governments to achieve their goals, in part by attempting to receive tax revenues raised by those governments. The change in overall state and local tax burdens would be a measure of the growth in the potential for distributional coalitions to derive rents from tax revenues. Higher taxes also have been observed to be an impediment to growth.[14] Hence the growth in state and local taxes as a percent of personal income in 1932 and 1983, T, is introduced as a variable.[15]

The results are again quite robust:

$$(2) \quad G = 295.776 - 0.410 \, A + 141.732 \, S - 1.965 \, U - 4.995 \, T,$$
$$(10.625) \quad (2.571) \qquad (8.098) \qquad (2.787) \qquad (1.832)$$

Over three-fourths of the considerable variation in growth rates is explainable in terms of the model. All variables have the expected signs and are statistically significant at the 1 percent level except the tax variable, which is significant at the 5 percent level.

The impact of these factors on the East North Central states is considerable, given the fact that the region had large values with respect to all four distributional coalition variables. Every state, for example, had much higher union membership than the national average, and the tax burden of all except Indiana rose considerably more than the national average. Three were older states than the national average as well.

By substituting national average levels of unionization, changing tax burdens and state age for the actual values, and using the coefficients estimated in (2), we can calculate counterfactual estimates of what growth would have been had the region been merely average with respect to these distributional coalition variables. These are the Variant I estimates in table 5. Likewise, we can estimate what the growth rate would have been if the union and tax burden measures had not changed in the region over time: In doing this we assume that 15 percent of the nonagricultural labor force was unionized in 1929 in each state. We also assume the states had the average age for all states.

The simulations reveal that the distributional coalition variables very sizably reduced growth in the region. The growth rates in Ohio, Michigan, and Illinois are estimated to have been one-third to over two-fifths higher, and the impact in Wisconsin and Indiana, though smaller, is still important. In particular, the extraordinary degree of unionization seemed to have an adverse impact on economic growth, with the rising tax burden a secondary factor. Had tax burdens and unionization remained at 1929 levels, the growth impact would have been even more remarkable, with the largest state, Illinois, having more than 80 percent higher growth than actually recorded. In these calculations the unionization factor again is stronger, but the rising tax burden is a very important secondary consideration.

The rise in the tax burden and the growth of unionization reflected a growing willingness among the people of the region to rely more on government to allocate resources, both in an absolute sense and relative to other states. The people of the region were becoming more "liberal" in the way that term is used in contemporary America. Evidence from presidential elections over the past century or so tends to confirm this (table 6). The proportion of voters supporting the Democratic party candidate (presumably the more "liberal" of the major candidates) is compared to the national average, with an index number of one hundred indicating support for that candidate equal the average, with a smaller number indicating relatively less support (a sign of greater conservatism). The results confirm that the region has gone from being distinctly more conservative than the national average to being slightly more liberal, with the move being continuous over

TABLE 5

Actual and Counterfactual Growth Rates, East North Central States, 1929–1985

Variable	Ohio	Indiana	Illinois	Michigan	Wisconsin
Variant I:					
Actual Growth Rate	121.8%	166.3%	101.7%	124.7%	152.6%
Impact If Variable Had Been At National Average:					
Change Tax Burden	5.0	–8.6	11.5	10.6	7.1
Union Membership as % of Labor Force	21.3	25.2	24.6	31.7	21.9
Years Since Statehood	13.0	7.7	6.9	–0.9	–5.5
Counterfactual Rate (Sum of 4 Rows)	161.0	190.6	144.6	166.1	176.1
Variant II:					
Impact If Variable Had Remained At 1929 Level:*					
Change Tax Burden	22.5	8.8	29.0	28.1	24.6
Union Membership As % of Labor Force	45.2	49.1	48.5	56.6	45.8
Years Since Statehood	13.0	7.7	6.9	–0.9	–5.5
Counterfactual Rate (Actual Rate + 3 Rows)	202.4	231.9	186.0	208.5	217.5

*Except for years for statehood, assumed to equal the national average.

SOURCES: Authors' calculations from regression equation; see text.

time, although heaviest during the New Deal era.

Regarding the "structuralist" hypothesis, we regressed the growth rate against the proportion of the population engaged in agricultural pursuits, F, as well as the proportion of the population engaged in manufacturing activities, M, for a mid-period year.[16] Modern structuralist thinking would suggest overreliance on these slower growing primary fields of production should impede real growth. The results, however, are far from convincing:

$$(3) \quad G = 187.127 - 4.046 \, M + 5.863 \, F, \quad \bar{R}^2 = .29.$$
$$\quad\quad\quad (5.274) \quad (1.591) \quad\quad (2.849)$$

TABLE 6

Index of Relative "Liberalism," East North Central States, 1880–1984

Presidential Election	% Voting Democratic, E.N.C. States	Democratic Vote in Region As % of National
1880	30.99%	64.5%
1900	30.26	66.5
1920	23.36	68.4
1940	50.69	92.6
1960	48.39	97.3
1980	41.36	100.9
1984	41.33	101.9

SOURCES: Authors' calculations from election data in U.S. Department of Commerce, *Historical Statistics in the United States, Colonial Times to 1970*, and the 1986 *Statistical Abstract of the United States*.

The manufacturing variable has the expected negative sign but is not significant at the 5 percent level; the agricultural variable has a positive sign and is significant at the 1 percent level. The overall explanatory power of the variables is weak, far less than for either of the other models. We would conclude that the "structuralist" type explanations are probably less convincing than either "convergence" or "distributional coalition" hypotheses.

Because of problems of multicolinearity, attempts to develop an expanded explanation, incorporating variables from all three models, were only partially successful; however, a model with the income, unionization, age of state, and south dummy variables could explain 88 percent of the total variation in growth rates. Some alternative forms of the reported variables worked about as well as the ones reported. For example, we calculated hours missed because of work stoppages as a percent of total labor hours for the twelve-year period 1953–64; the region had the highest "strike rate" of any region. That variable works well in model estimation, although it is colinear with the union variable.

The Impact of Unions on Employment and Growth: More Evidence

The indications of a very powerful negative impact on economic growth associated with the presence of a high degree of unionization of the labor force deserves further exploration. Presumably, the effect of union activity in the states of the Old Northwest would be reflected in higher wage rates for labor. Conventional economic theory argues that, *ceteris paribus*, an increase in wage rates will have a tendency to reduce levels of employment and raise unemployment in an area. Could this be the link through which a greater incidence of unionization has impeded the economic growth process in recent years in the East North Central states?

To provide some insight into that possibility, we have assembled data for the time period 1953–1982 that describe the wage levels of nonagricultural workers in the five East North Central states *relative* to national wage levels and the percent of national nonagricultural employment accounted for by the states in question. The wage rate data are expressed in index number form with one hundred being equal to the national average. The percentage share of employment has been indexed on 1953 (= 100) in order to show how employment levels in the East North Central states have changed *relative* to the nation over time.

The basic information is summarized in table 7. Turning first to the wage data, we are struck by two things. In 1953 the nonagricultural wage level exceeded that for the nation in all five states, although just barely in Wisconsin. This is not so surprising, given the generally higher income levels of the region. However, after 1953 nonagricultural worker wage rates rose more rapidly than they did throughout the United States, despite the decline in relative income levels. By 1982 nonagricultural wage rates in Ohio were 18.5 percent above the national average. In Indiana they were 15.2 percent higher. In Illinois the gap was 9.5 percent; in Michigan, 31.5 percent; in Wisconsin, 10.2 percent. In every instance this represented an increase in the relative wage rate for the state.

TABLE 7

Relative Wage Rates and Employment, Nonagricultural Employment,
East North Central States, 1953 and 1982

State	Relative Wage Rate		Employment Level	
	1953	1982	1953	1982
Ohio	110.2	118.5	100.0	75.1
Indiana	106.8	115.2	100.0	78.2
Illinois	105.1	109.2	100.0	74.3
Michigan	118.1	131.5	100.0	72.0
Wisconsin	100.6	110.2	100.0	94.8

SOURCE: United States Department of Labor, as reported in *Statistical Abstract of the United States*, various issues.

There are also similar dramatic movements in the relative share of nonagricultural employment in these states. With the exception of Wisconsin, with about a 5 percent decline, there is a 20-30 percent fall in the employment share, with Michigan showing the greatest deterioration and Indiana the least. This suggests the possibility of a systematic relationship between relative wage movements and employment shares. To test that hypothesis, we estimated a pooled time-series regression (N = 150) for the five East North Central states using the employment share, *E*, as the dependent variable and the relative wage, W, as the independent variable, with the following results:

$$(4) \quad E = 220.436 - 1.140 \ W, \ \bar{R}^2 = .80.$$
$$\quad\quad (41.739) \quad (24.533)$$

Statistically, expression (4) is impressive, accounting for 80 percent of the variation in the employment share in the affected states. To illustrate this relationship graphically, figure 1 is provided. Clearly, there is a strong linkage between relative wage rates and the share of overall nonagricultural employment found in the various states. In conjunction with our earlier findings, the clear implication would seem to be that higher levels of unionization have produced higher relative wage rates and lower relative levels of nonagricultural employment.

The negative relationship between relative wage rates and employment shares implies the somewhat paradoxical possibility that, *ceteris paribus*, high relative wage rates in a state will impact *negatively* on per capita income. To explore that possibility more thoroughly, we have employed a multistage least squares regression process (data for the period 1953–82 and $N = 150$) to estimate the relationship between per capita income levels, Y, the dependent variable, and relative wages, W; the portion of nonagricultural employment not explained by relative wage movements, denoted by the symbol E'; and average Aid to Families with Dependent Children (AFDC) benefits, a variable designed to measure the impact of another of the significant distributional coalitions in modern life. The AFDC payments variable is denoted as AD. The results of the estimation process are as follows:

$$(5) \quad Y = 151.223 + 0.552 \ E' - 0.523 \ W$$
$$\quad\quad (55.996) \quad (12.681) \quad (21.675)$$

$$\quad - \ .002 \ AD, \ \bar{R}^2 = .82$$
$$\quad (1.824)$$

Again, powerful statistical relationships are found. By itself the employment effects of movements in relative wage rates are strongly related, *in a negative fashion*, with income levels. On the other hand, the portion of nonagricultural employment not explained by movements in relative wage rates is positively associated with income levels. The greater the volume of such employment, the higher the level of per capita income. Finally, the AFDC benefit variable has a *negative* sign, suggesting that the ultimate impact of the distributional coalition that functions through the welfare system is to reduce levels of per capita income.[17]

Collectively, the statistical results reported in expression (5) provide significant confirmation of the hypothesis that the relative decline in the economic fortunes of the Old Northwest states in recent times are intimately associated with the phenomenon of distributional coalitions.

FIGURE 1

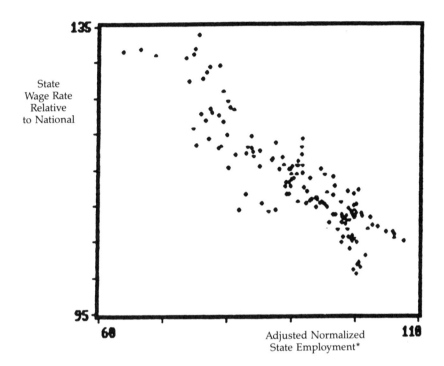

State
Wage Rate
Relative
to National

Adjusted Normalized
State Employment*

* Employment is normalized so that a state's percentage share of national nonagricultural employment in 1953 is equal to 100. Employment is also adjusted to control for individual state-variations in the share of employment that are unique to the state. This adjustment is done on the basis of a regression model that inlcudes individual state dummy variables.

WILL REGIONAL GENTRIFICATION OCCUR?

WILL THE REGIONAL DECLINE of the past half century reverse itself, or will it continue in the Old Northwest's third century? Predicting the future is hazardous, but there are two reasons, one empirical and the second theoretical, to believe that the regional economic decline will slow and possibly reverse itself at some time in the next generation (and certainly in the next half century).

Empirically, projecting relative economic decline at the rate observed since 1950 into the future leads to the conclusion that by the beginning of the third decade of the twenty-first century, per capita income in the Old Northwest would be about 20 percent below the national average, about the differential currently observed for the poorest region, the East South Central states. Since regional income differentials have been generally declining over time, it would seem very unlikely that the East North Central states will decline to 80 percent the per capita income level of the nation as a whole. Thus the degree of stagnation in income growth in the region relative to the nation as a whole should begin to lessen sometime in the generation ahead, and possibly the trend will reverse.

Market forces should work to ensure this. As average income per member of the labor force declines (either through high unemployment or lower incomes for employed workers), out-migration of resources will reduce resource supply in the East North Central region, raising compensation for those who remain. The extraordinary out-migration of the last quarter century suggests this process already is well under way.

The high wage nature of the region resulting from intense labor union activity has had the longer term effects of severely weakening membership in the labor unions, the most potent distributional coalition. Moreover, as other sections of the country age, coalitions building in those areas may rival the Old Northwest's in terms of impact. Thus the growth-retarding impact of such groups in other regions may, in time, rival those in the Old Northwest. Similarly, a structural retransformation is occurring in the region reflecting low rates of return on capital investment in heavy industry relative to returns on capital in the service and light manufacturing industries. Thus, to the extent the region's problems are "structural" in nature (and our empirical findings make us dubious of that contention), structural changes should reduce the region's relative backwardness over time.

Consequently, it is possible that the region may regain a measure of vitality, at least relative to other states, not because of aggressive new industrial policies enacted by growth-minded state governments, but rather by the forces of the market economy and the changing spatial patterns of special interest politics. If so, the first half of the third century may be brighter for the regional economy than the last half of the second.

Notes

1. See Richard A. Easterlin, "Interregional Differences in Per Capita Income, Population, and Total Income, 1840–1950," in William N. Parker, ed., *Trends in the American Economy in the Nineteenth Century*, Studies in Income and Wealth, vol. 24 (Princeton, N.J.: Princeton University Press for the National Bureau of Economic Research, 1960). For most of the twentieth century, state per capita income data can be found in U.S. Department of Commerce, Bureau of the Census, *Historical Statistics of the United States, Colonial Times to 1970* (Washington, D.C.: Government Printing Office, 1975.) We actually used various issues of the *Statistical Abstract of the United States* (because they provided average income statistics also by regions), and, for 1985, the April 1986 issue of the *Survey of Current Business*.

2. The price deflator for 1929 to 1980 was obtained in *Economic Report of the President*, 1986 (Washington, D.C.: Government Printing Office, 1986), 256; the 1985 number was obtained from *Economic Indicators*, July 1986, p.2. Earlier numbers were obtained from U.S. Department of Commerce, Bureau of the Census, *Historical Statistics of the United States, Colonial Times to 1970* (Washington, D.C.: Government Printing Office, 1975), 224, 211. Numbers were spliced and converted to a 1982 base by the authors.

3. Easterlin, for example, shows no growth in per capita income in the North Central region relative to the nation as a whole from 1840 to 1860. See his "Regional Income Trends, 1840–1950," in Seymour Harris, ed., *American Economic History* (New York: McGraw Hill, 1961), 528. For a good discussion of economic growth in the U.S. in both nineteenth and twentieth centuries, see Robert E. Gallman, "The Pace and Pattern of American Economic Growth," in Lance Davis, et al., *American Economic Growth: An Economist's History of the United States* (New York: Harper and Row, 1972.)

4. See, for example, Paul A. Samuelson, "International Trade and the Equalisation of Factor Prices," *Economic Journal*, June 1948, 58:163–84.

5. The adjustment to what we term a "steady-state equilibrium" may stop short of equalizing factor prices, however. Our views on this and on migration's role in income determination have been expressed elsewhere, for example, in "Population Transfers and the Post-Bellum Adjustment to Economic Dislocation, 1870–1920," *Journal of Economic History*, March 1980, 40:143–49.

6. Richard A. Easterlin, for example, has estimated that the East North Central states had net nonagricultural capital imports from 1840–1900 equal to 16 percent of the 1870 capital stock; by contrast the Northeast had net capital exports. See his "Regional Growth of Income: Long Term Tendencies," in Simon Kuznets, Ann Ratner Miller and Richard A. Easterlin, *Analyses of Economic Change*, vol. 2 of *Population Redistribution and Economic Growth: United States, 1870–1950* (Philadelphia: American Philosophical Society, 1960.)

7. On the importance of economic determinants in migration decisions, including data on migration of individuals from the five Old Northwest states, see our

"Mobility of Native Americans," *Journal of Economic History*, September 1971, 31:613–49.

8. Mancur Olson, *The Rise and Decline of Nations* (New Haven: Yale University Press, 1982).

9. This is all part of the literature on public choice. The classic pioneering study is James Buchanan and Gordon Tullock, *The Calculus of Consent* (Ann Arbor: University of Michigan Press, 1962).

10. Richard Vedder and Lowell Gallaway, "Rent Seeking, Distributional Coalitions, Taxes, Relative Prices and Economic Growth, *Public Choice*, vol. 50, forthcoming.

11. See Gallaway and Vedder, "Mobility of Native Americans," *Journal of Economic History,* September 1971, 31:613-49.

12. Nominal personal income per capita state estimates for 1929 and 1985 derived from standard Department of Commerce sources were deflated by the GNP price deflator.

13. As calculated by the National Bureau of Economic Research and reported in the 1956 *Statistical Abstract of the United States*, p. 237.

14. See, for example, Richard K. Vedder, "Rich States, Poor States: How High Taxes Inhibit Growth," *Journal of Contemporary Studies*, Fall 1982; and Lowell E. Gallaway and Richard K. Vedder, *Poverty, Income Distribution, the Family and Public Policy*, Study for the Joint Economic Committee of Congress (Washington, D.C.: Government Printing Office, 1986), chap. 14.

15. Nineteen thirty-two is used because a Census of Governments provided data for that date; unfortunately, 1929 data are not available. The 1932 data were derived from U.S. Bureau of the Census, *Historical Review of State and Local Government Finances* (Washington, D.C.: Government Printing Office, 1948); the 1983 fiscal year data were derived from the 1986 *Statistical Abstract of the United States*.

16. Specifically, we derived manufacturing workforce data for 1950 from the 1953 *Statistical Abstract of the United States*, and agricultural work force data for 1954 from U.S. Department of Agriculture, *Farm Labor Fact Book* (Washington, D.C.: Government Printing Office, 1959).

17. This finding is consistent with a growing body of literature that demonstrates the impact of the labor market disincentive effects associated with the provision of transfer payment income to members of the population. This literature is summarized in Gallaway and Vedder, *Poverty, Income Distribution, the Family and Public Policy* (Washington, D.C.: Government Printing Office, 1986).